Sand Chronicles

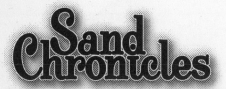

Shojo Beat

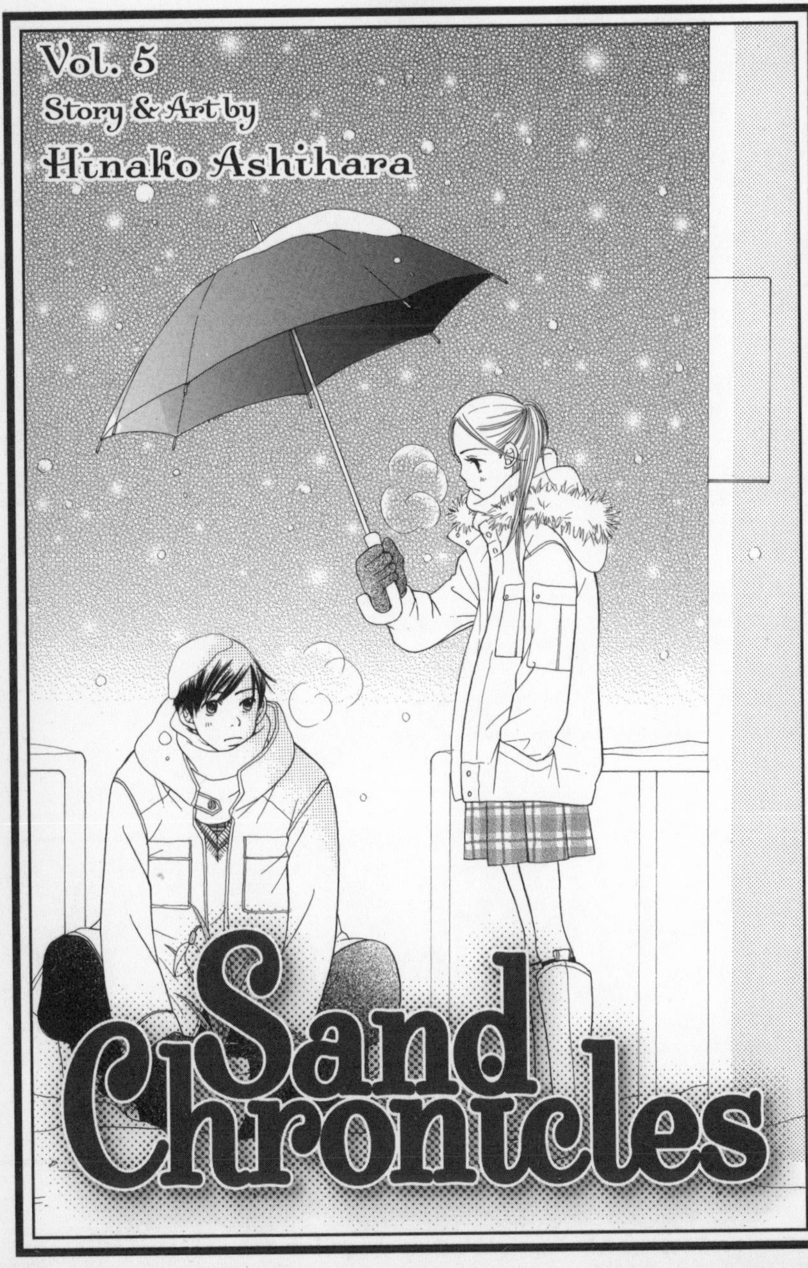
Vol. 5
Story & Art by
Hinako Ashihara
Sand Chronicles

Sand Chronicles

Volume 5

Contents

Summer, Age 17: Shadows—5

Winter, Age 17: First Love—87

Glossary—188

Story thus far...

After her parents' divorce, Ann moves to rural Shimane with her mother. When Ann's mother commits suicide, Ann's new friends, Daigo and wealthy siblings Fuji and Shika, are a great support to her. But then Ann moves back to Tokyo to live with her father, and time and distance put a strain on Ann and Daigo's romantic relationship. Eventually, Daigo suggests they cool things off between them.

Meanwhile, Fuji runs away from his elite private school and family. He is tormented by information that suggests he is the child of his mother's affair. (In fact, it is his sister.) A divorced woman in the midst of a custody battle takes Fuji in. Ann remains Fuji's only connection to his old life, and they spend more and more time together. Finally, at Ann's urging, Fuji returns home.

Meanwhile, Shika tells Daigo that she is in love with him. And then she tells Ann, as well...

Main characters

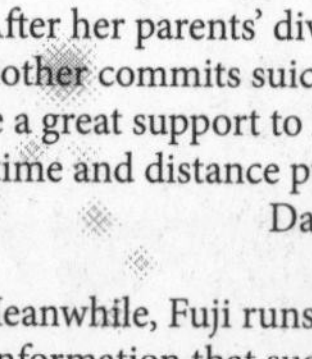

Shika Tsukishima
Fuji's sheltered younger sister.

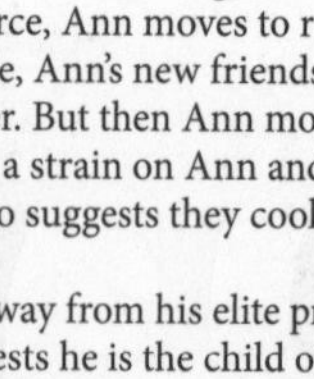

Fuji Tsukishima
The son of an elite family. A loner.

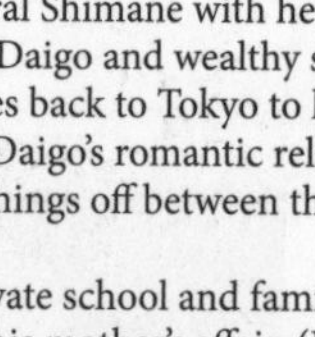

Daigo Kitamura
Boyish and gruff, but kind.

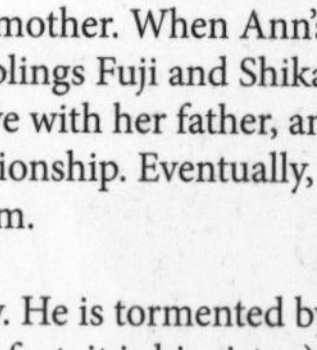

Ann Uekusa
Strongwilled and, like her mother, sensitive.

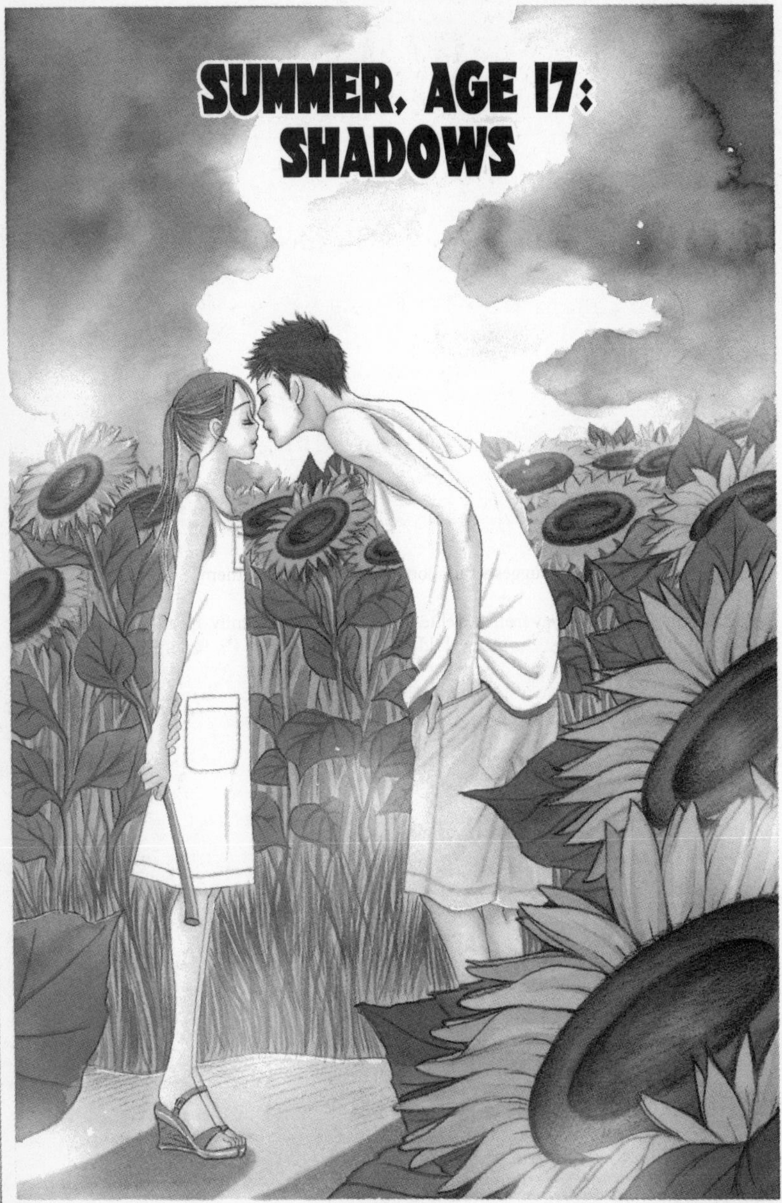
SUMMER, AGE 17:
SHADOWS

Sand Chronicles

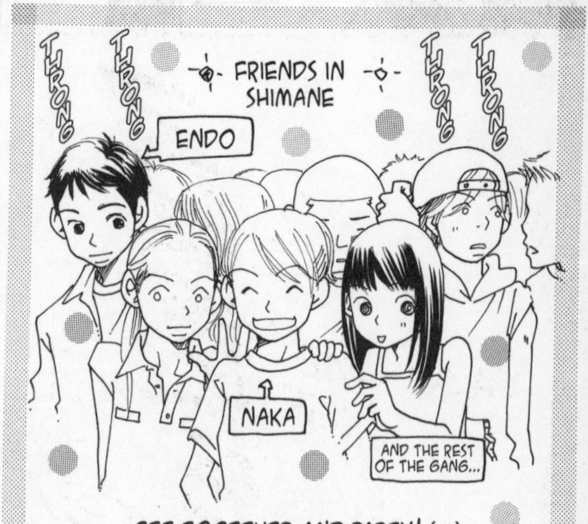
THRONG THRONG
FRIENDS IN SHIMANE
THRONG THRONG
ENDO
NAKA
AND THE REST OF THE GANG...
...GET TOGETHER AND PARTY! (...)

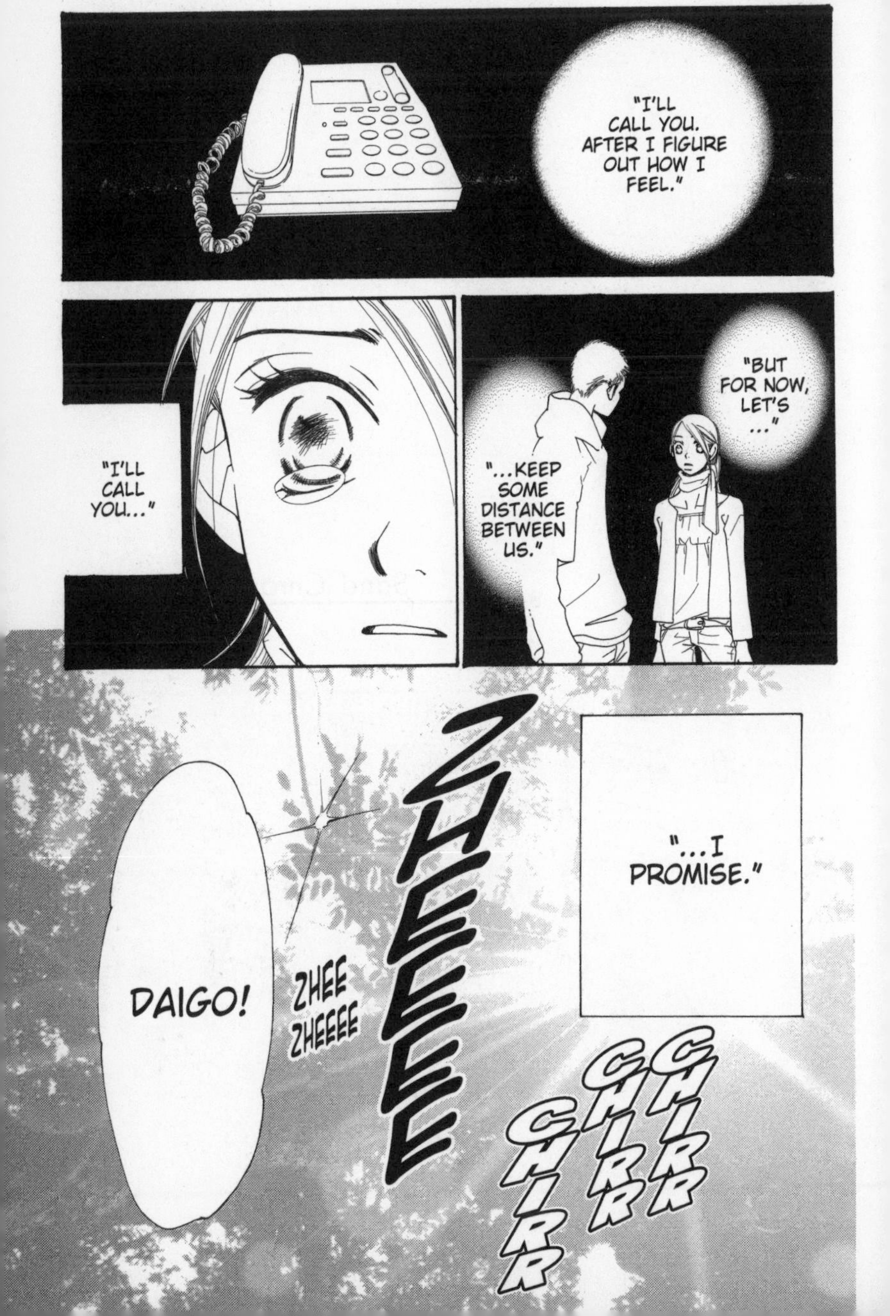
"I'LL CALL YOU. AFTER I FIGURE OUT HOW I FEEL."
"BUT FOR NOW, LET'S ..."
"...KEEP SOME DISTANCE BETWEEN US."
"I'LL CALL YOU..."
"...I PROMISE."
CHIRR CHIRR
CHIRR CHIRR
CHIRR CHIRR
ZHEEEEEE
ZHEE ZHEEEE
DAIGO!

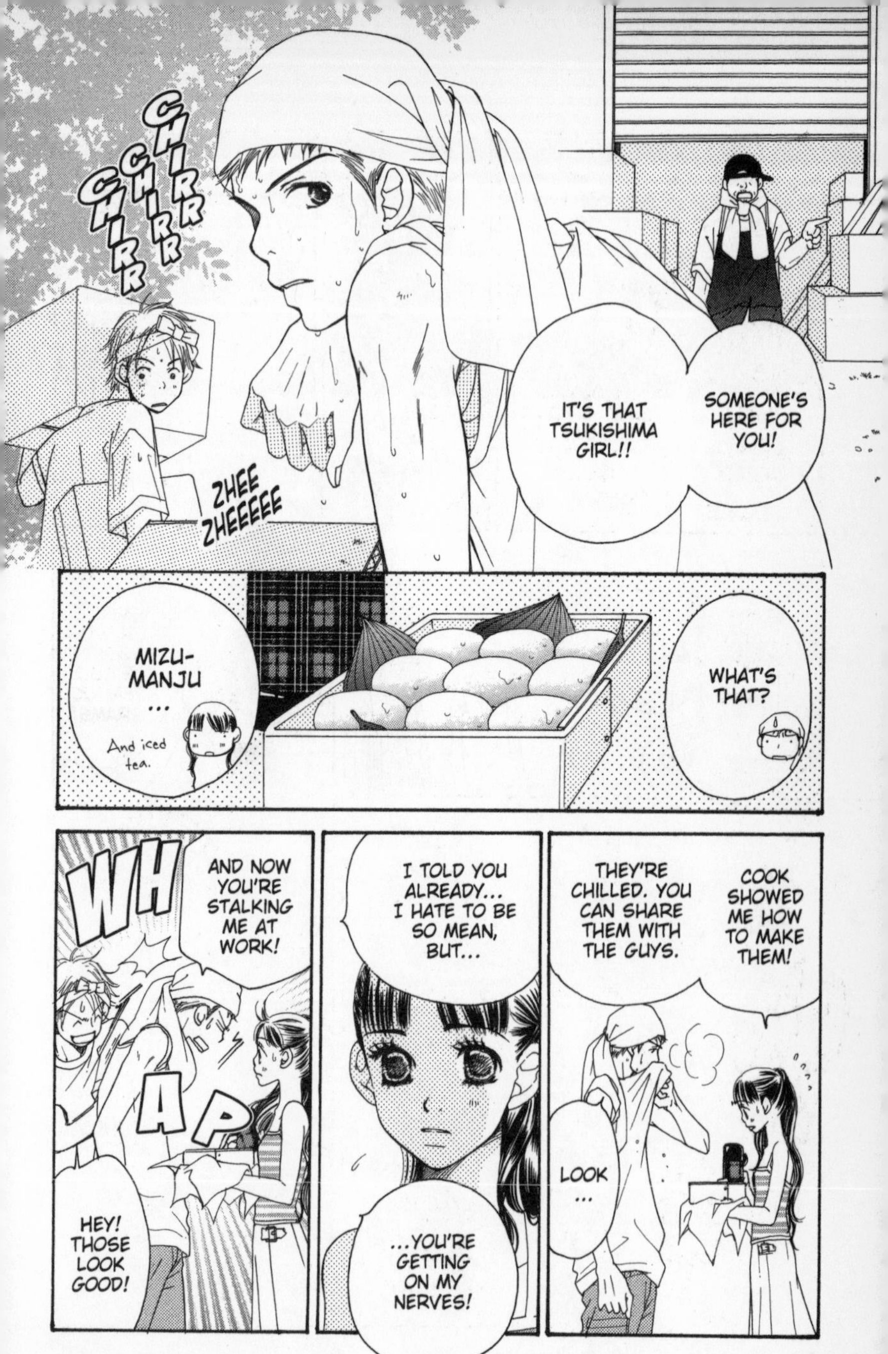
CHIRR CHIRR CHIRR
SOMEONE'S HERE FOR YOU!
IT'S THAT TSUKISHIMA GIRL!!
ZHEE ZHEEEEEE
WHAT'S THAT?
MIZU-MANJU ...
And iced tea.
COOK SHOWED ME HOW TO MAKE THEM!
THEY'RE CHILLED. YOU CAN SHARE THEM WITH THE GUYS.
LOOK ...
I TOLD YOU ALREADY... I HATE TO BE SO MEAN, BUT...
...YOU'RE GETTING ON MY NERVES!
WHAP
AND NOW YOU'RE STALKING ME AT WORK!
HEY! THOSE LOOK GOOD!

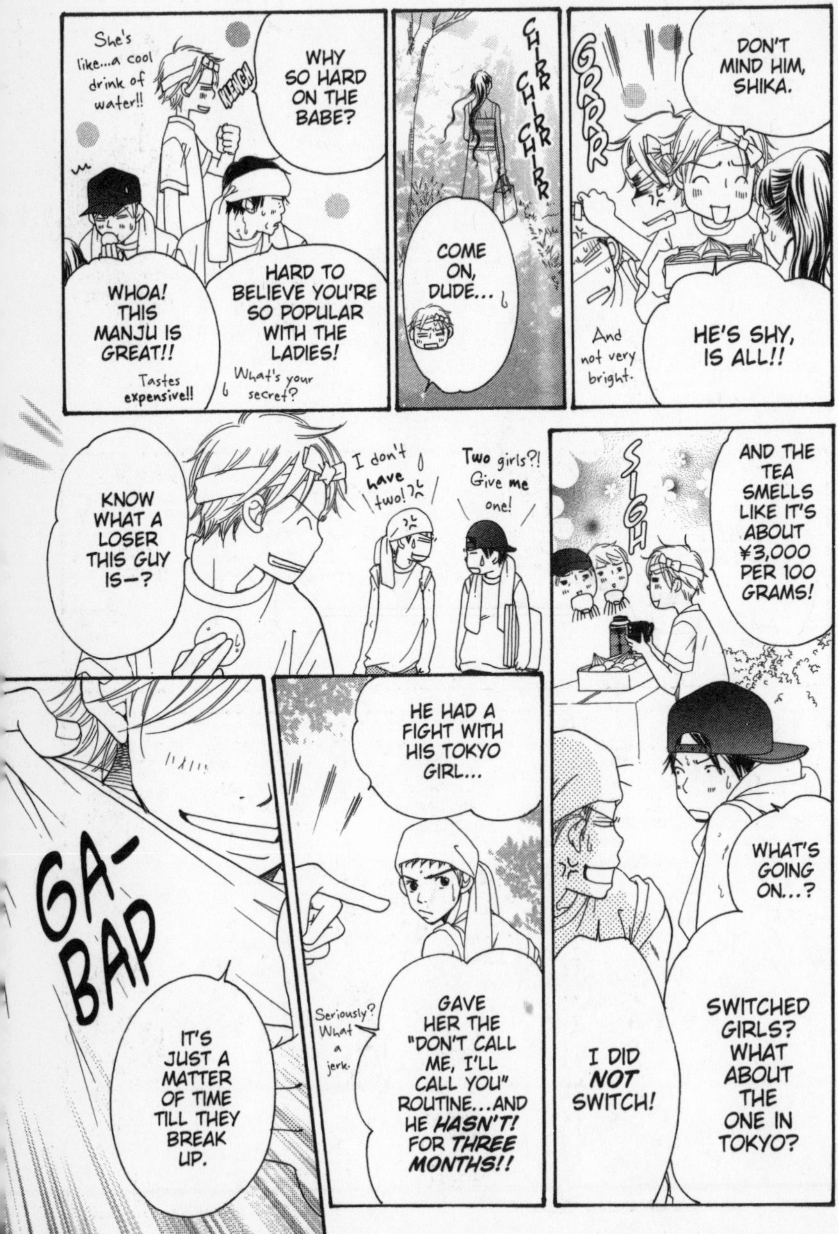
DON'T MIND HIM, SHIKA.
GRRRR
HE'S SHY, IS ALL!!
And not very bright.
CHIRR CHIRR CHIRR
COME ON, DUDE...
WHY SO HARD ON THE BABE?
She's like...a cool drink of water!!
KENCH
HARD TO BELIEVE YOU'RE SO POPULAR WITH THE LADIES!
What's your secret?
WHOA! THIS MANJU IS GREAT!!
Tastes expensive!!
AND THE TEA SMELLS LIKE IT'S ABOUT ¥3,000 PER 100 GRAMS!
SIGH
Two girls?! Give me one!
I don't have two!
KNOW WHAT A LOSER THIS GUY IS—?
WHAT'S GOING ON...?
SWITCHED GIRLS? WHAT ABOUT THE ONE IN TOKYO?
I DID NOT SWITCH!
HE HAD A FIGHT WITH HIS TOKYO GIRL...
GAVE HER THE "DON'T CALL ME, I'LL CALL YOU" ROUTINE...AND HE HASN'T! FOR THREE MONTHS!!
Seriously? What a jerk.
GA-BAP
IT'S JUST A MATTER OF TIME TILL THEY BREAK UP.

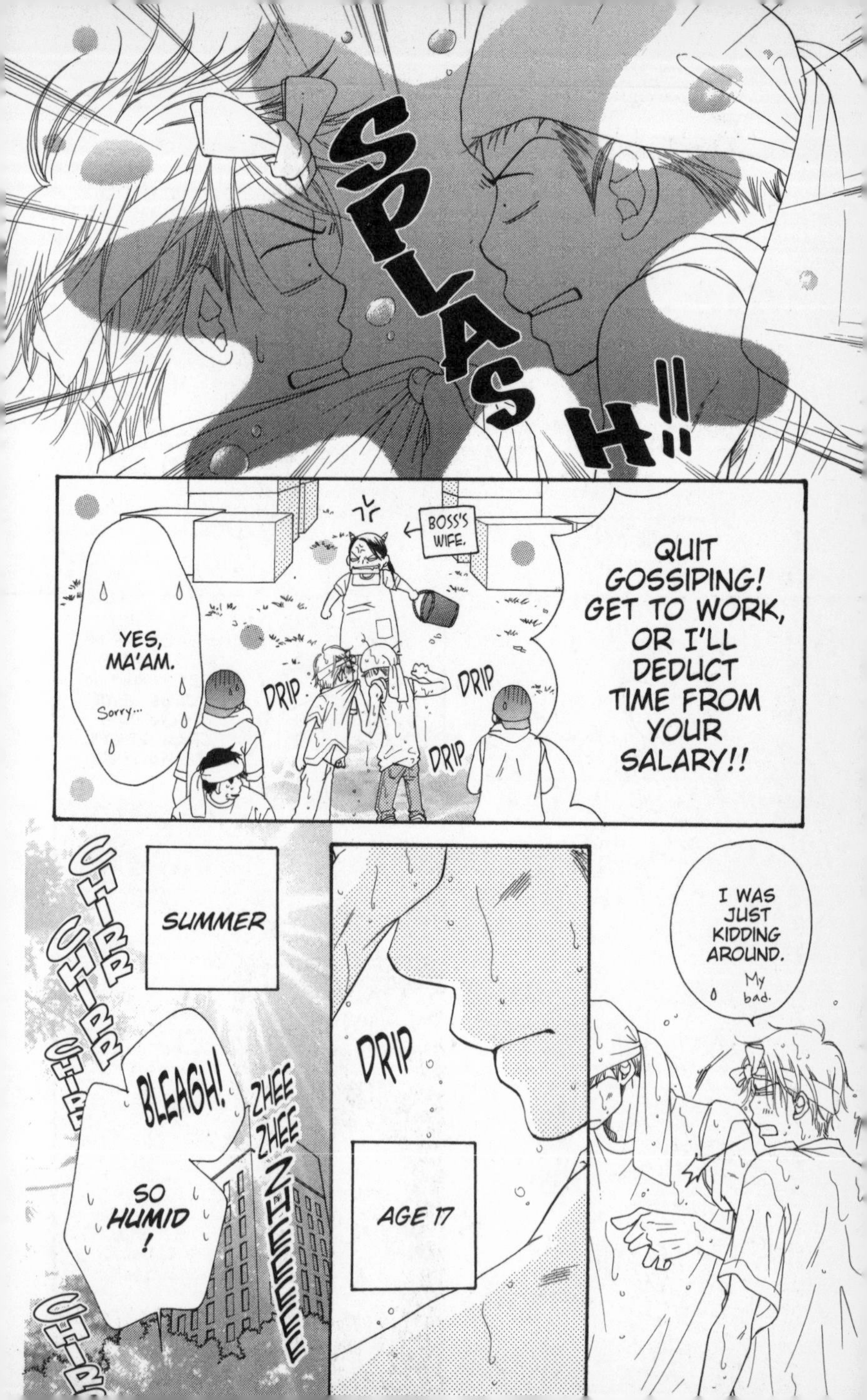
SPLASH!!
QUIT GOSSIPING! GET TO WORK, OR I'LL DEDUCT TIME FROM YOUR SALARY!!
BOSS'S WIFE.
DRIP
DRIP
DRIP
YES, MA'AM.
Sorry...
I WAS JUST KIDDING AROUND.
My bad.
DRIP
AGE 17
SUMMER
CHIRR
CHIRR
BLEAGH!
ZHEE ZHEE ZHEEEEE
SO HUMID!

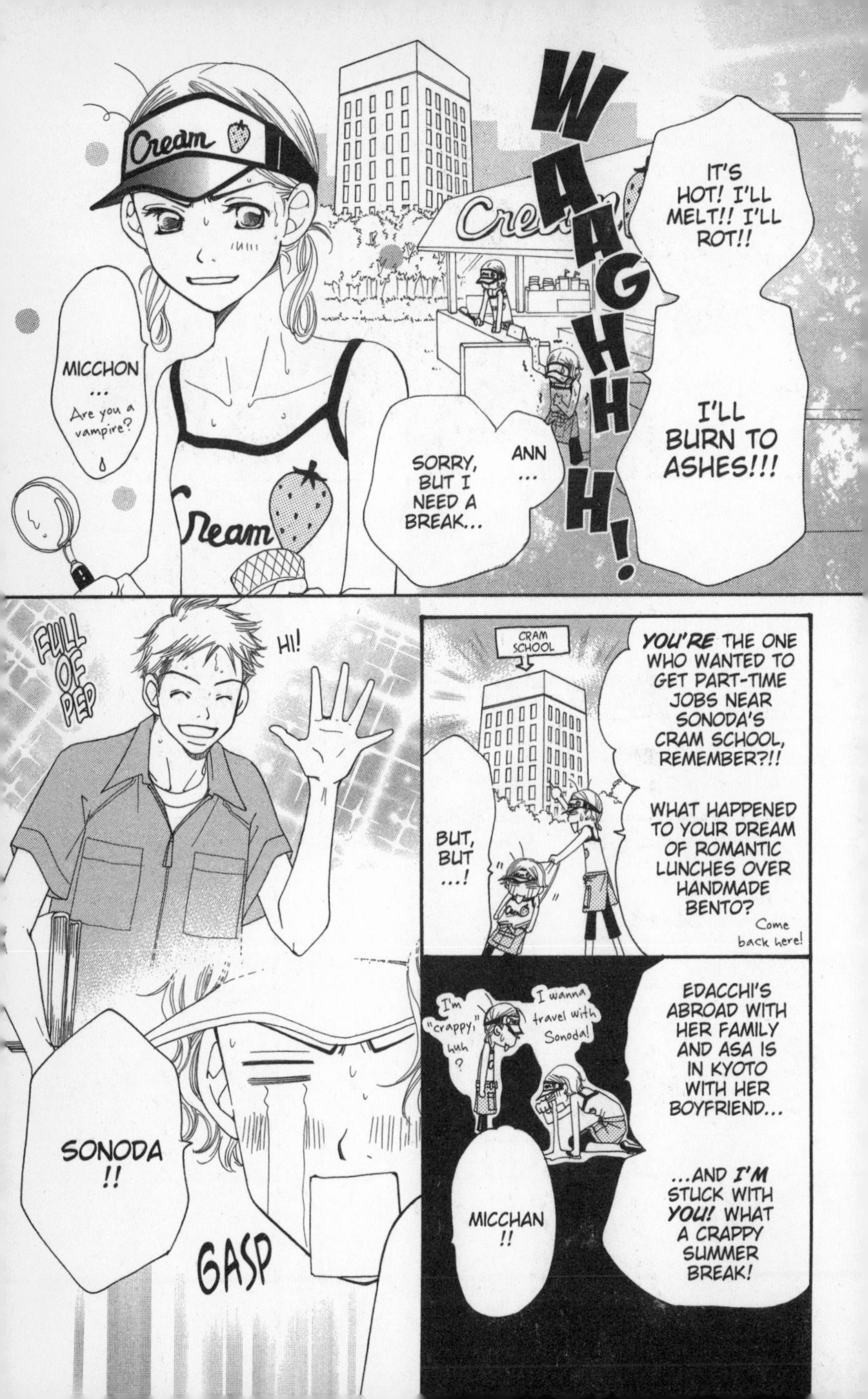
IT'S HOT! I'LL MELT!! I'LL ROT!!
I'LL BURN TO ASHES!!!
WAAGHHH!
ANN ...
SORRY, BUT I NEED A BREAK...
MICCHON ...
Are you a vampire?
CRAM SCHOOL
YOU'RE THE ONE WHO WANTED TO GET PART-TIME JOBS NEAR SONODA'S CRAM SCHOOL, REMEMBER?!!
WHAT HAPPENED TO YOUR DREAM OF ROMANTIC LUNCHES OVER HANDMADE BENTO?
BUT, BUT ...!
Come back here!
EDACCHI'S ABROAD WITH HER FAMILY AND ASA IS IN KYOTO WITH HER BOYFRIEND...
...AND I'M STUCK WITH YOU! WHAT A CRAPPY SUMMER BREAK!
I wanna travel with Sonoda!
I'm "crappy," huh?
MICCHAN!!
HI!
FULL OF PEP
SONODA!!
GASP

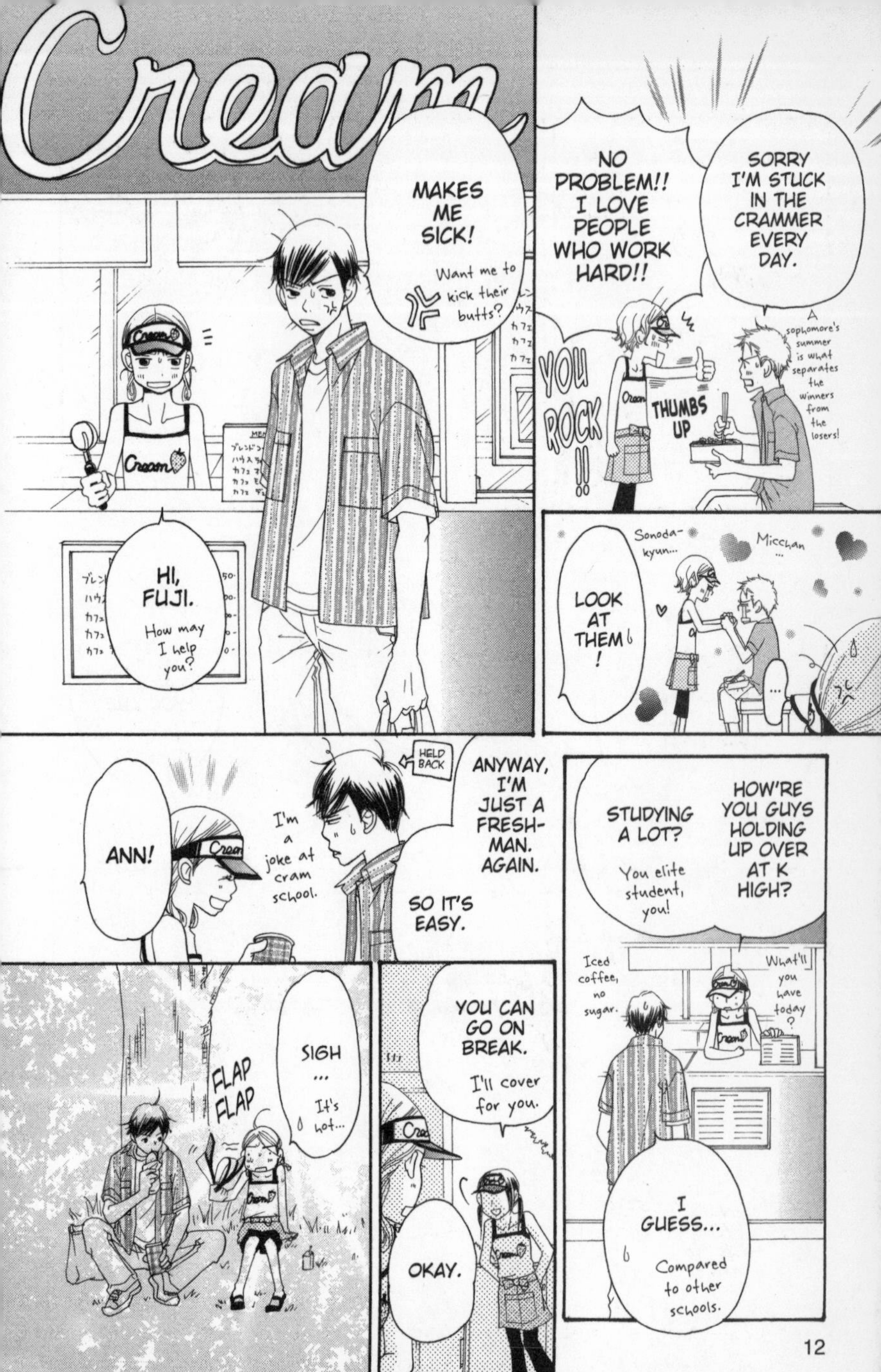
SORRY I'M STUCK IN THE CRAMMER EVERY DAY.
A sophomore's summer is what separates the winners from the losers!
NO PROBLEM!! I LOVE PEOPLE WHO WORK HARD!!
YOU ROCK!!
THUMBS UP
Micchan...
Sonoda-kyun...
LOOK AT THEM!
...
Cream
MAKES ME SICK!
Want me to kick their butts?
HI, FUJI.
How may I help you?
HOW'RE YOU GUYS HOLDING UP OVER AT K HIGH?
STUDYING A LOT?
You elite student, you!
What'll you have today?
Iced coffee, no sugar.
I GUESS...
Compared to other schools.
HELD BACK
ANYWAY, I'M JUST A FRESHMAN. AGAIN.
SO IT'S EASY.
I'm a joke at cram school.
ANN!
YOU CAN GO ON BREAK.
I'll cover for you.
OKAY.
SIGH...
It's hot...
FLAP FLAP

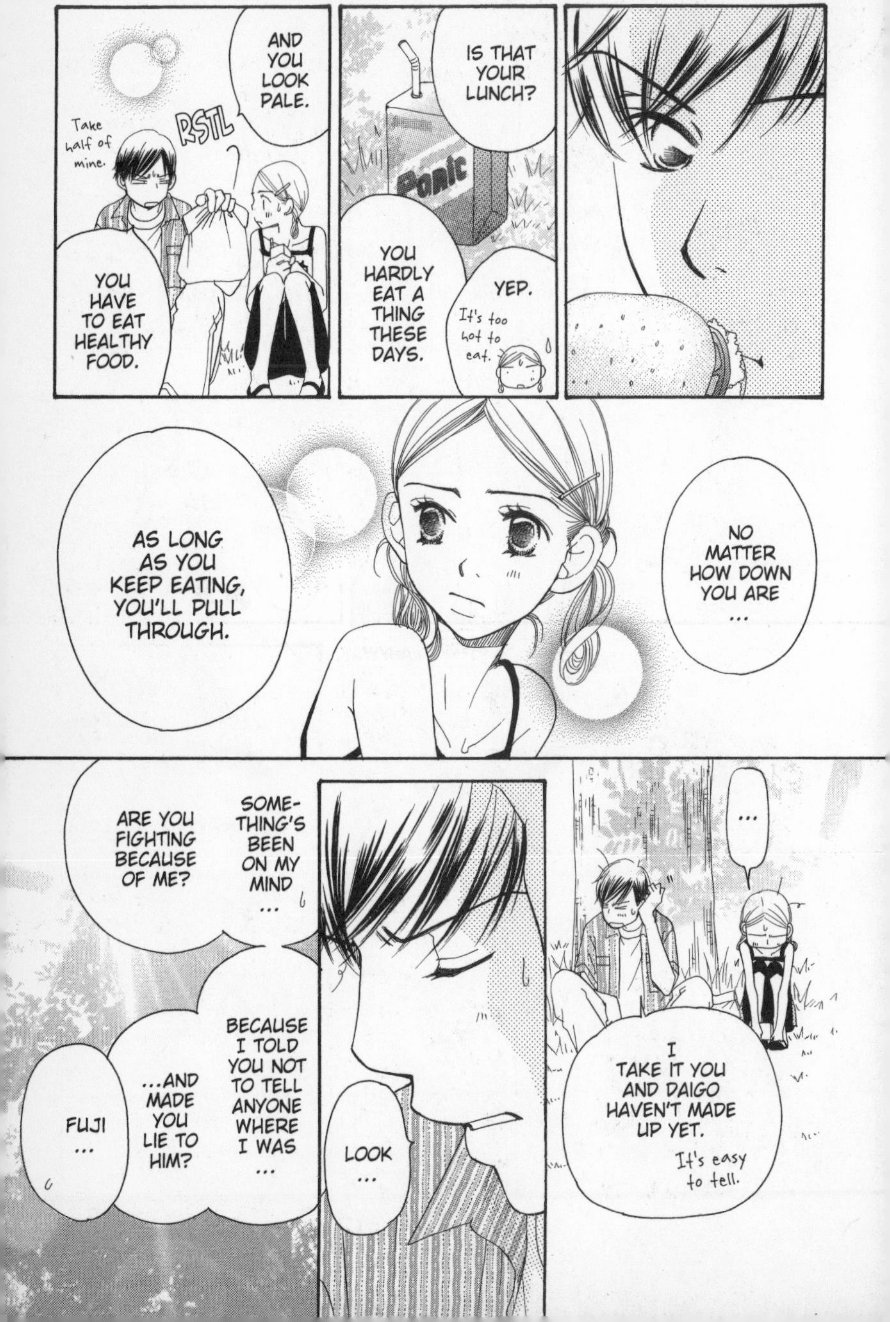
IS THAT YOUR LUNCH?
Ponic
YEP.
It's too hot to eat.
YOU HARDLY EAT A THING THESE DAYS.
AND YOU LOOK PALE.
RSTL
Take half of mine.
YOU HAVE TO EAT HEALTHY FOOD.
NO MATTER HOW DOWN YOU ARE ...
AS LONG AS YOU KEEP EATING, YOU'LL PULL THROUGH.
...
I TAKE IT YOU AND DAIGO HAVEN'T MADE UP YET.
It's easy to tell.
LOOK ...
SOME-THING'S BEEN ON MY MIND ...
ARE YOU FIGHTING BECAUSE OF ME?
BECAUSE I TOLD YOU NOT TO TELL ANYONE WHERE I WAS ...
...AND MADE YOU LIE TO HIM?
FUJI ...

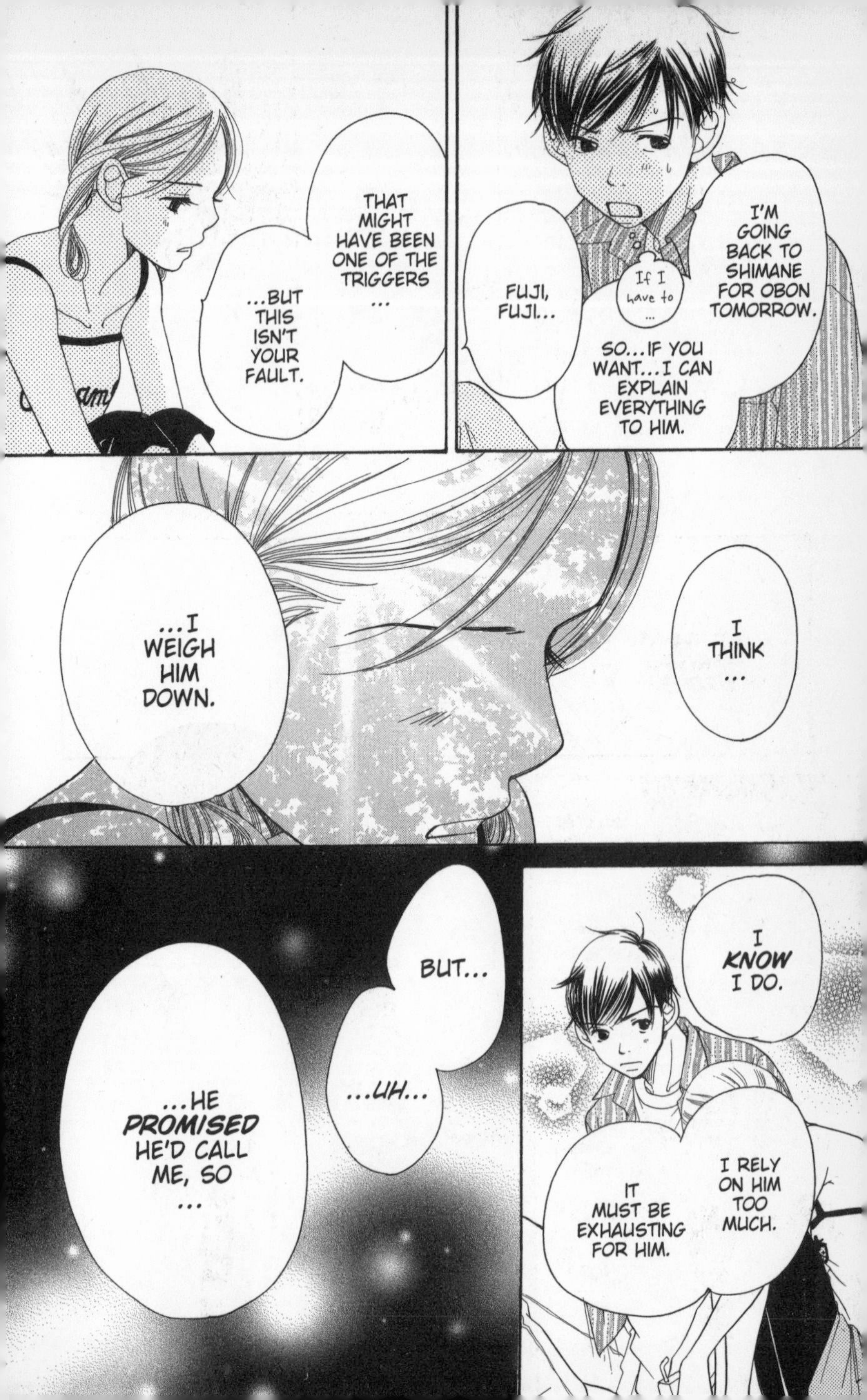
I'M GOING BACK TO SHIMANE FOR OBON TOMORROW.
If I have to ...
SO... IF YOU WANT... I CAN EXPLAIN EVERYTHING TO HIM.
FUJI, FUJI...
THAT MIGHT HAVE BEEN ONE OF THE TRIGGERS ...
...BUT THIS ISN'T YOUR FAULT.
I THINK ...
...I WEIGH HIM DOWN.
I *KNOW* I DO.
I RELY ON HIM TOO MUCH.
IT MUST BE EXHAUSTING FOR HIM.
BUT...
...UH...
...HE *PROMISED* HE'D CALL ME, SO ...

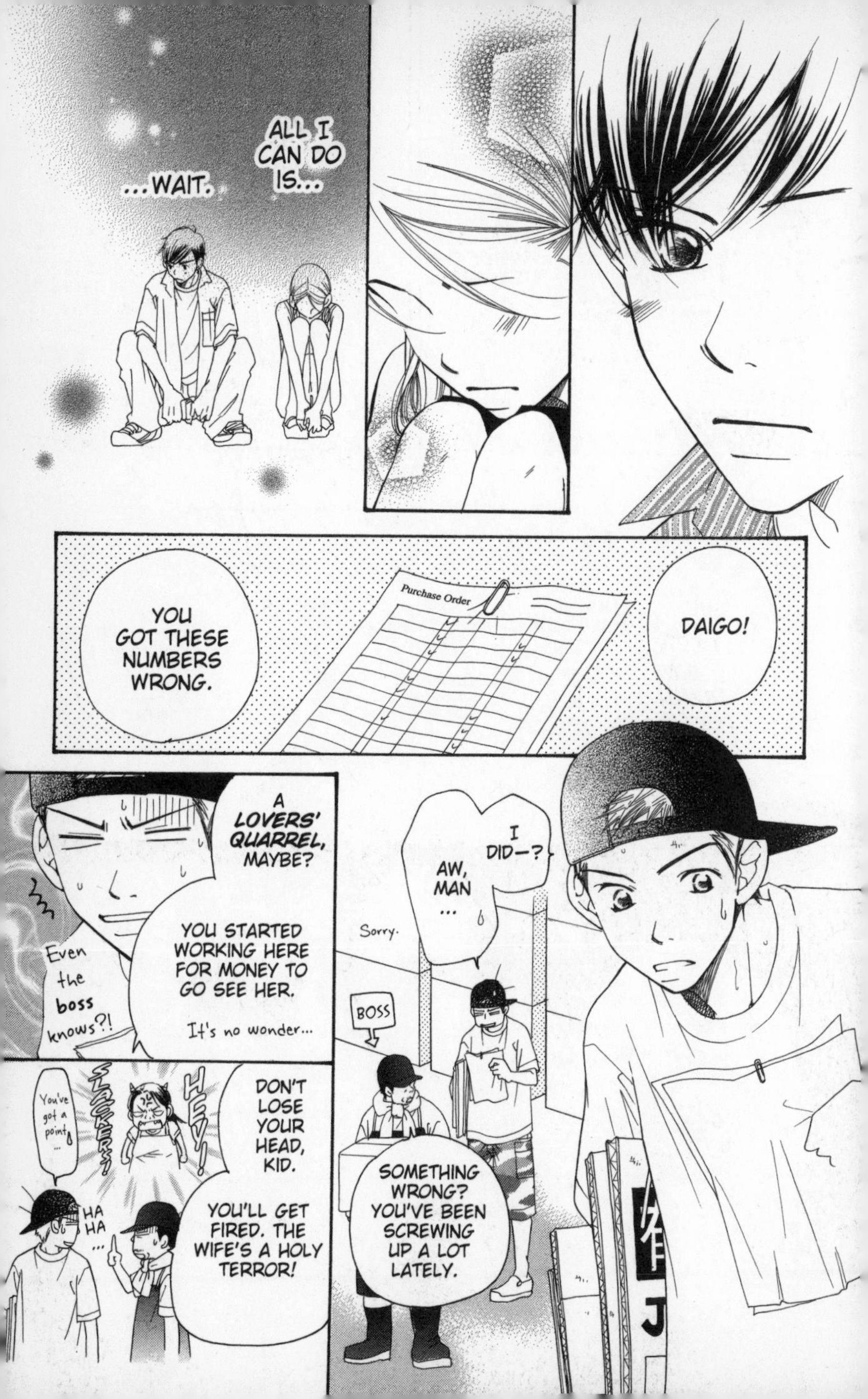
ALL I CAN DO IS...
...WAIT.
DAIGO!
Purchase Order
YOU GOT THESE NUMBERS WRONG.
I DID—?
AW, MAN...
Sorry.
BOSS
SOMETHING WRONG? YOU'VE BEEN SCREWING UP A LOT LATELY.
A *LOVERS' QUARREL,* MAYBE?
YOU STARTED WORKING HERE FOR MONEY TO GO SEE HER.
It's no wonder...
Even the **boss** knows?!
DON'T LOSE YOUR HEAD, KID.
YOU'LL GET FIRED. THE WIFE'S A HOLY TERROR!
HEY!
SLACKER!!
You've got a point...
HA HA...

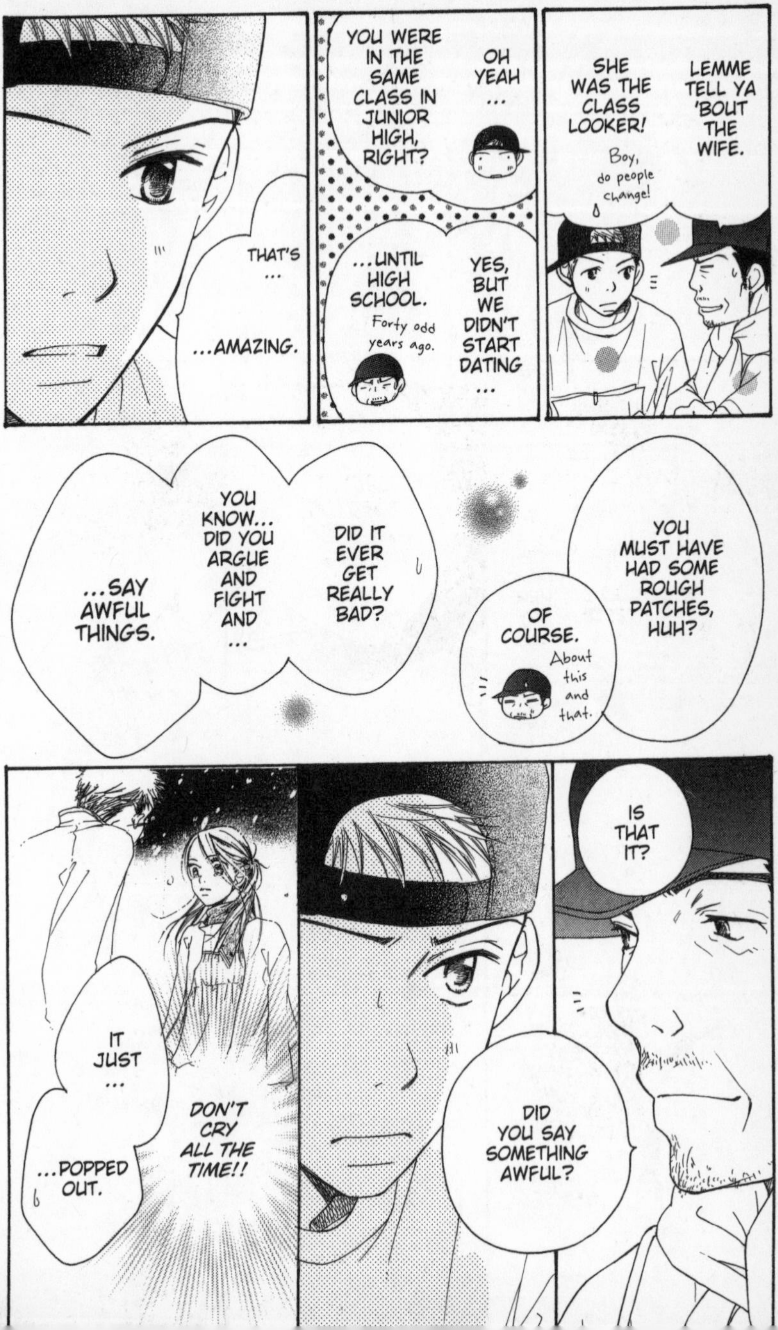
LEMME TELL YA 'BOUT THE WIFE.
SHE WAS THE CLASS LOOKER!
Boy, do people change!
OH YEAH ...
YOU WERE IN THE SAME CLASS IN JUNIOR HIGH, RIGHT?
YES, BUT WE DIDN'T START DATING ...
...UNTIL HIGH SCHOOL.
Forty odd years ago.
THAT'S ...
...AMAZING.
YOU MUST HAVE HAD SOME ROUGH PATCHES, HUH?
OF COURSE.
About this and that.
DID IT EVER GET REALLY BAD?
YOU KNOW... DID YOU ARGUE AND FIGHT AND ...
...SAY AWFUL THINGS.
IS THAT IT?
DID YOU SAY SOMETHING AWFUL?
IT JUST ...
DON'T CRY ALL THE TIME!!
...POPPED OUT.

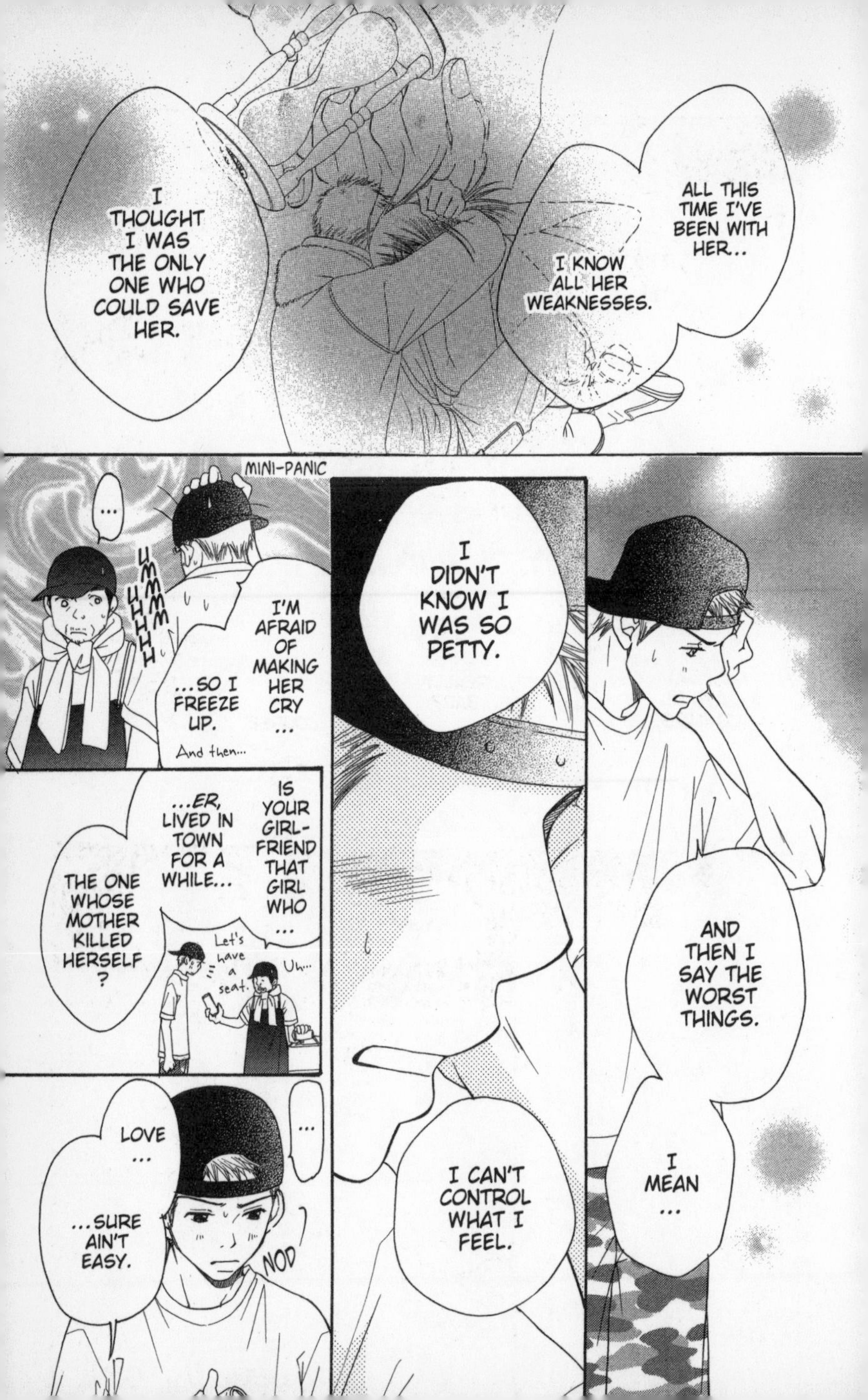
ALL THIS TIME I'VE BEEN WITH HER...
I KNOW ALL HER WEAKNESSES.
I THOUGHT I WAS THE ONLY ONE WHO COULD SAVE HER.
AND THEN I SAY THE WORST THINGS.
I MEAN...
I DIDN'T KNOW I WAS SO PETTY.
I CAN'T CONTROL WHAT I FEEL.
MINI-PANIC
I'M AFRAID OF MAKING HER CRY...
...SO I FREEZE UP.
UMMM UHHHH
...
And then...
IS YOUR GIRLFRIEND THAT GIRL WHO...
...ER, LIVED IN TOWN FOR A WHILE...
THE ONE WHOSE MOTHER KILLED HERSELF?
Uh...
Let's have a seat.
...
LOVE...
...SURE AIN'T EASY.
NOD

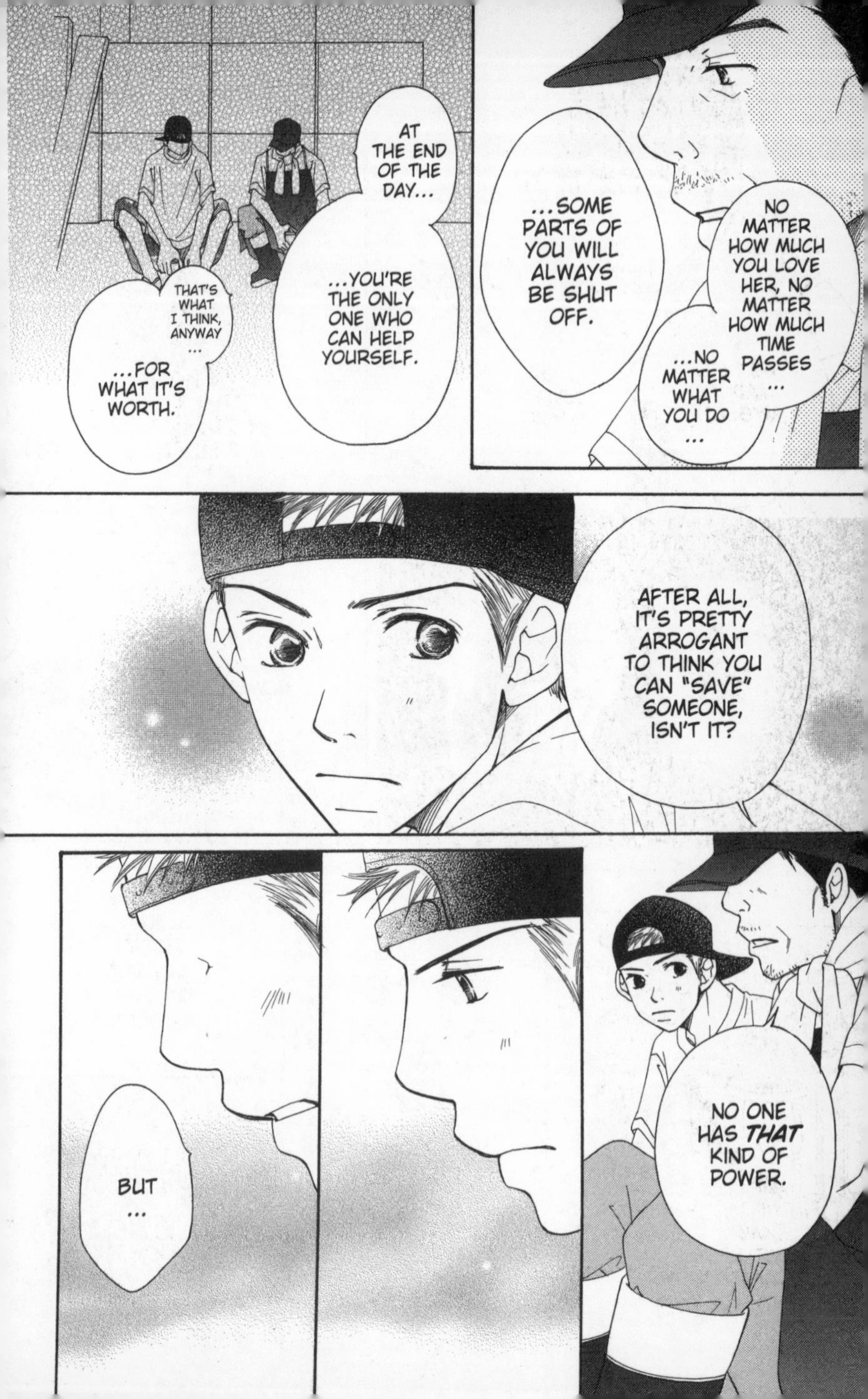
NO MATTER HOW MUCH YOU LOVE HER, NO MATTER HOW MUCH TIME PASSES...
...NO MATTER WHAT YOU DO...
...SOME PARTS OF YOU WILL ALWAYS BE SHUT OFF.
AT THE END OF THE DAY...
...YOU'RE THE ONLY ONE WHO CAN HELP YOURSELF.
THAT'S WHAT I THINK, ANYWAY...
...FOR WHAT IT'S WORTH.
AFTER ALL, IT'S PRETTY ARROGANT TO THINK YOU CAN "SAVE" SOMEONE, ISN'T IT?
NO ONE HAS *THAT* KIND OF POWER.
BUT...

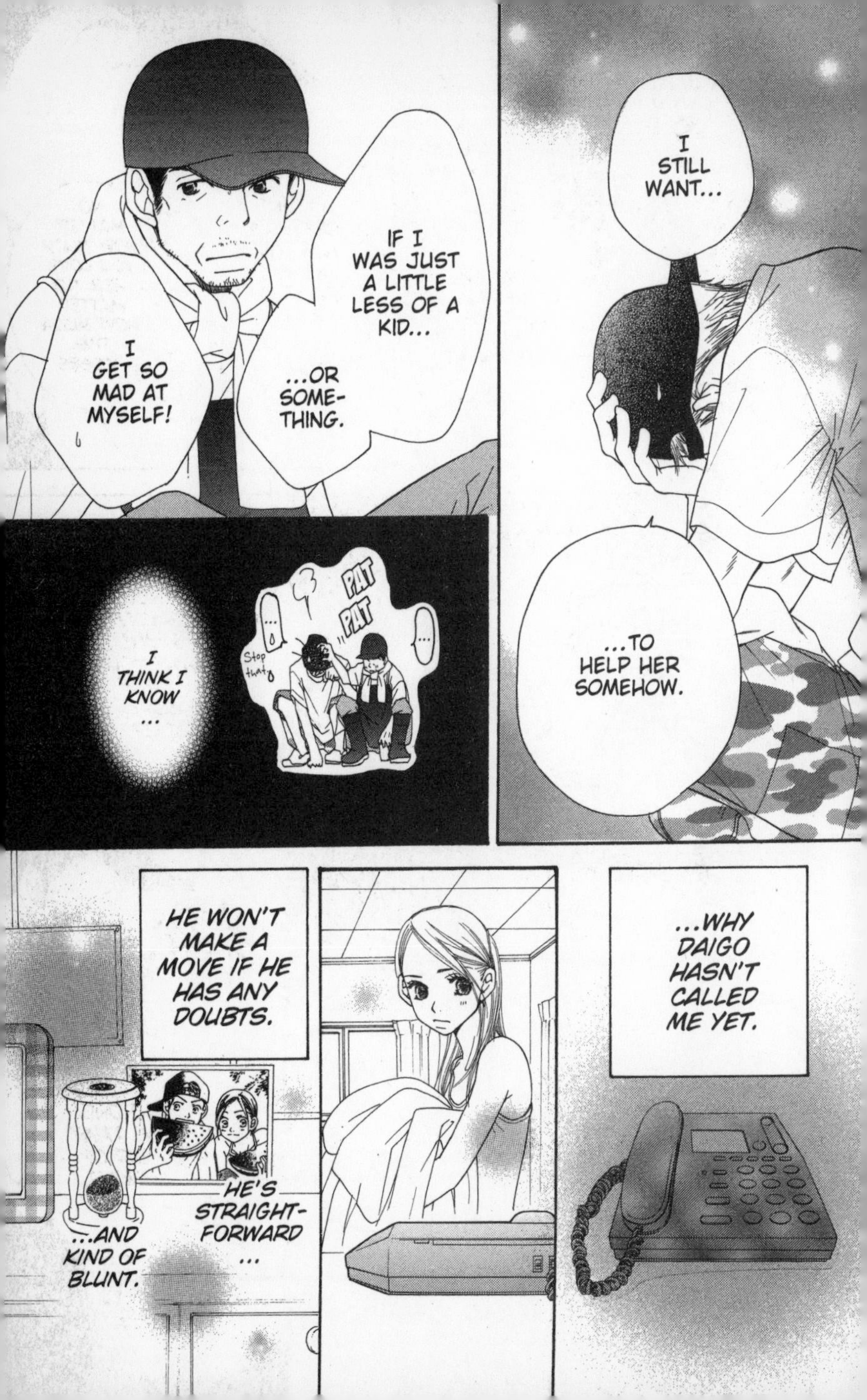
I STILL WANT...
...TO HELP HER SOMEHOW.
IF I WAS JUST A LITTLE LESS OF A KID...
...OR SOME-THING.
I GET SO MAD AT MYSELF!
...
PAT PAT
...
Stop that
I THINK I KNOW ...
...WHY DAIGO HASN'T CALLED ME YET.
HE WON'T MAKE A MOVE IF HE HAS ANY DOUBTS.
HE'S STRAIGHT-FORWARD ...
...AND KIND OF BLUNT.

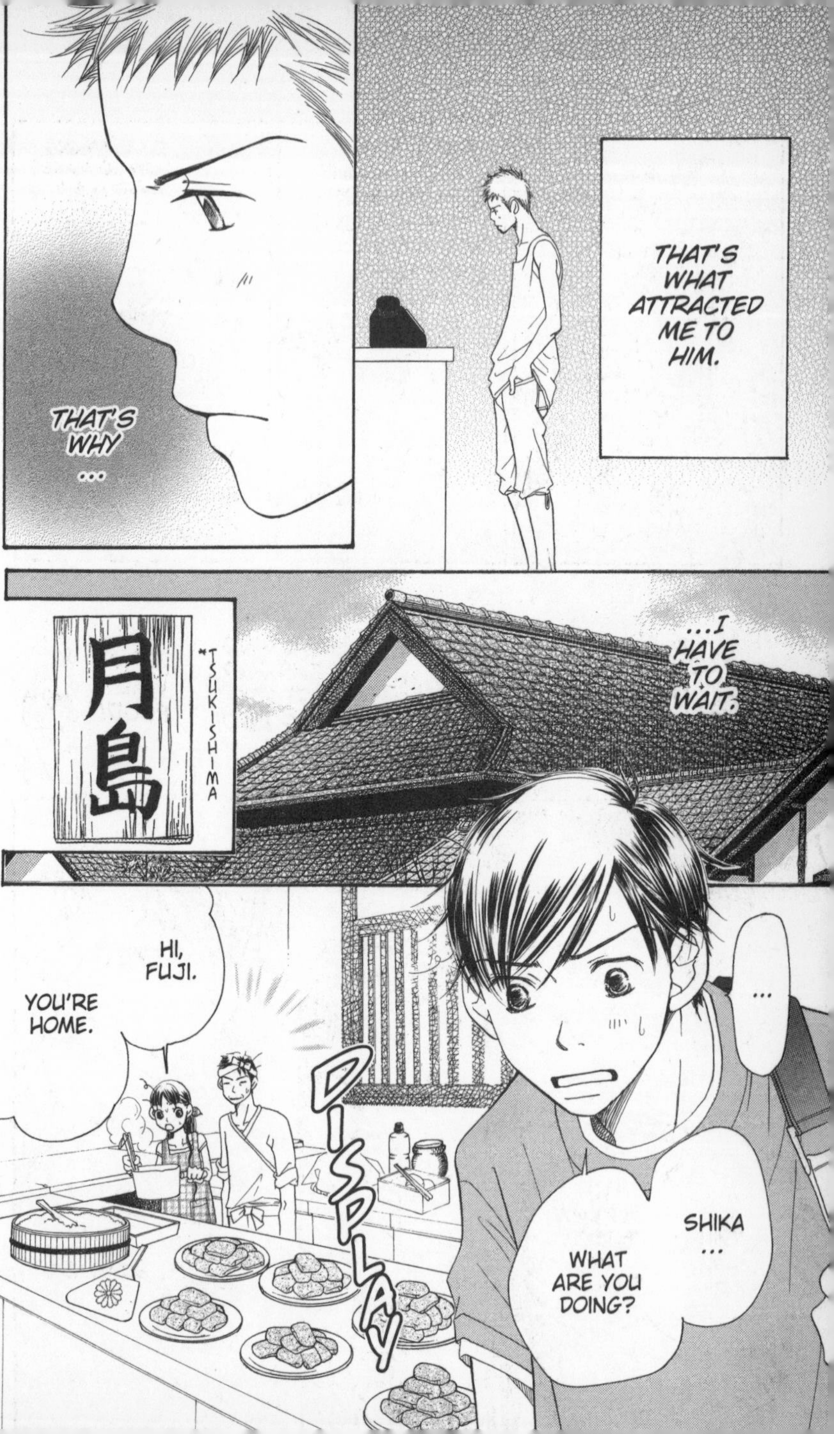
THAT'S WHAT ATTRACTED ME TO HIM.
THAT'S WHY ...
...I HAVE TO WAIT.
月島
*TSUKISHIMA
HI, FUJI.
YOU'RE HOME.
DISPLAY
...
SHIKA ...
WHAT ARE YOU DOING?

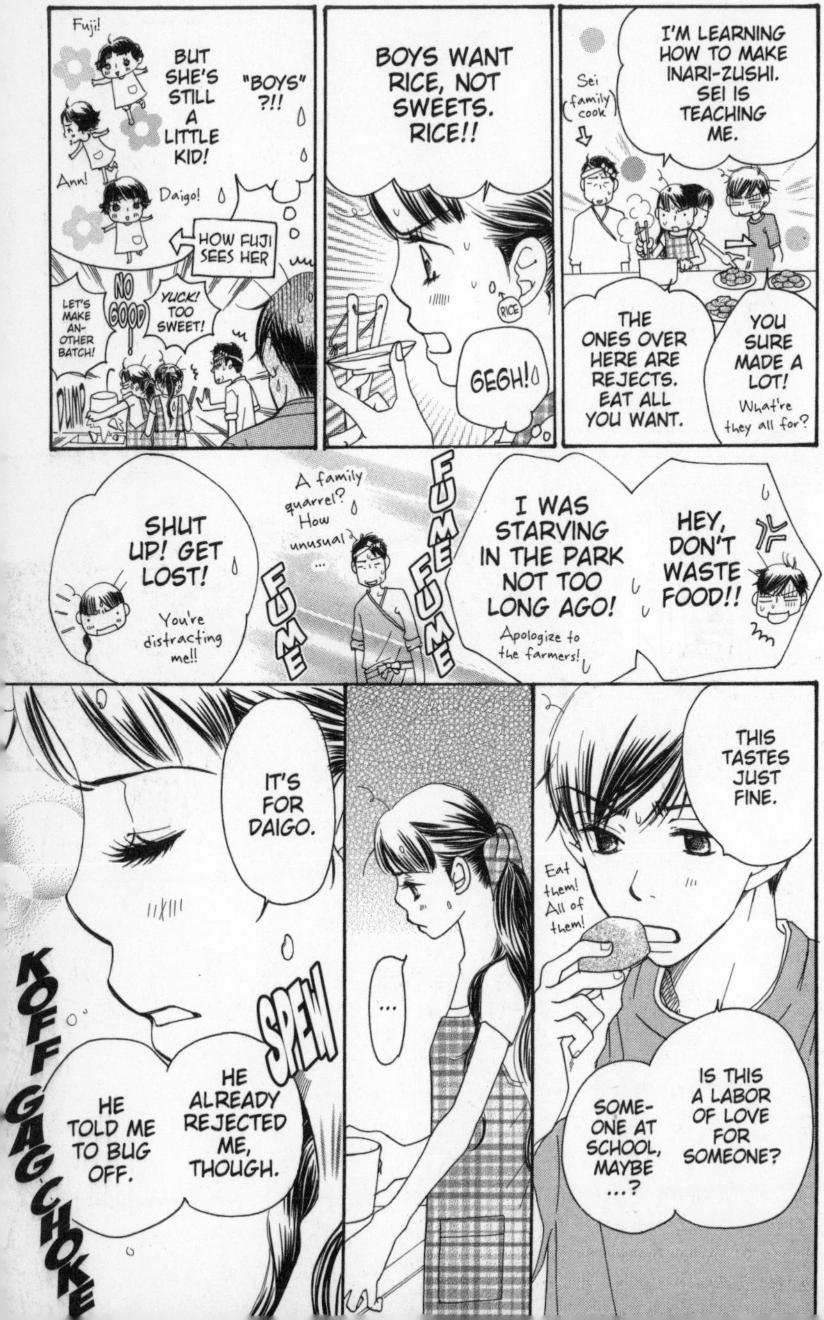
I'M LEARNING HOW TO MAKE INARI-ZUSHI. SEI IS TEACHING ME.
Sei (family cook)
YOU SURE MADE A LOT!
What're they all for?
THE ONES OVER HERE ARE REJECTS. EAT ALL YOU WANT.
BOYS WANT RICE, NOT SWEETS. RICE!!
RICE
GEGH!
"BOYS"?!!
BUT SHE'S STILL A LITTLE KID!
Fuji!
Ann!
Daigo!
HOW FUJI SEES HER
YUCK! TOO SWEET!
NO GOOD!
LET'S MAKE AN-OTHER BATCH!
DUMP
HEY, DON'T WASTE FOOD!!
I WAS STARVING IN THE PARK NOT TOO LONG AGO!
Apologize to the farmers!
FUME FUME
A family quarrel? How unusual...
FUME
SHUT UP! GET LOST!
You're distracting me!!
THIS TASTES JUST FINE.
Eat them! All of them!
IS THIS A LABOR OF LOVE FOR SOMEONE?
SOME-ONE AT SCHOOL, MAYBE ...?
...
IT'S FOR DAIGO.
SPEW
HE ALREADY REJECTED ME, THOUGH.
HE TOLD ME TO BUG OFF.
KOFF GAG CHOKE

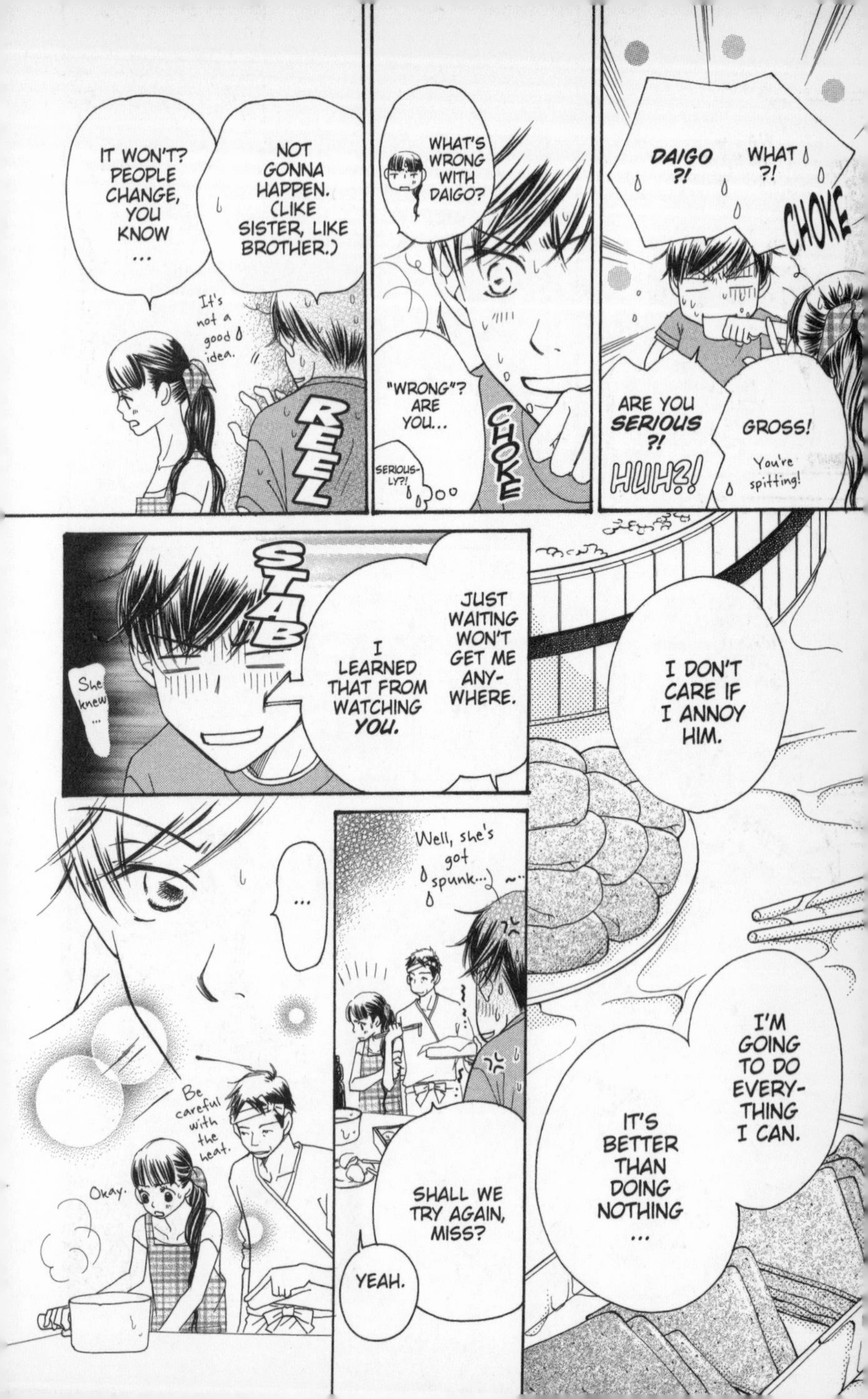
WHAT ?!
DAIGO ?!
CHOKE
GROSS!
You're spitting!
ARE YOU SERIOUS ?!
HUH?!
WHAT'S WRONG WITH DAIGO?
CHOKE
"WRONG"? ARE YOU...
SERIOUSLY?!
NOT GONNA HAPPEN. (LIKE SISTER, LIKE BROTHER.)
IT WON'T? PEOPLE CHANGE, YOU KNOW ...
REEL
It's not a good idea.
I DON'T CARE IF I ANNOY HIM.
I'M GOING TO DO EVERY-THING I CAN.
IT'S BETTER THAN DOING NOTHING ...
JUST WAITING WON'T GET ME ANY-WHERE.
I LEARNED THAT FROM WATCHING YOU.
STAB
She knew ...
Well, she's got spunk...
SHALL WE TRY AGAIN, MISS?
YEAH.
...
Be careful with the heat.
Okay.

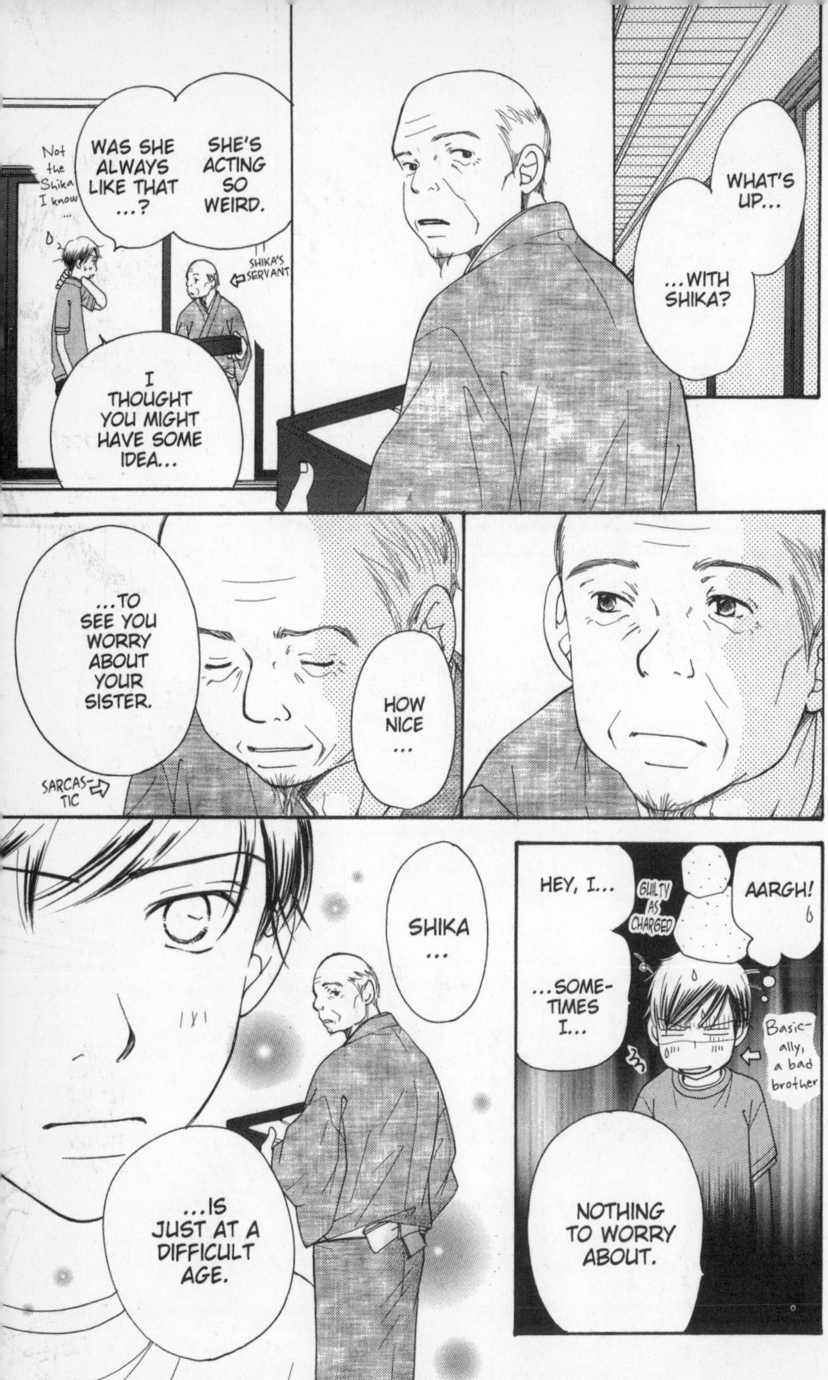
WHAT'S UP...
...WITH SHIKA?
SHE'S ACTING SO WEIRD.
WAS SHE ALWAYS LIKE THAT ...?
Not the Shika I know ...
SHIKA'S SERVANT
I THOUGHT YOU MIGHT HAVE SOME IDEA...
HOW NICE ...
...TO SEE YOU WORRY ABOUT YOUR SISTER.
SARCASTIC
AARGH!
HEY, I...
GUILTY AS CHARGED
...SOMETIMES I...
Basically, a bad brother
NOTHING TO WORRY ABOUT.
SHIKA ...
...IS JUST AT A DIFFICULT AGE.

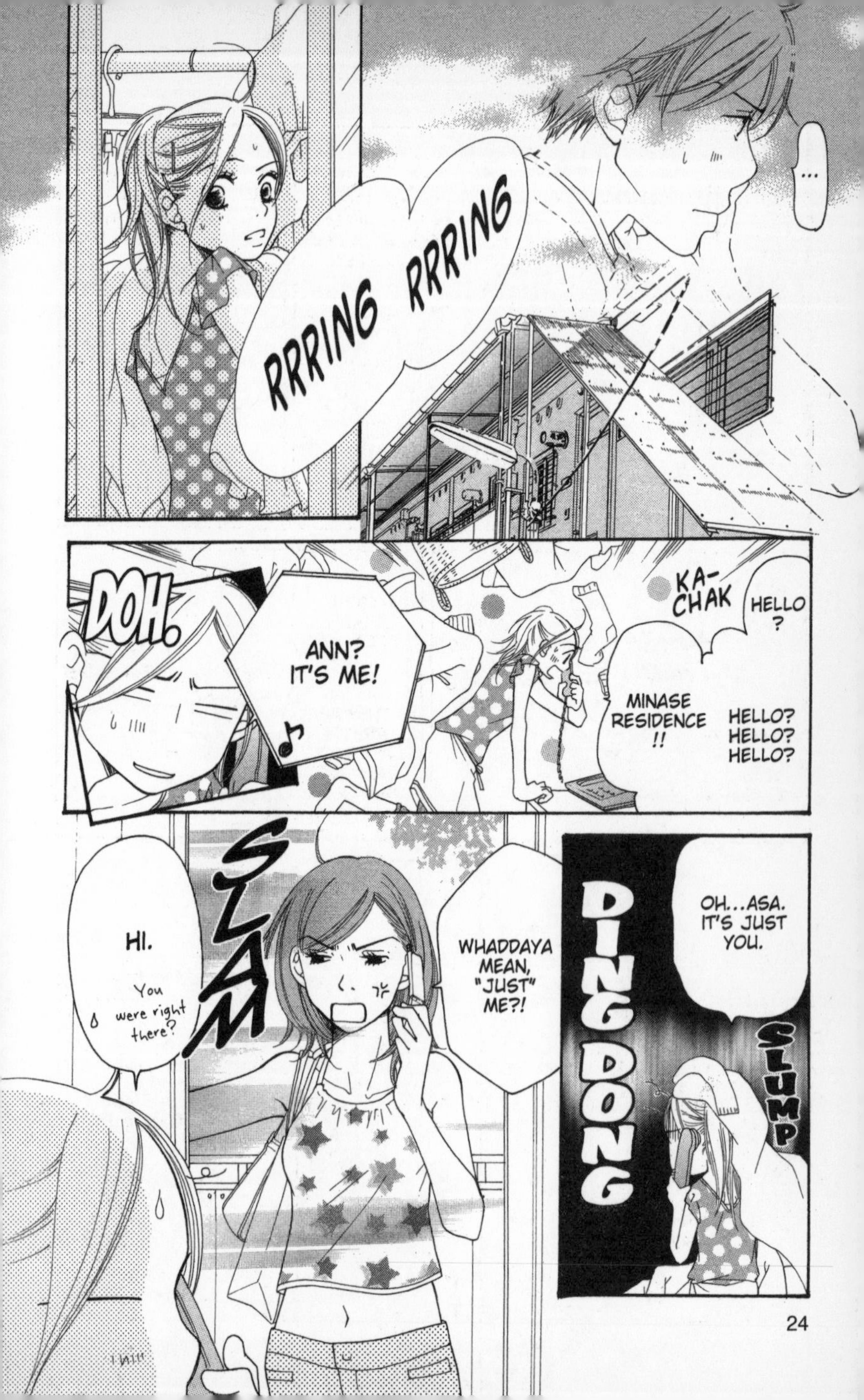
…
RRRING RRRING
KA-CHAK
HELLO?
MINASE RESIDENCE!!
HELLO? HELLO? HELLO?
ANN? IT'S ME! ♪
DOH.
DING DONG
OH…ASA. IT'S JUST YOU.
SLUMP
SLAM
WHADDAYA MEAN, "JUST" ME?!
HI.
You were right there?

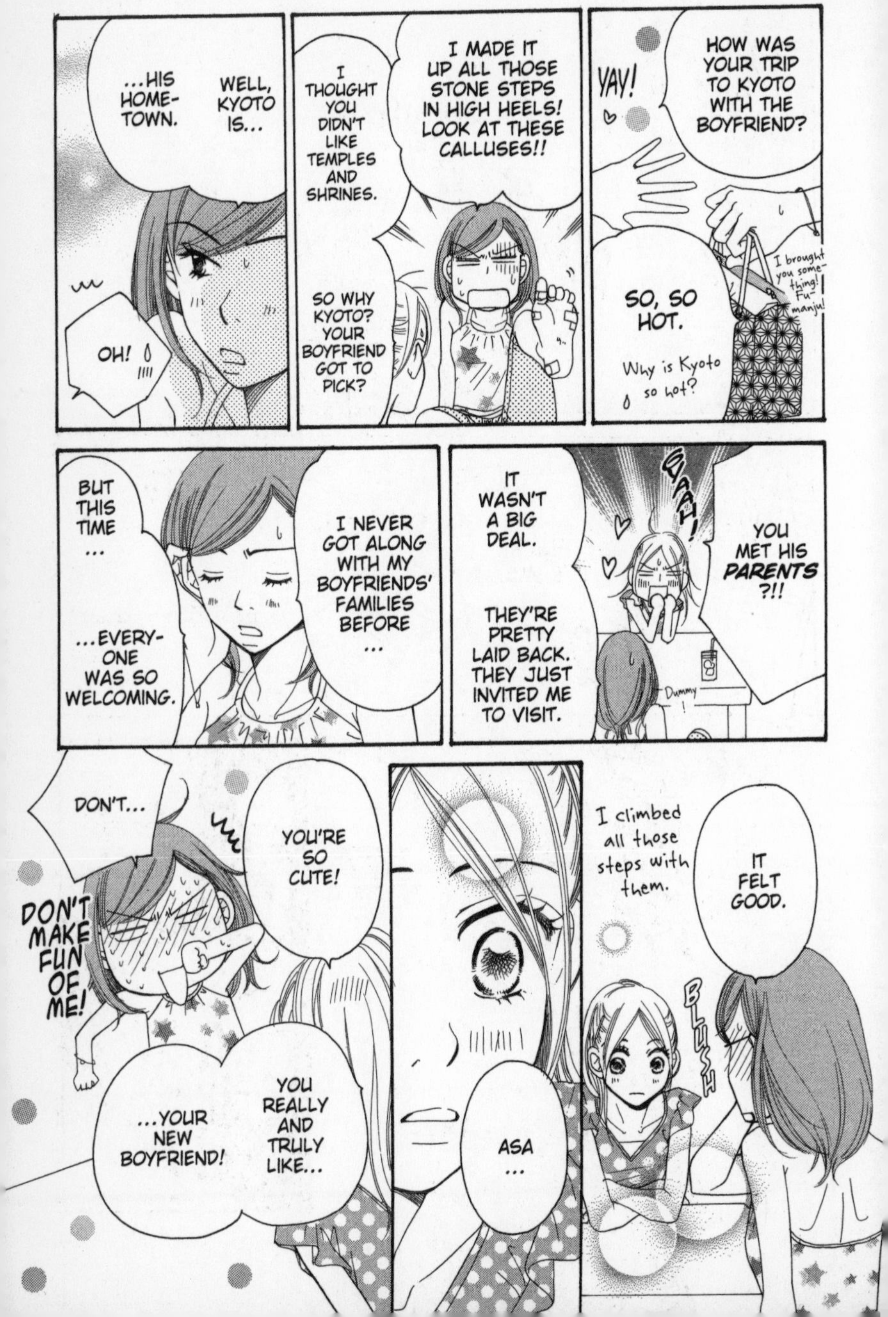
HOW WAS YOUR TRIP TO KYOTO WITH THE BOYFRIEND?
YAY!
I brought you something! Fu-manju!
SO, SO HOT.
Why is Kyoto so hot?
I MADE IT UP ALL THOSE STONE STEPS IN HIGH HEELS! LOOK AT THESE CALLUSES!!
I THOUGHT YOU DIDN'T LIKE TEMPLES AND SHRINES.
SO WHY KYOTO? YOUR BOYFRIEND GOT TO PICK?
WELL, KYOTO IS...
...HIS HOMETOWN.
OH!
YOU MET HIS PARENTS?!!
GYAAH!
Dummy!
IT WASN'T A BIG DEAL.
THEY'RE PRETTY LAID BACK. THEY JUST INVITED ME TO VISIT.
I NEVER GOT ALONG WITH MY BOYFRIENDS' FAMILIES BEFORE...
BUT THIS TIME...
...EVERYONE WAS SO WELCOMING.
IT FELT GOOD.
I climbed all those steps with them.
BLUSH
ASA...
YOU REALLY AND TRULY LIKE...
...YOUR NEW BOYFRIEND!
YOU'RE SO CUTE!
DON'T...
DON'T MAKE FUN OF ME!

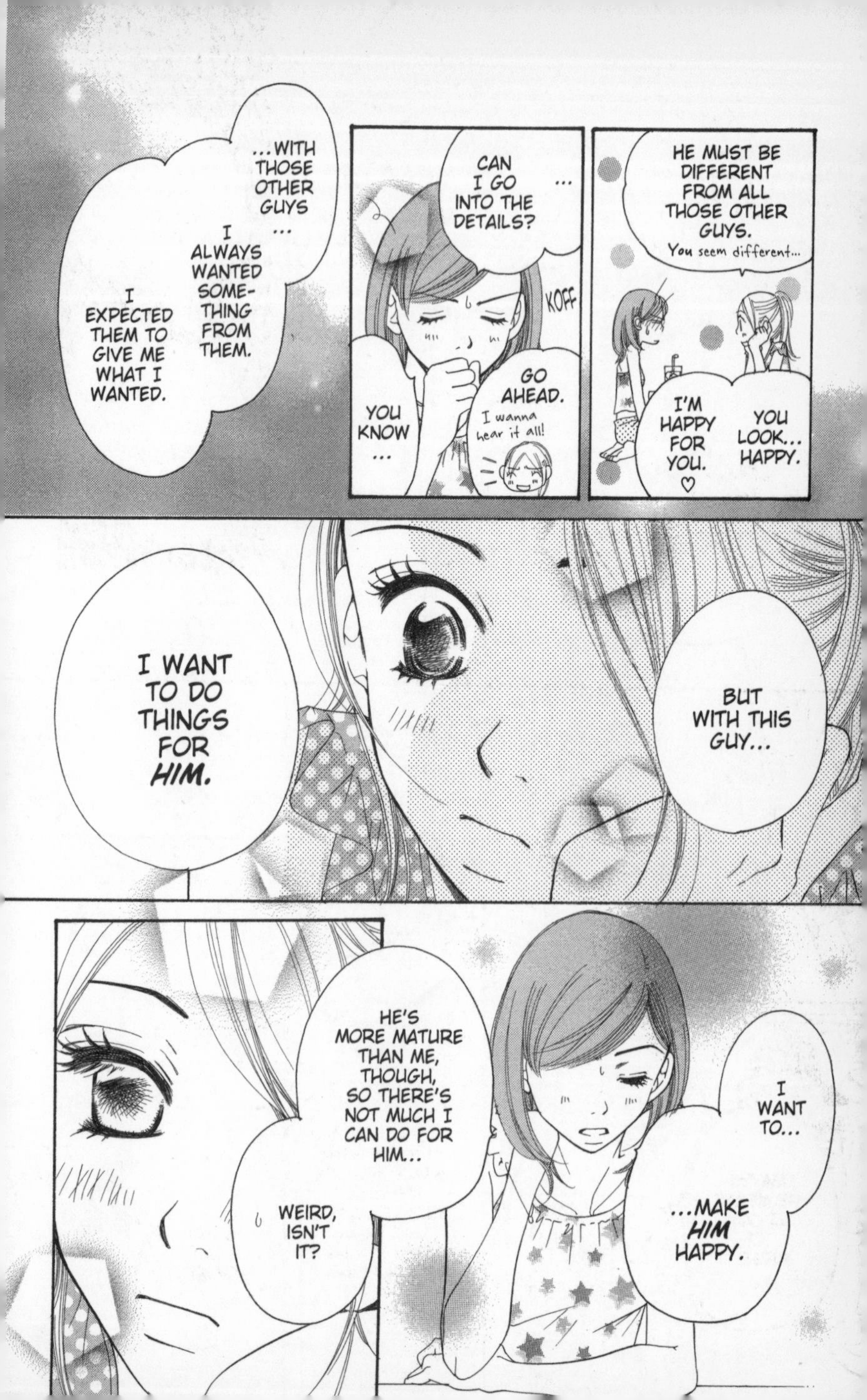

HE MUST BE DIFFERENT FROM ALL THOSE OTHER GUYS.
You seem different...
YOU LOOK... HAPPY.
I'M HAPPY FOR YOU. ♡
CAN I GO INTO THE DETAILS?
...
KOFF
GO AHEAD.
I wanna hear it all!
YOU KNOW ...
...WITH THOSE OTHER GUYS ...
I ALWAYS WANTED SOMETHING FROM THEM.
I EXPECTED THEM TO GIVE ME WHAT I WANTED.
BUT WITH THIS GUY...
I WANT TO DO THINGS FOR ***HIM.***
I WANT TO...
...MAKE ***HIM*** HAPPY.
HE'S MORE MATURE THAN ME, THOUGH, SO THERE'S NOT MUCH I CAN DO FOR HIM...
WEIRD, ISN'T IT?

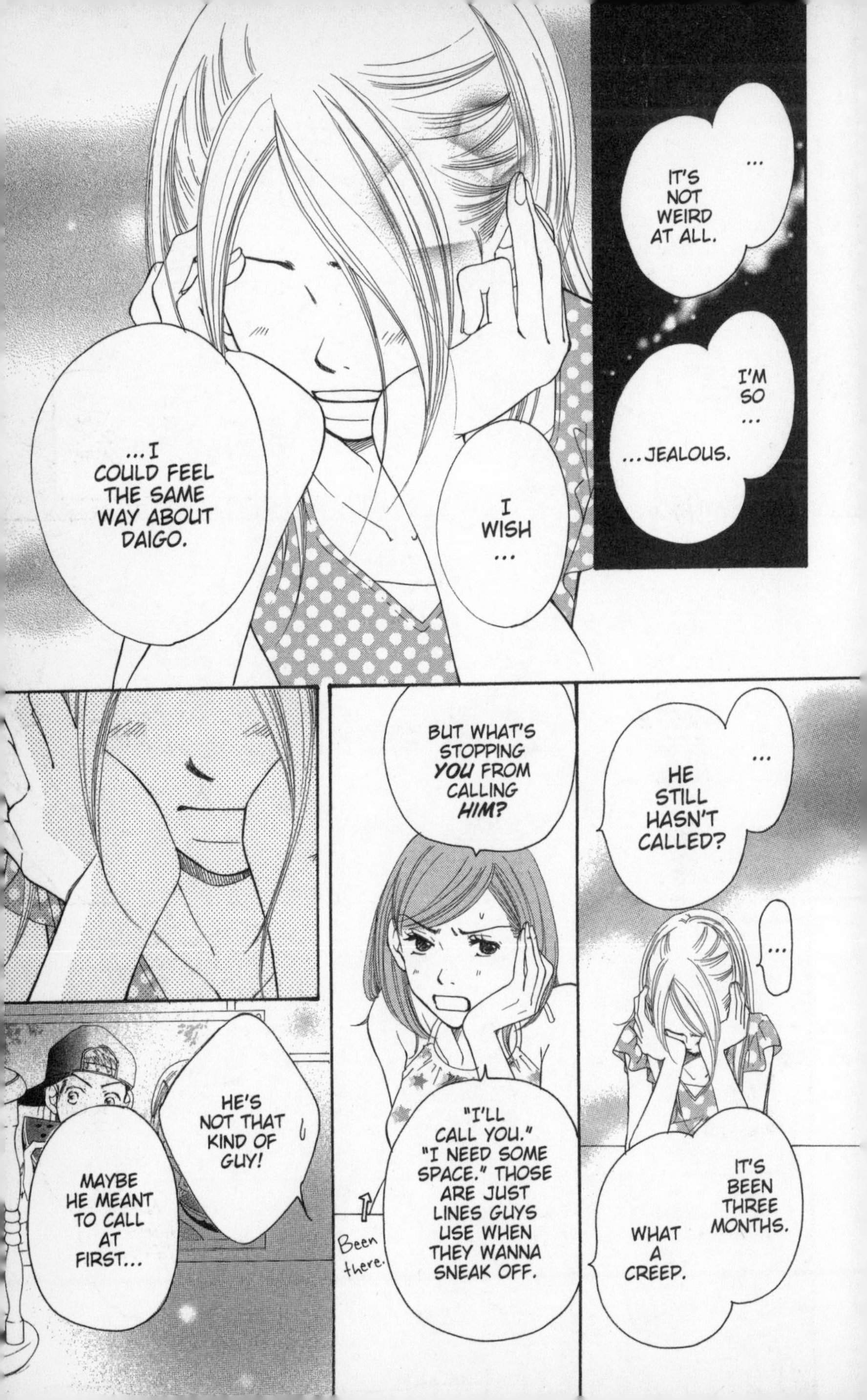
...
IT'S NOT WEIRD AT ALL.
I'M SO...
...JEALOUS.
I WISH...
...I COULD FEEL THE SAME WAY ABOUT DAIGO.
...
HE STILL HASN'T CALLED?
...
IT'S BEEN THREE MONTHS.
WHAT A CREEP.
BUT WHAT'S STOPPING *YOU* FROM CALLING *HIM*?
"I'LL CALL YOU." "I NEED SOME SPACE." THOSE ARE JUST LINES GUYS USE WHEN THEY WANNA SNEAK OFF.
Been there.
HE'S NOT THAT KIND OF GUY!
MAYBE HE MEANT TO CALL AT FIRST...

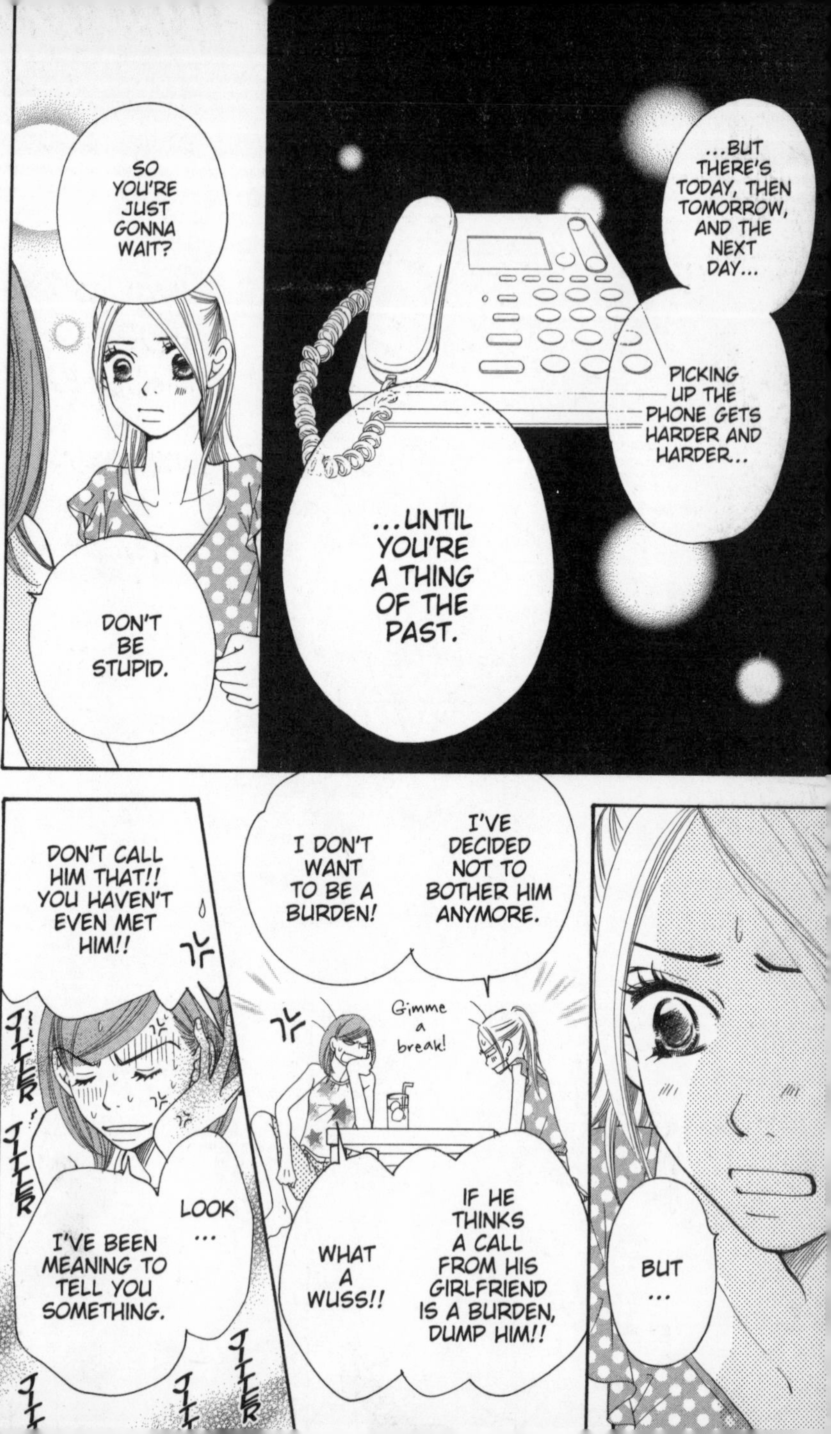
...BUT THERE'S TODAY, THEN TOMORROW, AND THE NEXT DAY...
PICKING UP THE PHONE GETS HARDER AND HARDER...
...UNTIL YOU'RE A THING OF THE PAST.
SO YOU'RE JUST GONNA WAIT?
DON'T BE STUPID.
BUT ...
I'VE DECIDED NOT TO BOTHER HIM ANYMORE.
I DON'T WANT TO BE A BURDEN!
Gimme a break!
IF HE THINKS A CALL FROM HIS GIRLFRIEND IS A BURDEN, DUMP HIM!!
WHAT A WUSS!!
DON'T CALL HIM THAT!! YOU HAVEN'T EVEN MET HIM!!
JITTER JITTER
LOOK ...
I'VE BEEN MEANING TO TELL YOU SOMETHING.
JITTER JITTER

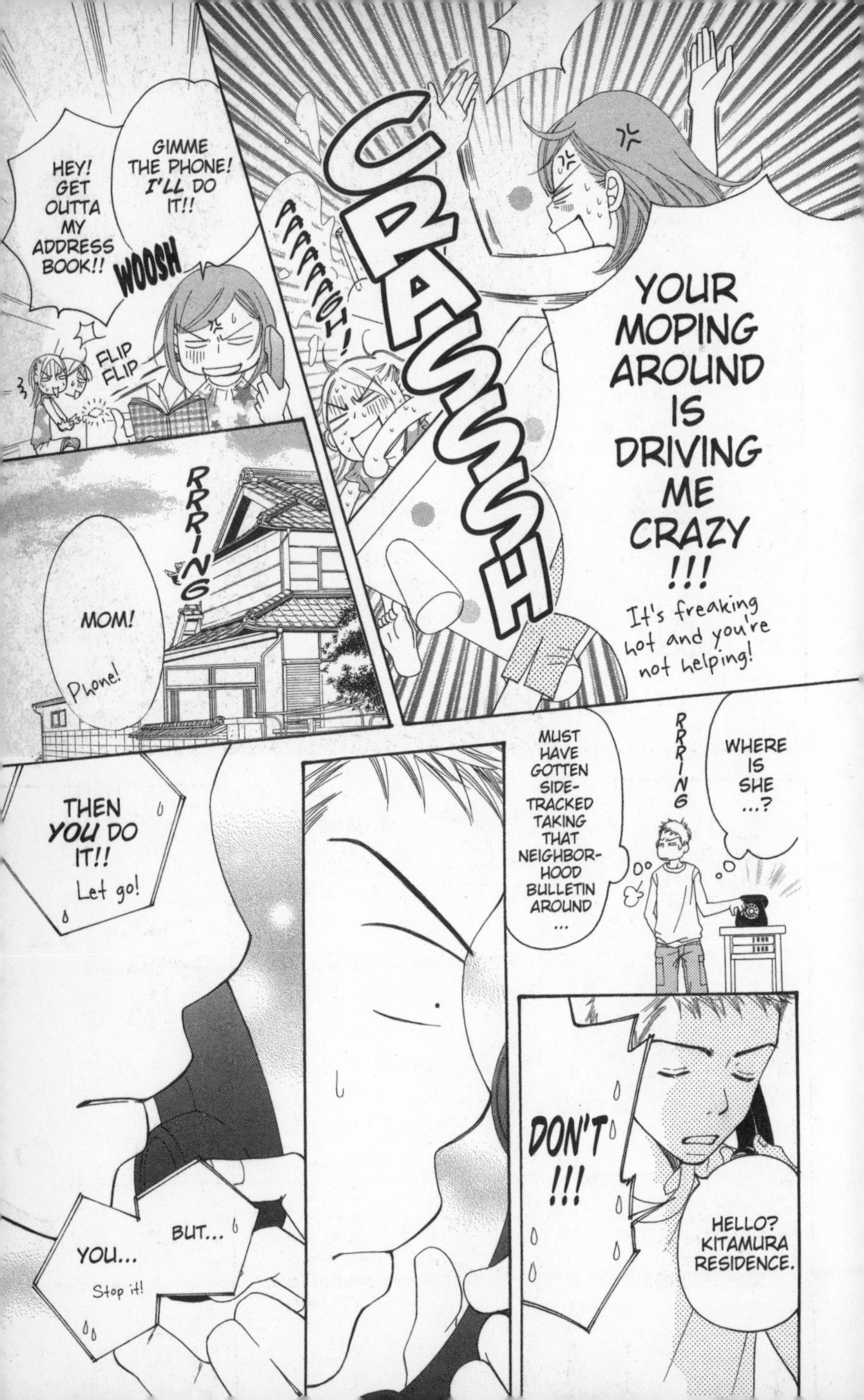
YOUR MOPING AROUND IS DRIVING ME CRAZY!!!
It's freaking hot and you're not helping!
AAAAAAAAGH!
CRASSSSH
GIMME THE PHONE! I'LL DO IT!!
HEY! GET OUTTA MY ADDRESS BOOK!!
WOOSH
FLIP FLIP
RRRING
MOM!
Phone!
WHERE IS SHE ...?
RRRING
MUST HAVE GOTTEN SIDE-TRACKED TAKING THAT NEIGHBOR-HOOD BULLETIN AROUND ...
HELLO? KITAMURA RESIDENCE.
DON'T!!!
THEN YOU DO IT!!
Let go!
BUT...
YOU...
Stop it!

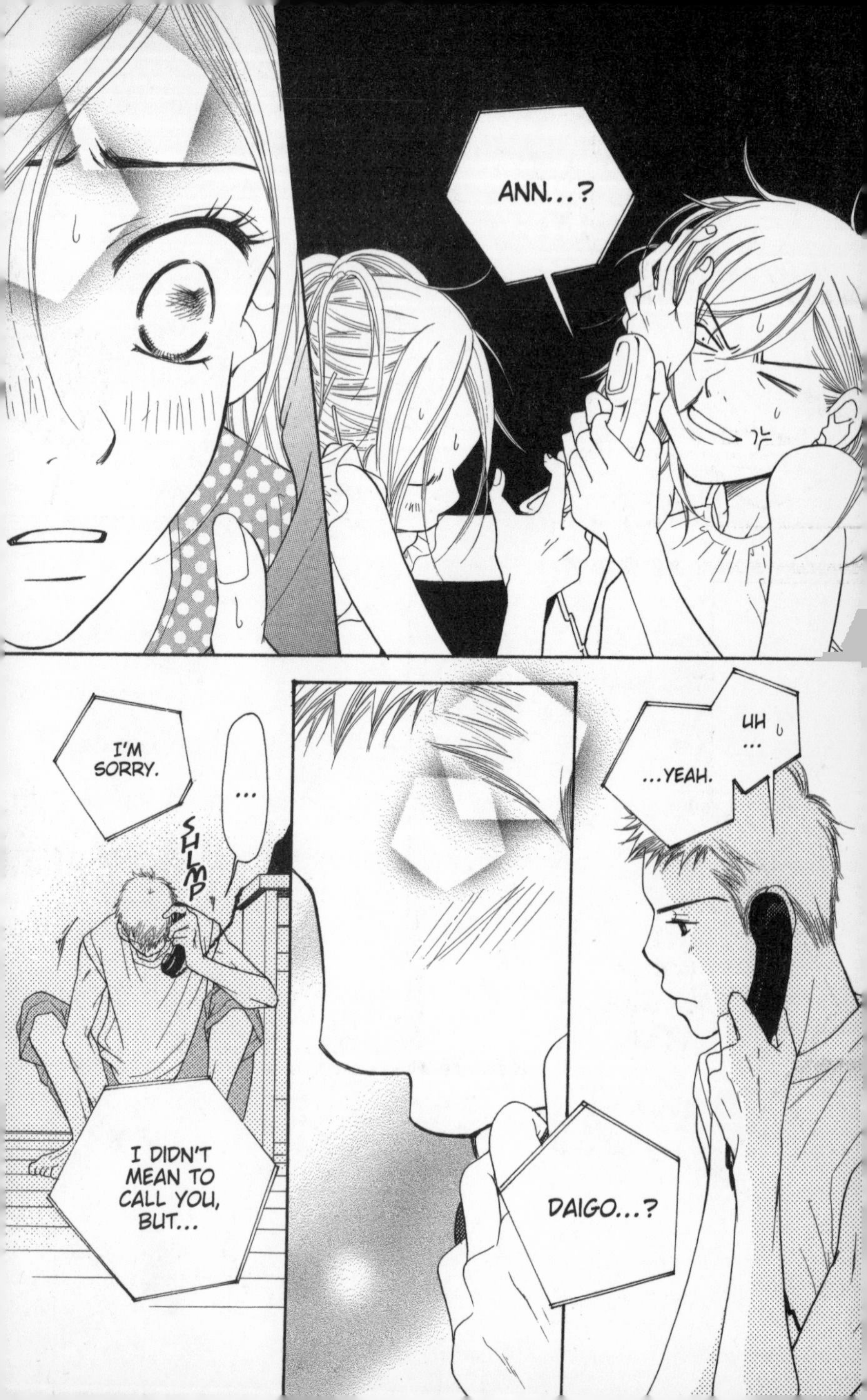
ANN...?
UH ...
...YEAH.
DAIGO...?
...
I'M SORRY.
SHLMP
I DIDN'T MEAN TO CALL YOU, BUT...

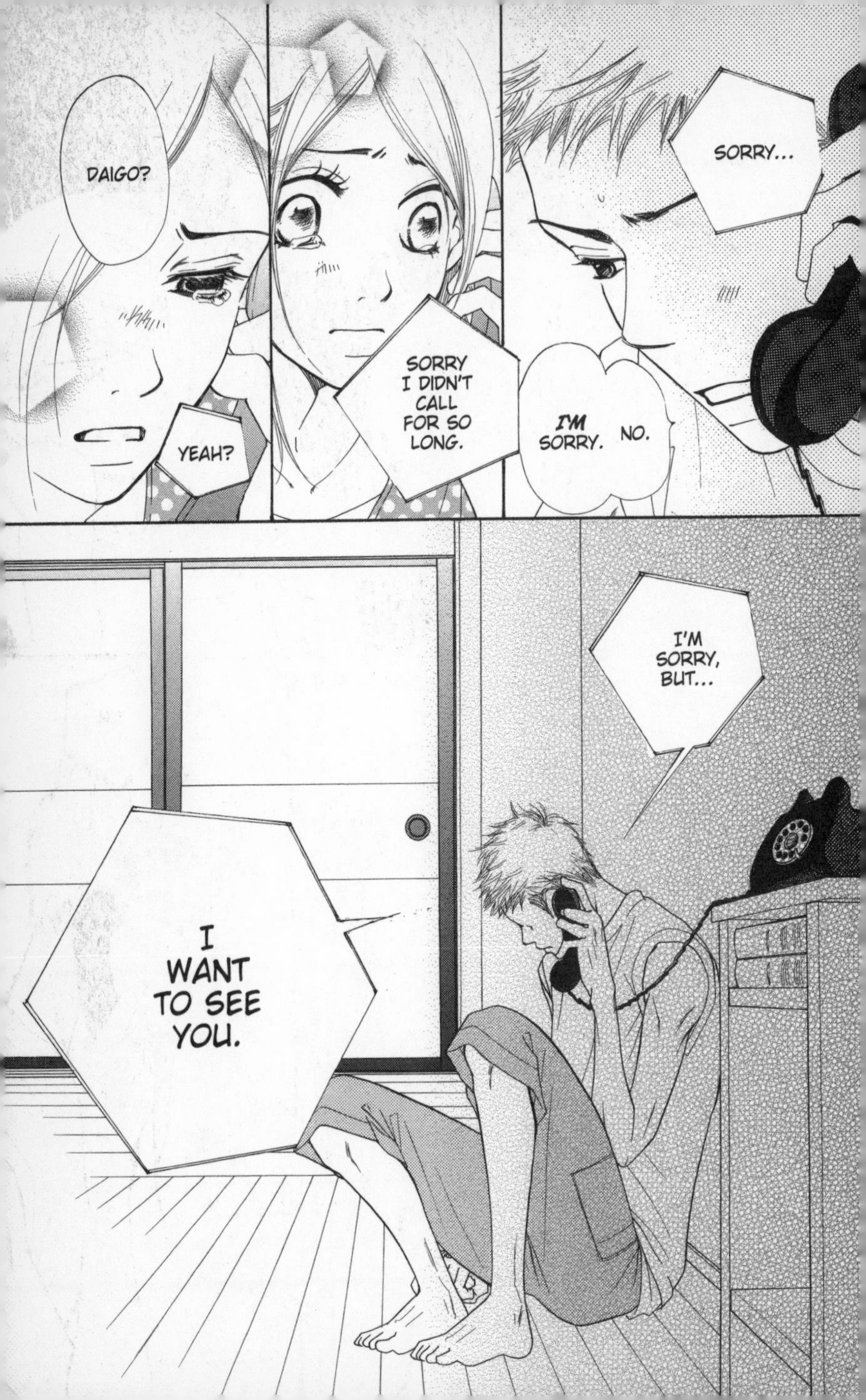
SORRY...
NO.
I'M SORRY.
SORRY I DIDN'T CALL FOR SO LONG.
DAIGO?
YEAH?
I'M SORRY, BUT...
I WANT TO SEE YOU.

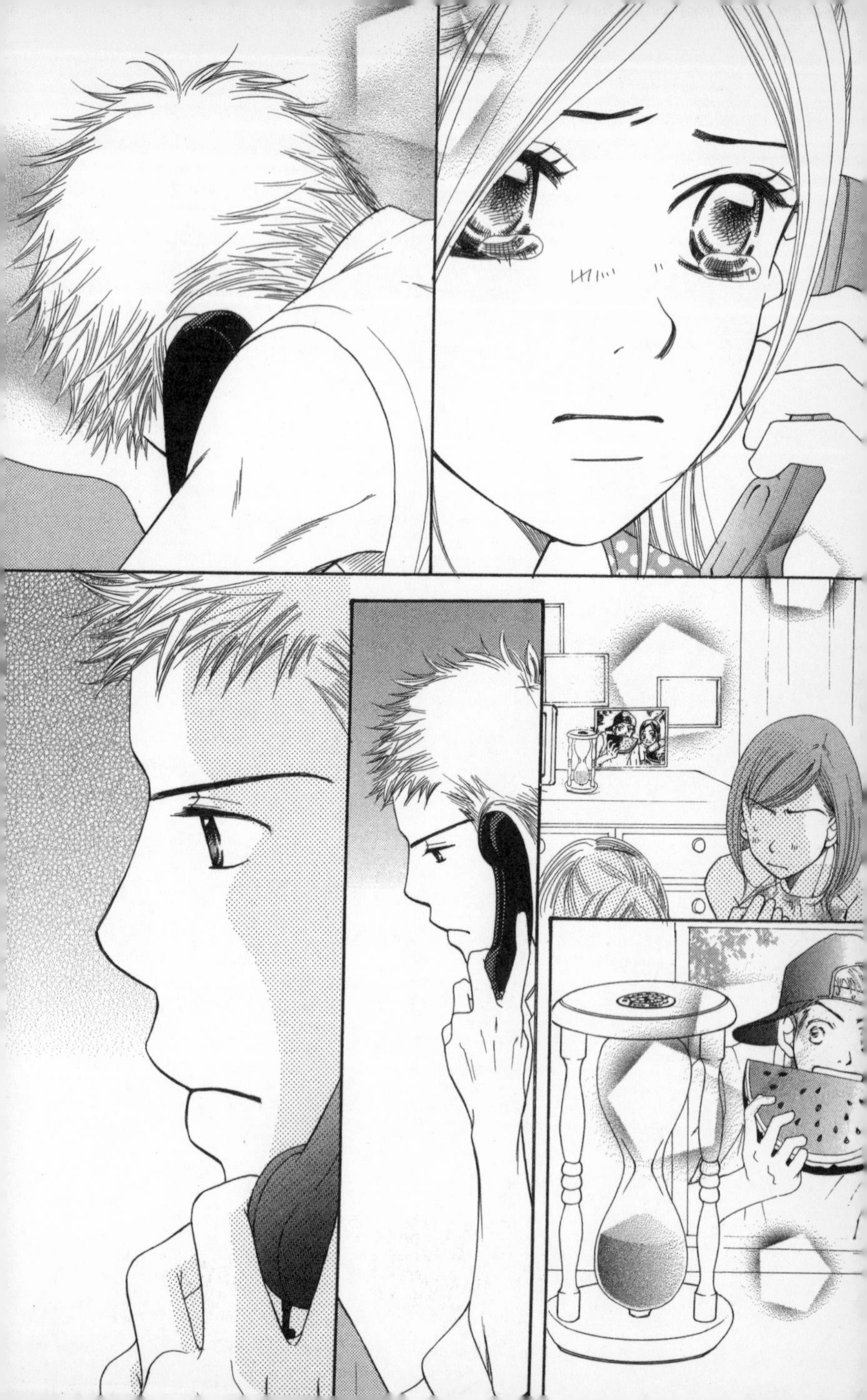

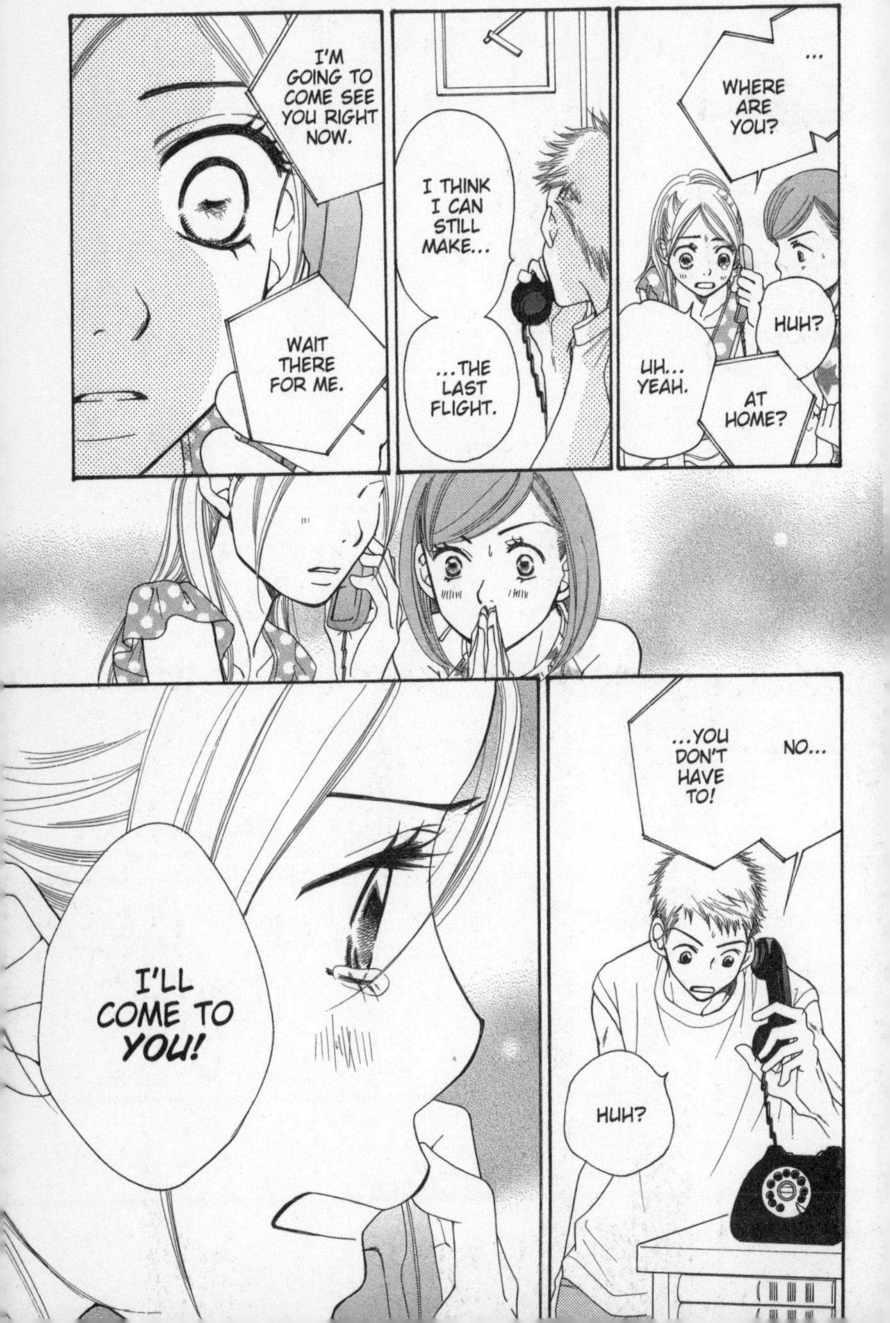
...
WHERE ARE YOU?
HUH?
AT HOME?
UH... YEAH.
I THINK I CAN STILL MAKE...
...THE LAST FLIGHT.
I'M GOING TO COME SEE YOU RIGHT NOW.
WAIT THERE FOR ME.
NO...
...YOU DON'T HAVE TO!
HUH?
I'LL COME TO YOU!

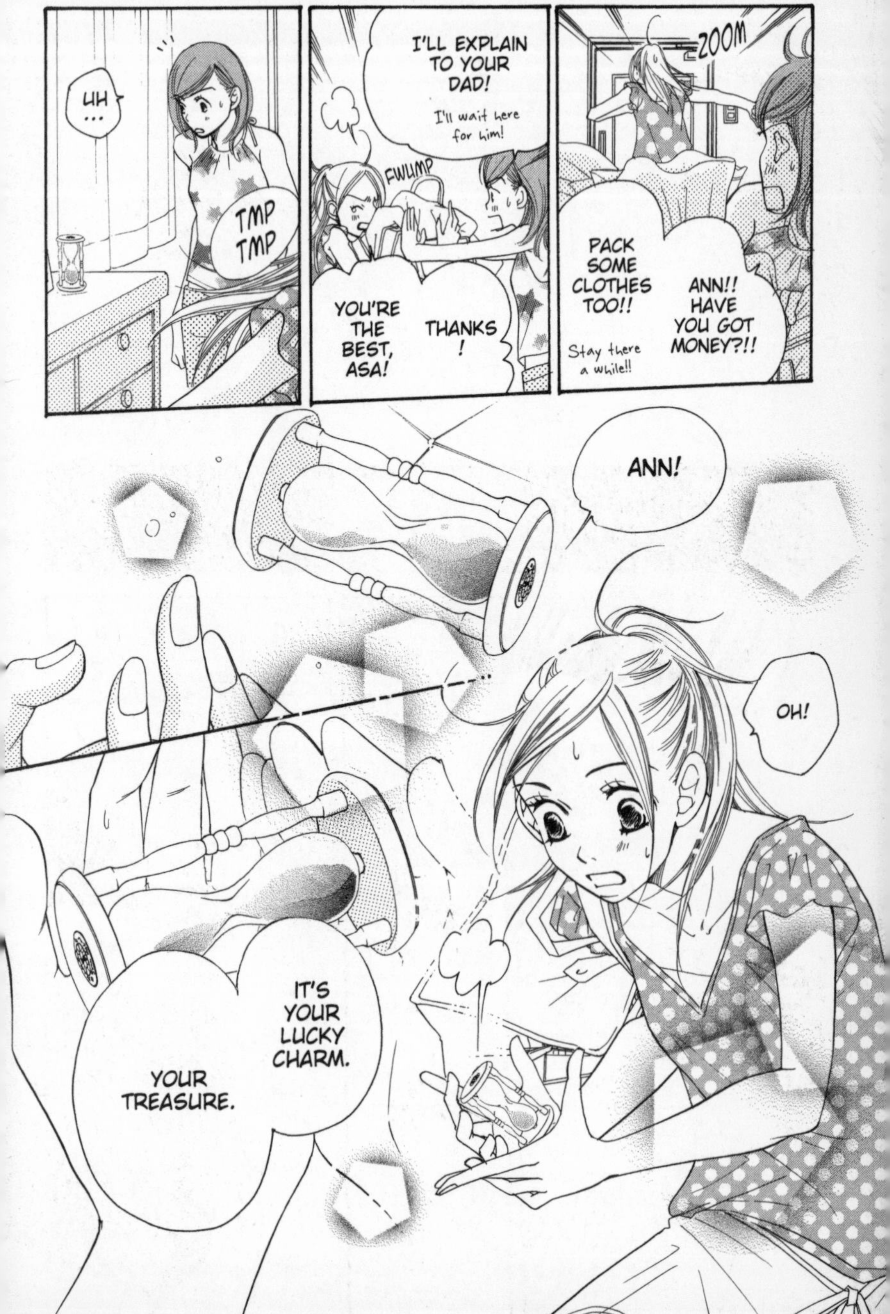
ZOOM
ANN!! HAVE YOU GOT MONEY?!!
PACK SOME CLOTHES TOO!!
Stay there a while!!
I'LL EXPLAIN TO YOUR DAD!
I'll wait here for him!
FWUMP
THANKS!
YOU'RE THE BEST, ASA!
UH...
TMP TMP
ANN!
OH!
IT'S YOUR LUCKY CHARM.
YOUR TREASURE.

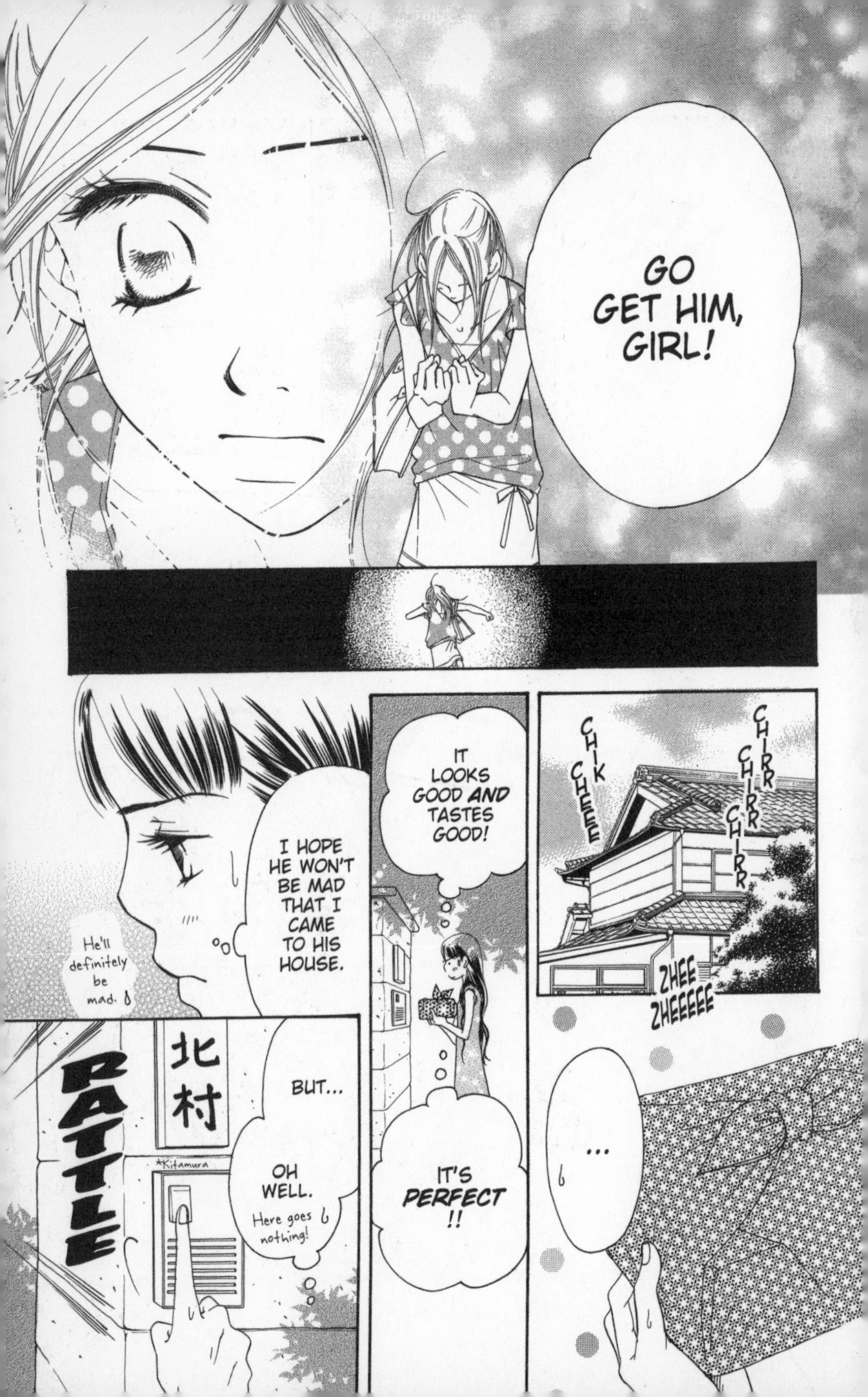
GO GET HIM, GIRL!
CHIRR CHIRR CHIRR
CHIK CHEEE
ZHEE ZHEEEEE
...
IT LOOKS GOOD AND TASTES GOOD!
IT'S PERFECT!!
I HOPE HE WON'T BE MAD THAT I CAME TO HIS HOUSE.
He'll definitely be mad.
BUT...
OH WELL.
Here goes nothing!
北村
*Kitamura
RATTLE

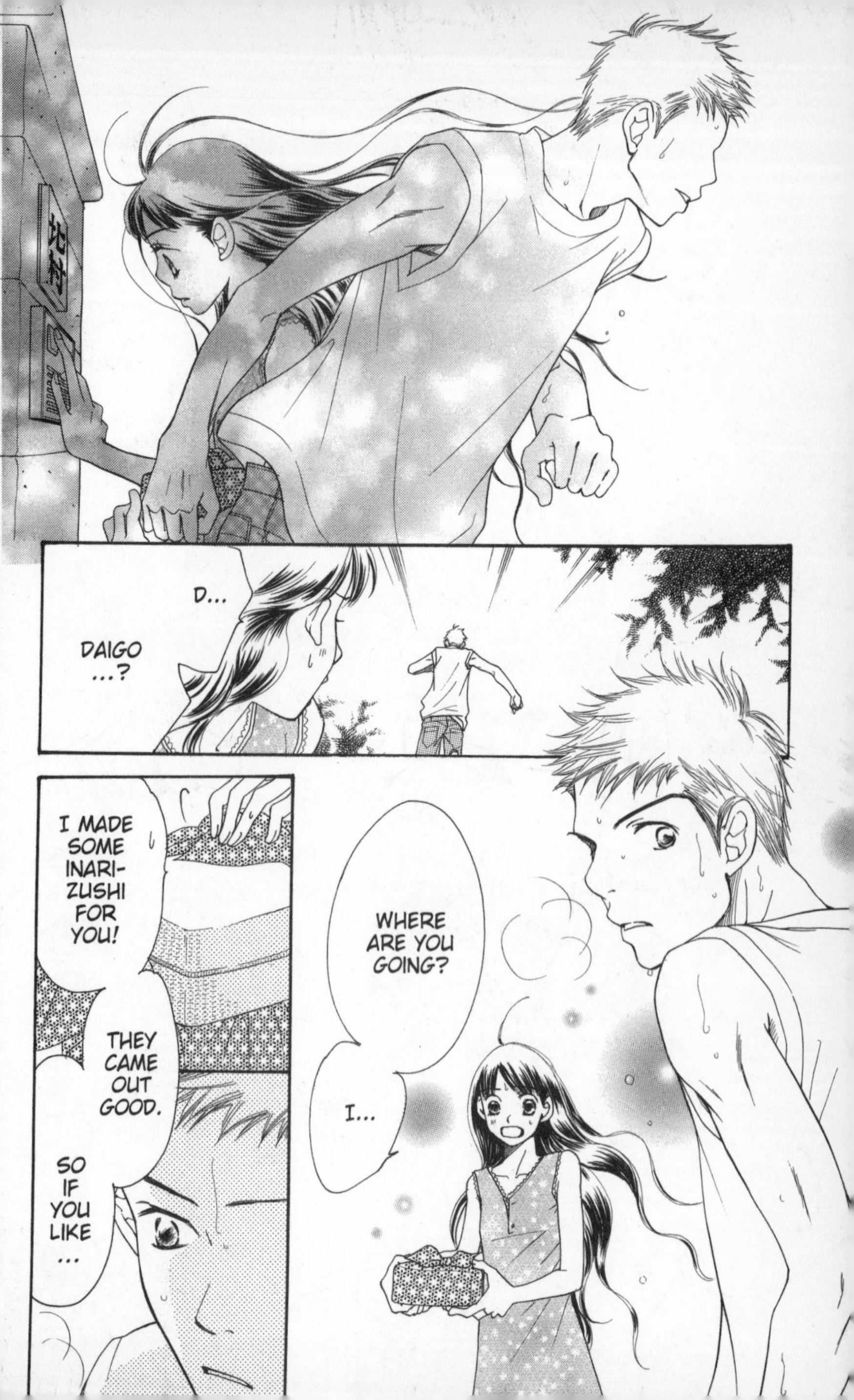
D...
DAIGO ...?
WHERE ARE YOU GOING?
I...
I MADE SOME INARI-ZUSHI FOR YOU!
THEY CAME OUT GOOD.
SO IF YOU LIKE ...

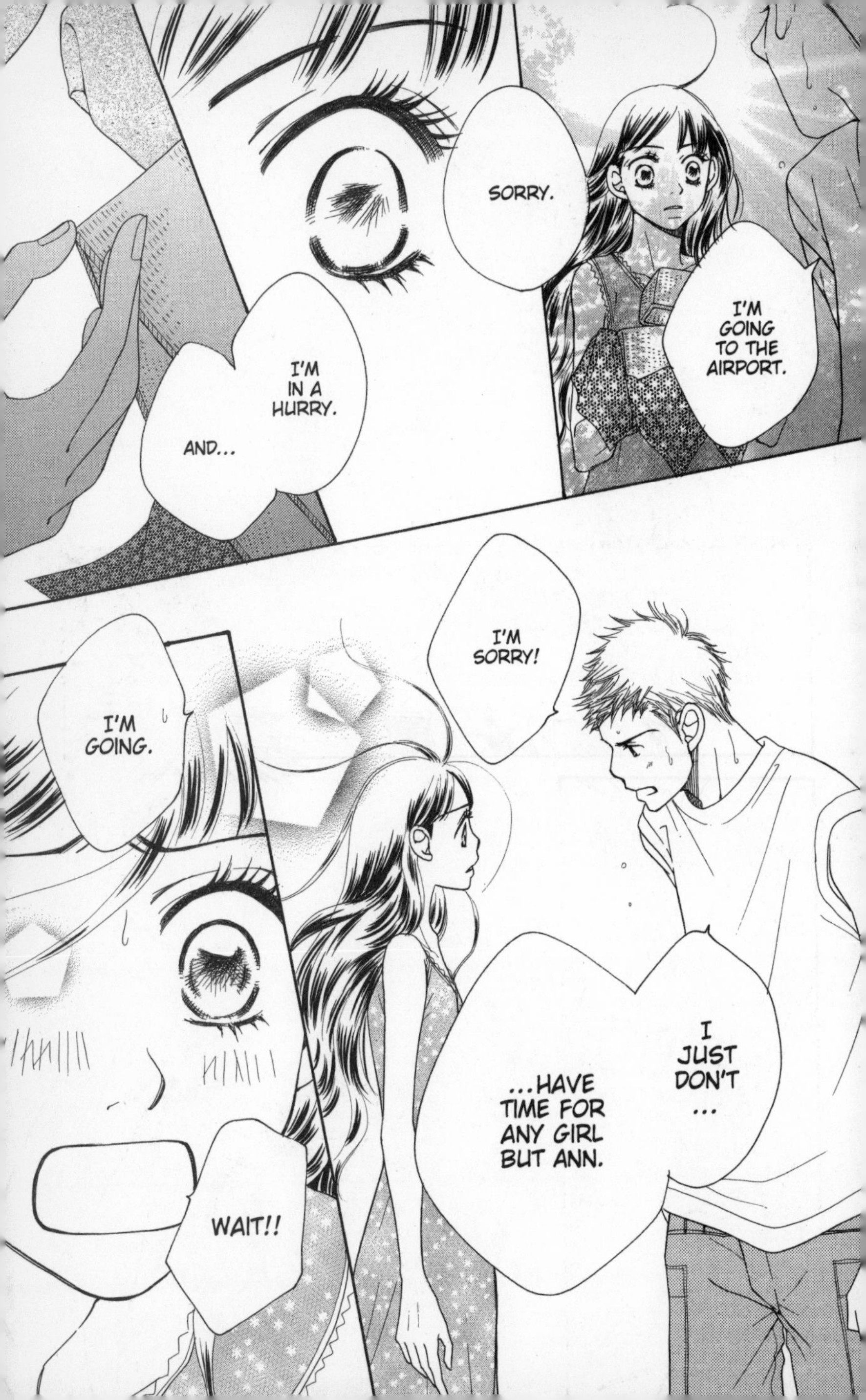
I'M GOING TO THE AIRPORT.
SORRY.
I'M IN A HURRY.
AND...
I'M SORRY!
I JUST DON'T...
...HAVE TIME FOR ANY GIRL BUT ANN.
I'M GOING.
WAIT!!

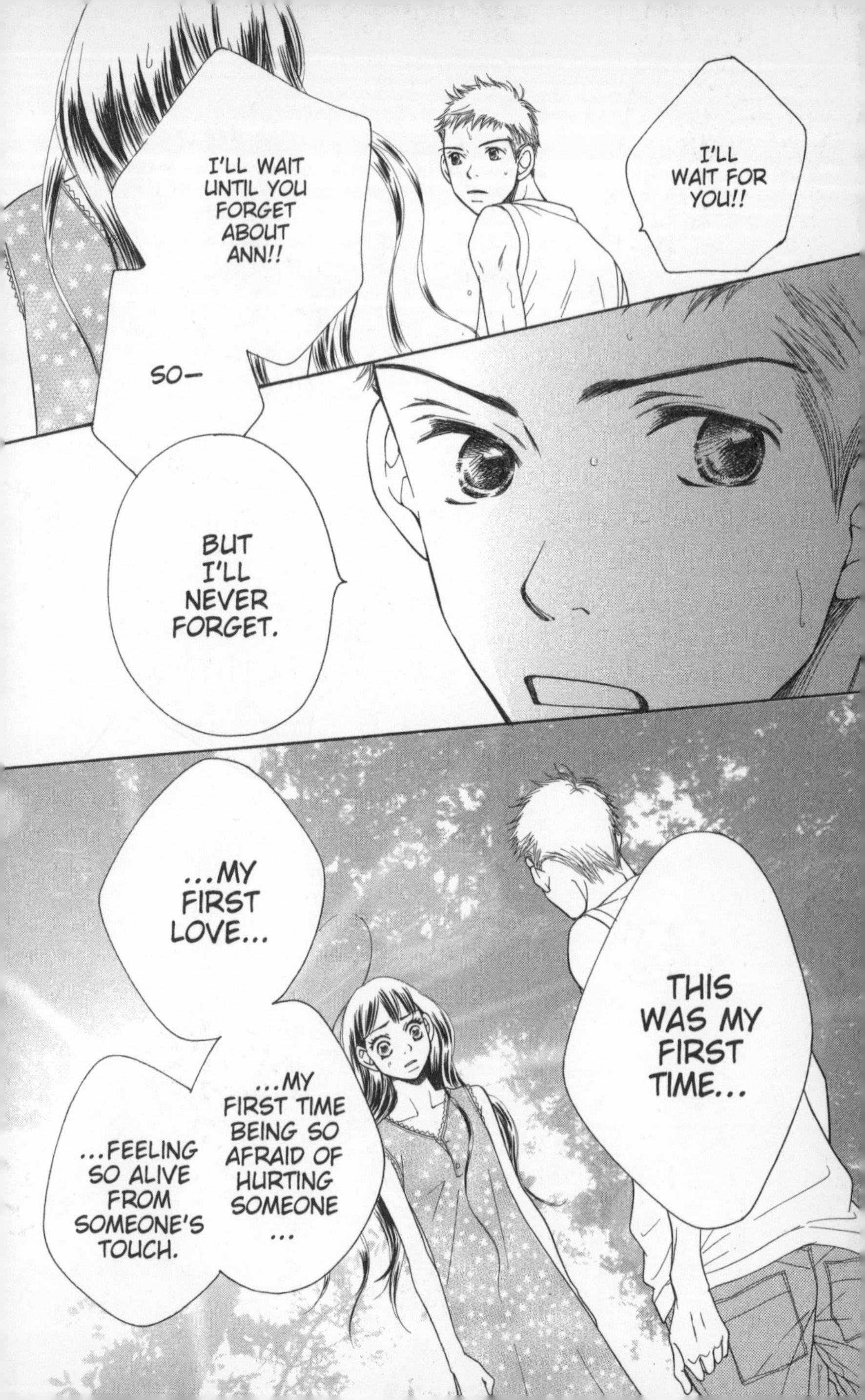
I'LL WAIT FOR YOU!!
I'LL WAIT UNTIL YOU FORGET ABOUT ANN!!
SO—
BUT I'LL NEVER FORGET.
THIS WAS MY FIRST TIME...
...MY FIRST LOVE...
...MY FIRST TIME BEING SO AFRAID OF HURTING SOMEONE...
...FEELING SO ALIVE FROM SOMEONE'S TOUCH.

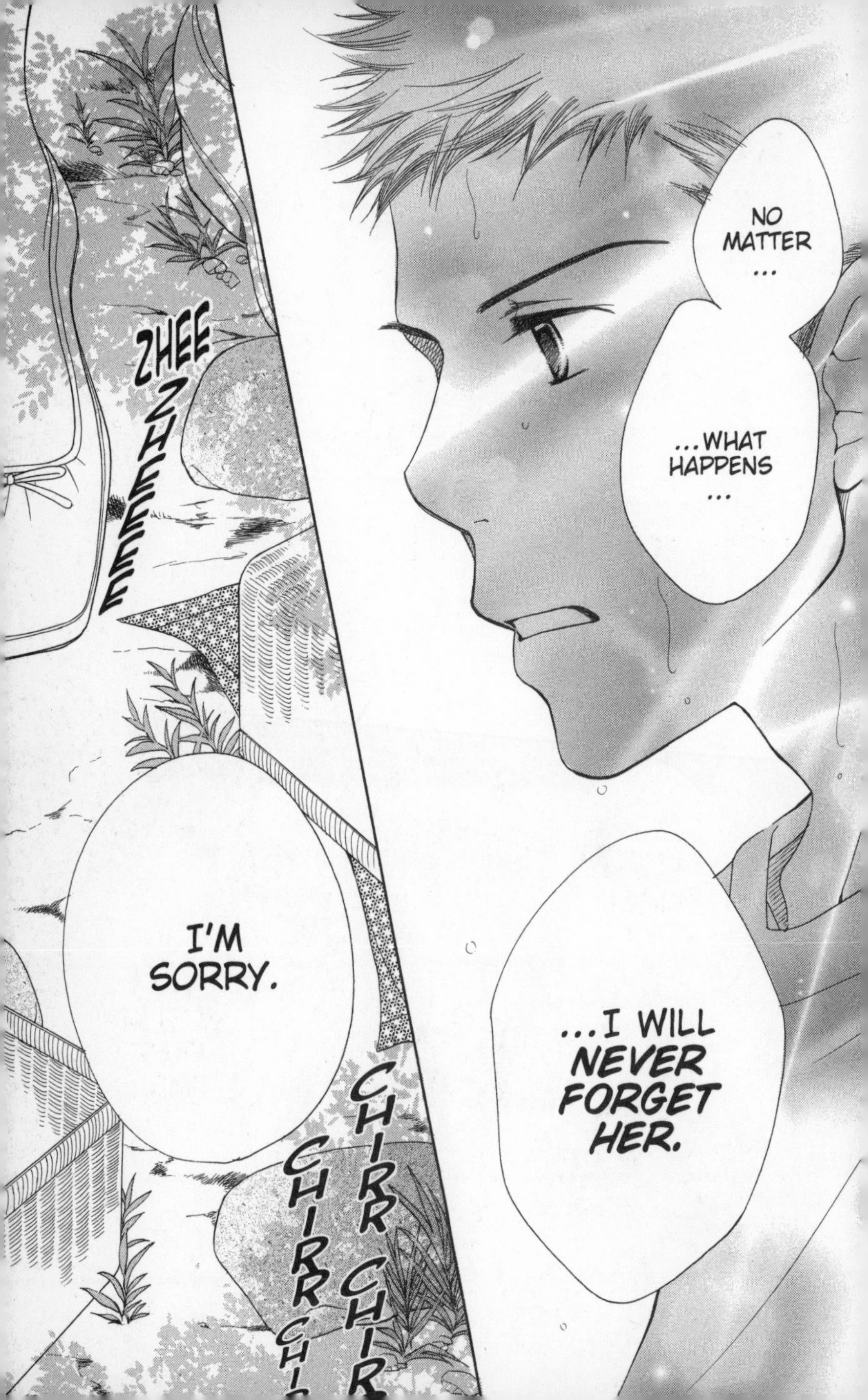
NO MATTER ...
...WHAT HAPPENS ...
...I WILL NEVER FORGET HER.
ZHEE ZHEEEEEE
I'M SORRY.
CHIRR CHIR
CHIRR CHI

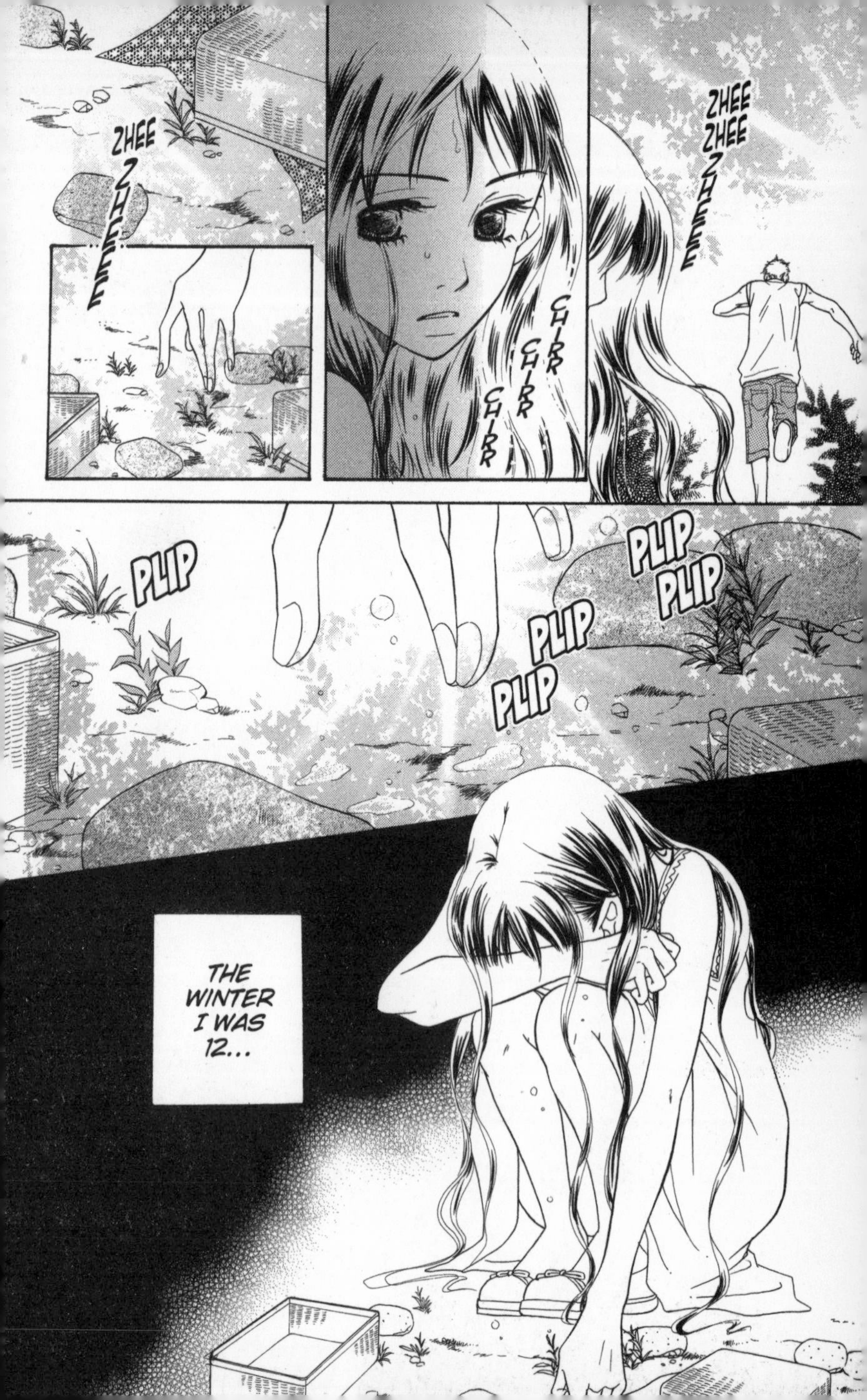
ZHEE ZHEE ZHEEEE
CHIRR CHIRR CHIRR
ZHEE ZHEEEE
PLIP PLIP
PLIP PLIP
PLIP
THE WINTER I WAS 12...

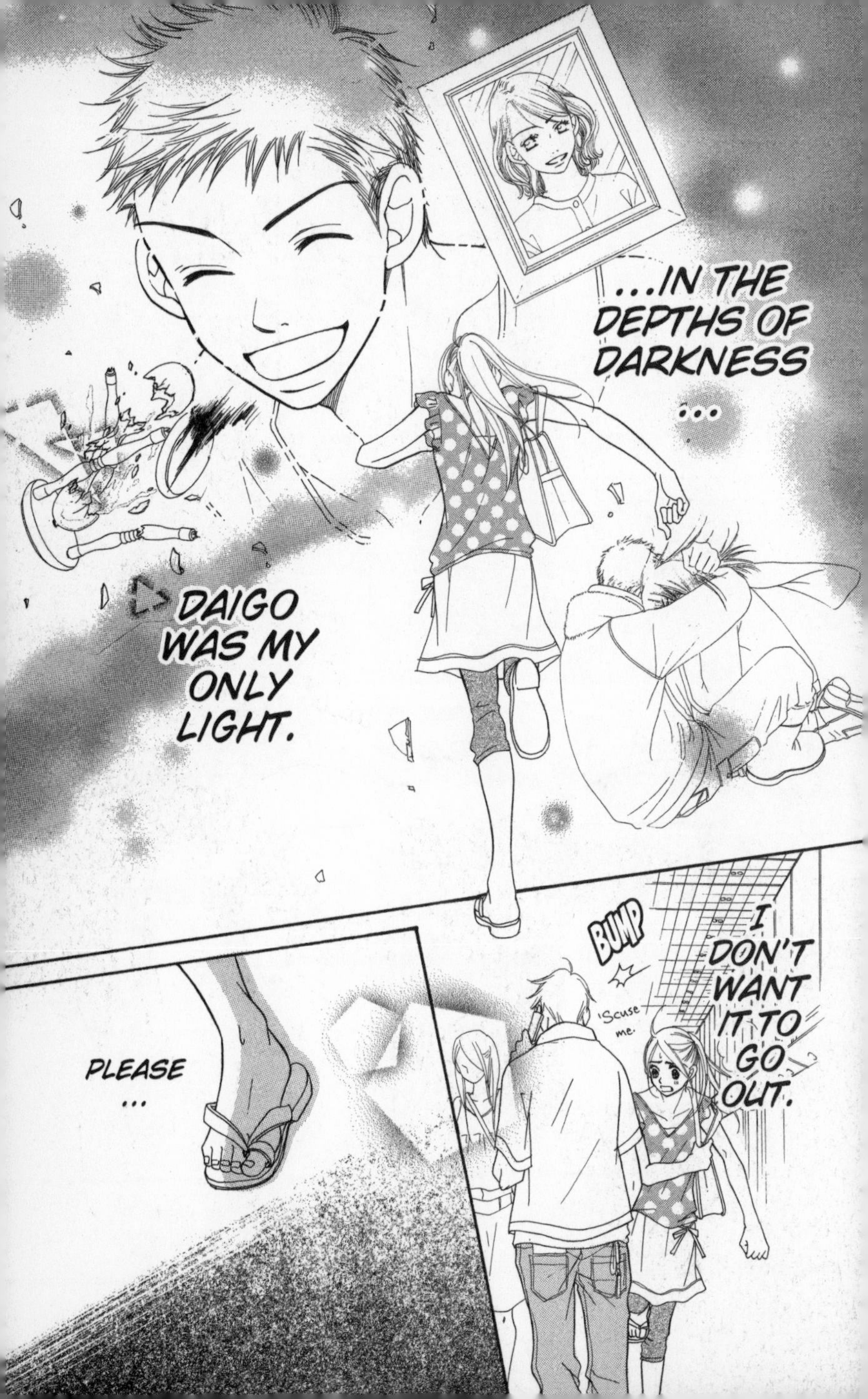
...IN THE DEPTHS OF DARKNESS ...
DAIGO WAS MY ONLY LIGHT.
BUMP
'Scuse me.
I DON'T WANT IT TO GO OUT.
PLEASE ...

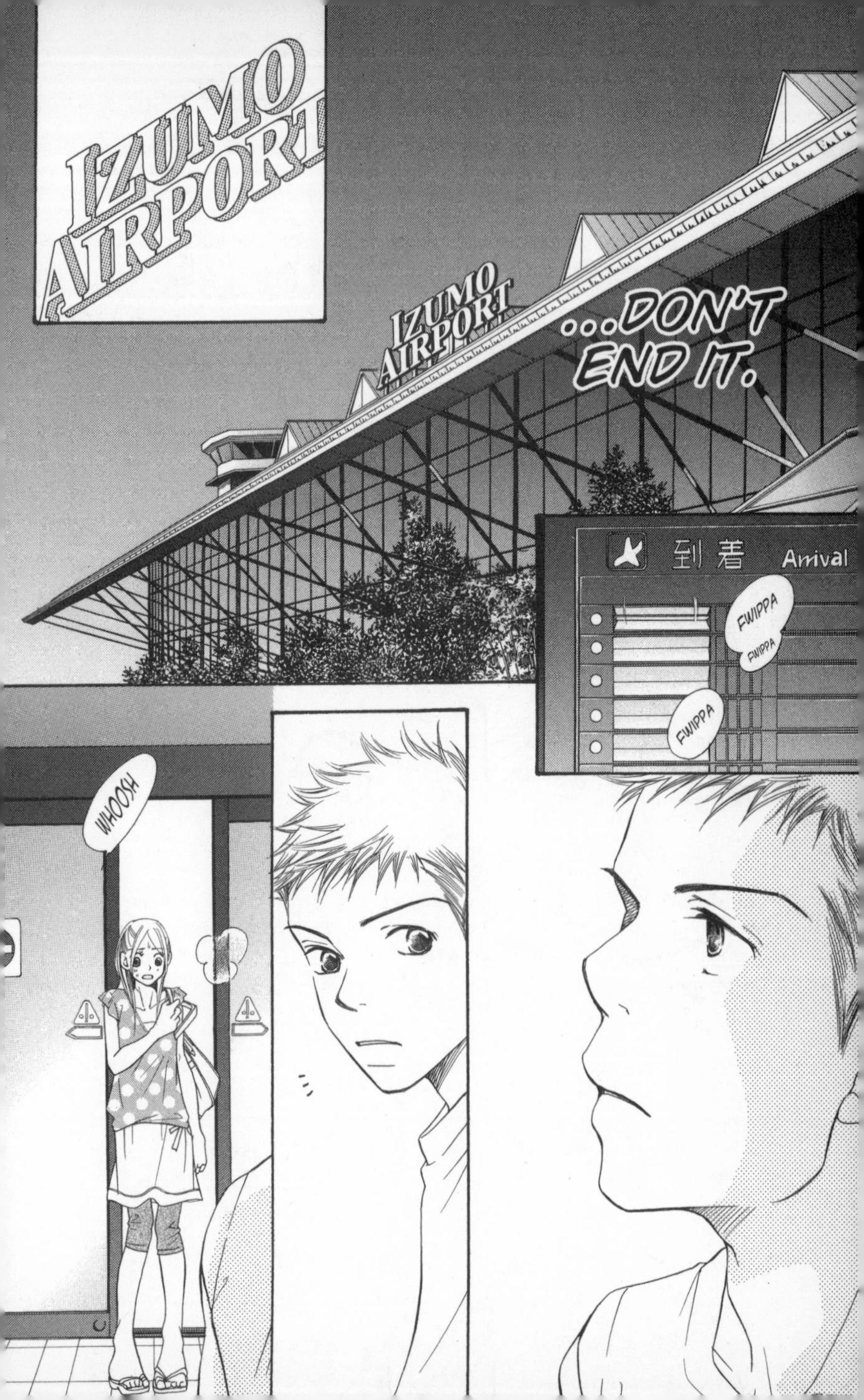
IZUMO AIRPORT
IZUMO AIRPORT
...DON'T END IT.
到着 Arrival
FWIPPA
FWIPPA
FWIPPA
WHOOSH

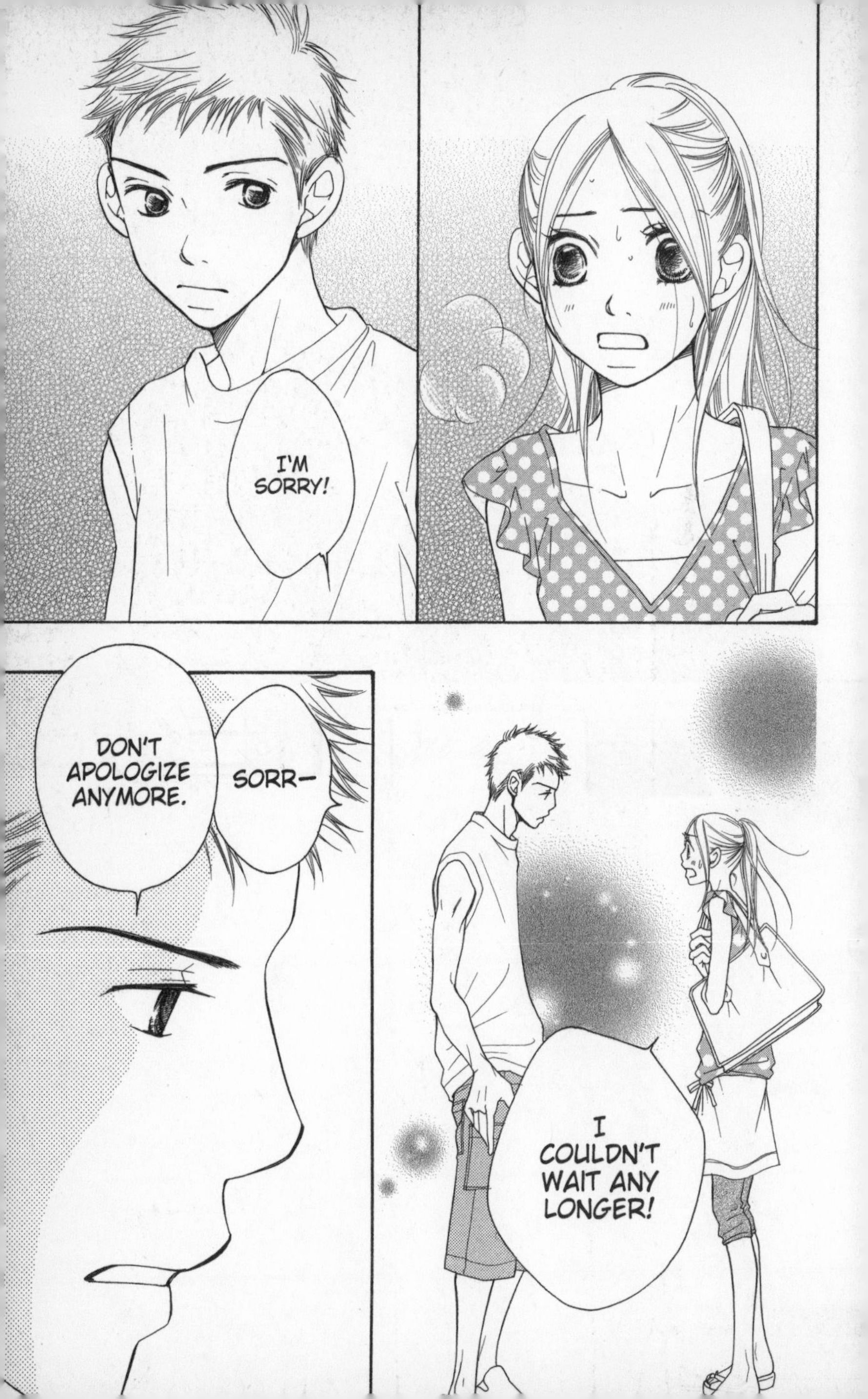
I'M SORRY!
I COULDN'T WAIT ANY LONGER!
SORR—
DON'T APOLOGIZE ANYMORE.

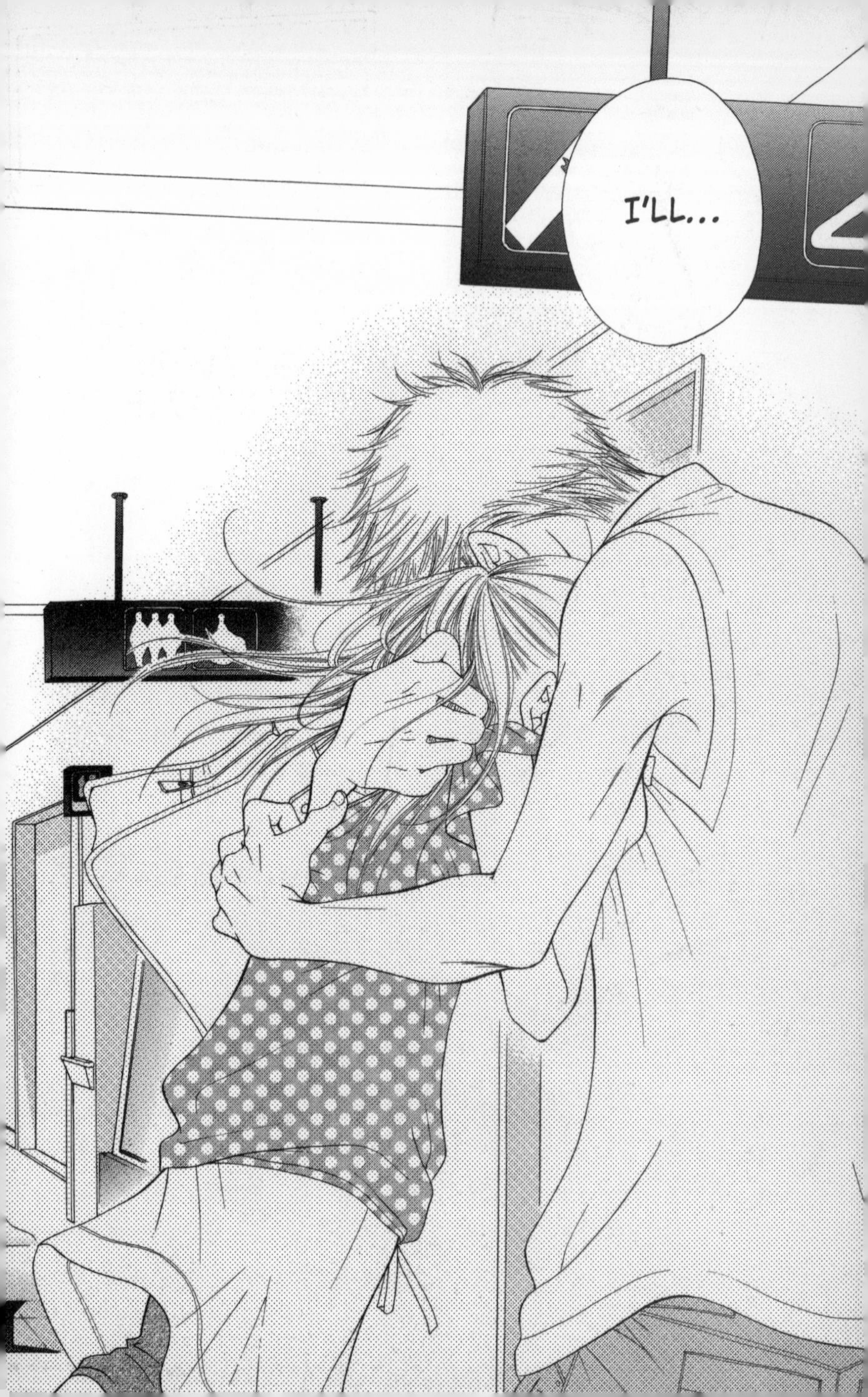
I'LL...

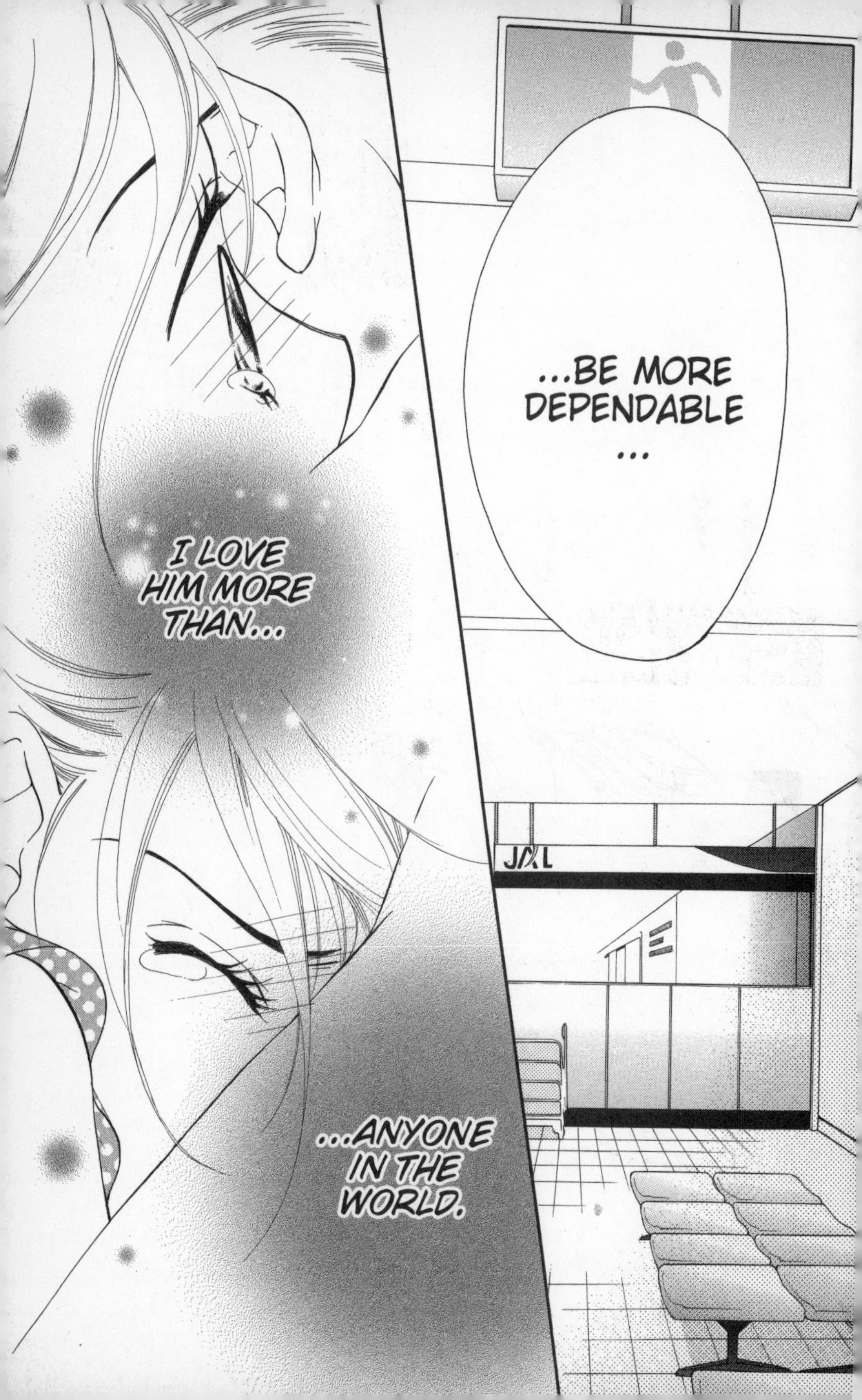
...BE MORE DEPENDABLE ...
I LOVE HIM MORE THAN...
...ANYONE IN THE WORLD.

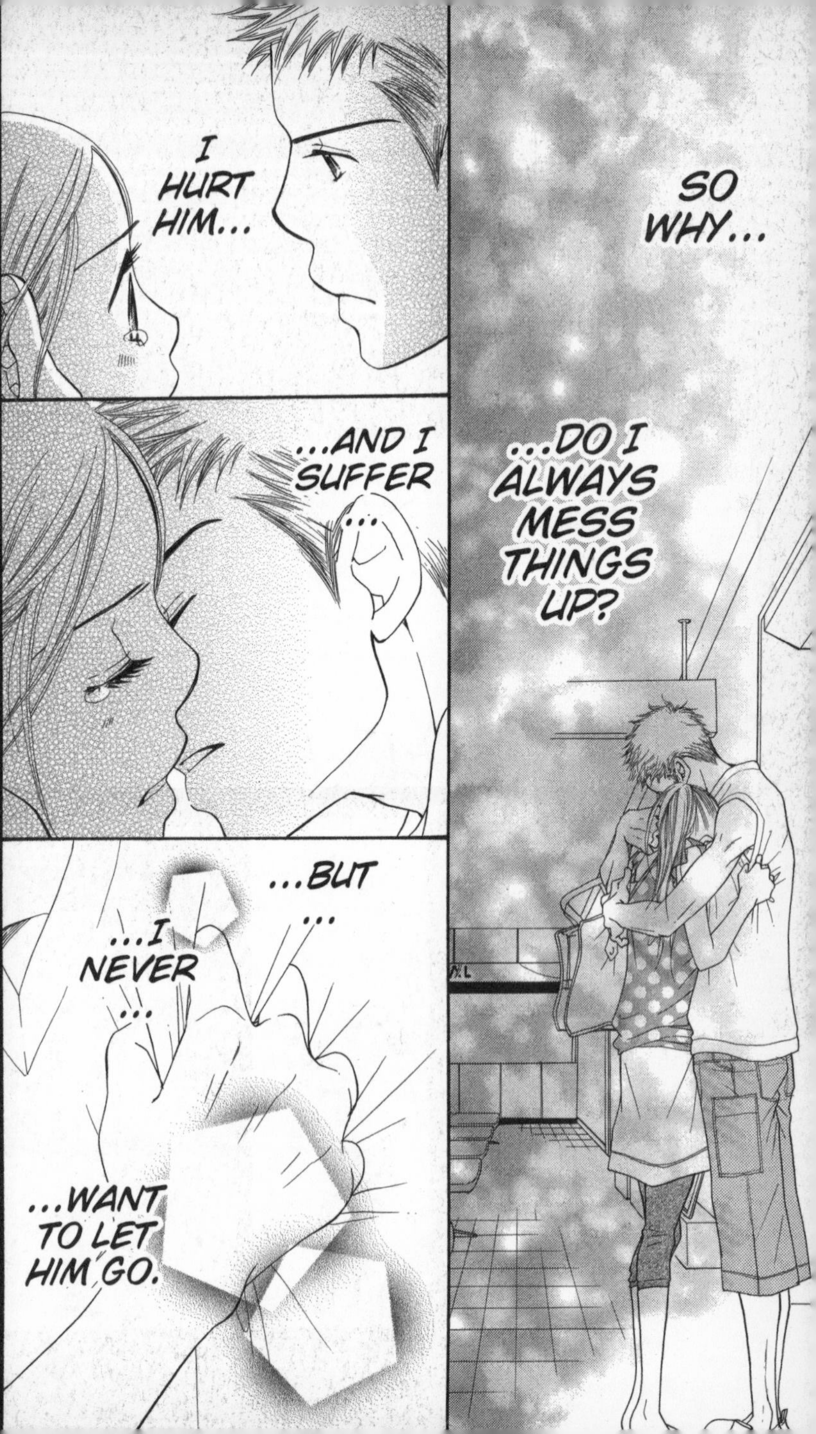
SO WHY...
...DO I ALWAYS MESS THINGS UP?
I HURT HIM...
...AND I SUFFER...
...BUT...
...I NEVER...
...WANT TO LET HIM GO.

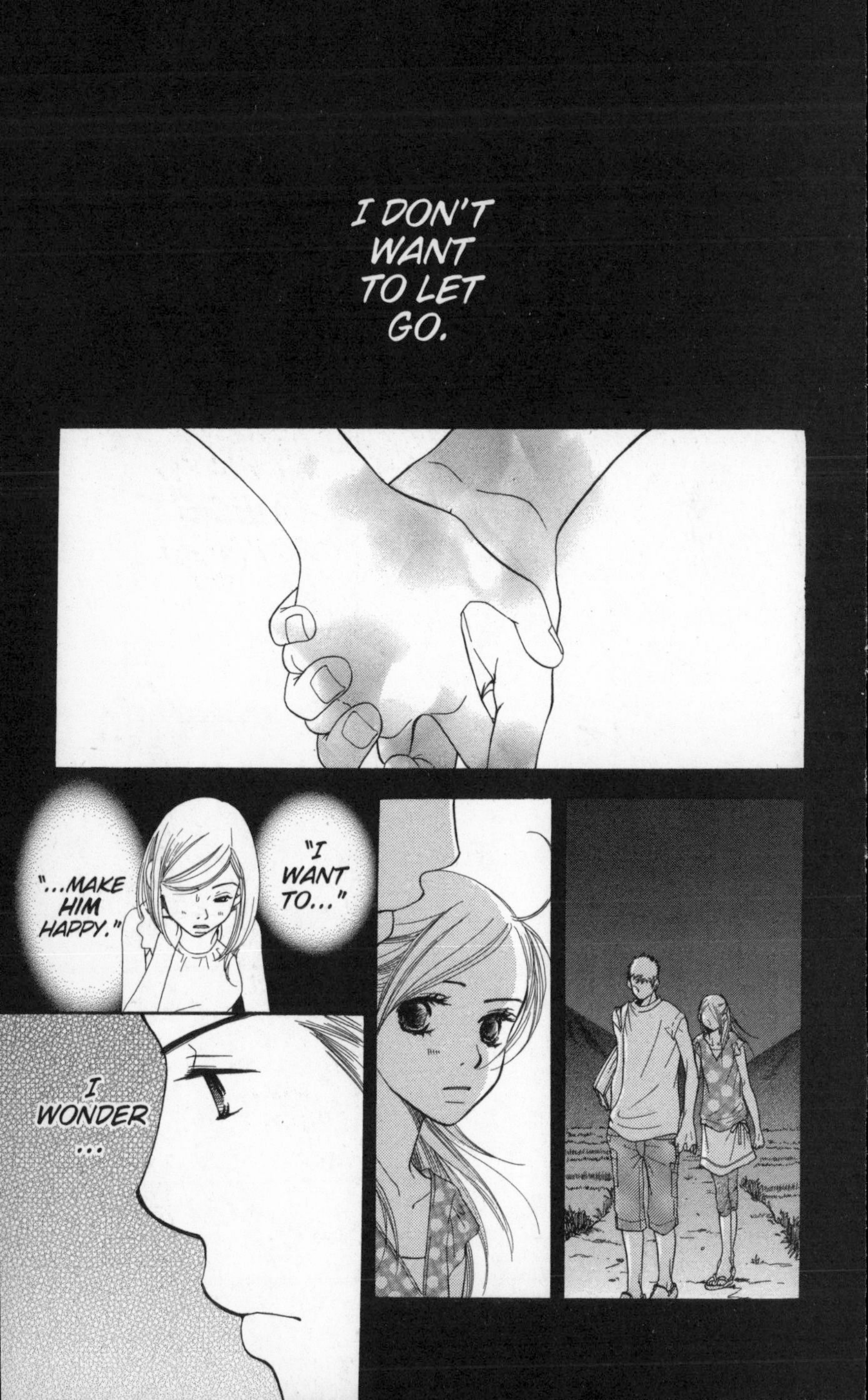
I DON'T WANT TO LET GO.
"I WANT TO..."
"...MAKE HIM HAPPY."
I WONDER ...

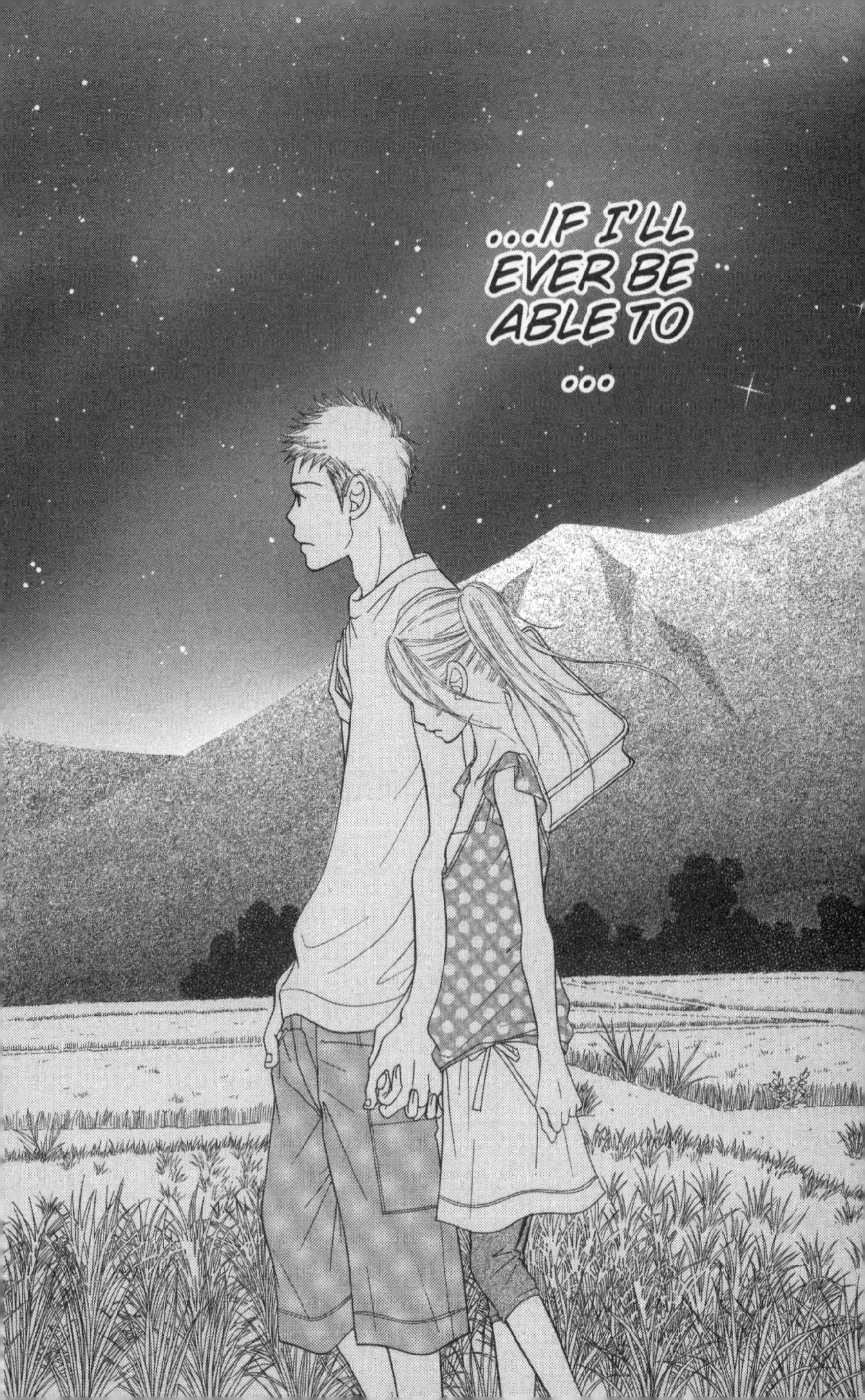
...IF I'LL EVER BE ABLE TO ...

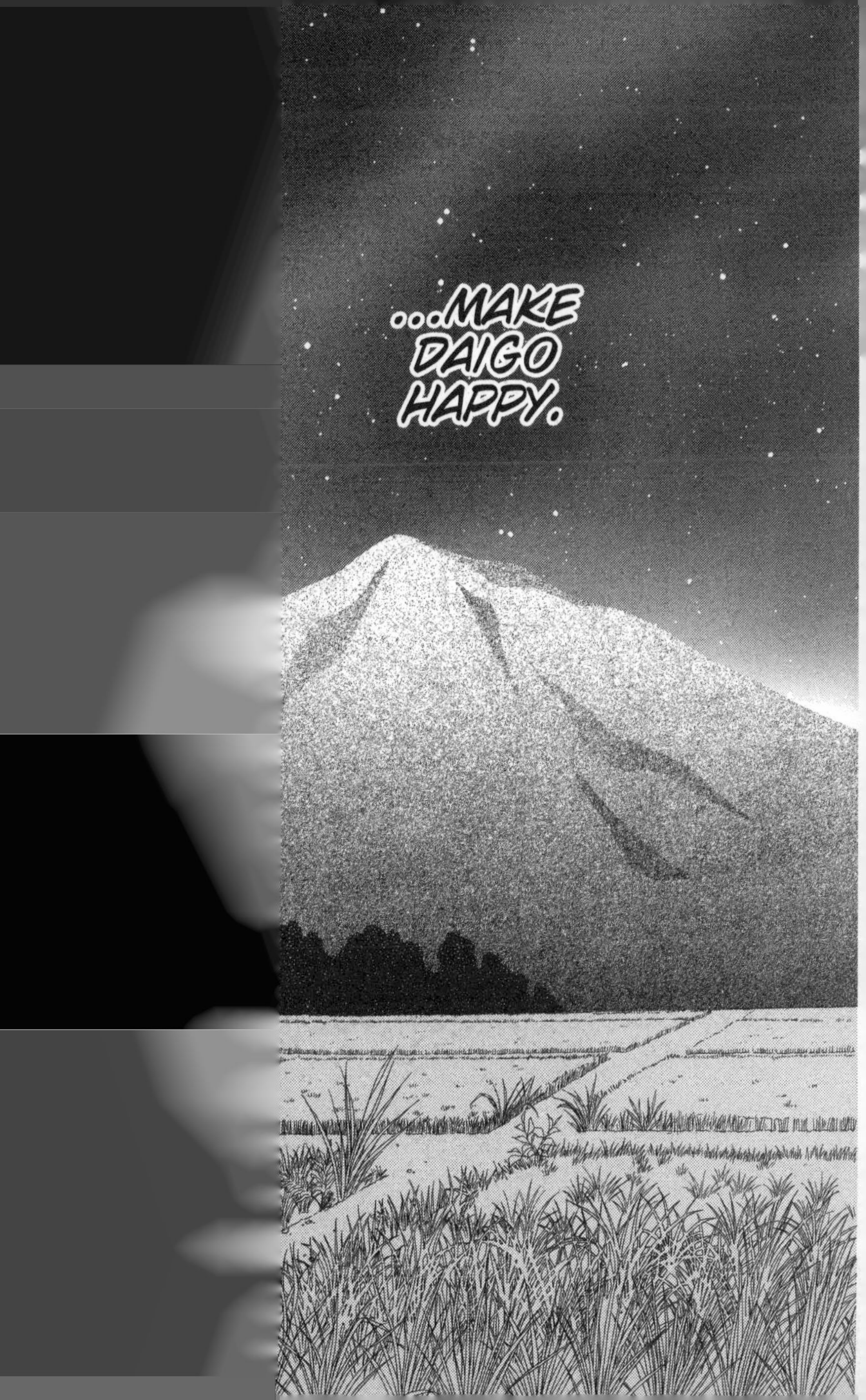
...MAKE DAIGO HAPPY.

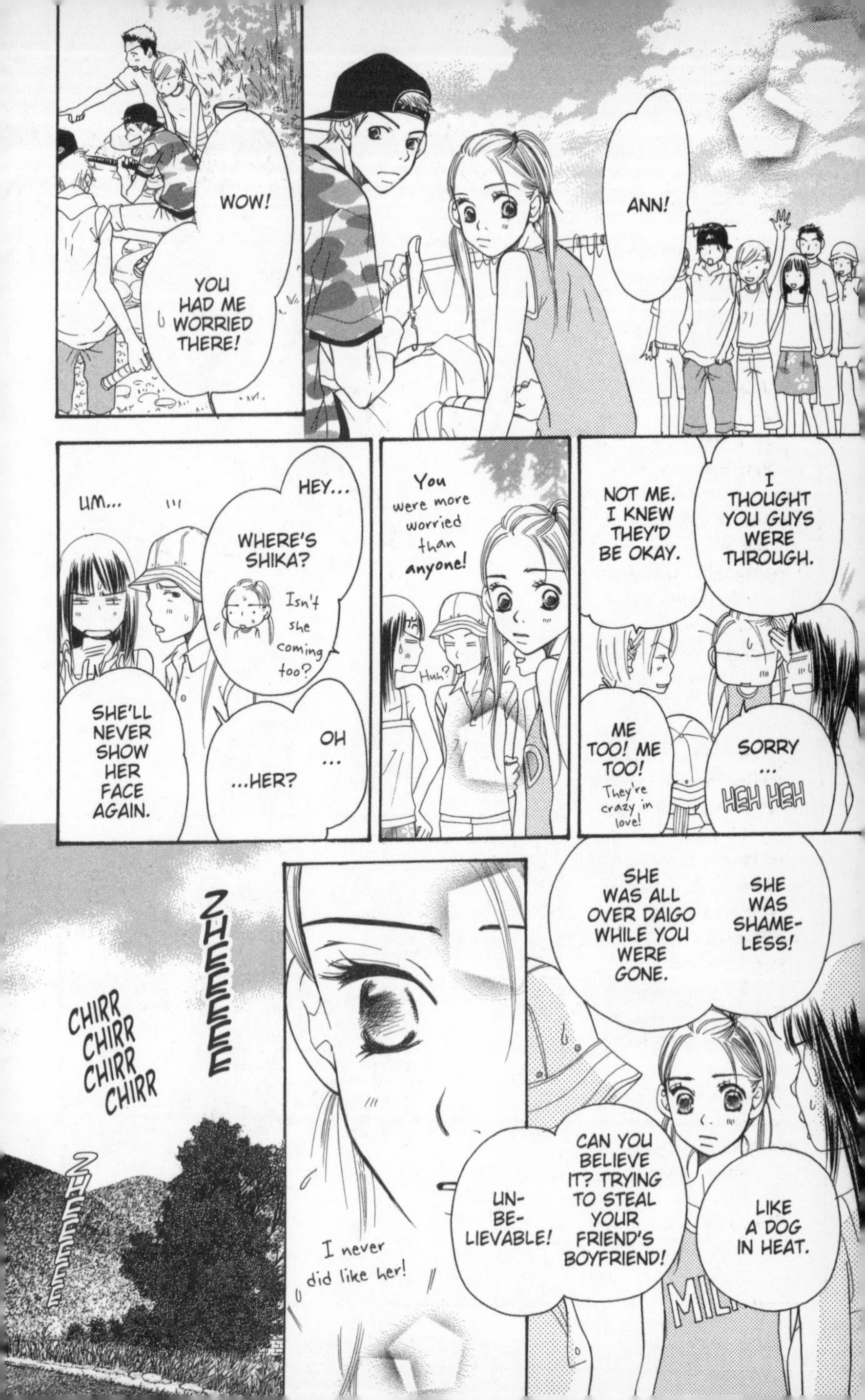
ANN!
WOW!
YOU HAD ME WORRIED THERE!
I THOUGHT YOU GUYS WERE THROUGH.
NOT ME. I KNEW THEY'D BE OKAY.
SORRY... HEH HEH
ME TOO! ME TOO!
They're crazy in love!
You were more worried than anyone!
Huh?
HEY... WHERE'S SHIKA?
Isn't she coming too?
UM...
OH ...
...HER?
SHE'LL NEVER SHOW HER FACE AGAIN.
SHE WAS SHAME-LESS!
SHE WAS ALL OVER DAIGO WHILE YOU WERE GONE.
LIKE A DOG IN HEAT.
CAN YOU BELIEVE IT? TRYING TO STEAL YOUR FRIEND'S BOYFRIEND!
UN-BE-LIEVABLE!
I never did like her!
ZHEEEEEE
CHIRR CHIRR CHIRR CHIRR
ZHEEEEEE

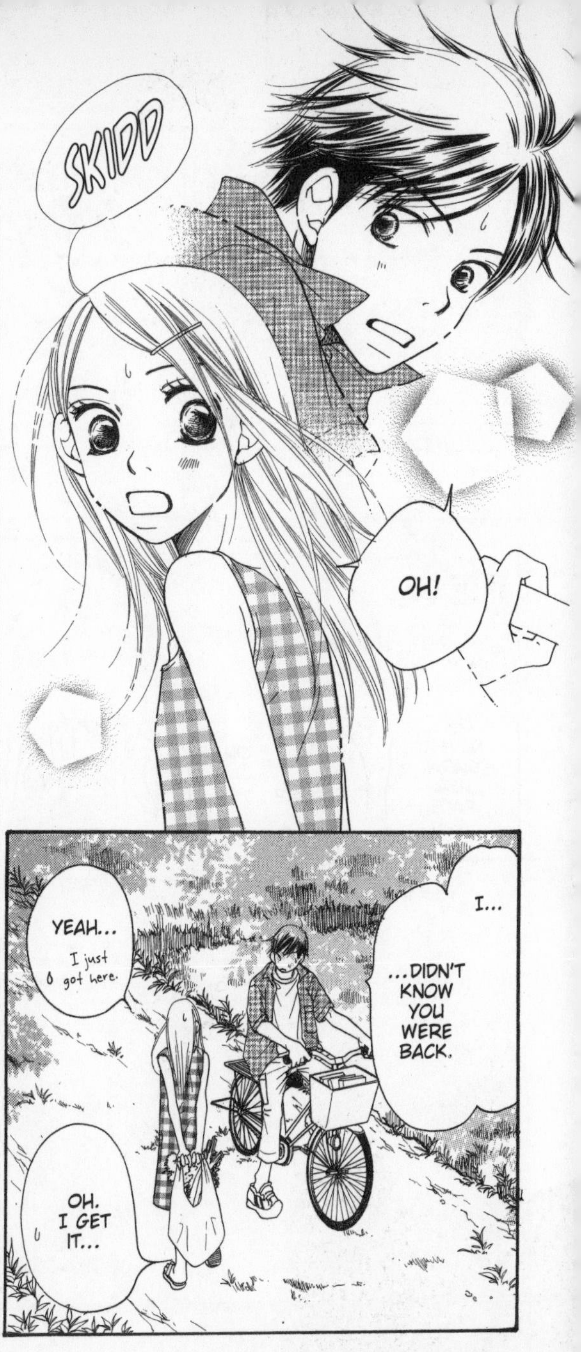
SKIDD
OH!
I...
...DIDN'T KNOW YOU WERE BACK.
YEAH...
I just got here.
OH. I GET IT...

Summer, Age 17: Shadows

Welcome to Volume 5! ♪ Volume 5! Volume 5! (I'm so excited!).

When I was little, I had a recurring dream that I was being chased. What does that mean?

Even though this is a tale of summer, it's pretty dark and heavy. All the main characters are having a rough time...

This summer ('04) is setting records for high temperatures. I worked on this script with the air conditioner going full blast. I didn't think it was working very well, but when I stepped outside to get something to eat, I was shocked. It was 103 degrees out... Impossible...

With the earth heating up like this, those of us who can't handle the heat won't survive!

I've got to toughen up!

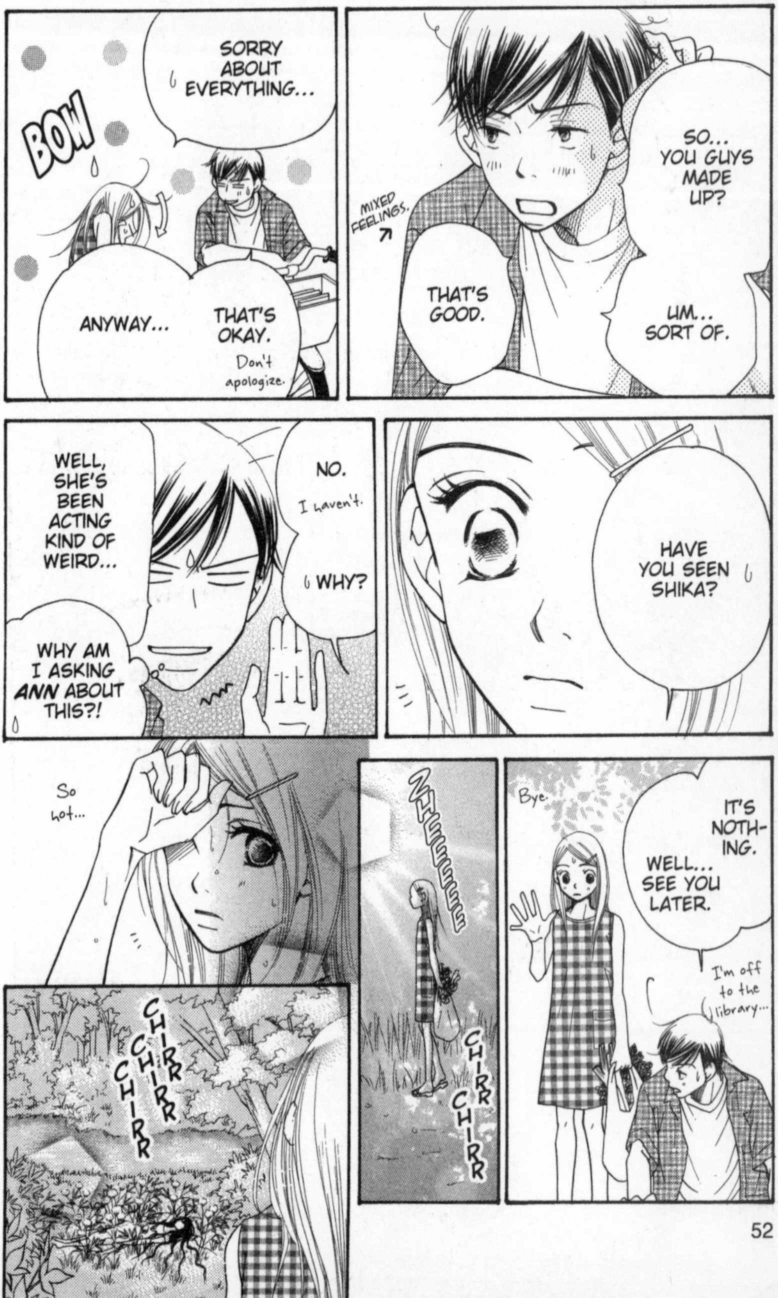
SO... YOU GUYS MADE UP?
UM... SORT OF.
MIXED FEELINGS.
THAT'S GOOD.
SORRY ABOUT EVERYTHING...
BOW
THAT'S OKAY.
Don't apologize.
ANYWAY...
HAVE YOU SEEN SHIKA?
NO.
I haven't.
WHY?
WELL, SHE'S BEEN ACTING KIND OF WEIRD...
WHY AM I ASKING ANN ABOUT THIS?!
Bye.
IT'S NOTHING. WELL... SEE YOU LATER.
I'm off to the library...
ZHEEEEEE
CHIRR CHIRR
So hot...
CHIRR CHIRR CHIRR

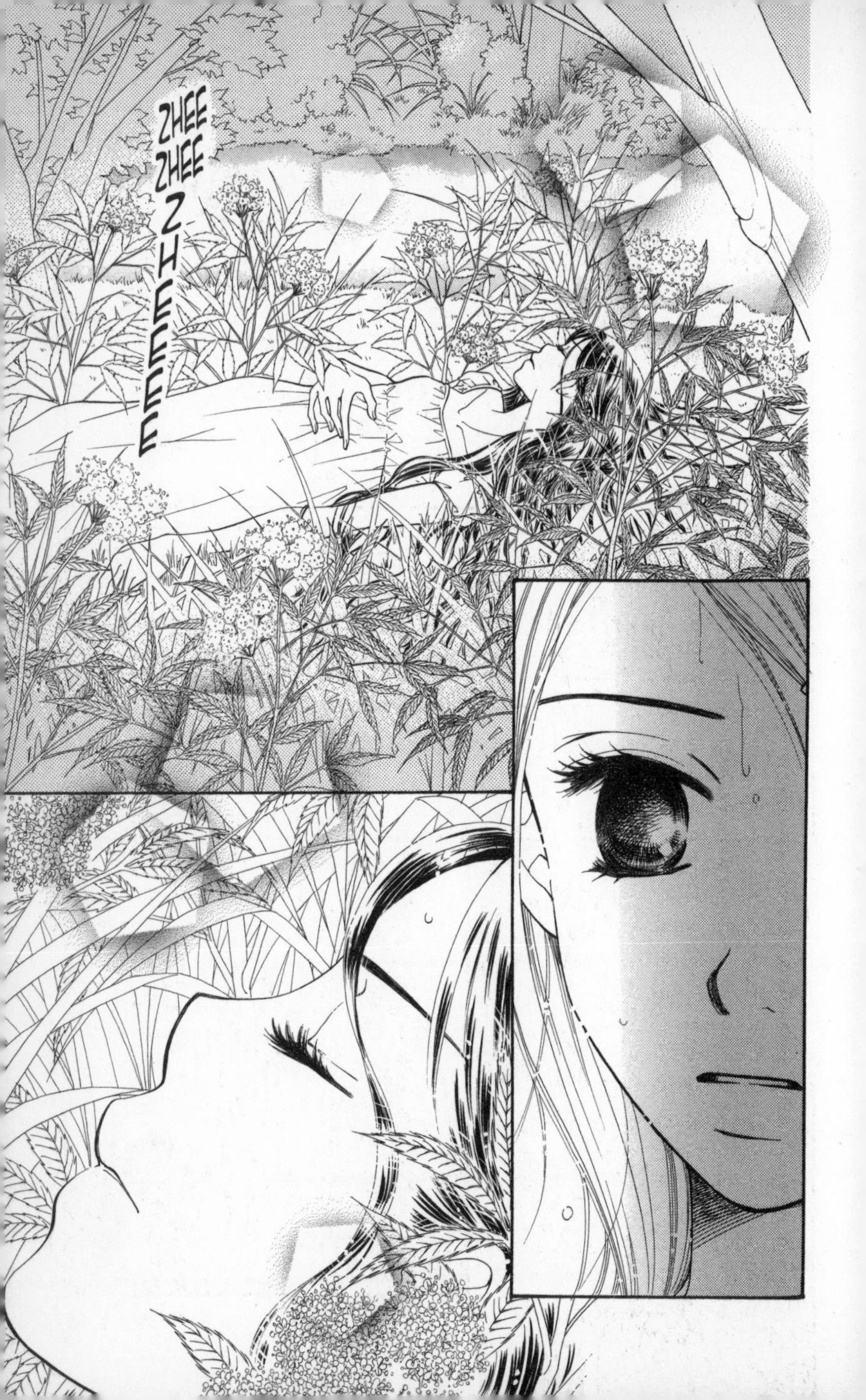
ZHEE ZHEE ZHEEEEE

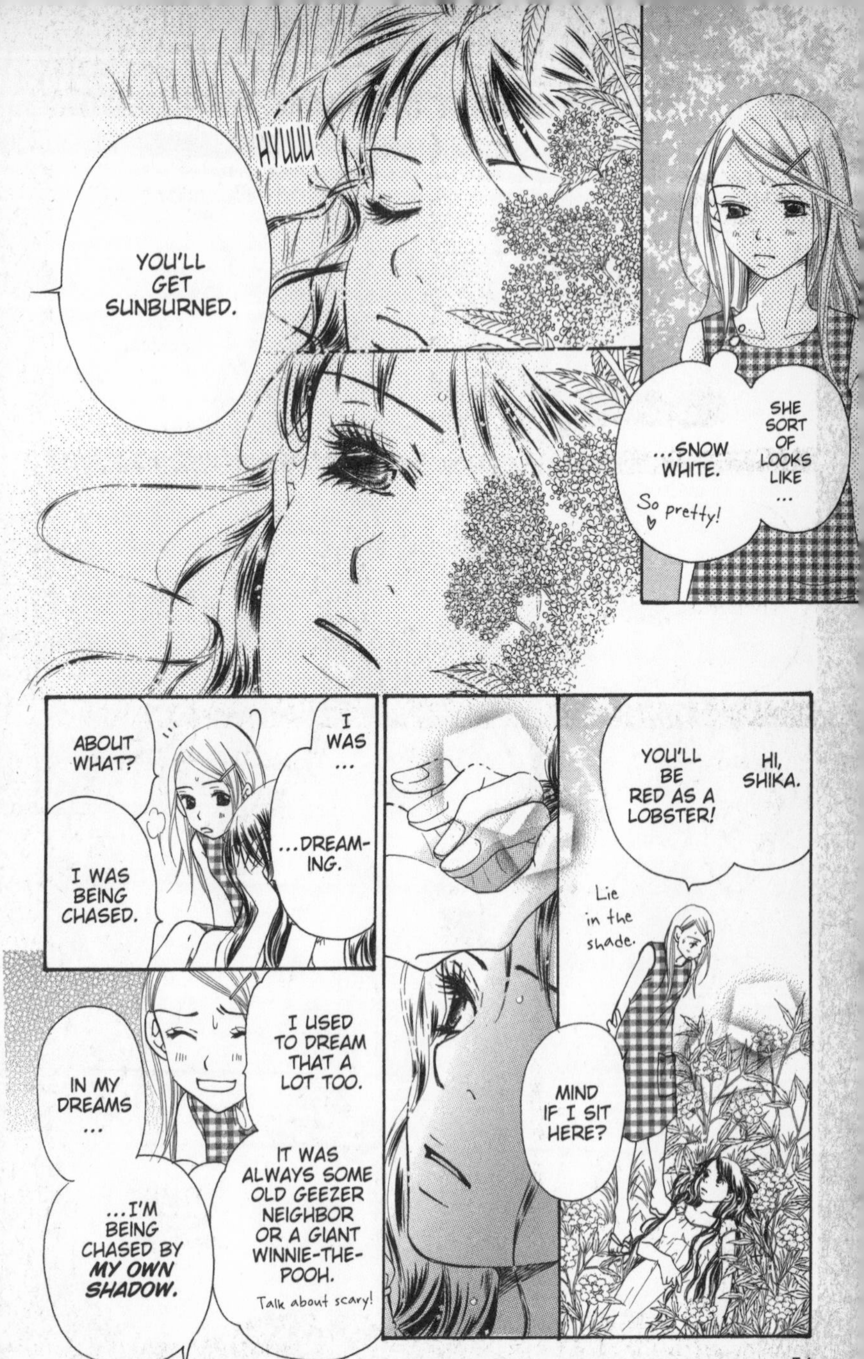
SHE SORT OF LOOKS LIKE ...
...SNOW WHITE.
So pretty!
HYUUU
YOU'LL GET SUNBURNED.
HI, SHIKA.
YOU'LL BE RED AS A LOBSTER!
Lie in the shade.
MIND IF I SIT HERE?
I WAS ...
...DREAMING.
ABOUT WHAT?
I WAS BEING CHASED.
I USED TO DREAM THAT A LOT TOO.
IT WAS ALWAYS SOME OLD GEEZER NEIGHBOR OR A GIANT WINNIE-THE-POOH.
Talk about scary!
IN MY DREAMS ...
...I'M BEING CHASED BY MY OWN SHADOW.

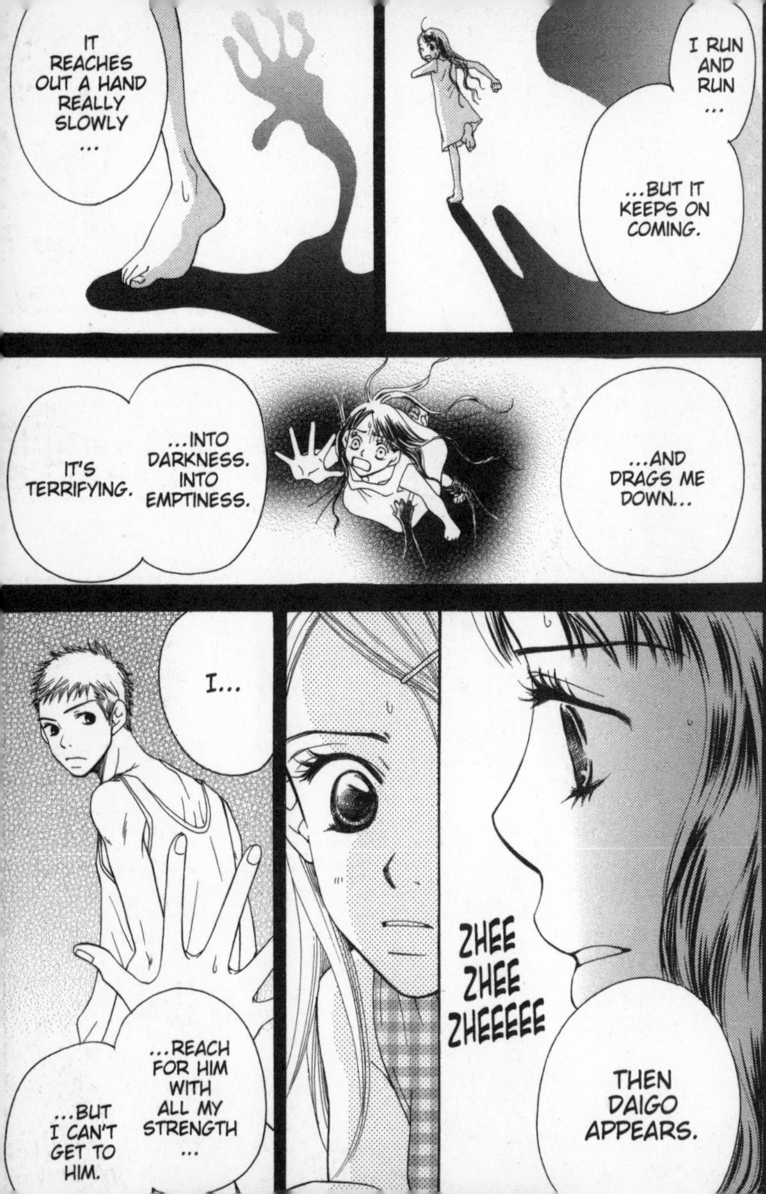
I RUN AND RUN ...
...BUT IT KEEPS ON COMING.
IT REACHES OUT A HAND REALLY SLOWLY ...
...AND DRAGS ME DOWN...
...INTO DARKNESS. INTO EMPTINESS.
IT'S TERRIFYING.
THEN DAIGO APPEARS.
ZHEE ZHEE ZHEEEEEE
I...
...REACH FOR HIM WITH ALL MY STRENGTH ...
...BUT I CAN'T GET TO HIM.

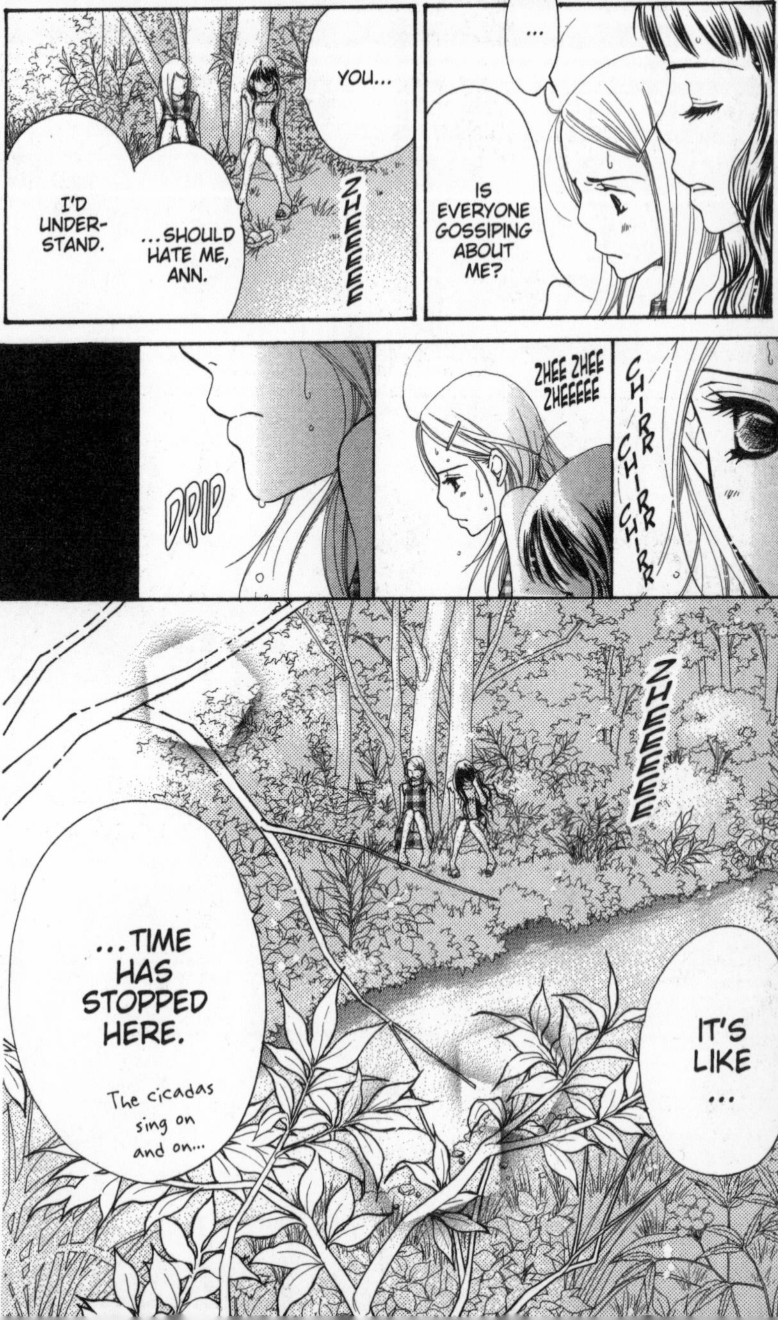
...
IS EVERYONE GOSSIPING ABOUT ME?
YOU...
ZHEEEEE
...SHOULD HATE ME, ANN.
I'D UNDER-STAND.
CHIRR CHIRR CHIRR
ZHEE ZHEE ZHEEEEE
DRIP
ZHEEEEEE
IT'S LIKE ...
...TIME HAS STOPPED HERE.
The cicadas sing on and on...

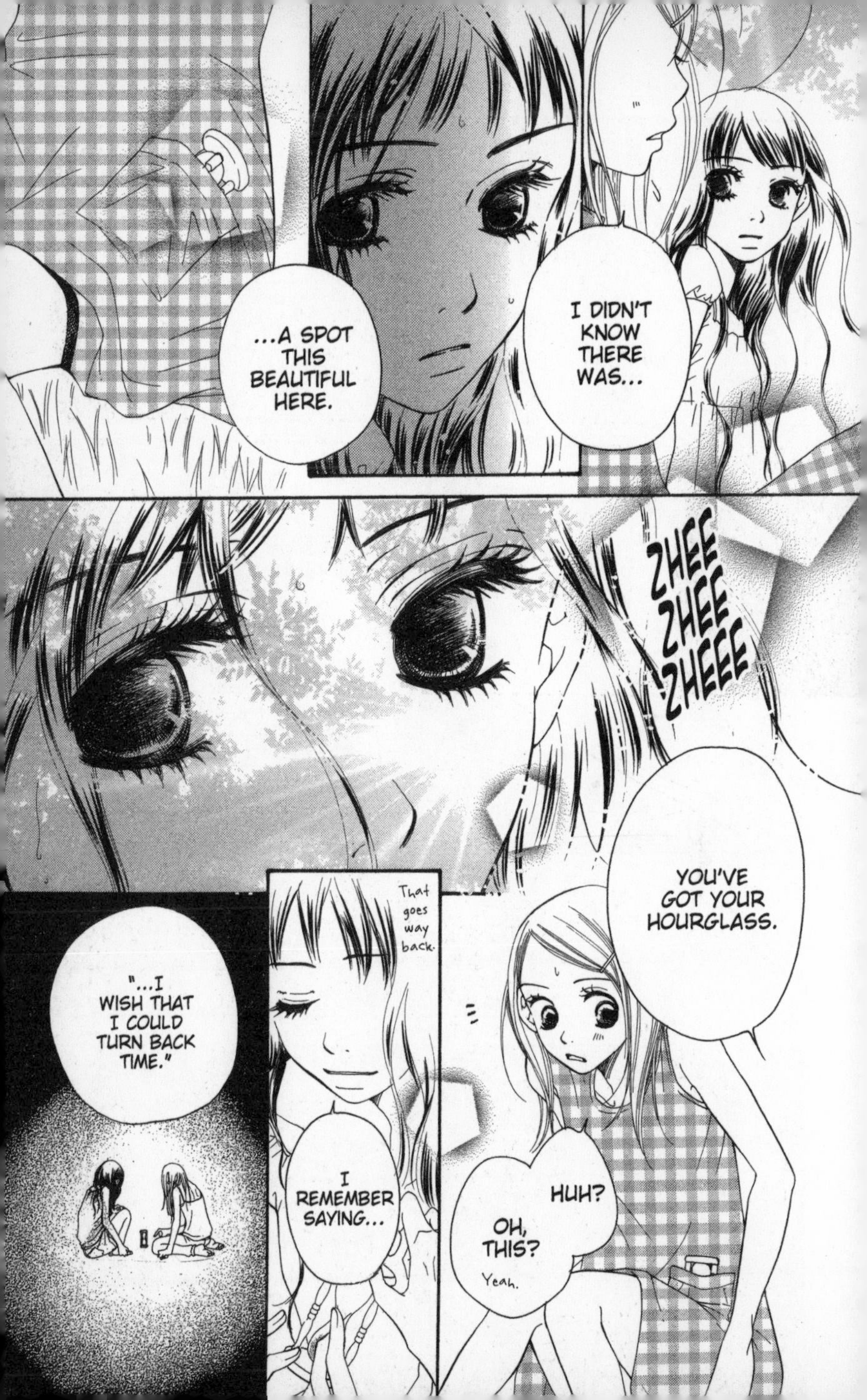
I DIDN'T KNOW THERE WAS...
...A SPOT THIS BEAUTIFUL HERE.
ZHEE ZHEE ZHEEE
YOU'VE GOT YOUR HOURGLASS.
HUH?
OH, THIS?
Yeah.
That goes way back.
I REMEMBER SAYING...
"...I WISH THAT I COULD TURN BACK TIME."

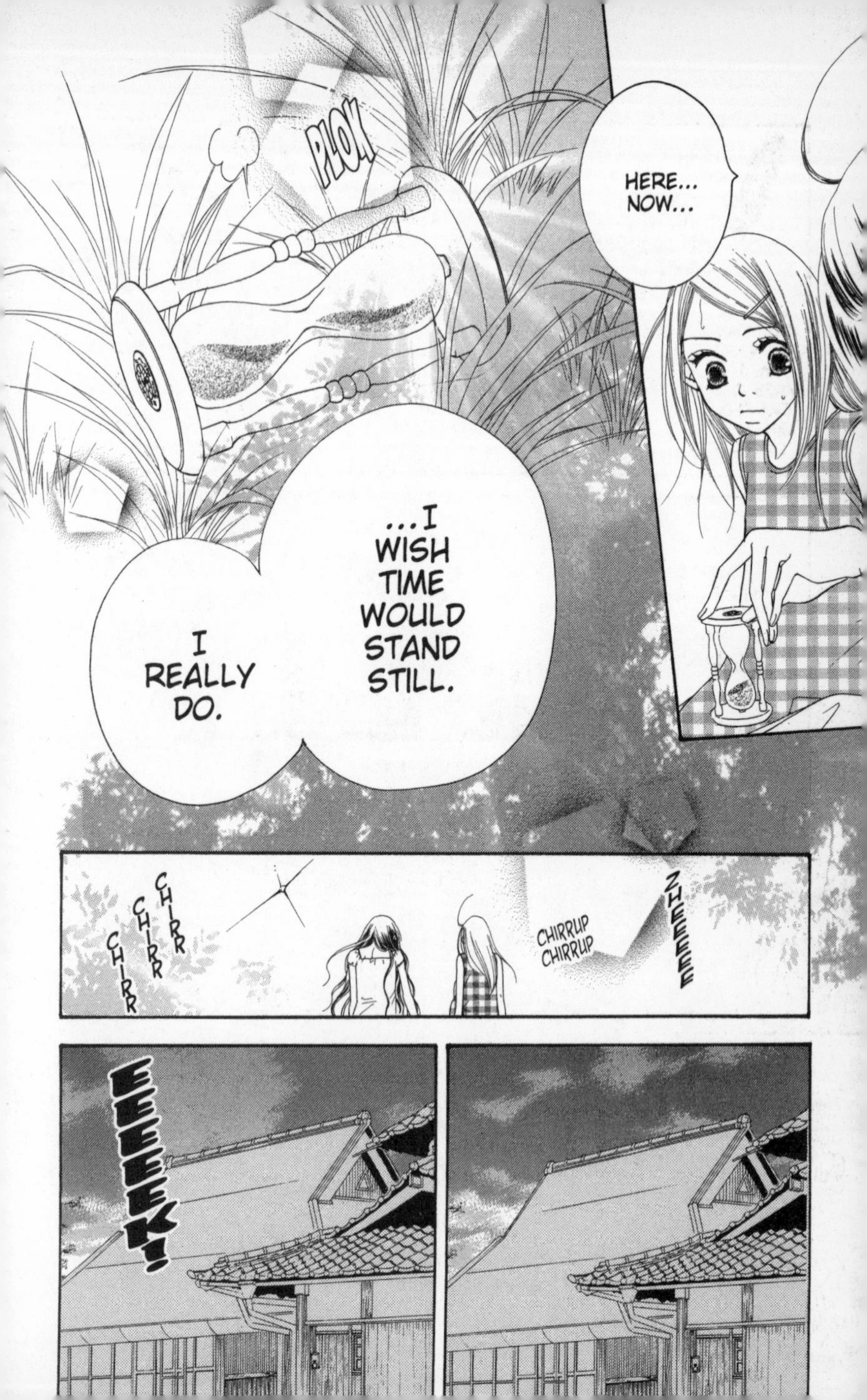
HERE... NOW...
PLOK
...I WISH TIME WOULD STAND STILL.
I REALLY DO.
ZHEEEEE
CHIRRUP CHIRRUP
CHIRR CHIRR CHIRR
EEEEEEK!

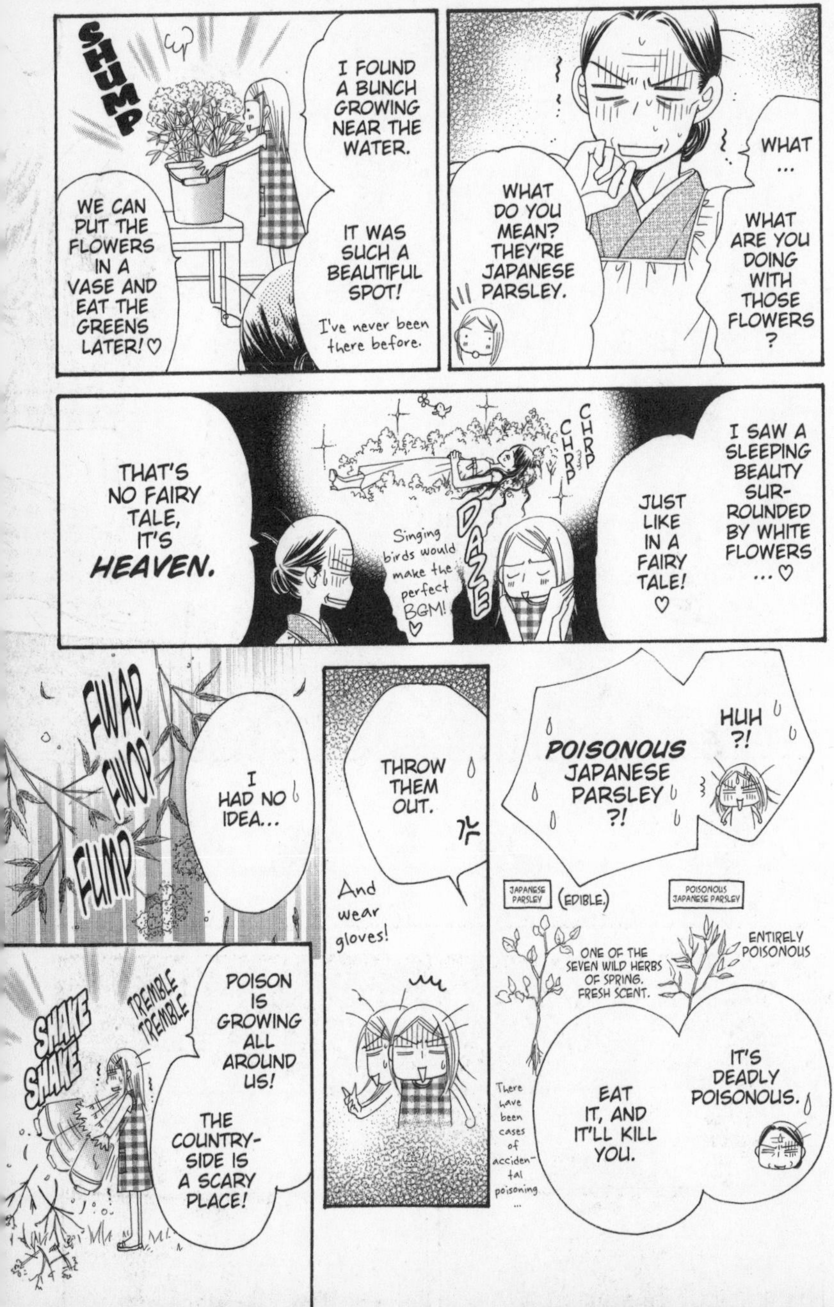
WHAT ...
WHAT ARE YOU DOING WITH THOSE FLOWERS?
WHAT DO YOU MEAN? THEY'RE JAPANESE PARSLEY.
I FOUND A BUNCH GROWING NEAR THE WATER.
IT WAS SUCH A BEAUTIFUL SPOT!
I've never been there before.
SHUMP
WE CAN PUT THE FLOWERS IN A VASE AND EAT THE GREENS LATER! ♡
I SAW A SLEEPING BEAUTY SUR-ROUNDED BY WHITE FLOWERS ... ♡
JUST LIKE IN A FAIRY TALE! ♡
CHRP CHRP
DAZE
Singing birds would make the perfect BGM! ♡
THAT'S NO FAIRY TALE, IT'S HEAVEN.
HUH ?!
POISONOUS JAPANESE PARSLEY ?!
JAPANESE PARSLEY
(EDIBLE.)
ONE OF THE SEVEN WILD HERBS OF SPRING. FRESH SCENT.
POISONOUS JAPANESE PARSLEY
ENTIRELY POISONOUS
IT'S DEADLY POISONOUS.
EAT IT, AND IT'LL KILL YOU.
There have been cases of acciden-tal poisoning ...
THROW THEM OUT.
And wear gloves!
FWAP FWOP FUMP
I HAD NO IDEA...
POISON IS GROWING ALL AROUND US!
THE COUNTRY-SIDE IS A SCARY PLACE!
TREMBLE TREMBLE
SHAKE SHAKE

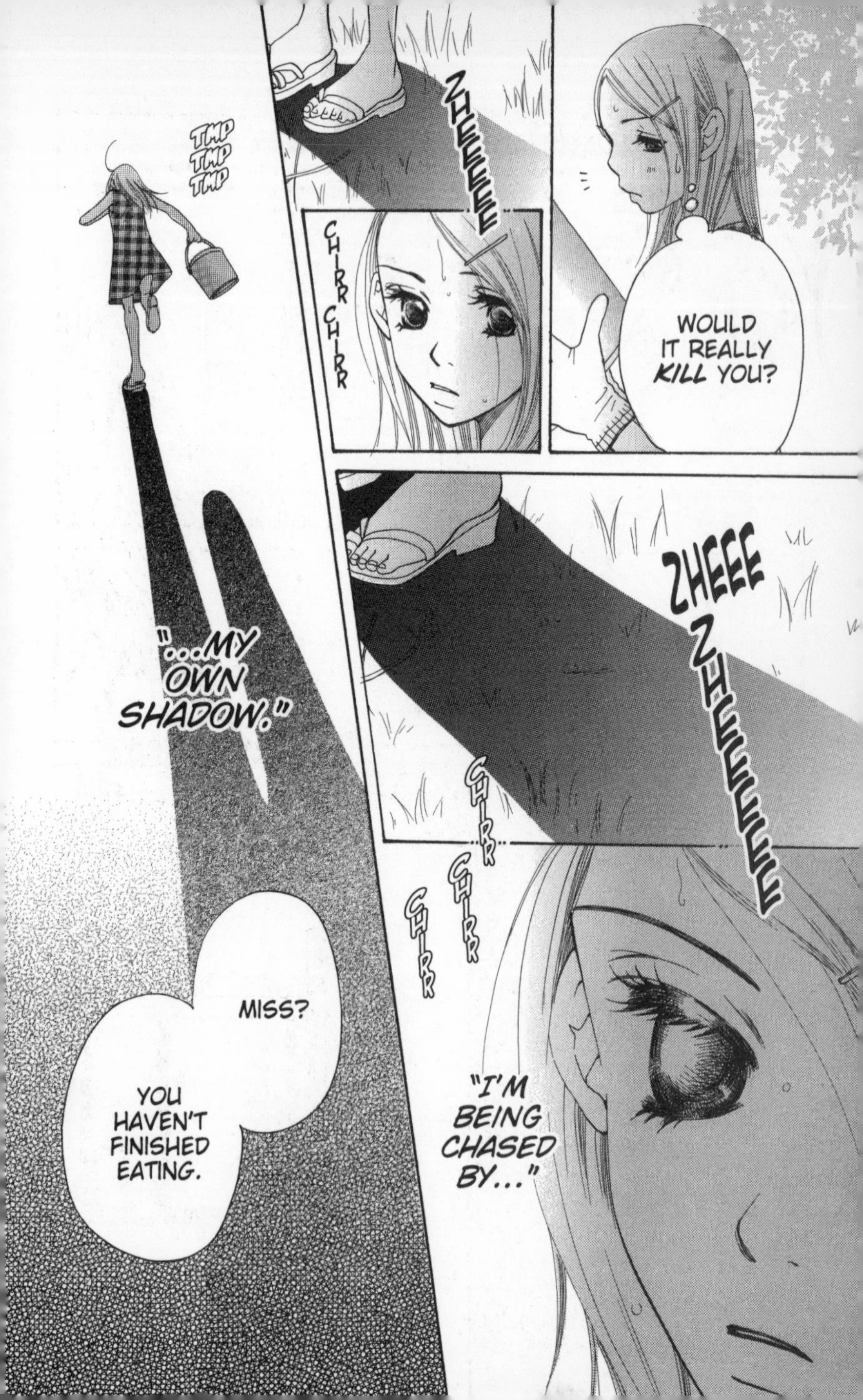

WOULD IT REALLY *KILL* YOU?
ZHEEEEE
CHIRR CHIRR
ZHEEE
ZHEEEEEEE
CHIRR
CHIRR
CHIRR
"I'M BEING CHASED BY..."
TMP TMP TMP
"...MY OWN SHADOW."
MISS?
YOU HAVEN'T FINISHED EATING.

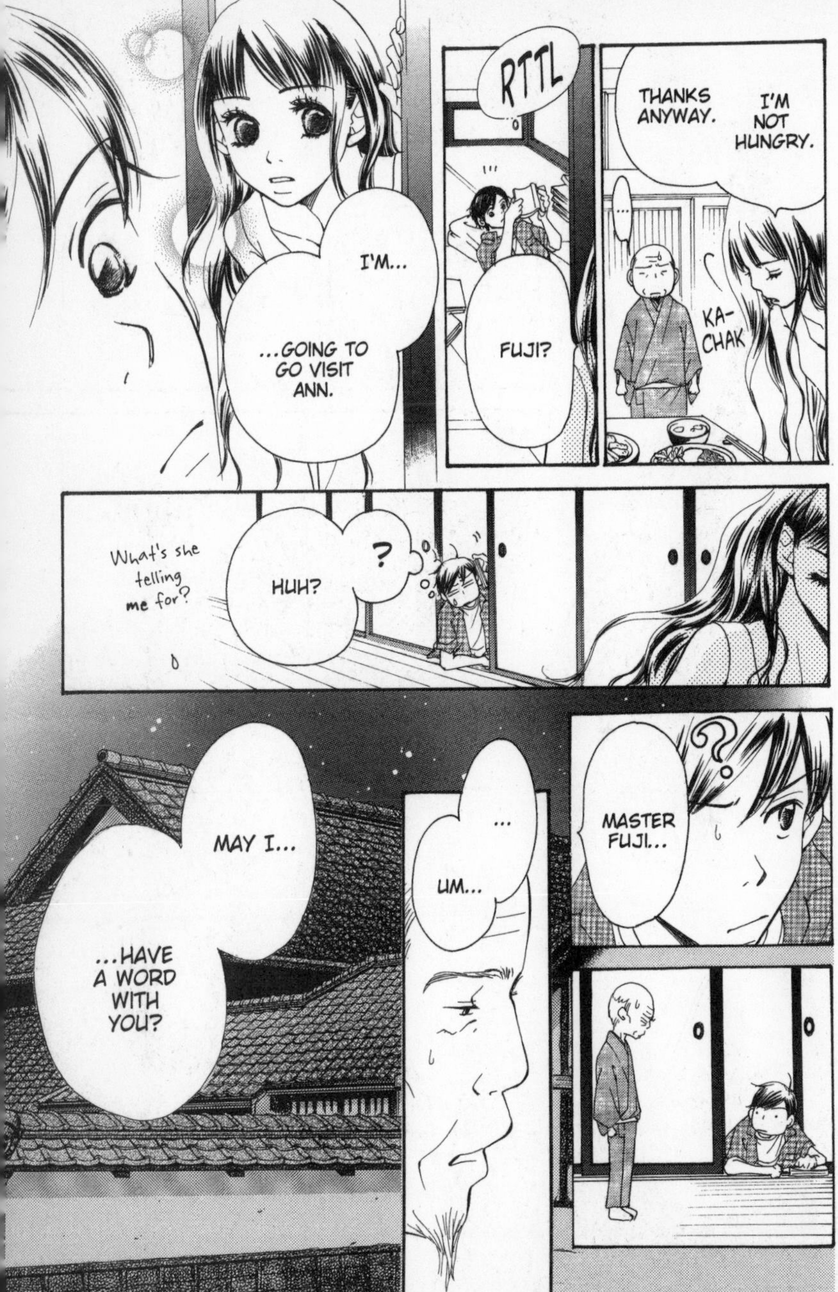
I'M NOT HUNGRY.
THANKS ANYWAY.
...
KA-CHAK
RTTL
FUJI?
I'M...
...GOING TO GO VISIT ANN.
HUH?
What's she telling me for?
MASTER FUJI...
...
UM...
MAY I...
...HAVE A WORD WITH YOU?

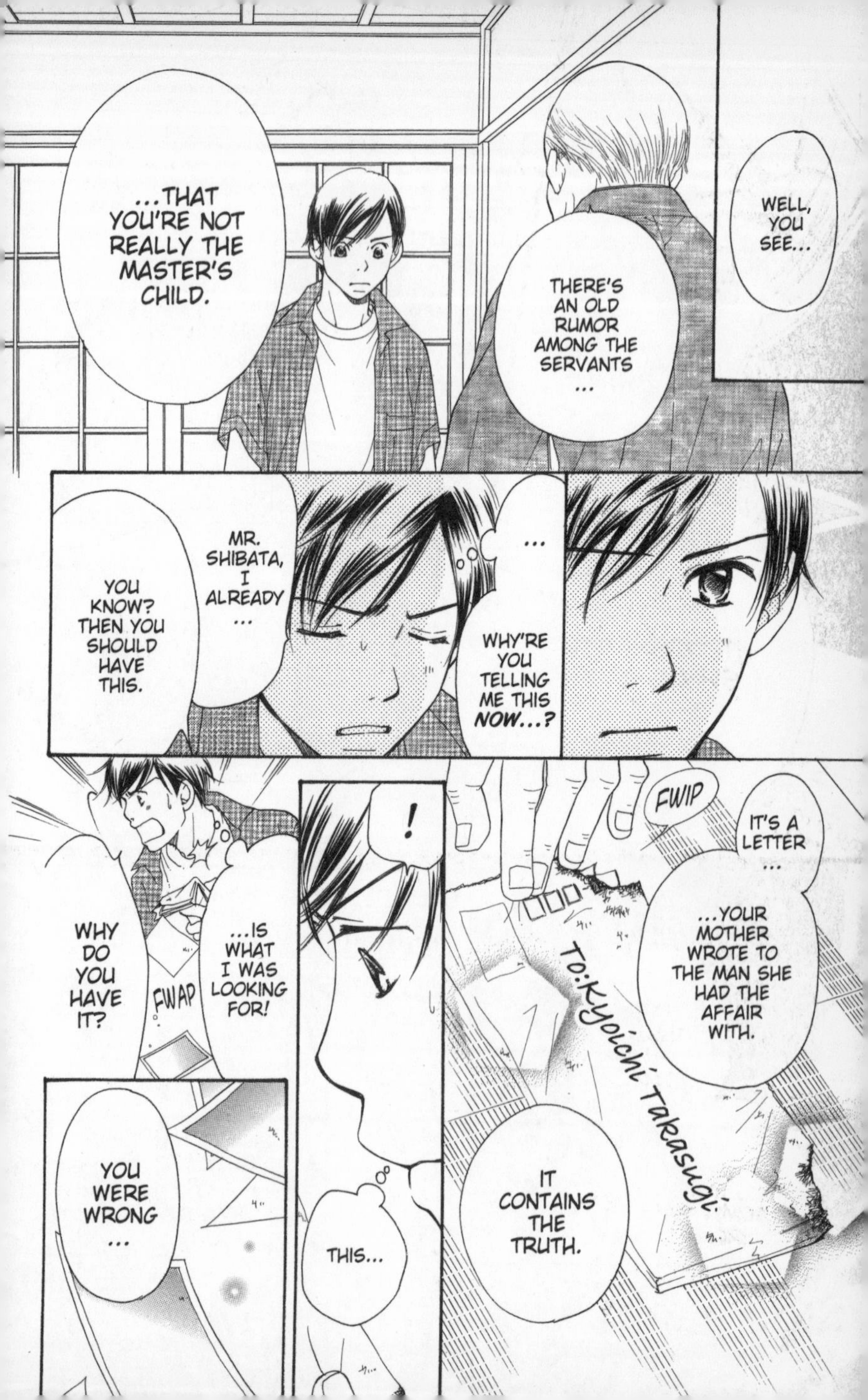
WELL, YOU SEE...
THERE'S AN OLD RUMOR AMONG THE SERVANTS...
...THAT YOU'RE NOT REALLY THE MASTER'S CHILD.
...
WHY'RE YOU TELLING ME THIS *NOW*...?
MR. SHIBATA, I ALREADY...
YOU KNOW? THEN YOU SHOULD HAVE THIS.
FWIP
IT'S A LETTER...
...YOUR MOTHER WROTE TO THE MAN SHE HAD THE AFFAIR WITH.
To: Kyoichi Takasugi
IT CONTAINS THE TRUTH.
!
THIS...
...IS WHAT I WAS LOOKING FOR!
FWAP
WHY DO YOU HAVE IT?
YOU WERE WRONG...

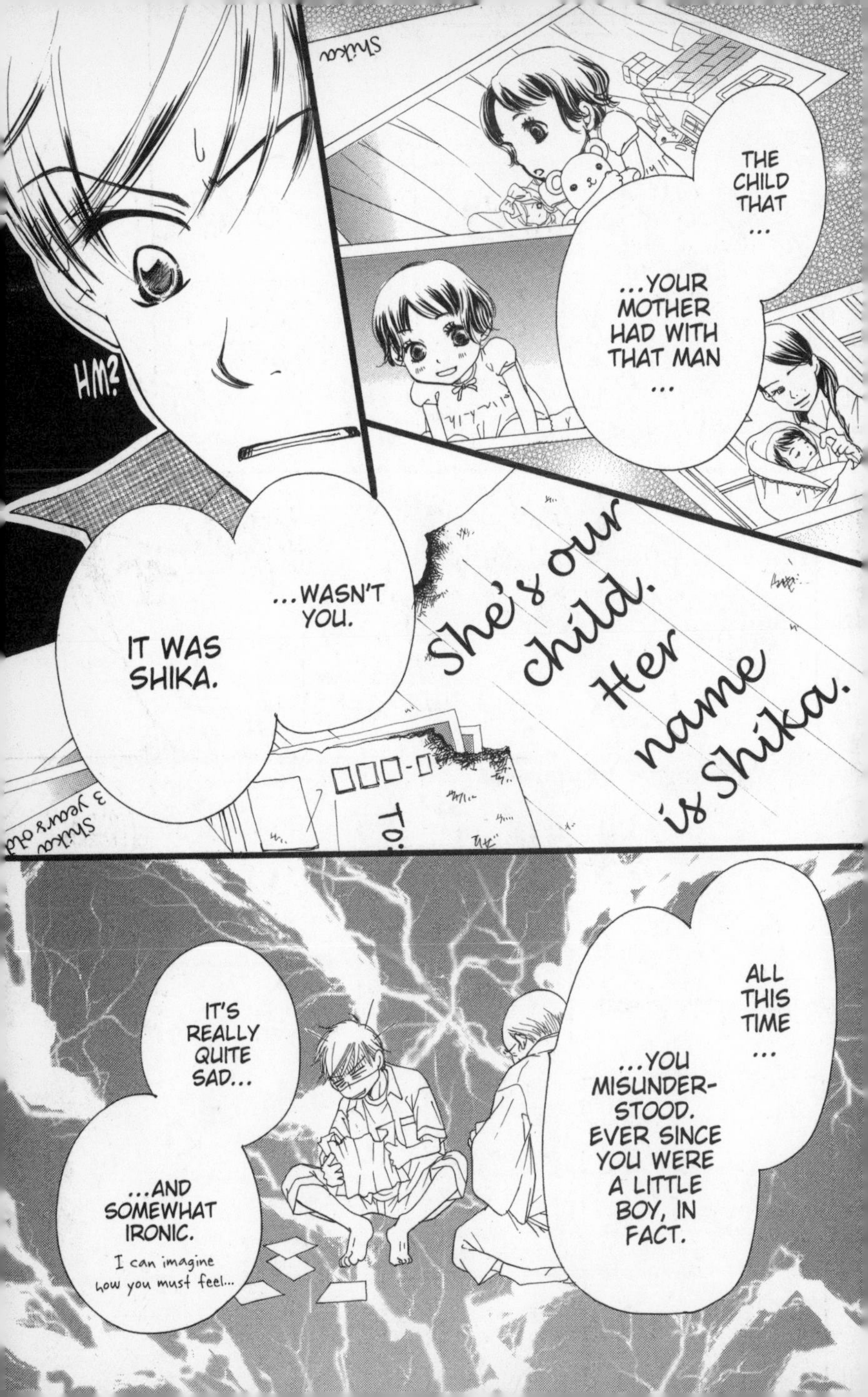
Shika
THE CHILD THAT ...
...YOUR MOTHER HAD WITH THAT MAN ...
HM?
She's our child. Her name is Shika.
...WASN'T YOU.
IT WAS SHIKA.
Shika 3 years old
To:
ALL THIS TIME ...
...YOU MISUNDERSTOOD. EVER SINCE YOU WERE A LITTLE BOY, IN FACT.
IT'S REALLY QUITE SAD...
...AND SOMEWHAT IRONIC.
I can imagine how you must feel...

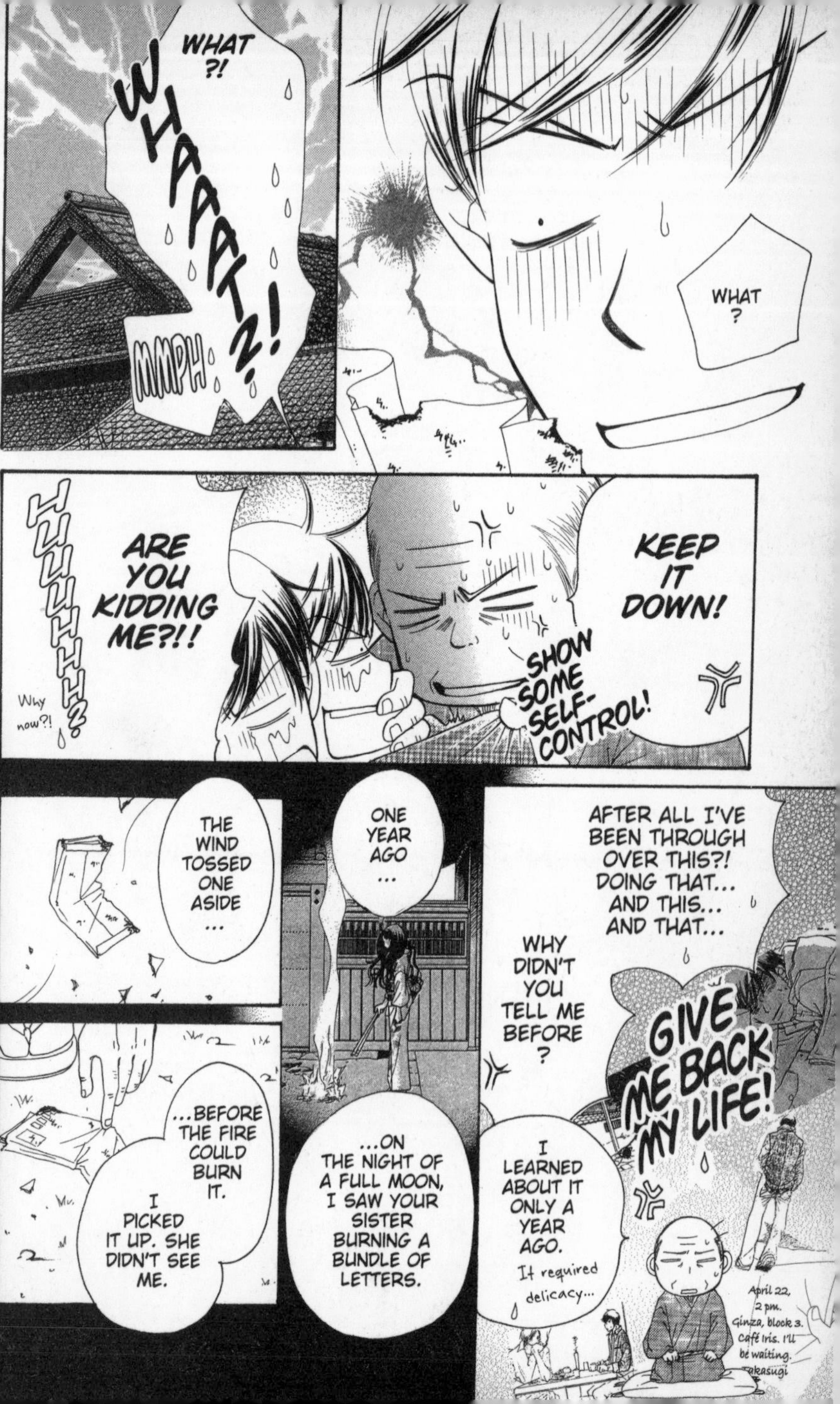
WHAT ?
WHAT ?!
WHAAAT?!
MMPH
KEEP IT DOWN!
SHOW SOME SELF-CONTROL!
ARE YOU KIDDING ME?!!
HUUUHHH?!
Why now?!
AFTER ALL I'VE BEEN THROUGH OVER THIS?! DOING THAT... AND THIS... AND THAT...
WHY DIDN'T YOU TELL ME BEFORE ?
GIVE ME BACK MY LIFE!
I LEARNED ABOUT IT ONLY A YEAR AGO.
It required delicacy...
April 22, 2 pm. Ginza, block 3. Café Iris. I'll be waiting. Takasugi
ONE YEAR AGO ...
...ON THE NIGHT OF A FULL MOON, I SAW YOUR SISTER BURNING A BUNDLE OF LETTERS.
THE WIND TOSSED ONE ASIDE ...
...BEFORE THE FIRE COULD BURN IT.
I PICKED IT UP. SHE DIDN'T SEE ME.

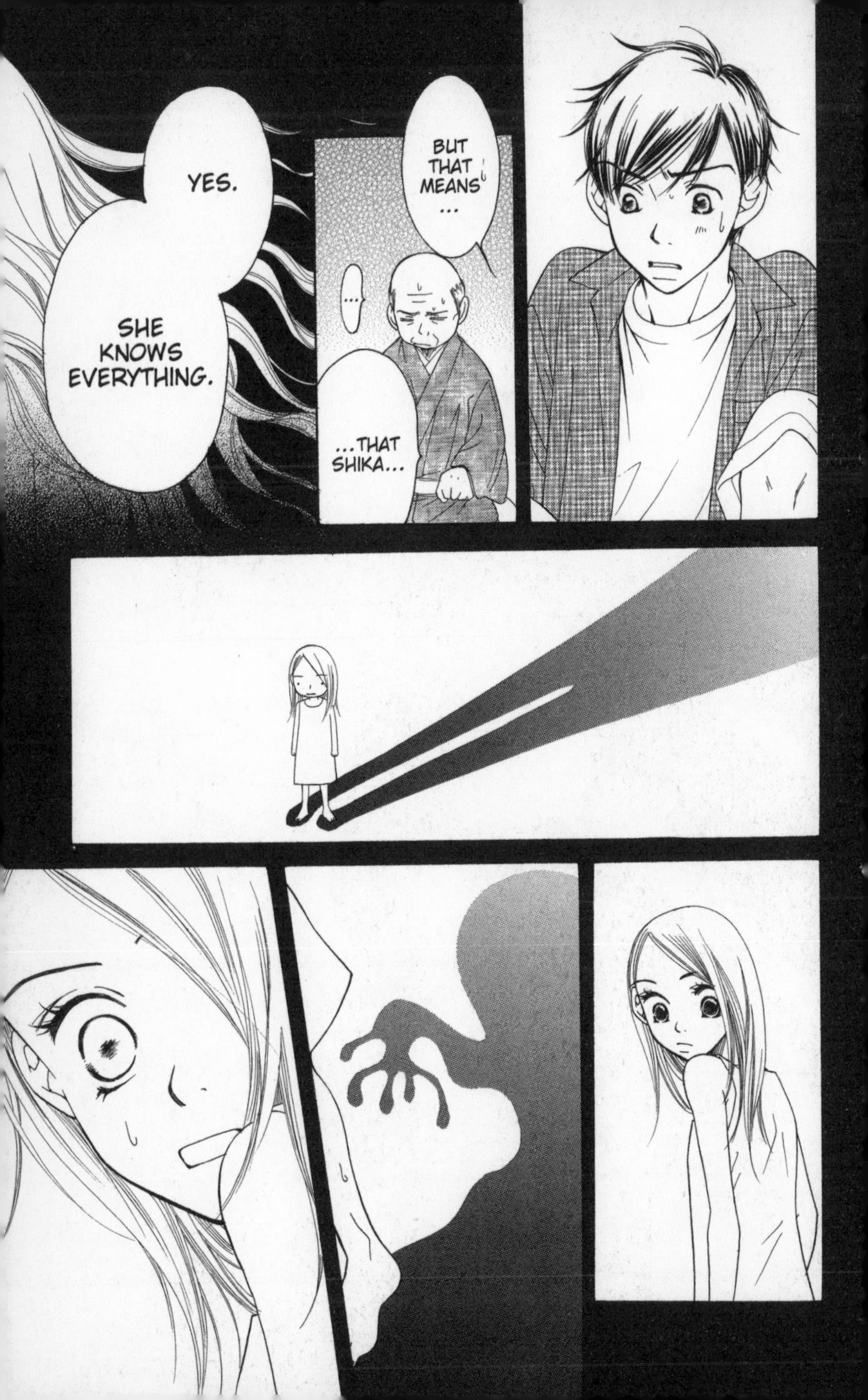
BUT THAT MEANS ...
...
...THAT SHIKA...
YES.
SHE KNOWS EVERYTHING.

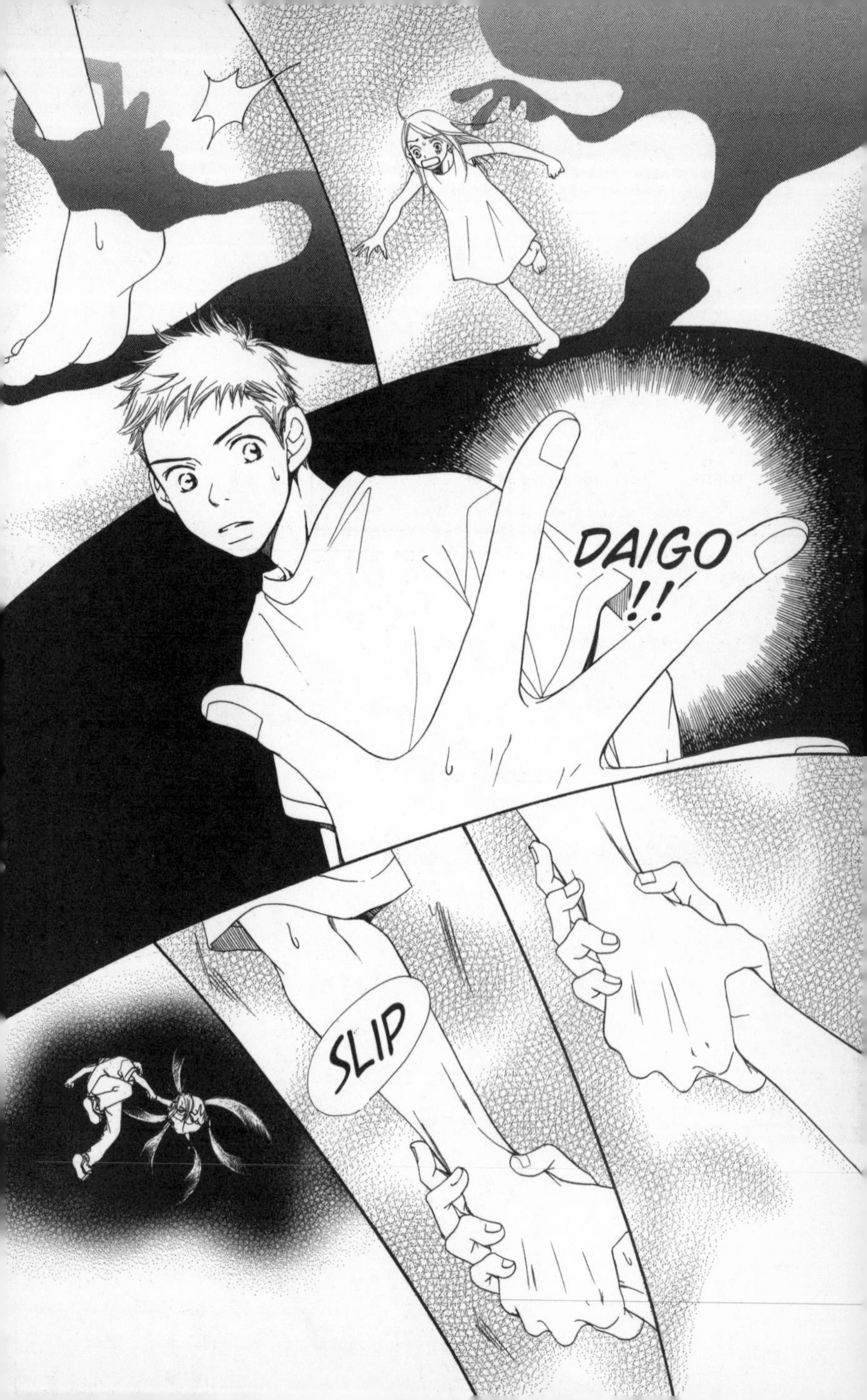
DAIGO !!
SLIP

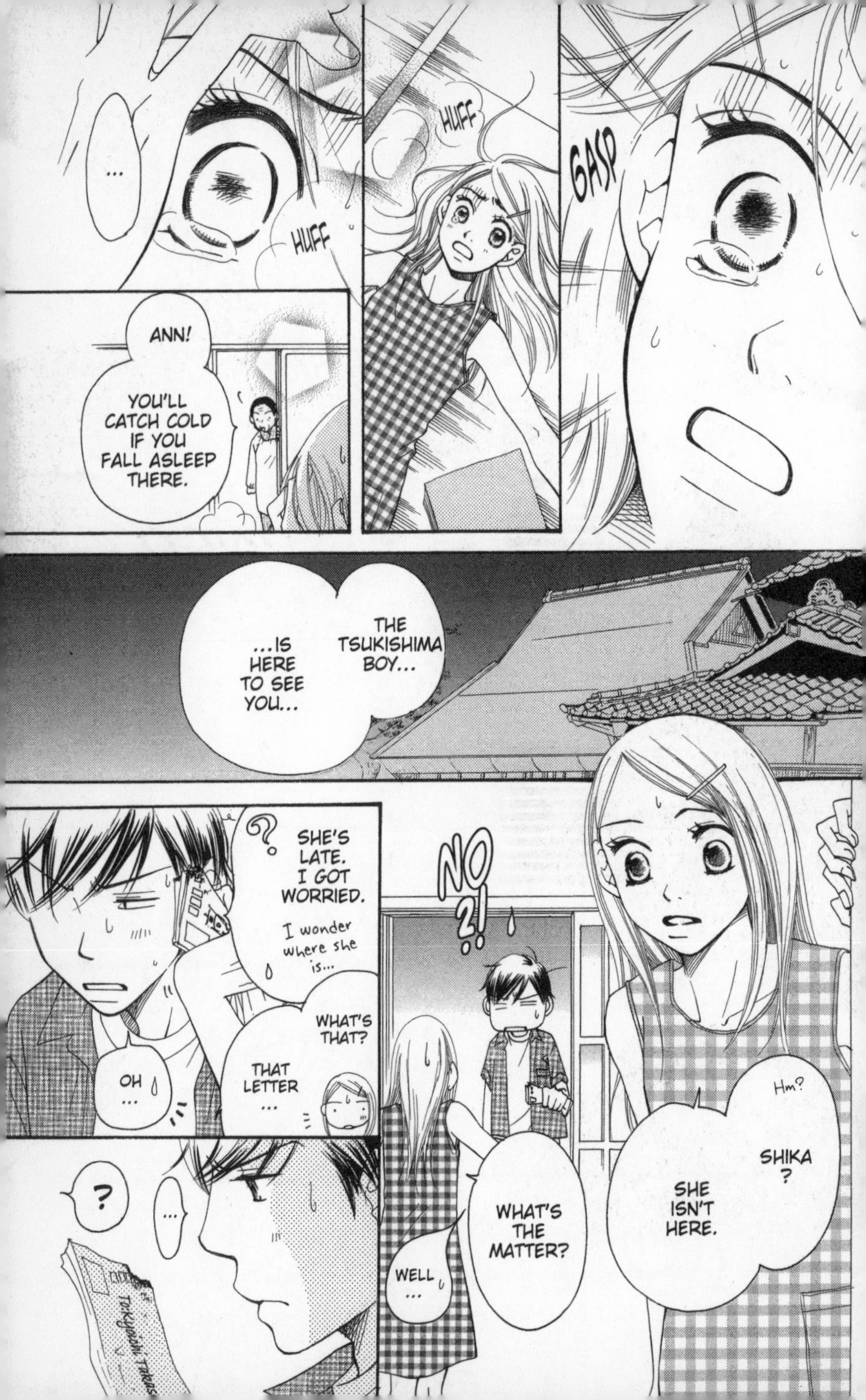
GASP
HUFF
HUFF
...
ANN!
YOU'LL CATCH COLD IF YOU FALL ASLEEP THERE.
THE TSUKISHIMA BOY...
...IS HERE TO SEE YOU...
NO?!
Hm?
SHIKA?
SHE ISN'T HERE.
WHAT'S THE MATTER?
WELL...
?
SHE'S LATE. I GOT WORRIED.
I wonder where she is...
WHAT'S THAT?
THAT LETTER...
OH...
...
?

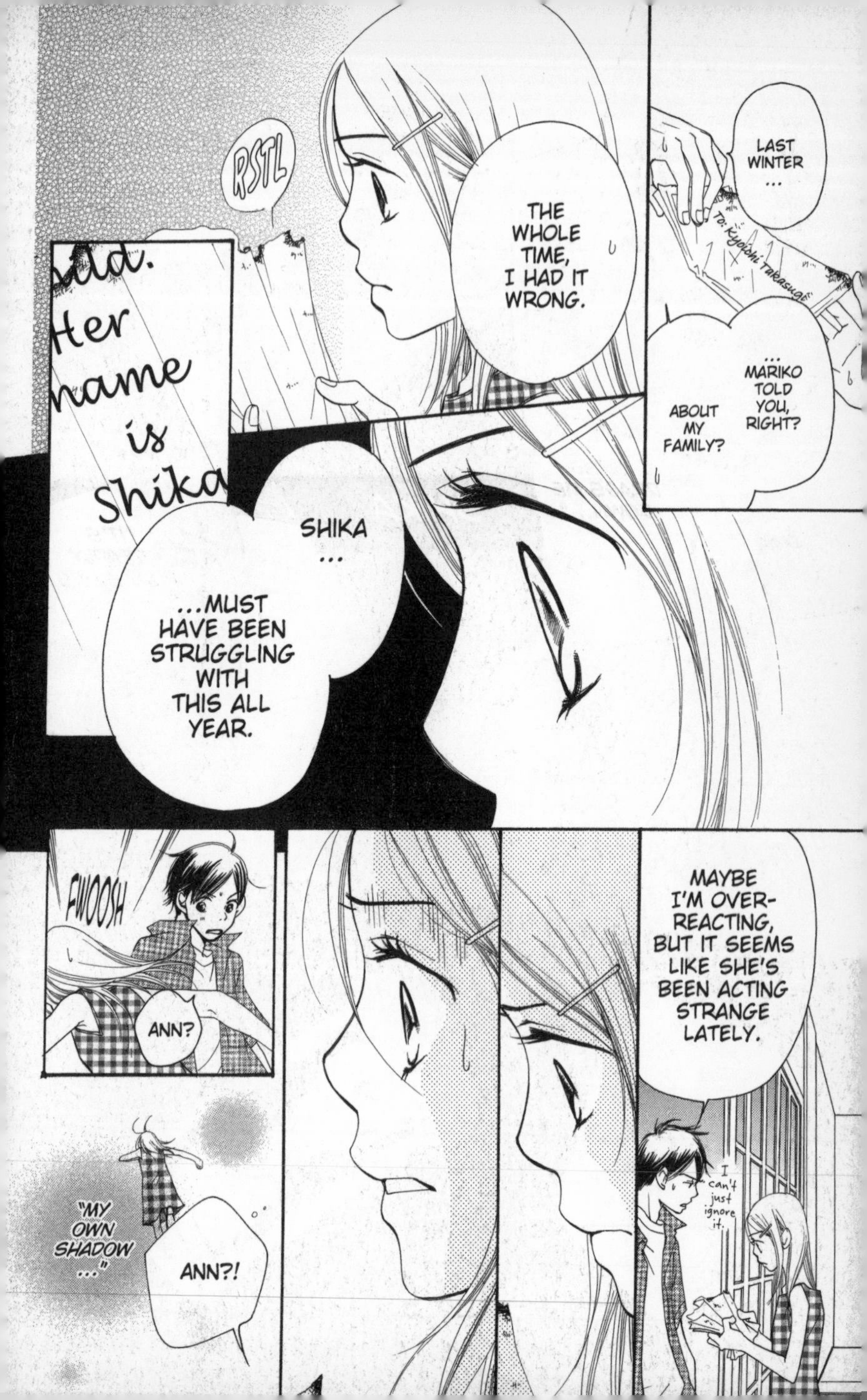
LAST WINTER...
To: Kyoichi Takasugi
...MARIKO TOLD YOU, RIGHT?
ABOUT MY FAMILY?
THE WHOLE TIME, I HAD IT WRONG.
RSTL
Her name is Shika
SHIKA...
...MUST HAVE BEEN STRUGGLING WITH THIS ALL YEAR.
MAYBE I'M OVER-REACTING, BUT IT SEEMS LIKE SHE'S BEEN ACTING STRANGE LATELY.
I can't just ignore it.
FWOOSH
ANN?
"MY OWN SHADOW..."
ANN?!

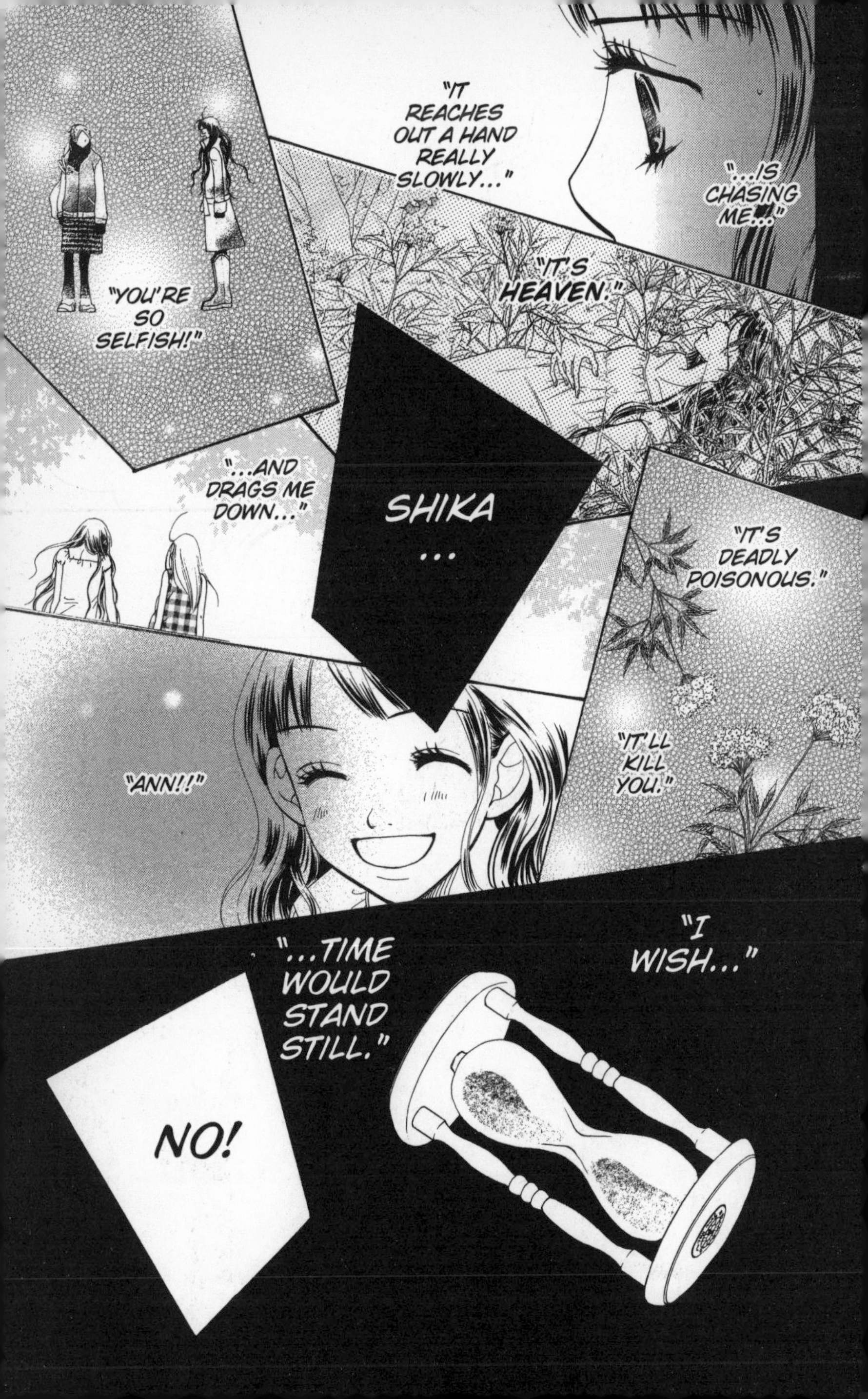
"...IS CHASING ME..."
"IT REACHES OUT A HAND REALLY SLOWLY..."
"YOU'RE SO SELFISH!"
"IT'S HEAVEN."
"IT'S DEADLY POISONOUS."
SHIKA ...
"...AND DRAGS ME DOWN..."
"IT'LL KILL YOU."
"ANN!!"
"I WISH..."
"...TIME WOULD STAND STILL."
NO!

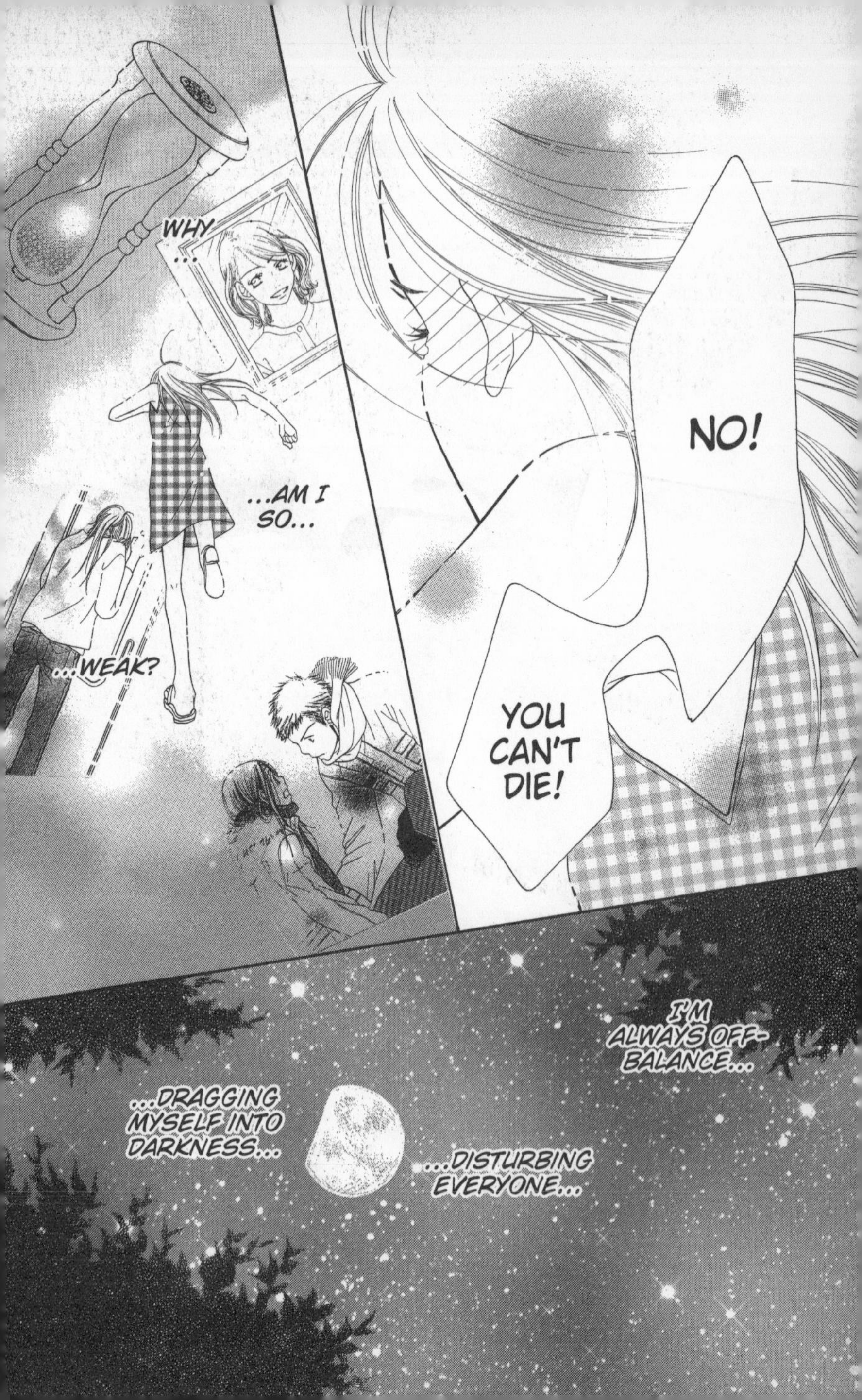
NO!
YOU CAN'T DIE!
WHY...
...AM I SO...
...WEAK?
I'M ALWAYS OFF-BALANCE...
...DISTURBING EVERYONE...
...DRAGGING MYSELF INTO DARKNESS...

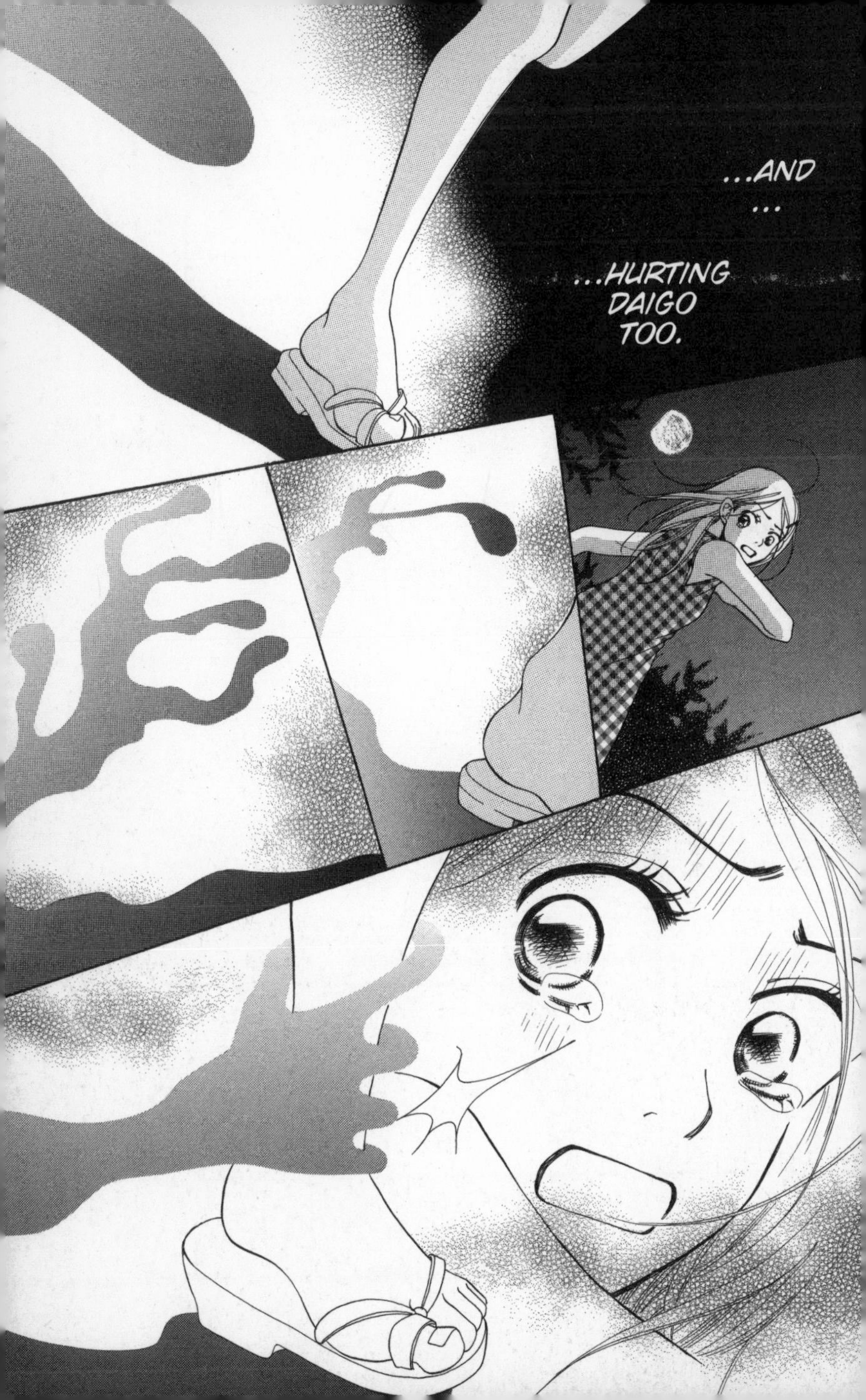
...AND
...
...HURTING DAIGO TOO.

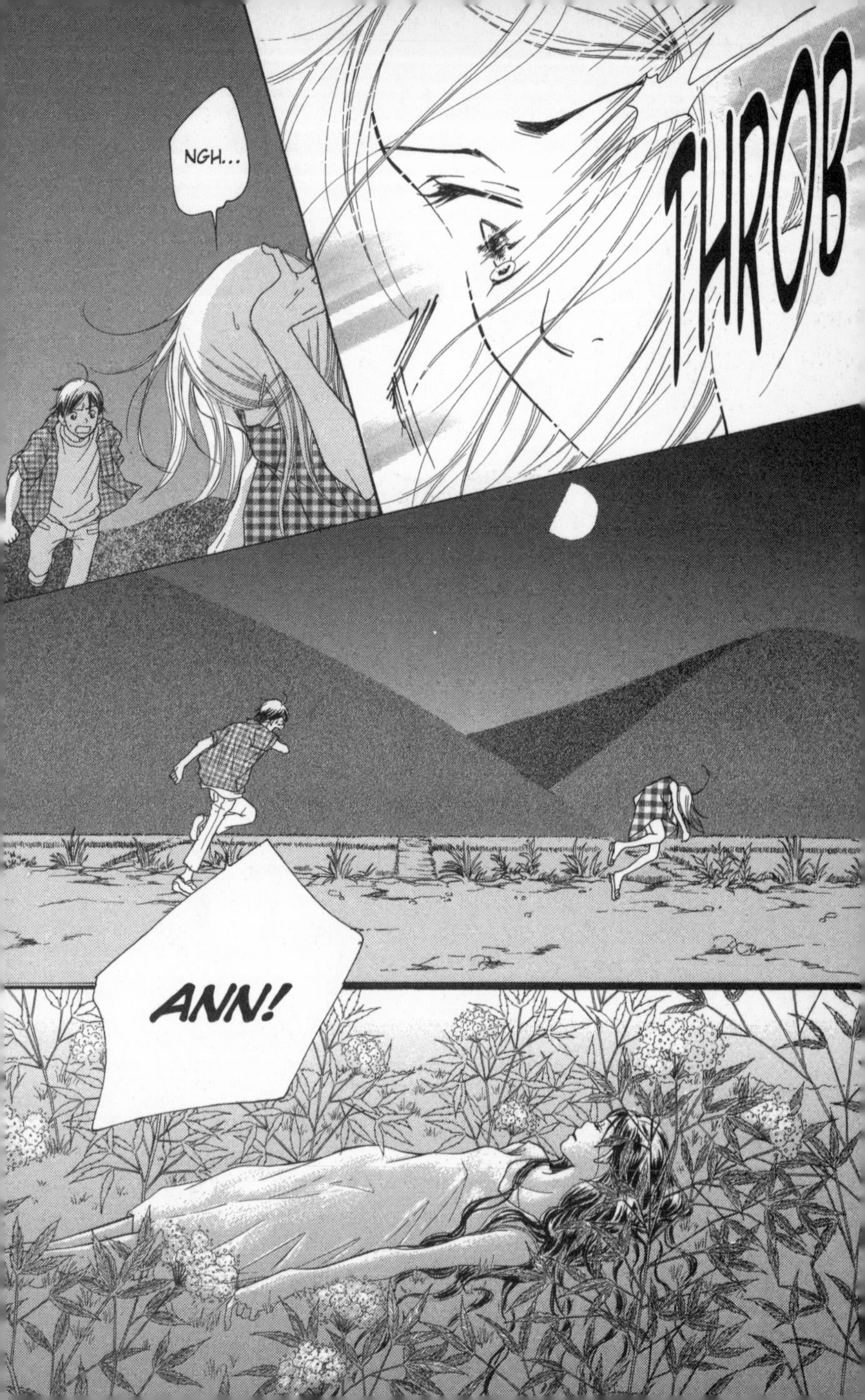
THROB
NGH...
ANN!

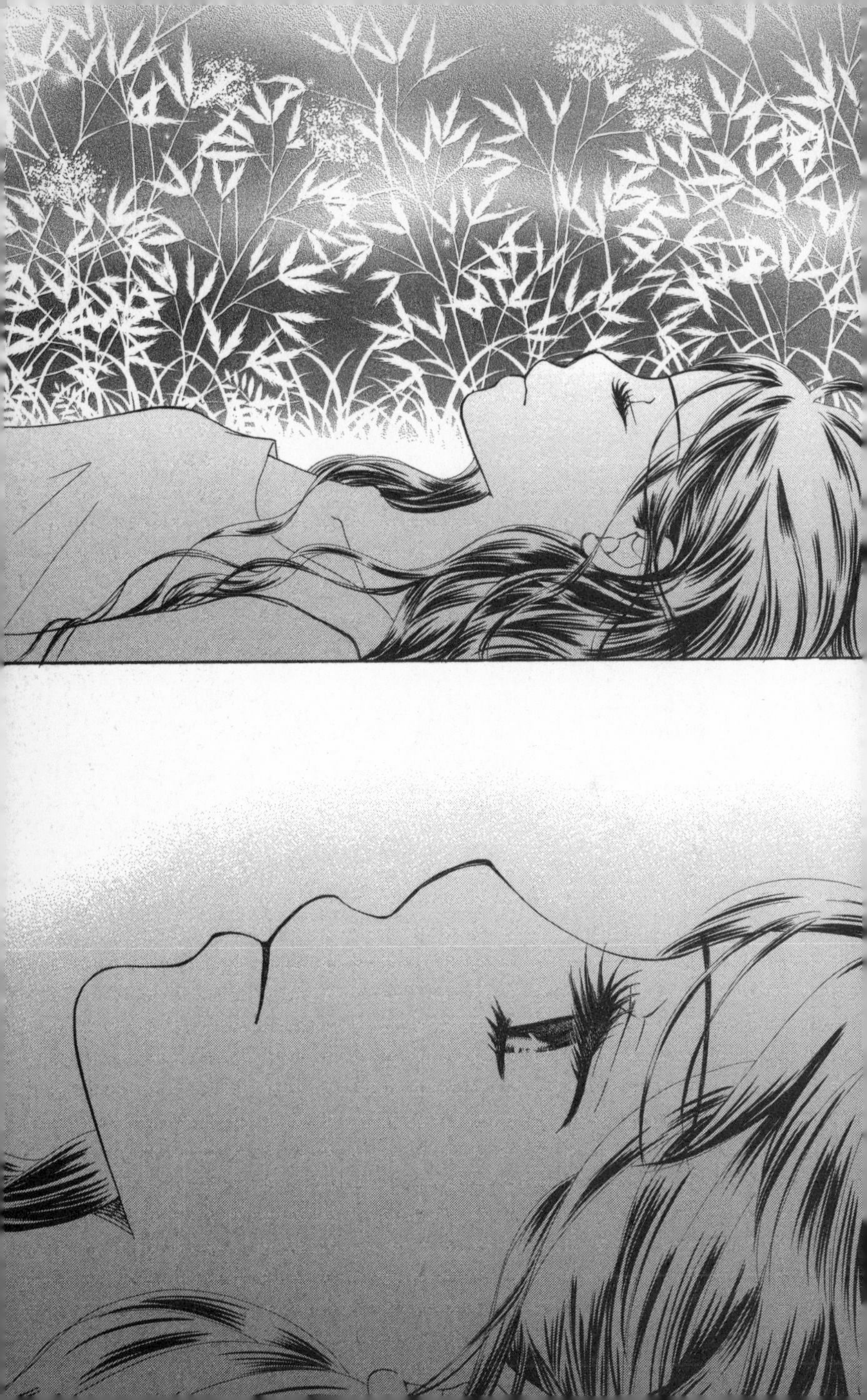

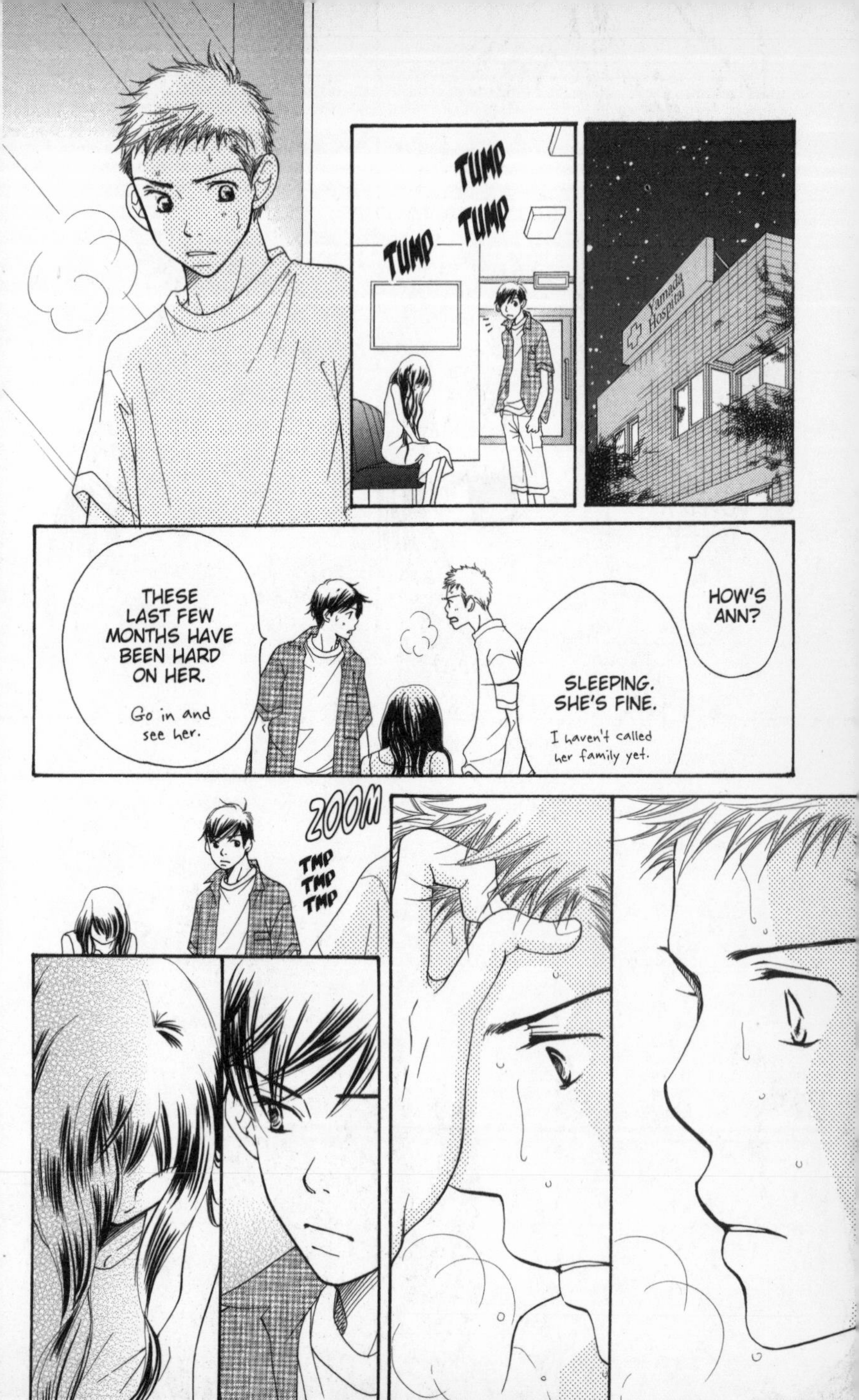
Yamada Hospital
TUMP
TUMP
TUMP
TUMP
HOW'S ANN?
SLEEPING. SHE'S FINE.
I haven't called her family yet.
THESE LAST FEW MONTHS HAVE BEEN HARD ON HER.
Go in and see her.
ZOOM
TMP TMP TMP

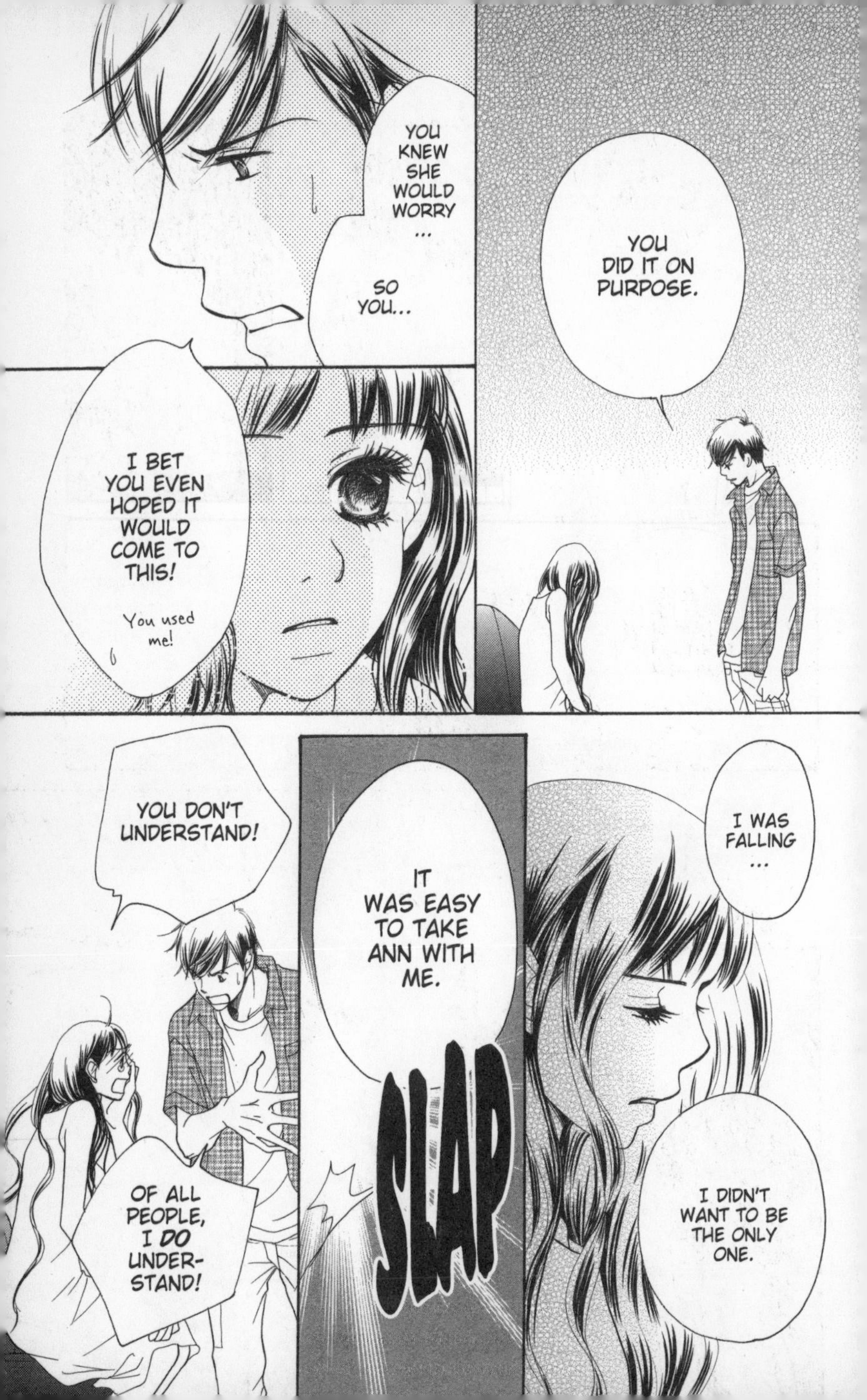
YOU DID IT ON PURPOSE.
YOU KNEW SHE WOULD WORRY...
SO YOU...
I BET YOU EVEN HOPED IT WOULD COME TO THIS!
You used me!
I WAS FALLING...
I DIDN'T WANT TO BE THE ONLY ONE.
IT WAS EASY TO TAKE ANN WITH ME.
SLAP
YOU DON'T UNDERSTAND!
OF ALL PEOPLE, I *DO* UNDERSTAND!

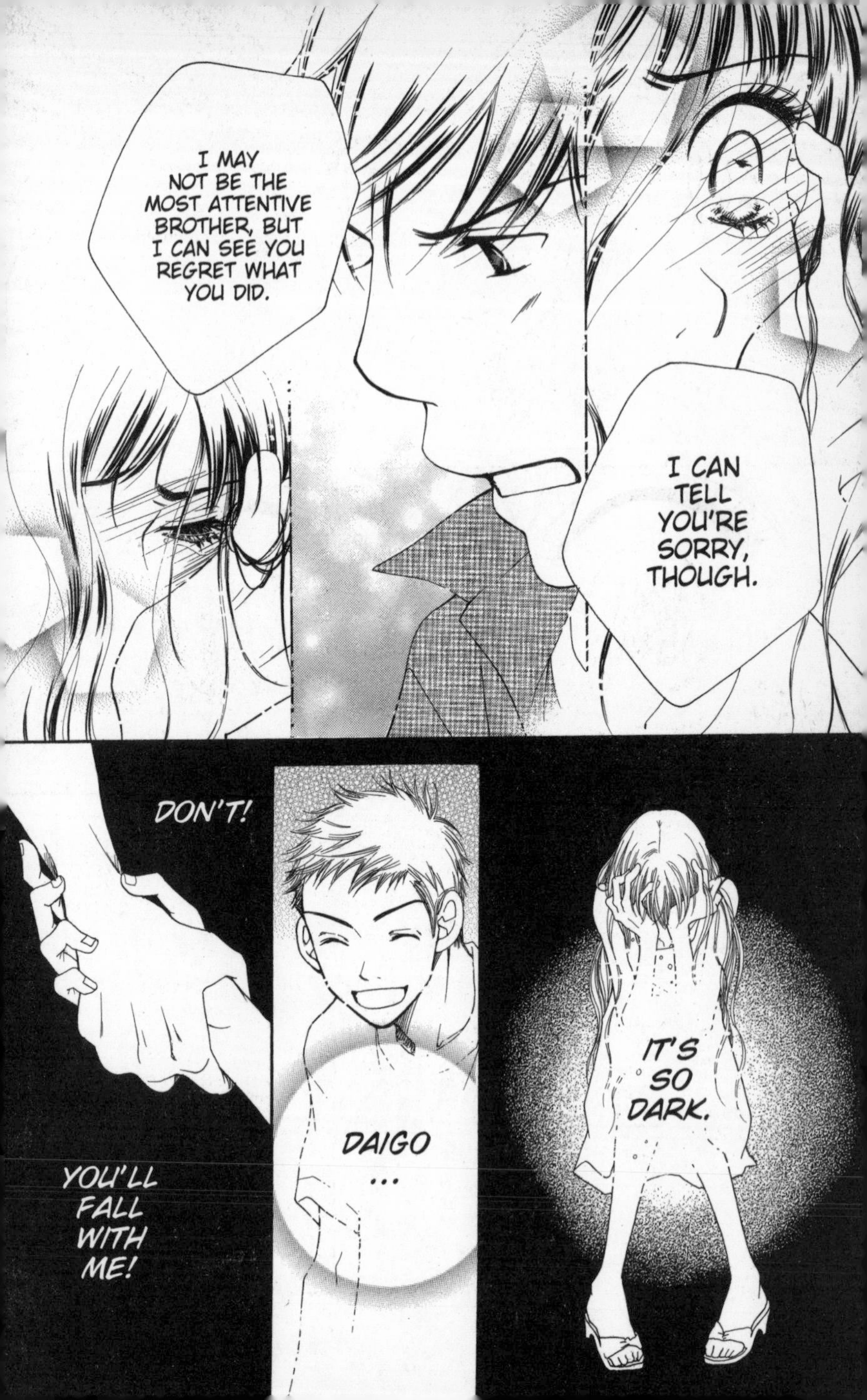
I MAY NOT BE THE MOST ATTENTIVE BROTHER, BUT I CAN SEE YOU REGRET WHAT YOU DID.
I CAN TELL YOU'RE SORRY, THOUGH.
IT'S SO DARK.
DAIGO ...
DON'T!
YOU'LL FALL WITH ME!

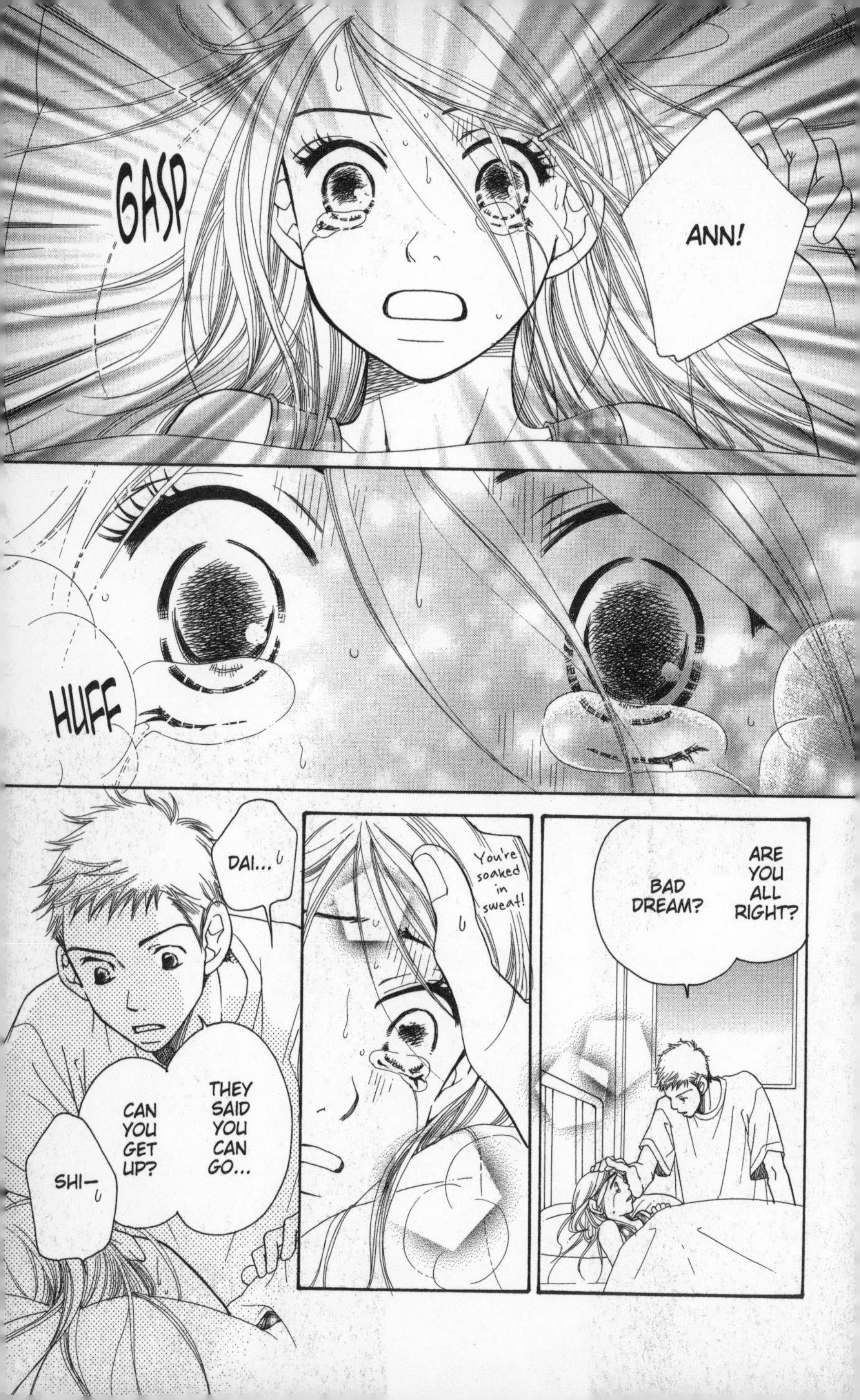
ANN!
GASP
HUFF
ARE YOU ALL RIGHT?
BAD DREAM?
You're soaked in sweat!
DAI...
THEY SAID YOU CAN GO...
CAN YOU GET UP?
SHI—

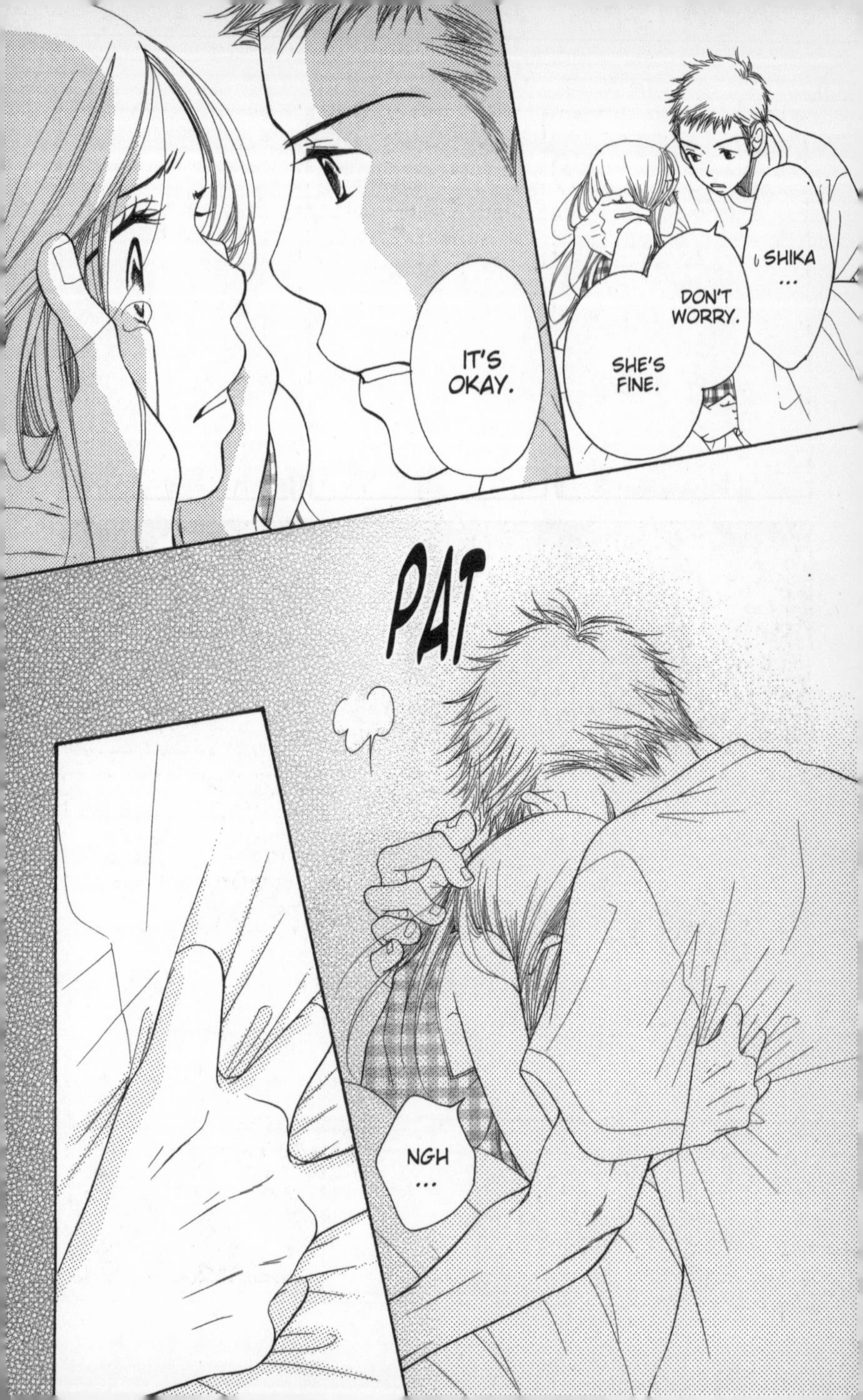
SHIKA ...
DON'T WORRY.
SHE'S FINE.
IT'S OKAY.
PAT
NGH ...

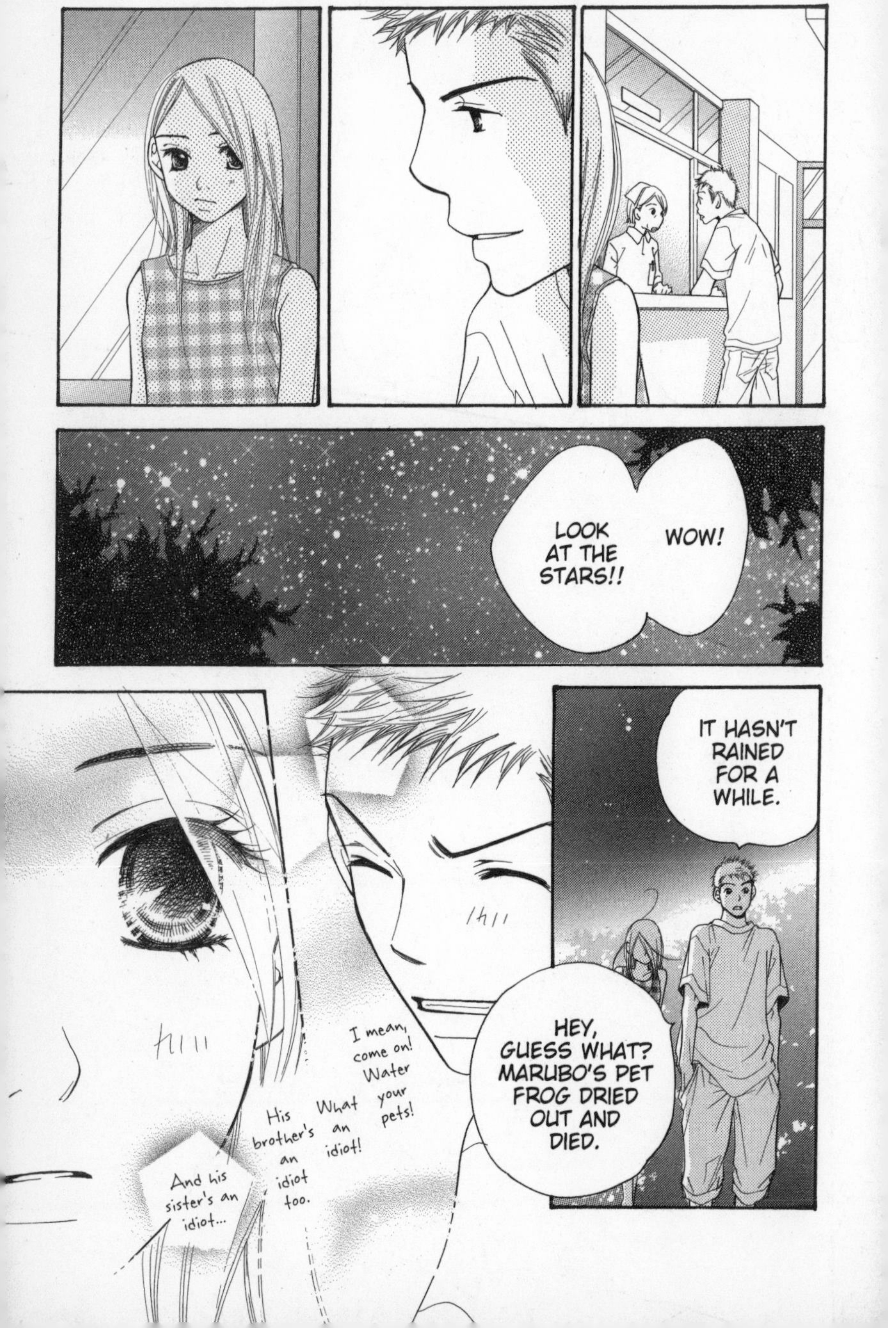
WOW!
LOOK AT THE STARS!!
IT HASN'T RAINED FOR A WHILE.
HEY, GUESS WHAT? MARUBO'S PET FROG DRIED OUT AND DIED.
I mean, come on! Water your pets!
What an idiot!
His brother's an idiot too.
And his sister's an idiot...

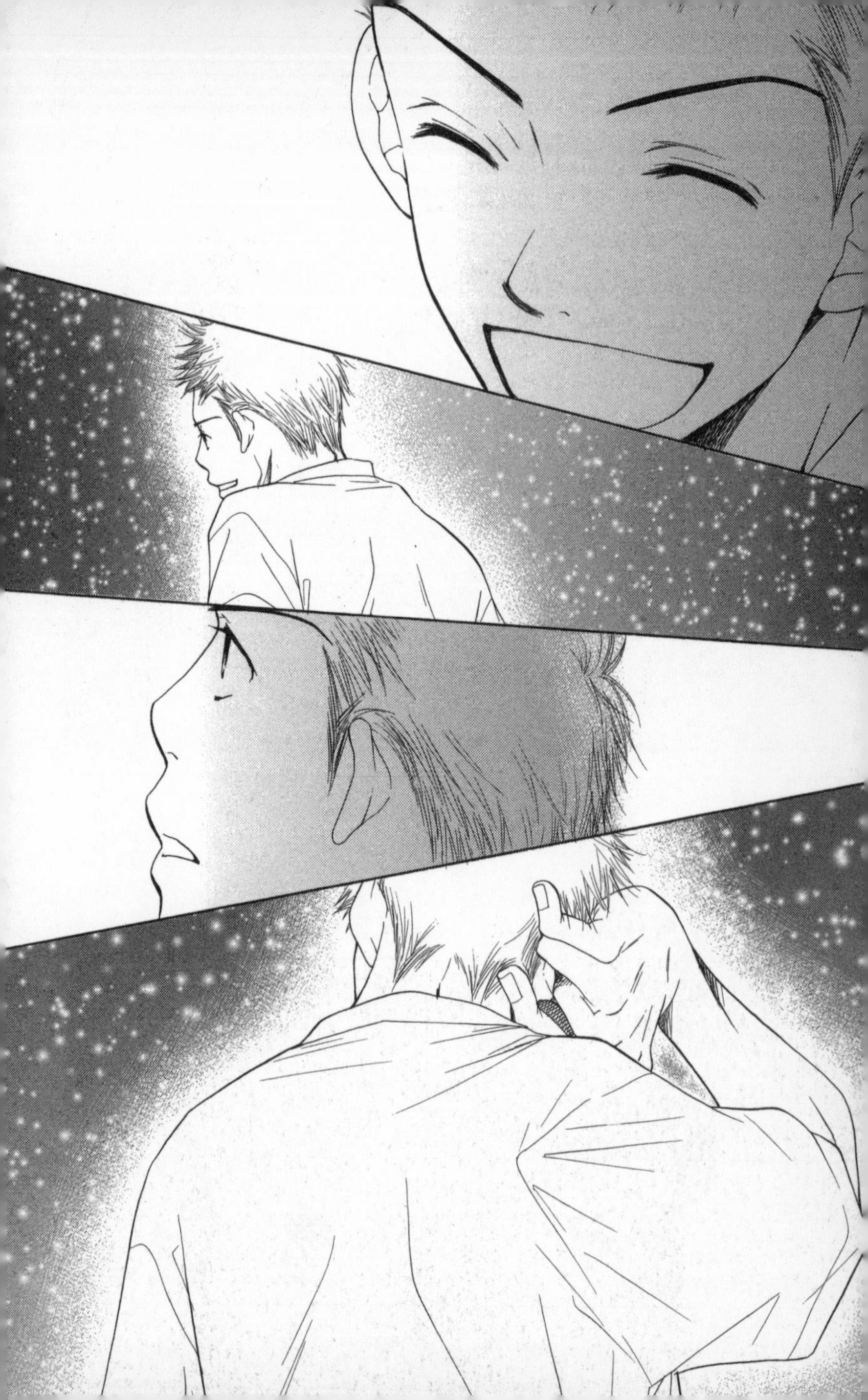

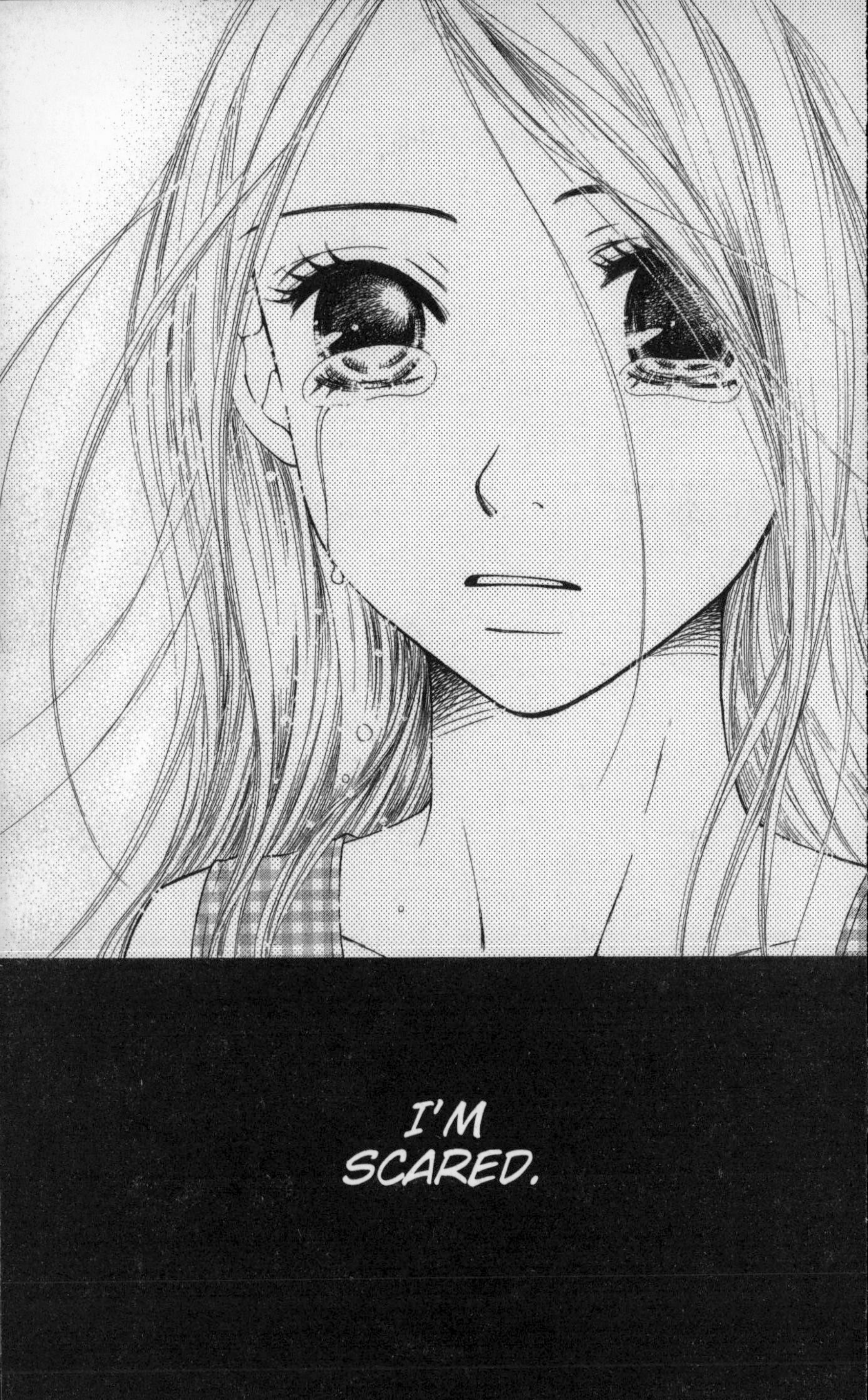
I'M SCARED.

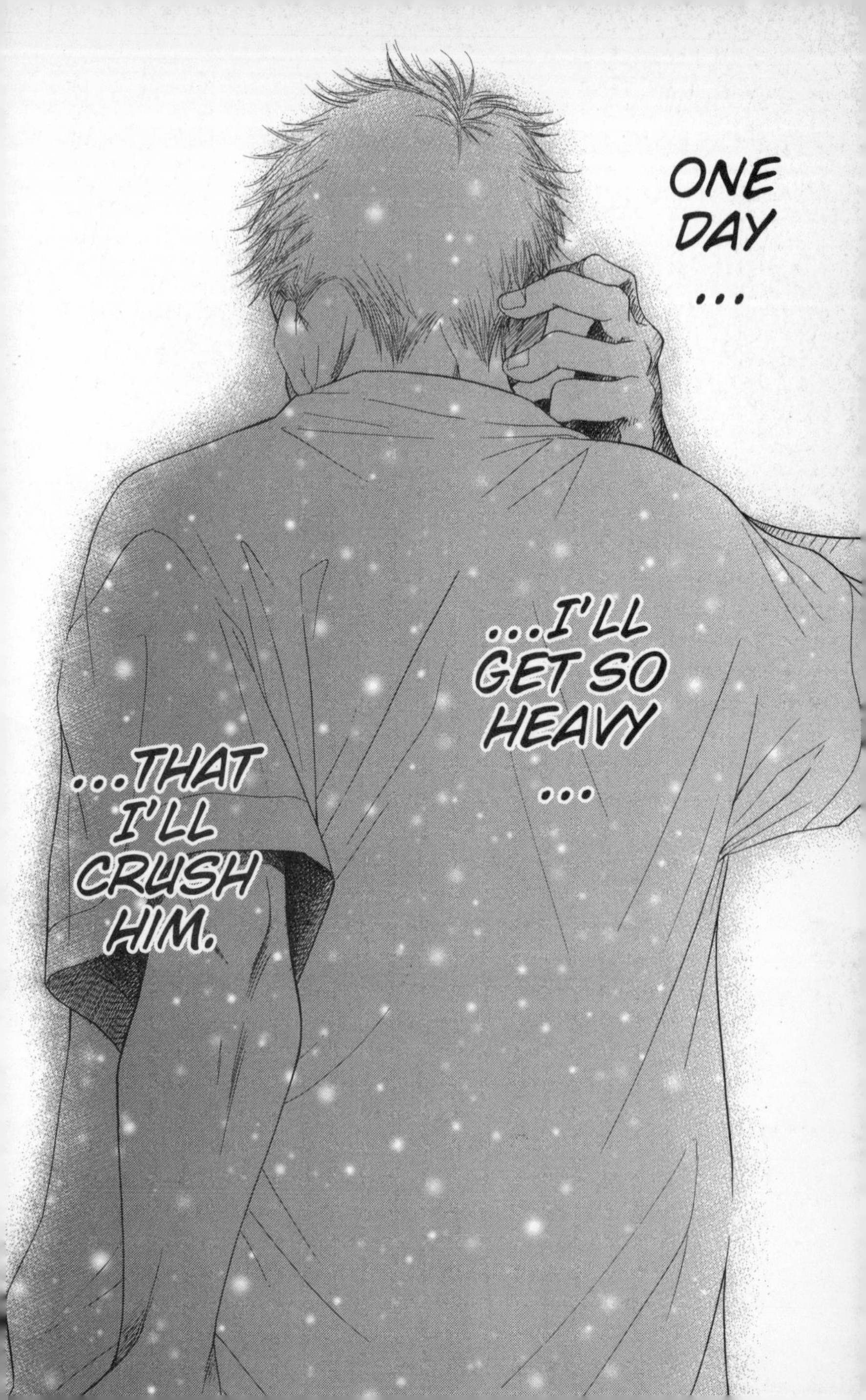
ONE DAY ...
...I'LL GET SO HEAVY ...
...THAT I'LL CRUSH HIM.

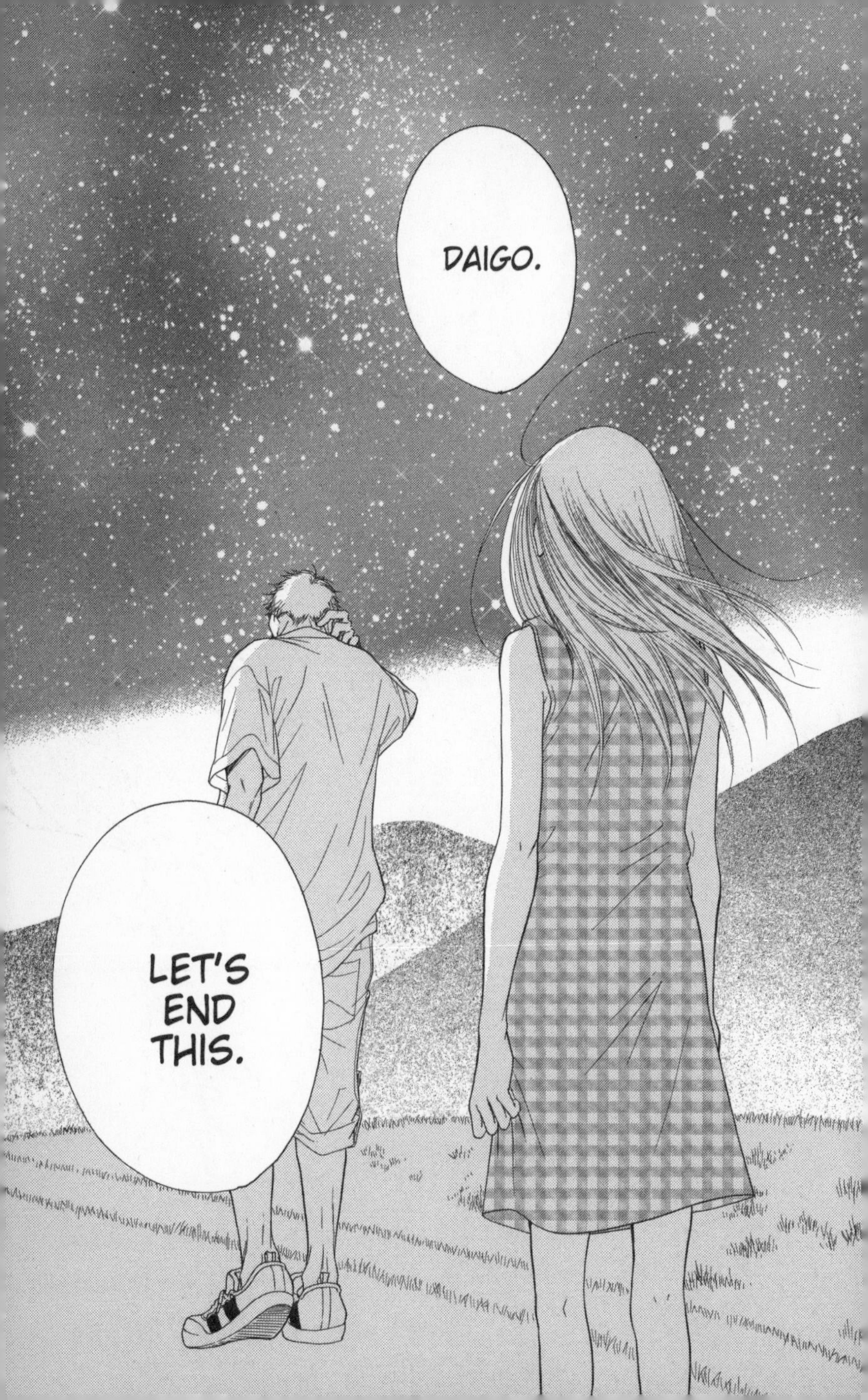
DAIGO.
LET'S END THIS.

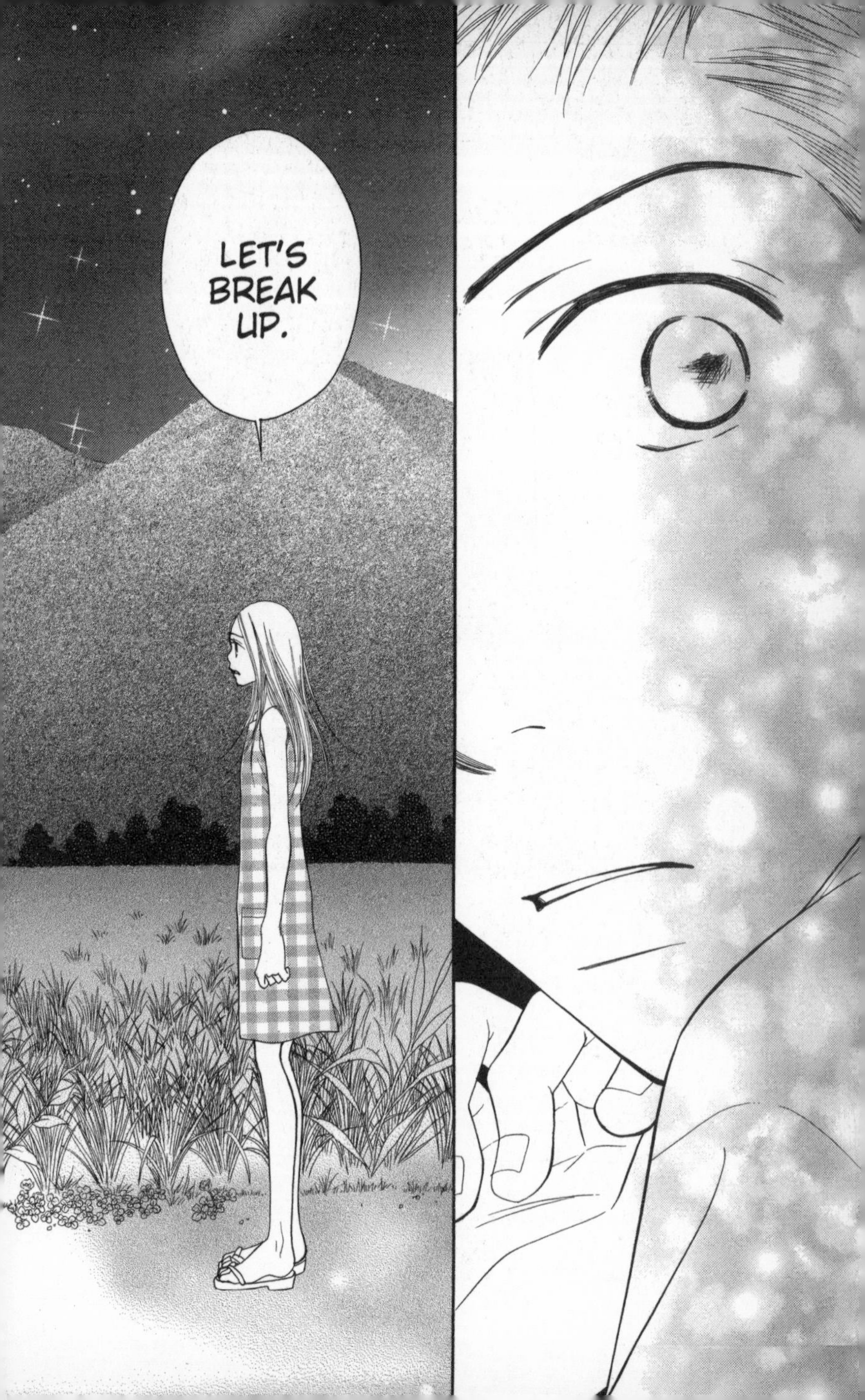
LET'S BREAK UP.

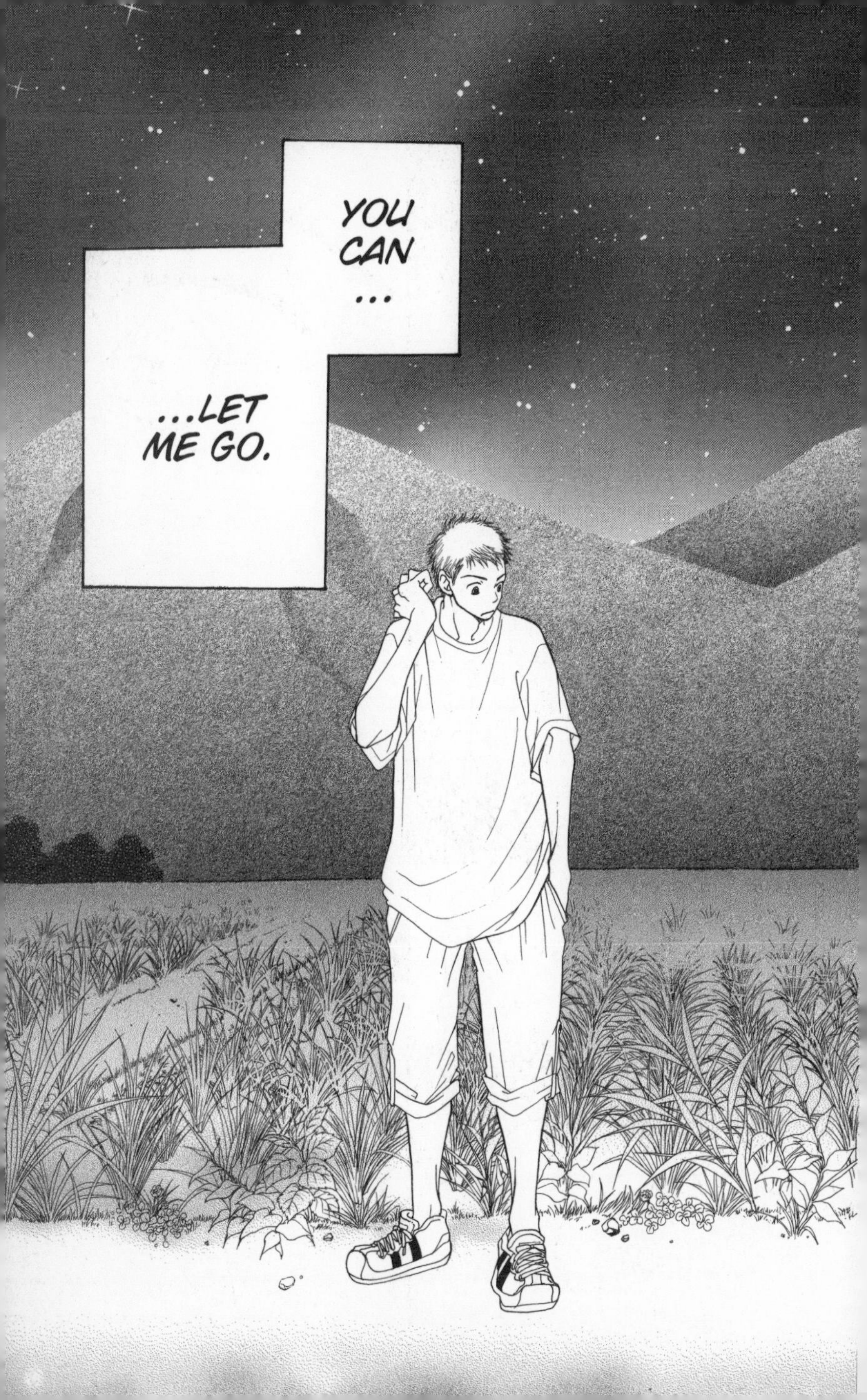
YOU CAN ...
...LET ME GO.

Sand Chronicles

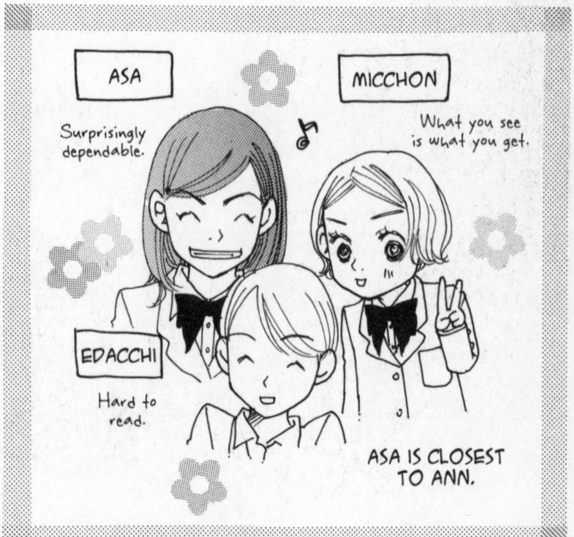
ASA
Surprisingly dependable.
MICCHON
What you see is what you get.
EDACCHI
Hard to read.
ASA IS CLOSEST TO ANN.

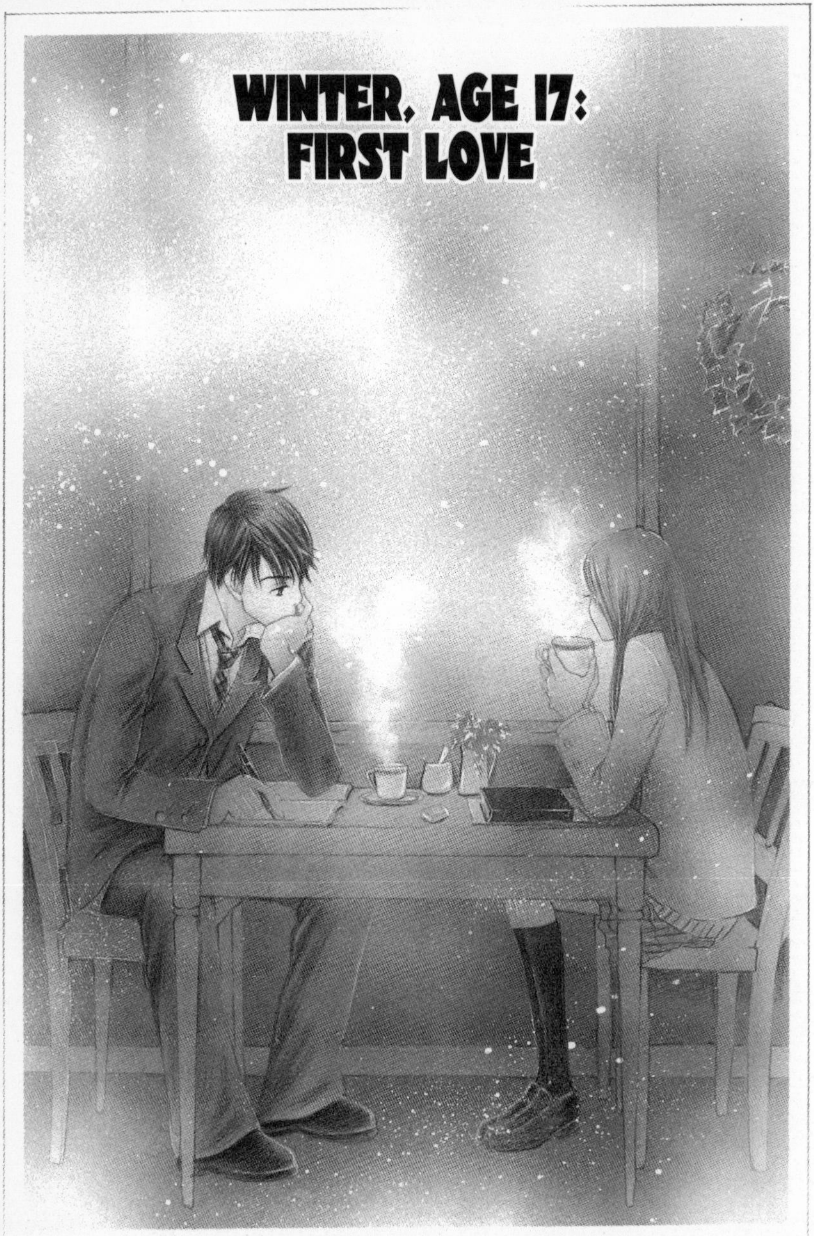
WINTER, AGE 17:
FIRST LOVE

Sand Chronicles

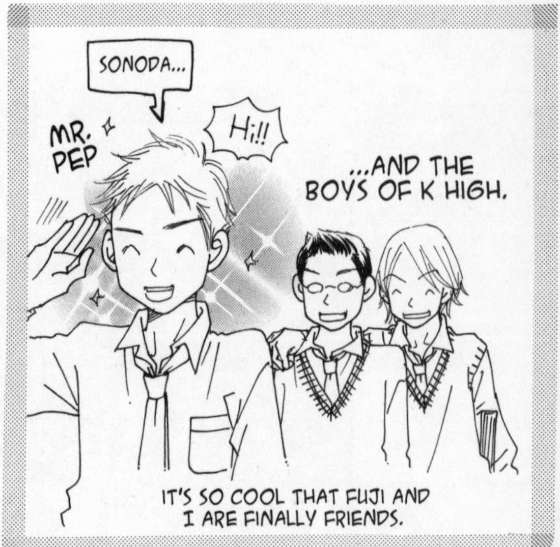
SONODA...
Hi!!
MR. PEP
...AND THE BOYS OF K HIGH.
IT'S SO COOL THAT FUJI AND I ARE FINALLY FRIENDS.

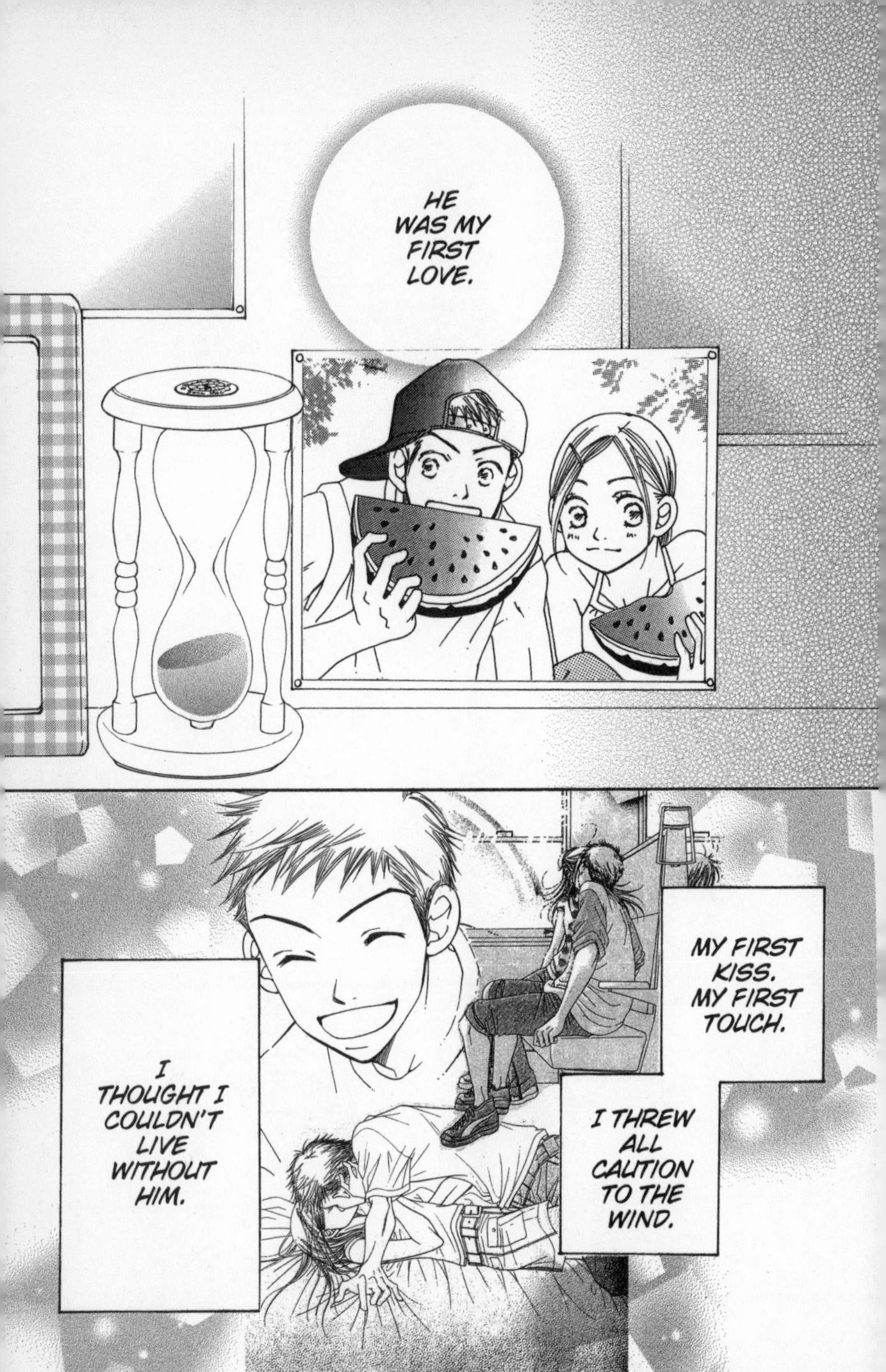
HE WAS MY FIRST LOVE.
MY FIRST KISS. MY FIRST TOUCH.
I THREW ALL CAUTION TO THE WIND.
I THOUGHT I COULDN'T LIVE WITHOUT HIM.

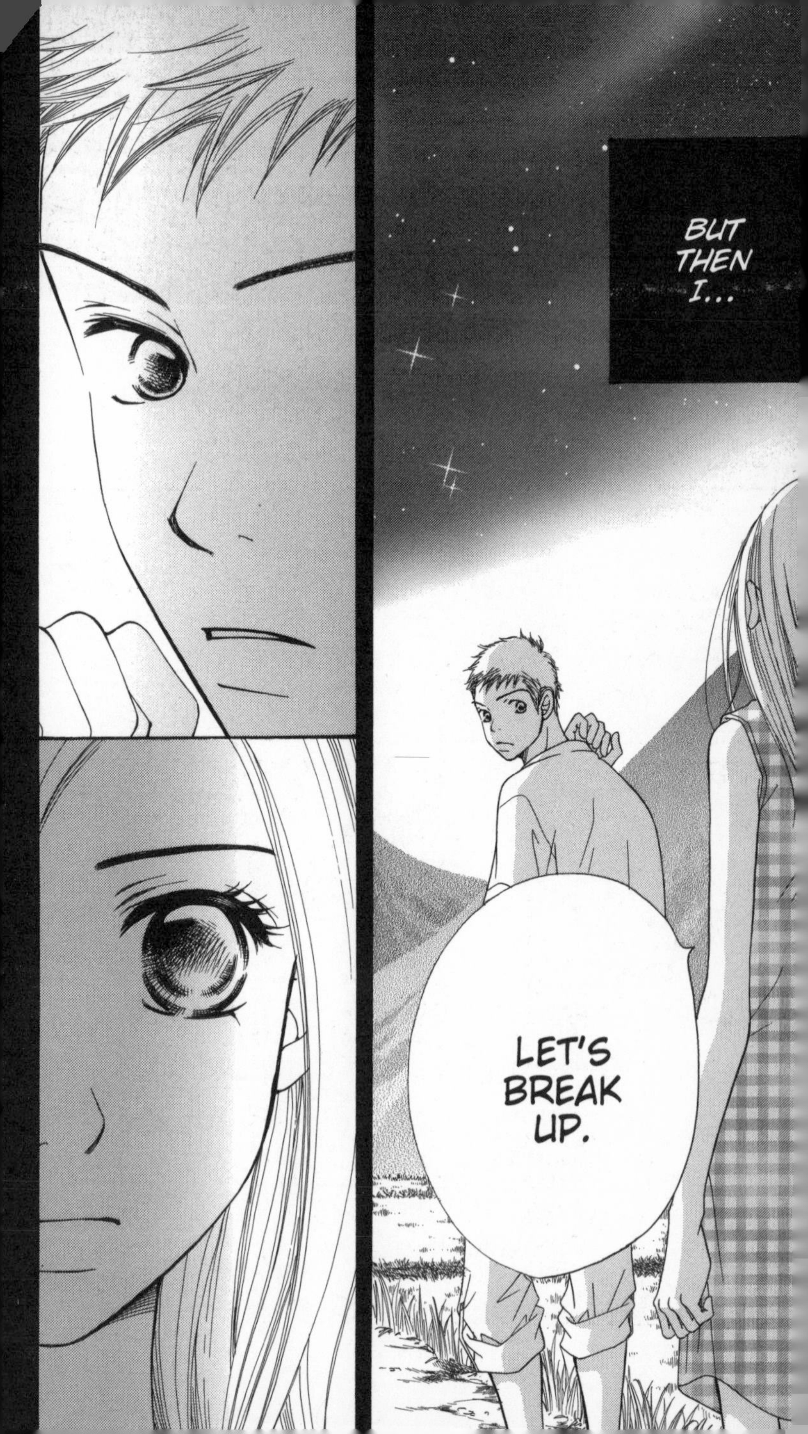
BUT THEN I...
LET'S BREAK UP.

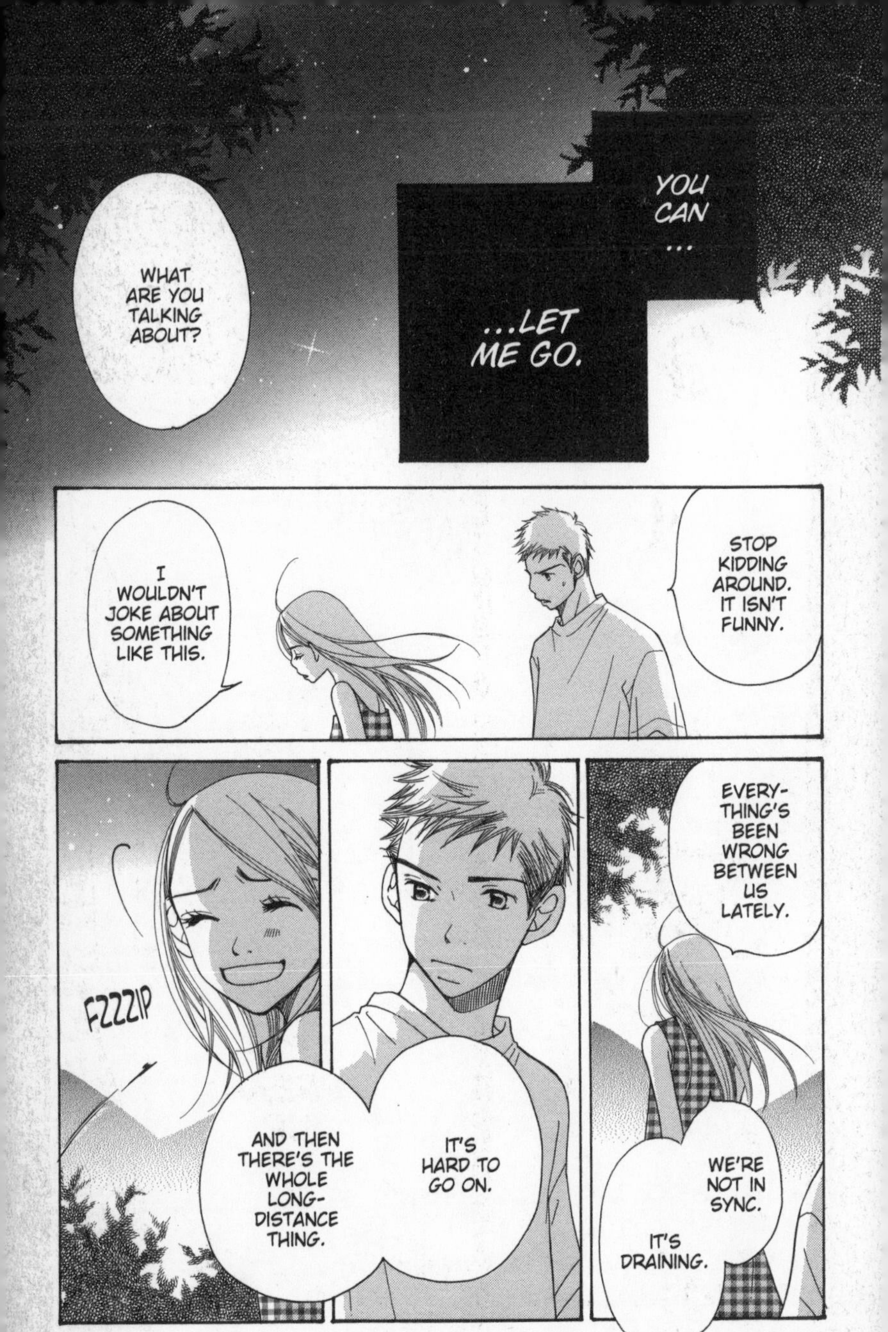
YOU CAN...
...LET ME GO.
WHAT ARE YOU TALKING ABOUT?
STOP KIDDING AROUND. IT ISN'T FUNNY.
I WOULDN'T JOKE ABOUT SOMETHING LIKE THIS.
EVERYTHING'S BEEN WRONG BETWEEN US LATELY.
WE'RE NOT IN SYNC.
IT'S DRAINING.
IT'S HARD TO GO ON.
AND THEN THERE'S THE WHOLE LONG-DISTANCE THING.
FZZZIP

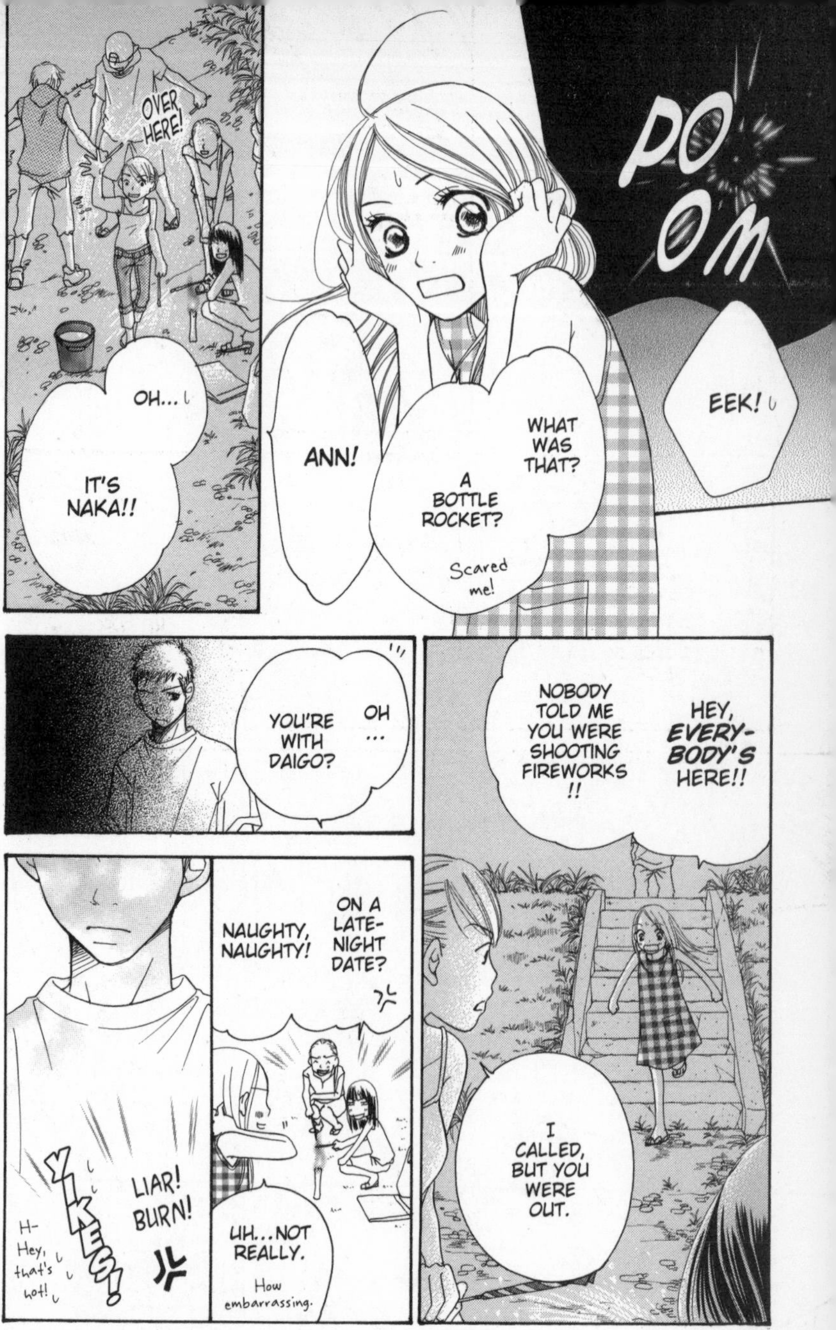
POOM
EEK!
WHAT WAS THAT?
A BOTTLE ROCKET?
Scared me!
ANN!
OVER HERE!
OH...
IT'S NAKA!!
HEY, EVERYBODY'S HERE!!
NOBODY TOLD ME YOU WERE SHOOTING FIREWORKS!!
I CALLED, BUT YOU WERE OUT.
OH...
YOU'RE WITH DAIGO?
ON A LATE-NIGHT DATE?
NAUGHTY, NAUGHTY!
UH...NOT REALLY.
How embarrassing.
LIAR! BURN!
YIKES!
H-Hey, that's hot!

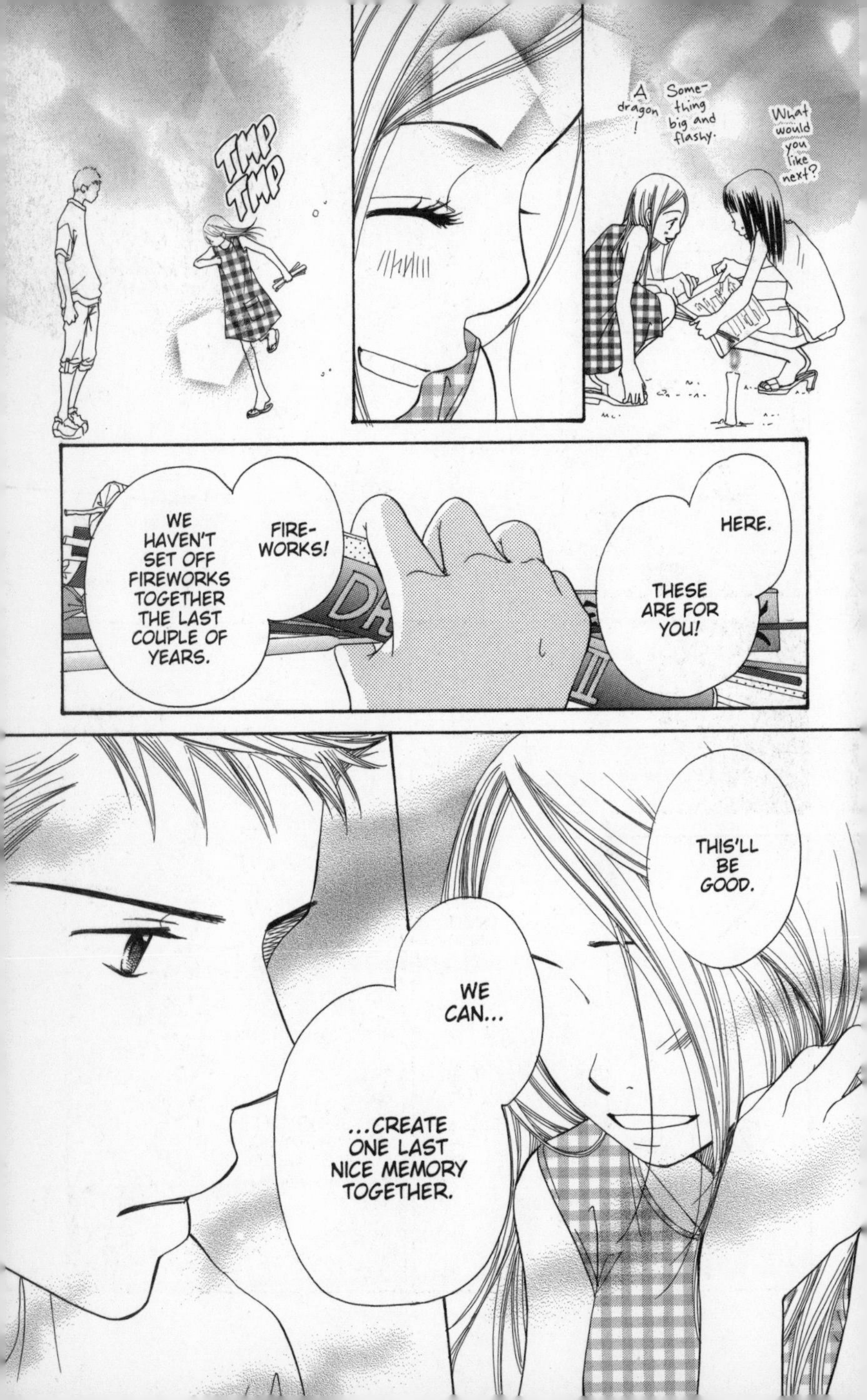
What would you like next?
Something big and flashy.
A dragon!
TMP TMP
HERE.
THESE ARE FOR YOU!
FIREWORKS!
WE HAVEN'T SET OFF FIREWORKS TOGETHER THE LAST COUPLE OF YEARS.
THIS'LL BE GOOD.
WE CAN...
...CREATE ONE LAST NICE MEMORY TOGETHER.

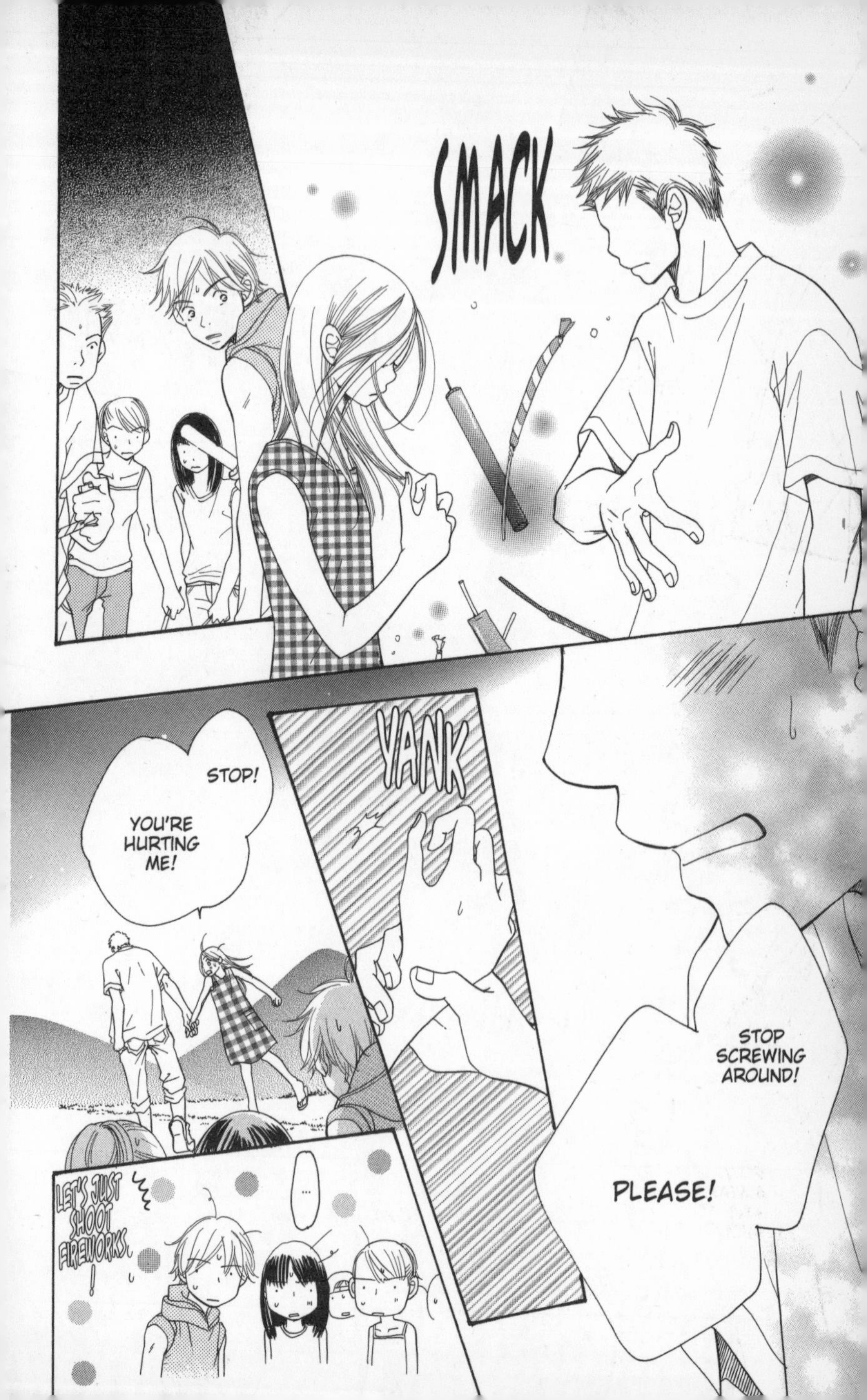
SMACK
STOP SCREWING AROUND!
PLEASE!
YANK
STOP!
YOU'RE HURTING ME!
...
LET'S JUST SHOOT FIREWORKS!

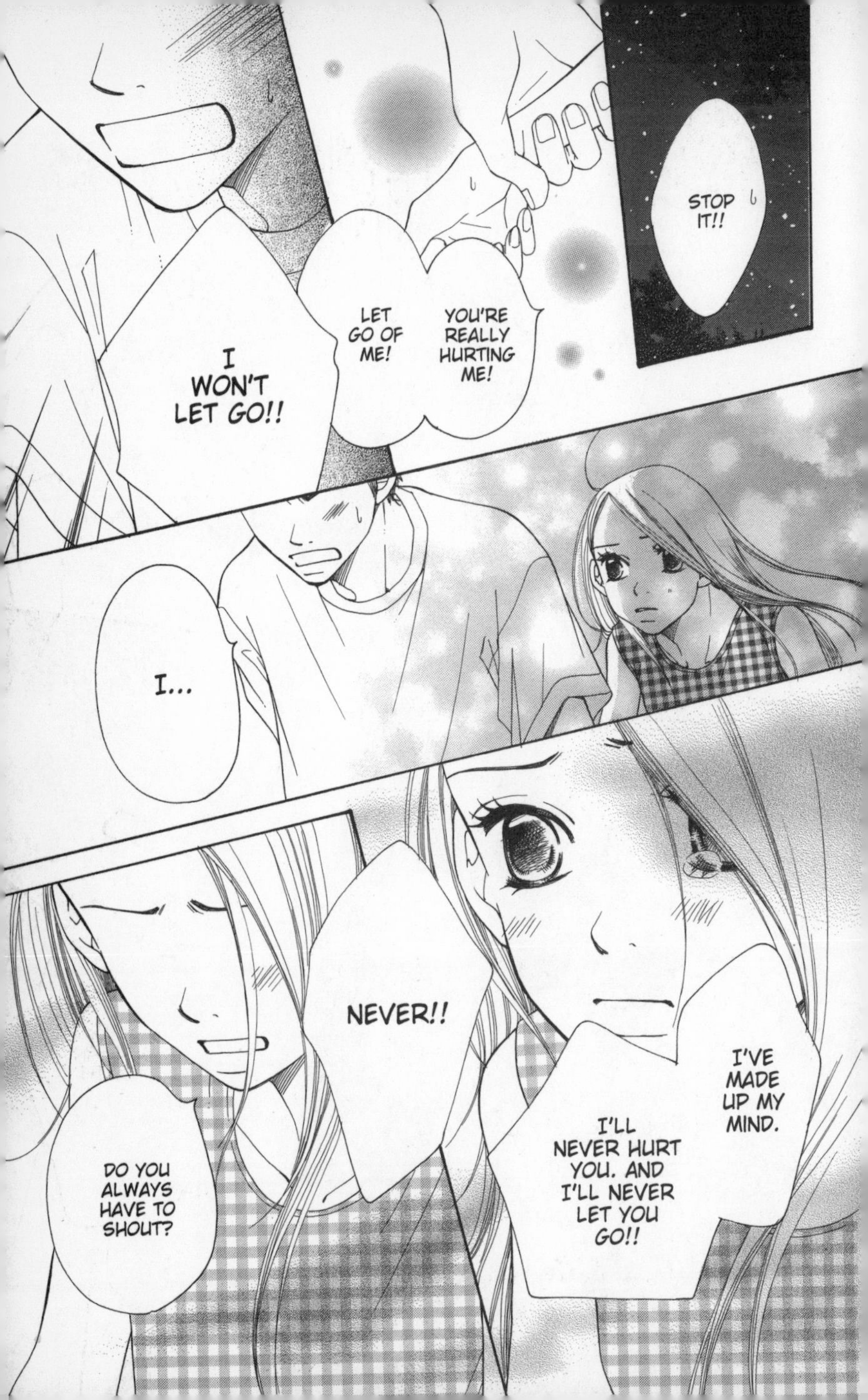
STOP IT!!
YOU'RE REALLY HURTING ME!
LET GO OF ME!
I WON'T LET GO!!
I...
I'VE MADE UP MY MIND.
I'LL NEVER HURT YOU. AND I'LL NEVER LET YOU GO!!
NEVER!!
DO YOU ALWAYS HAVE TO SHOUT?

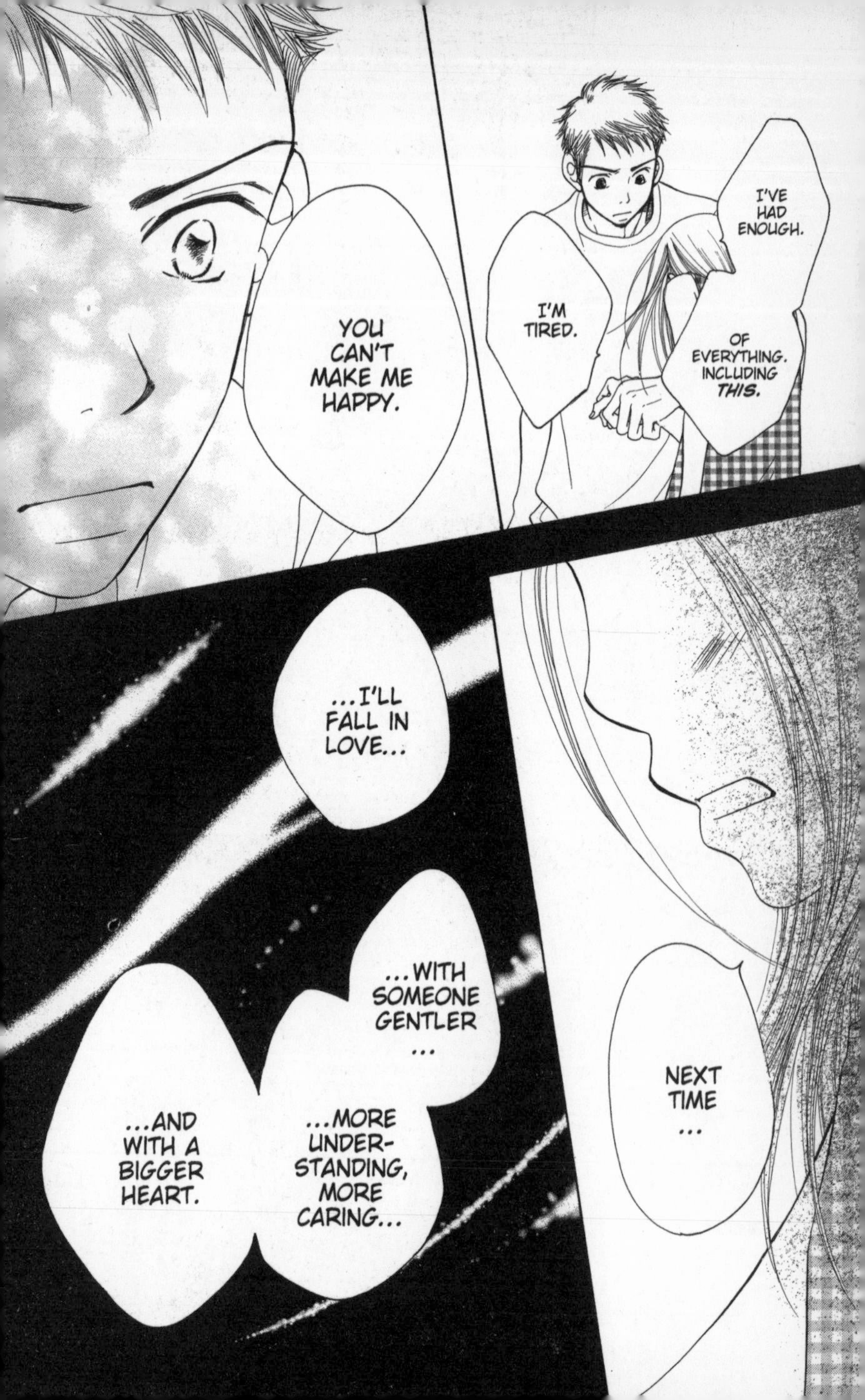
I'VE HAD ENOUGH.
I'M TIRED.
OF EVERYTHING. INCLUDING *THIS.*
YOU CAN'T MAKE ME HAPPY.
NEXT TIME ...
...I'LL FALL IN LOVE...
...WITH SOMEONE GENTLER ...
...MORE UNDER-STANDING, MORE CARING...
...AND WITH A BIGGER HEART.

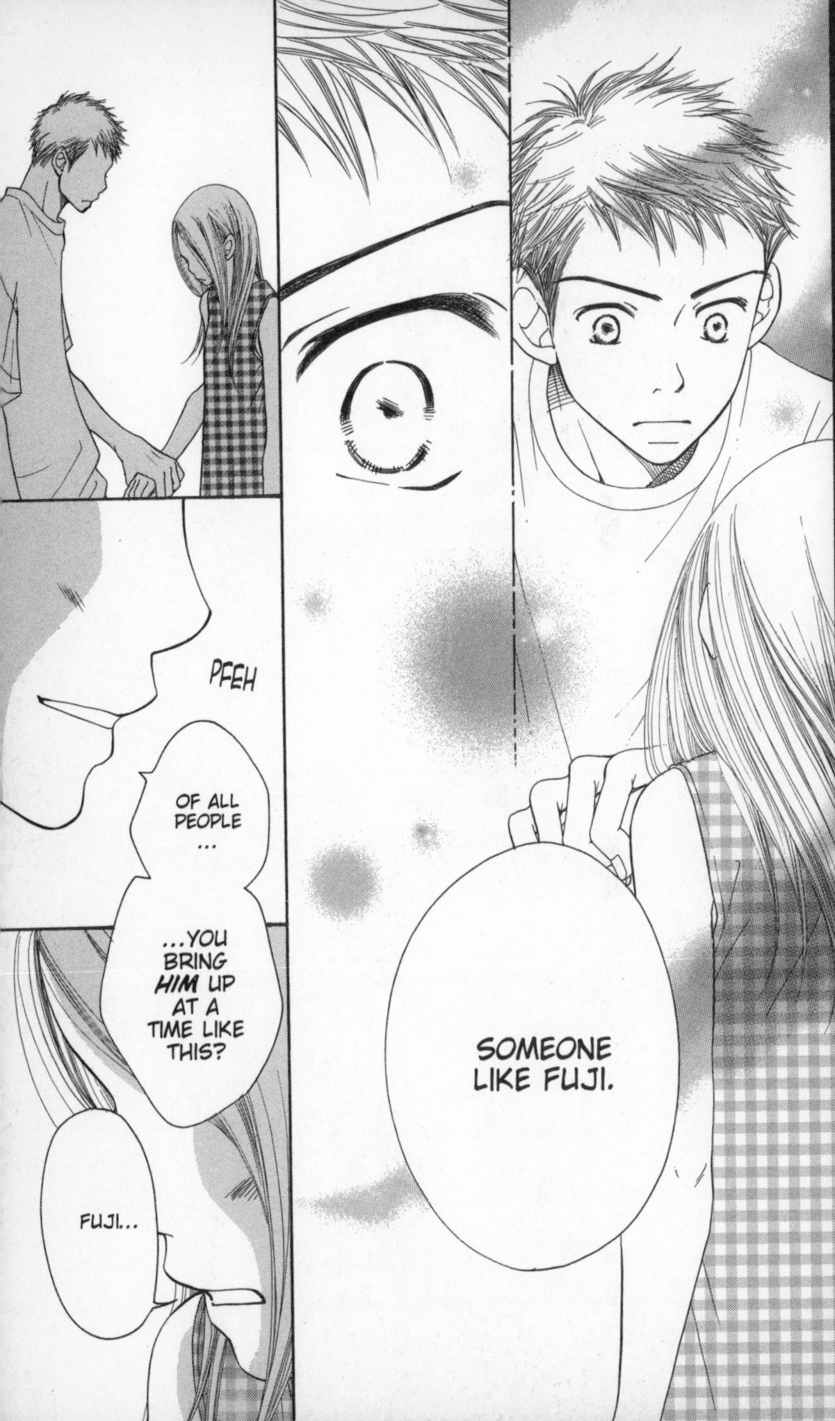
SOMEONE LIKE FUJI.
PFEH
OF ALL PEOPLE ...
...YOU BRING ***HIM*** UP AT A TIME LIKE THIS?
FUJI...

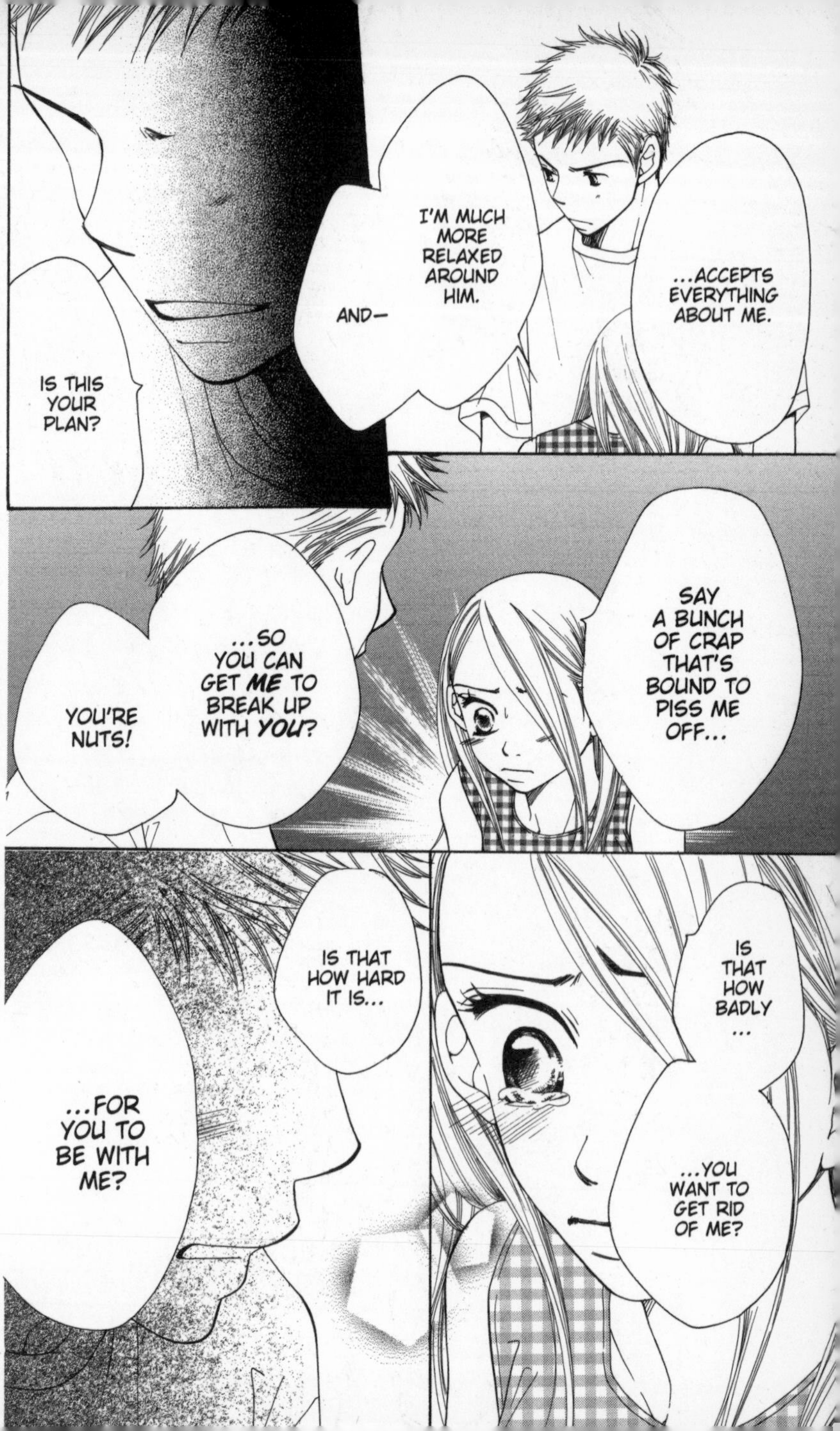
...ACCEPTS EVERYTHING ABOUT ME.
I'M MUCH MORE RELAXED AROUND HIM.
AND—
IS THIS YOUR PLAN?
SAY A BUNCH OF CRAP THAT'S BOUND TO PISS ME OFF...
...SO YOU CAN GET *ME* TO BREAK UP WITH *YOU*?
YOU'RE NUTS!
IS THAT HOW BADLY ...
...YOU WANT TO GET RID OF ME?
IS THAT HOW HARD IT IS...
...FOR YOU TO BE WITH ME?

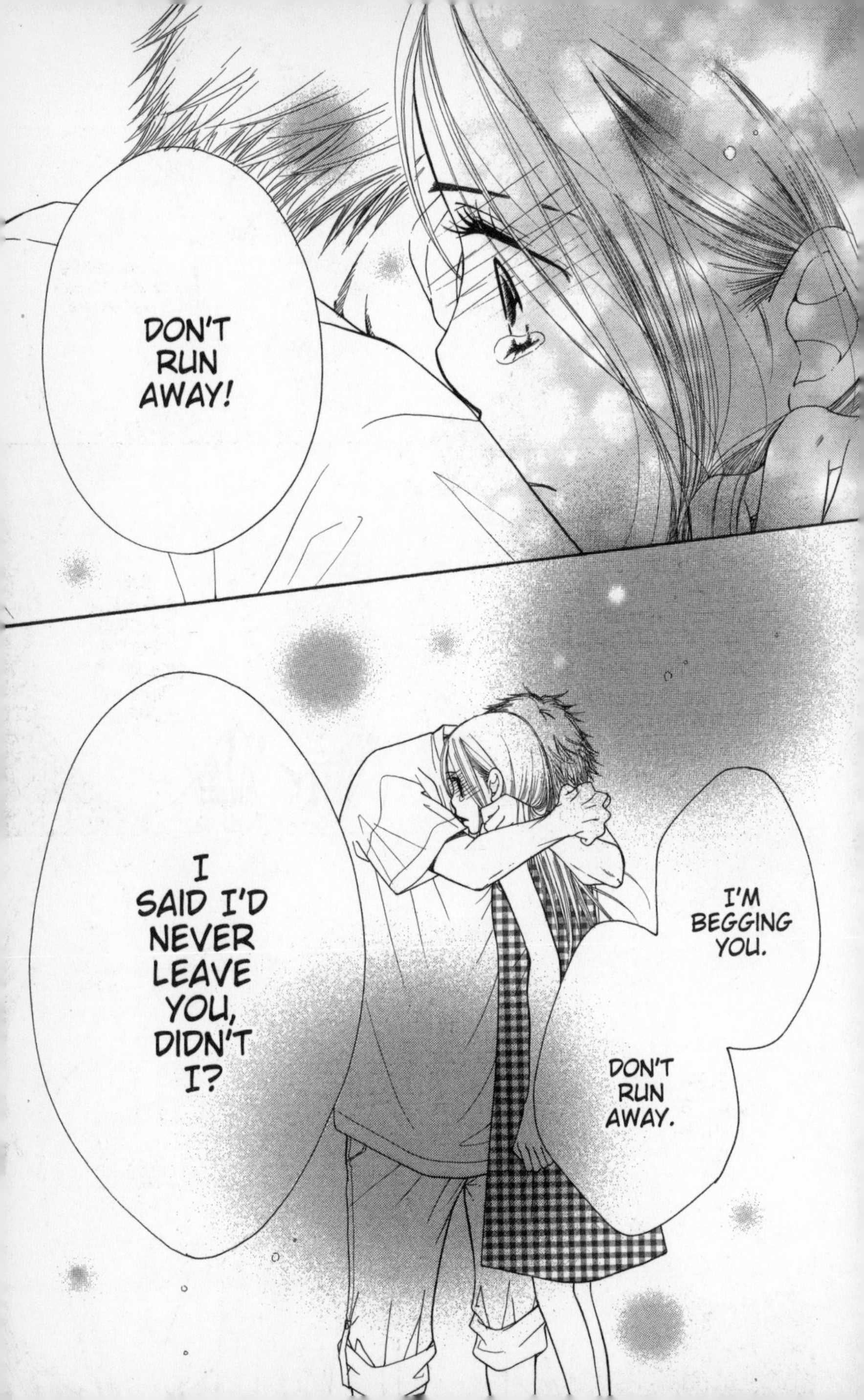
DON'T RUN AWAY!
I'M BEGGING YOU. DON'T RUN AWAY.
I SAID I'D NEVER LEAVE YOU, DIDN'T I?

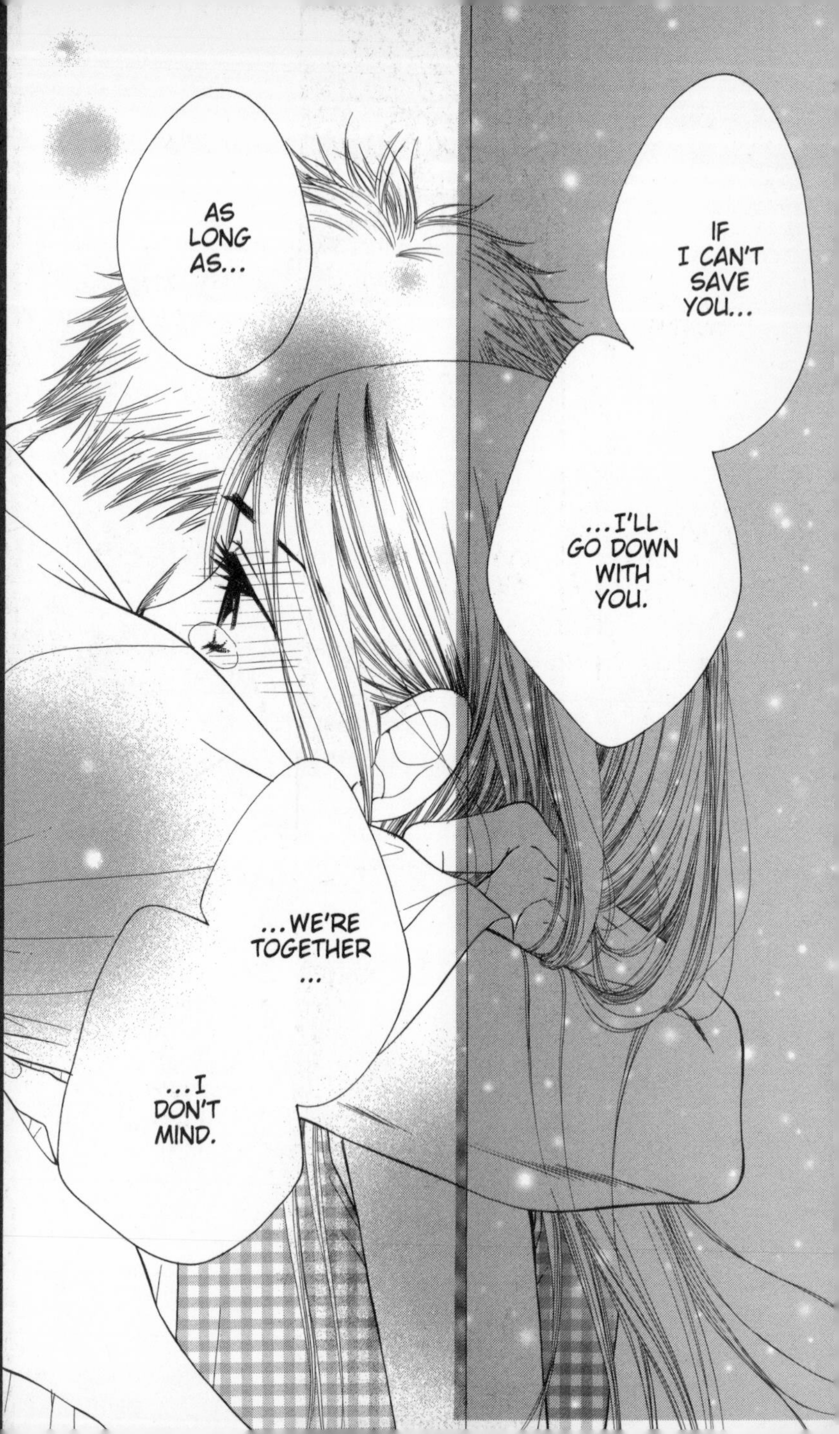
IF I CAN'T SAVE YOU...
...I'LL GO DOWN WITH YOU.
AS LONG AS...
...WE'RE TOGETHER...
...I DON'T MIND.

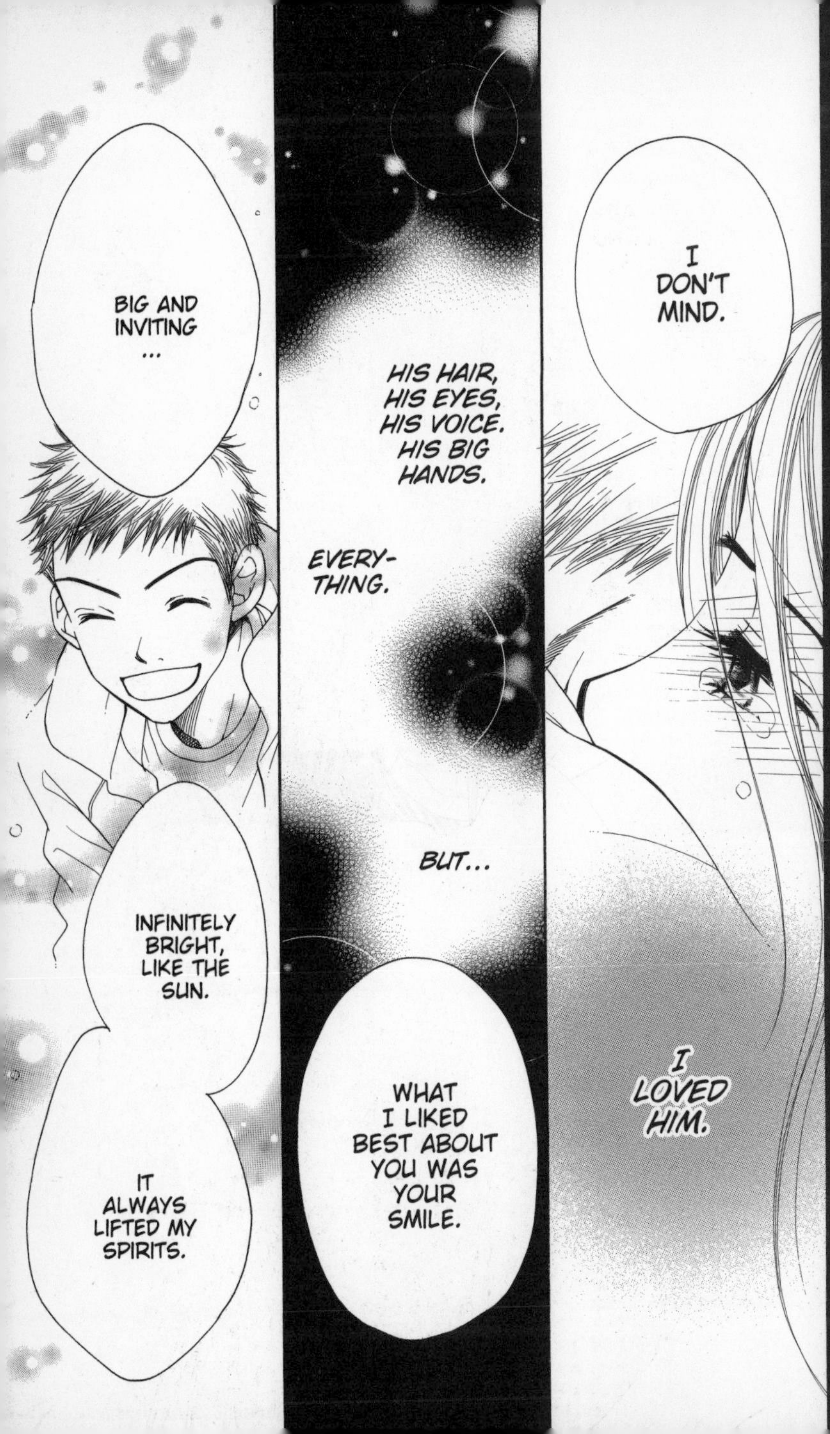
I DON'T MIND.
I LOVED HIM.
HIS HAIR, HIS EYES, HIS VOICE. HIS BIG HANDS.
EVERY-THING.
BUT...
WHAT I LIKED BEST ABOUT YOU WAS YOUR SMILE.
BIG AND INVITING ...
INFINITELY BRIGHT, LIKE THE SUN.
IT ALWAYS LIFTED MY SPIRITS.

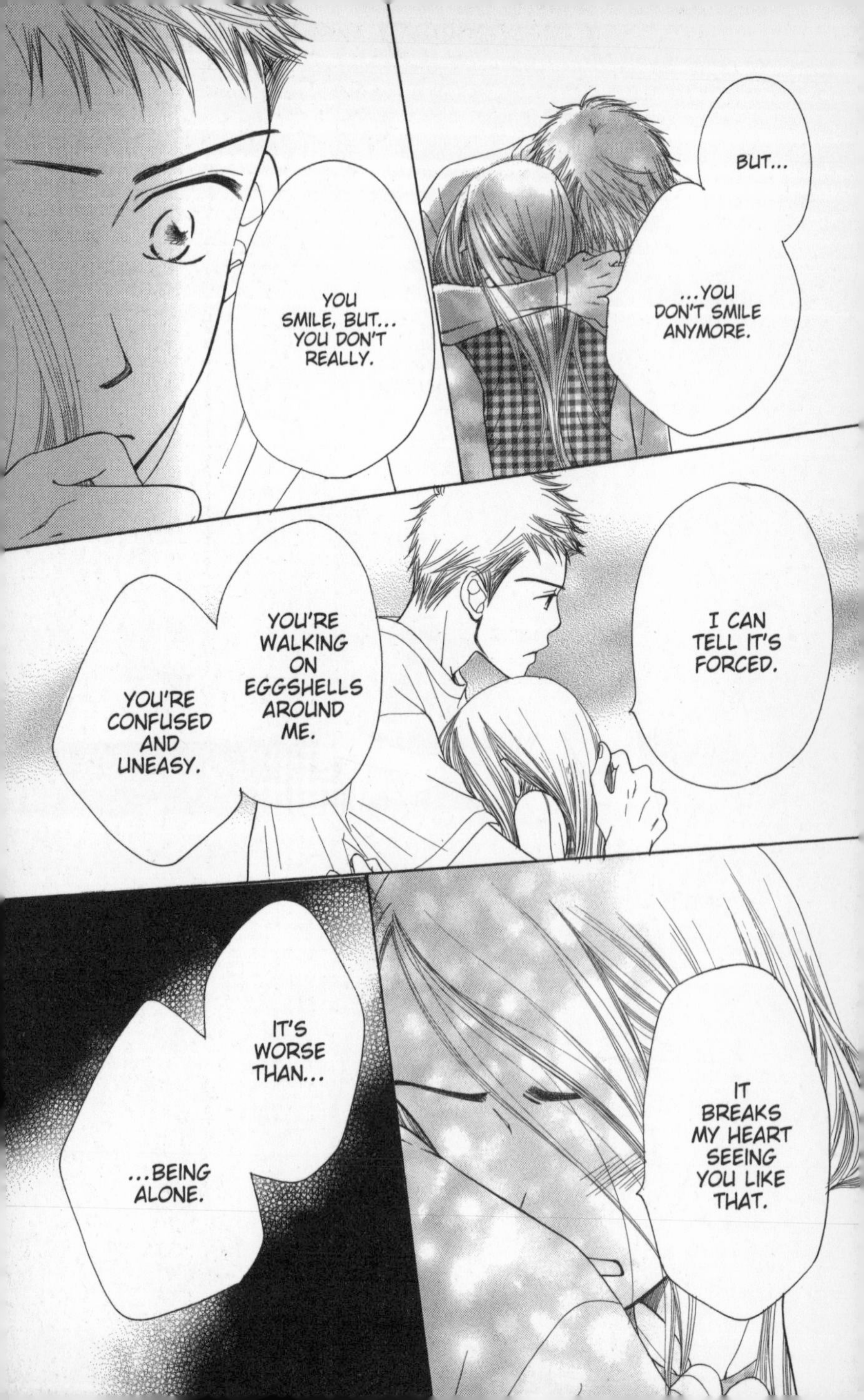
BUT...
...YOU DON'T SMILE ANYMORE.
YOU SMILE, BUT... YOU DON'T REALLY.
I CAN TELL IT'S FORCED.
YOU'RE WALKING ON EGGSHELLS AROUND ME.
YOU'RE CONFUSED AND UNEASY.
IT BREAKS MY HEART SEEING YOU LIKE THAT.
IT'S WORSE THAN...
...BEING ALONE.

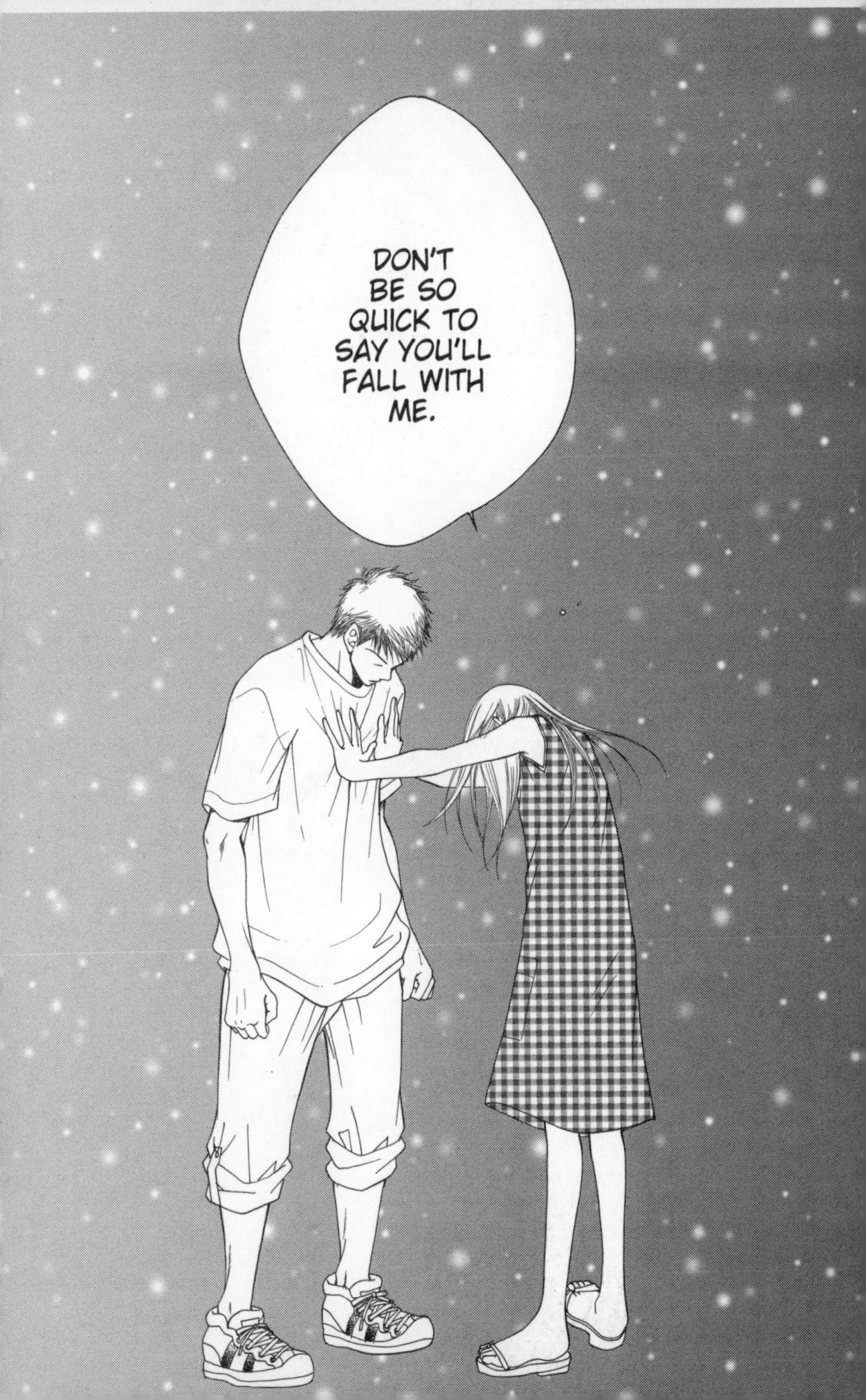
DON'T BE SO QUICK TO SAY YOU'LL FALL WITH ME.

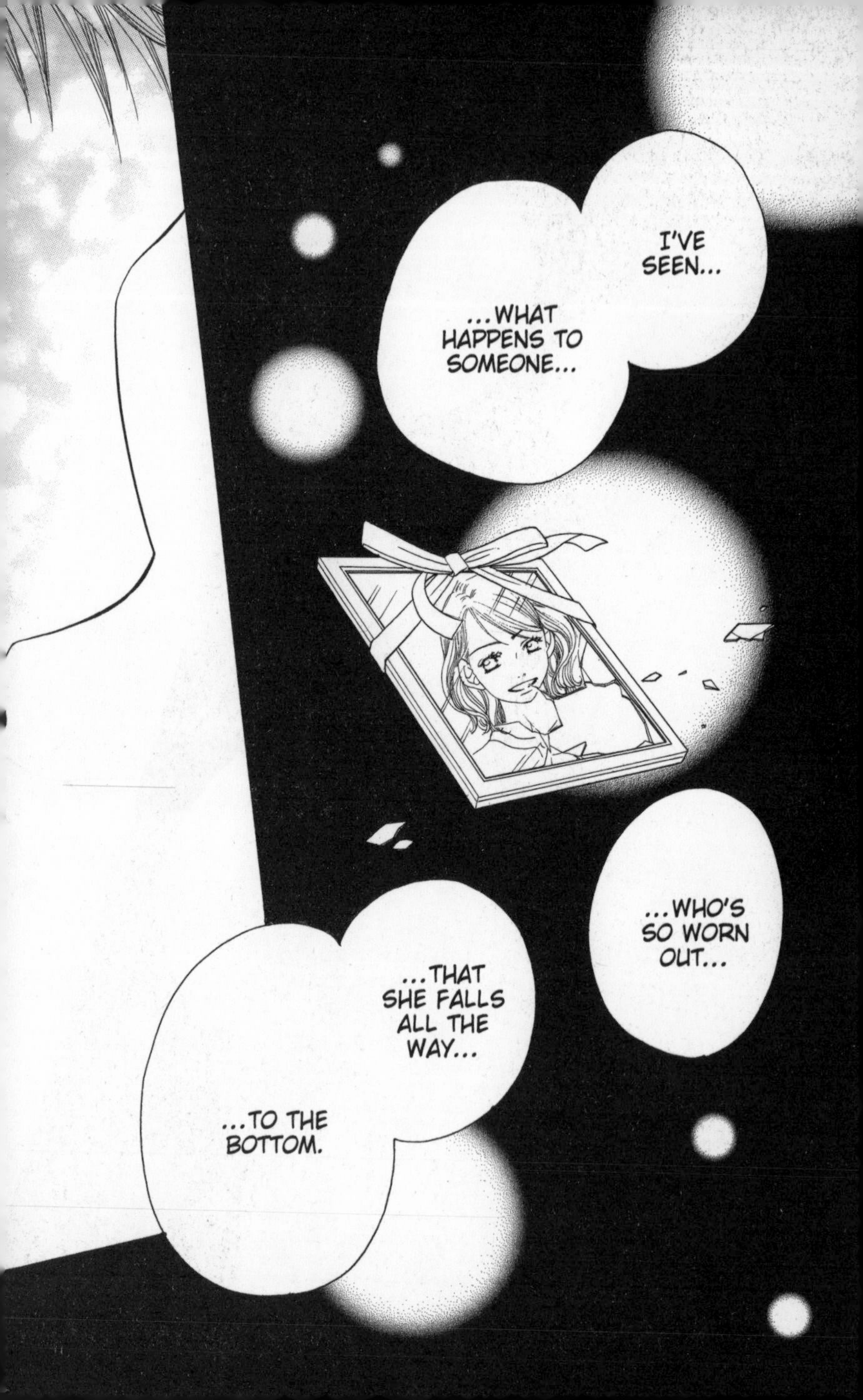
I'VE SEEN...
...WHAT HAPPENS TO SOMEONE...
...WHO'S SO WORN OUT...
...THAT SHE FALLS ALL THE WAY...
...TO THE BOTTOM.

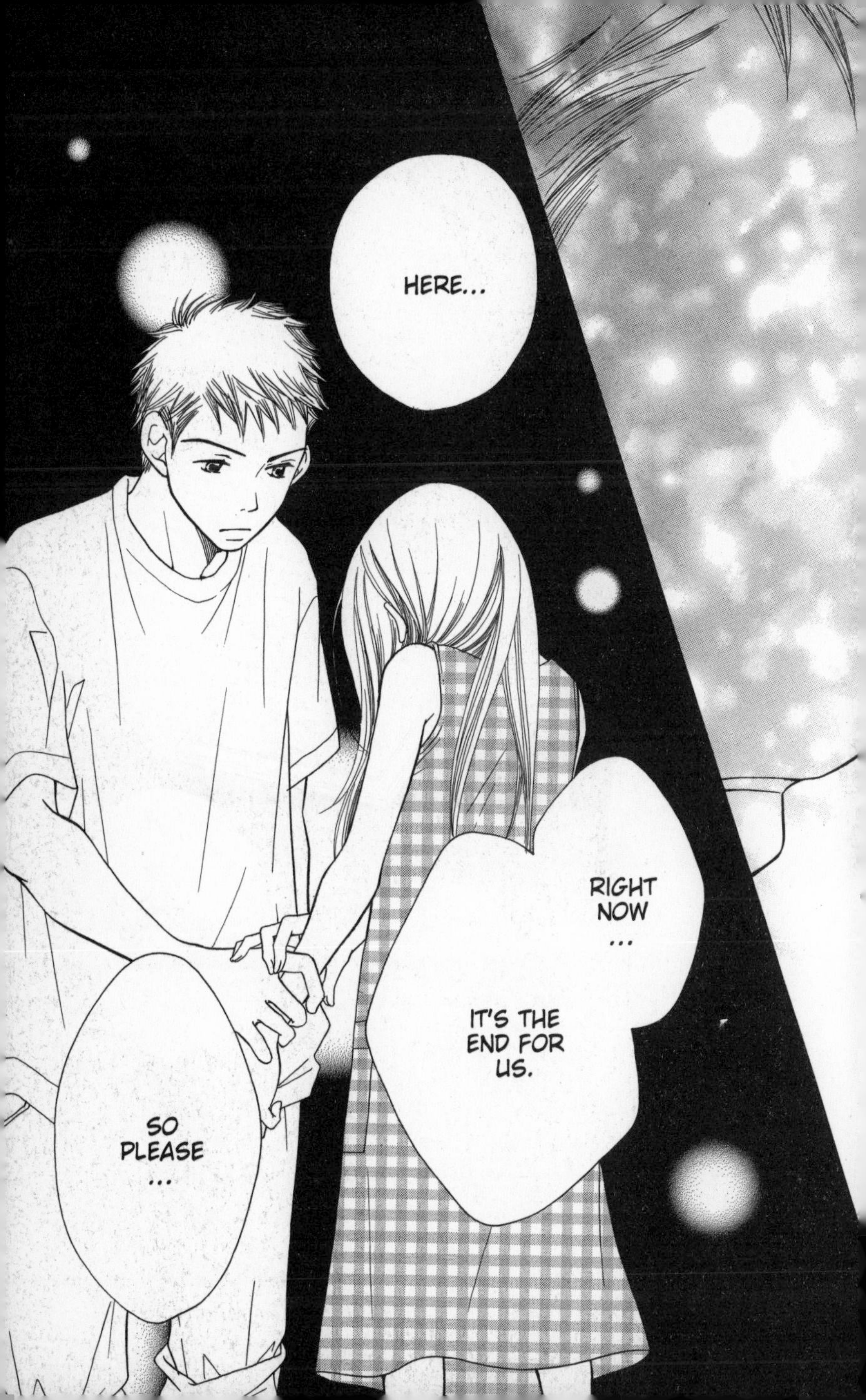
HERE...
RIGHT NOW ...
IT'S THE END FOR US.
SO PLEASE ...

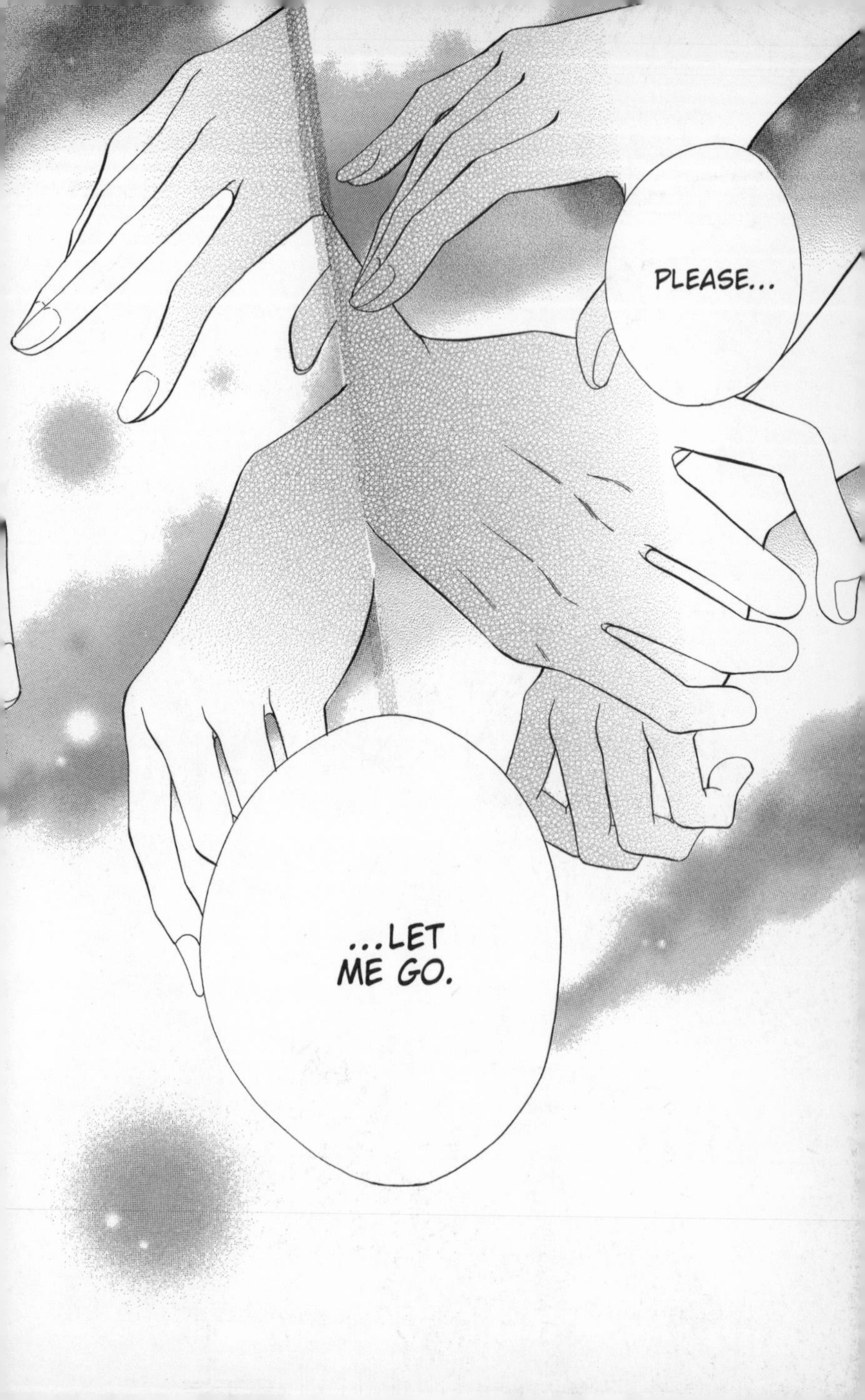
PLEASE...
...LET ME GO.

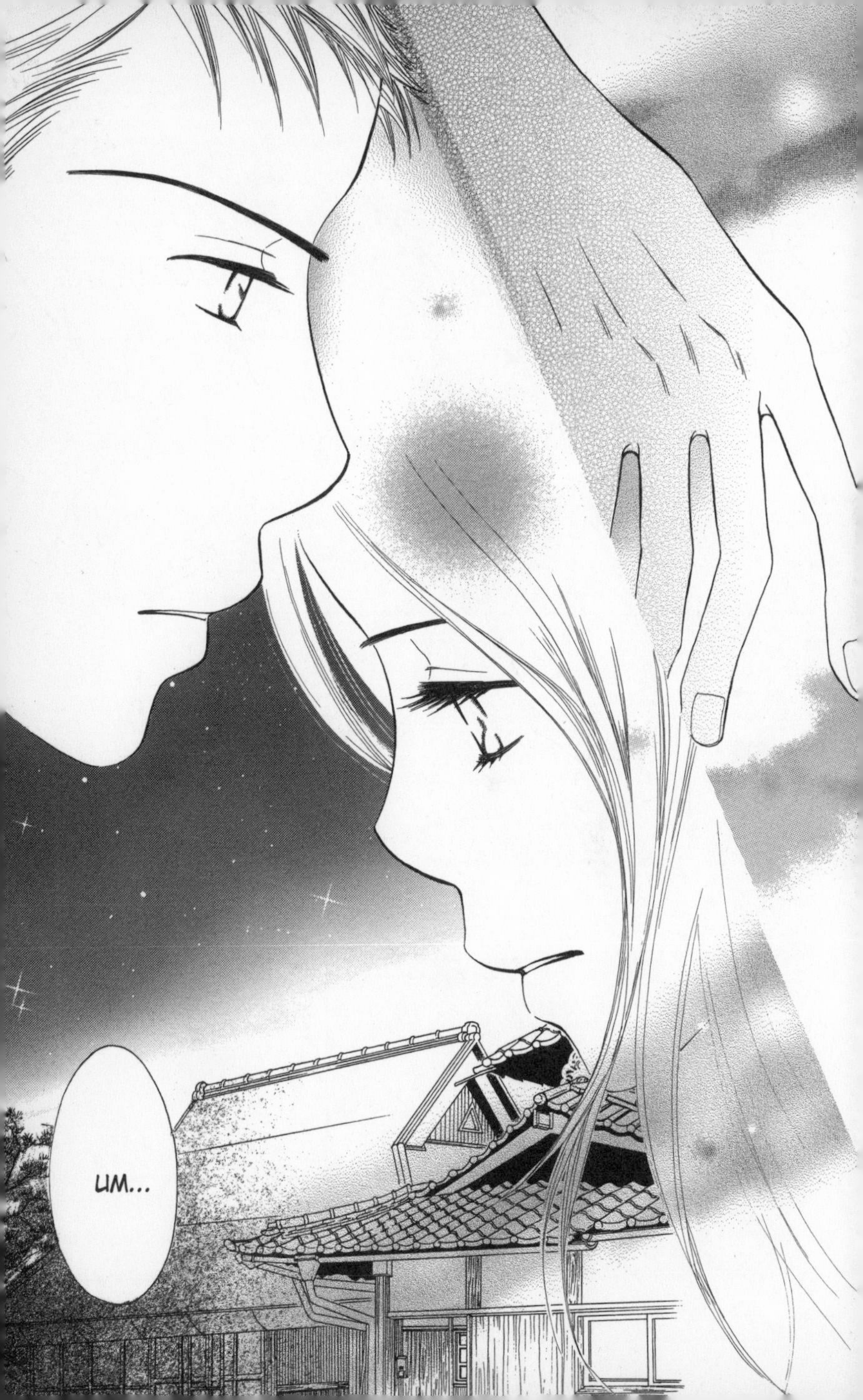
UM...

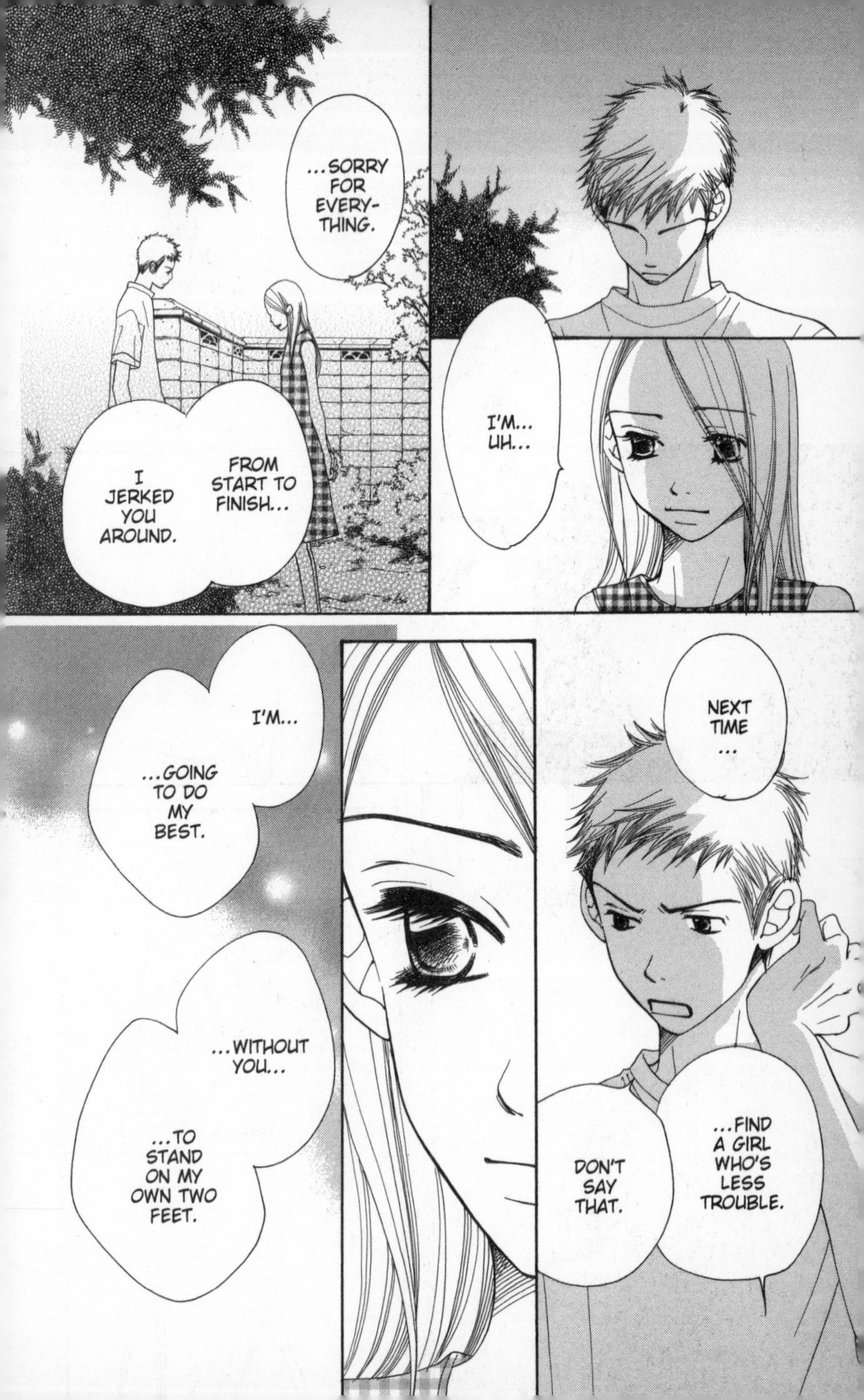
I'M... UH...
...SORRY FOR EVERY-THING.
FROM START TO FINISH...
I JERKED YOU AROUND.
NEXT TIME...
...FIND A GIRL WHO'S LESS TROUBLE.
DON'T SAY THAT.
I'M...
...GOING TO DO MY BEST.
...WITHOUT YOU...
...TO STAND ON MY OWN TWO FEET.

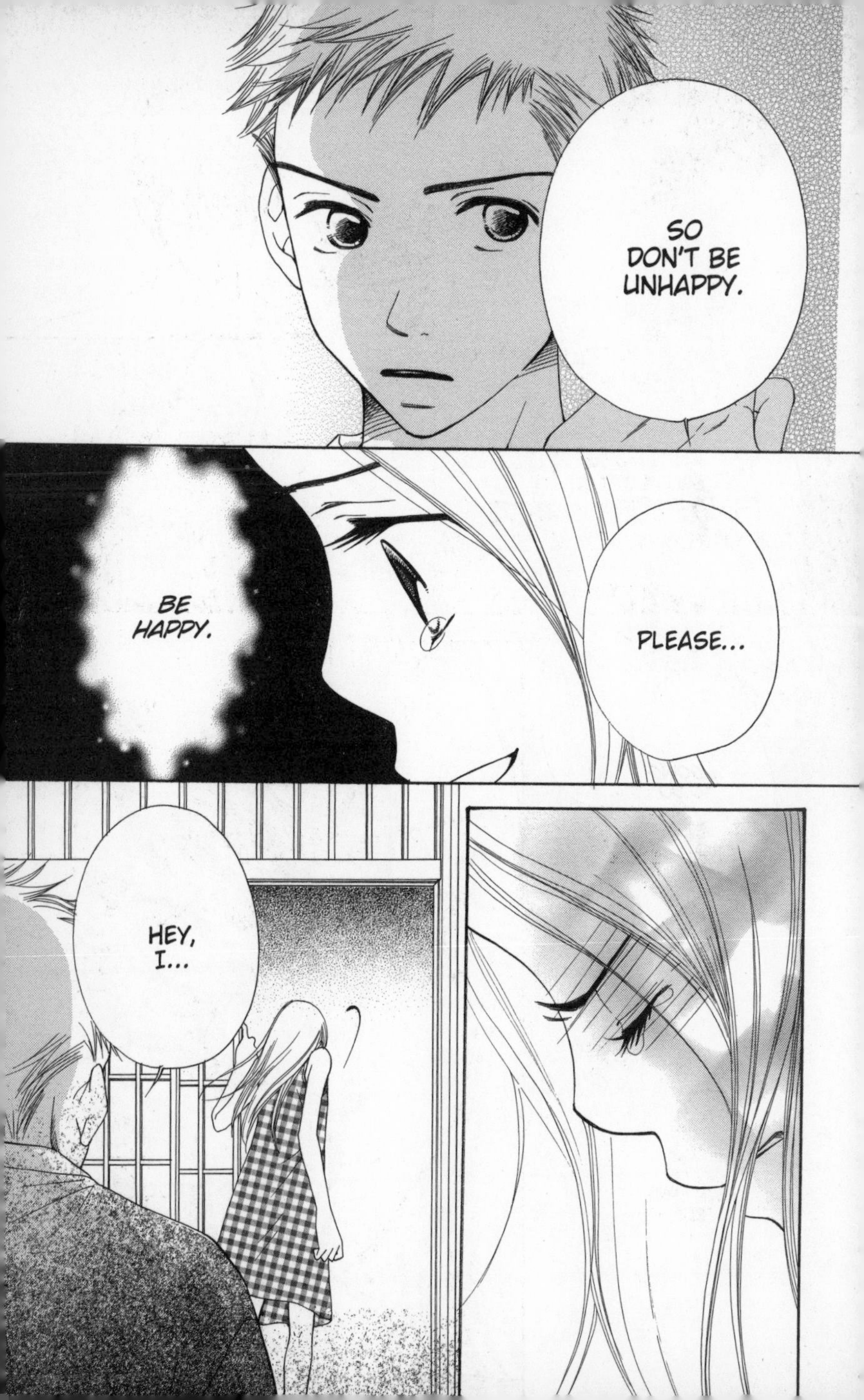
SO DON'T BE UNHAPPY.
PLEASE...
BE HAPPY.
HEY, I...

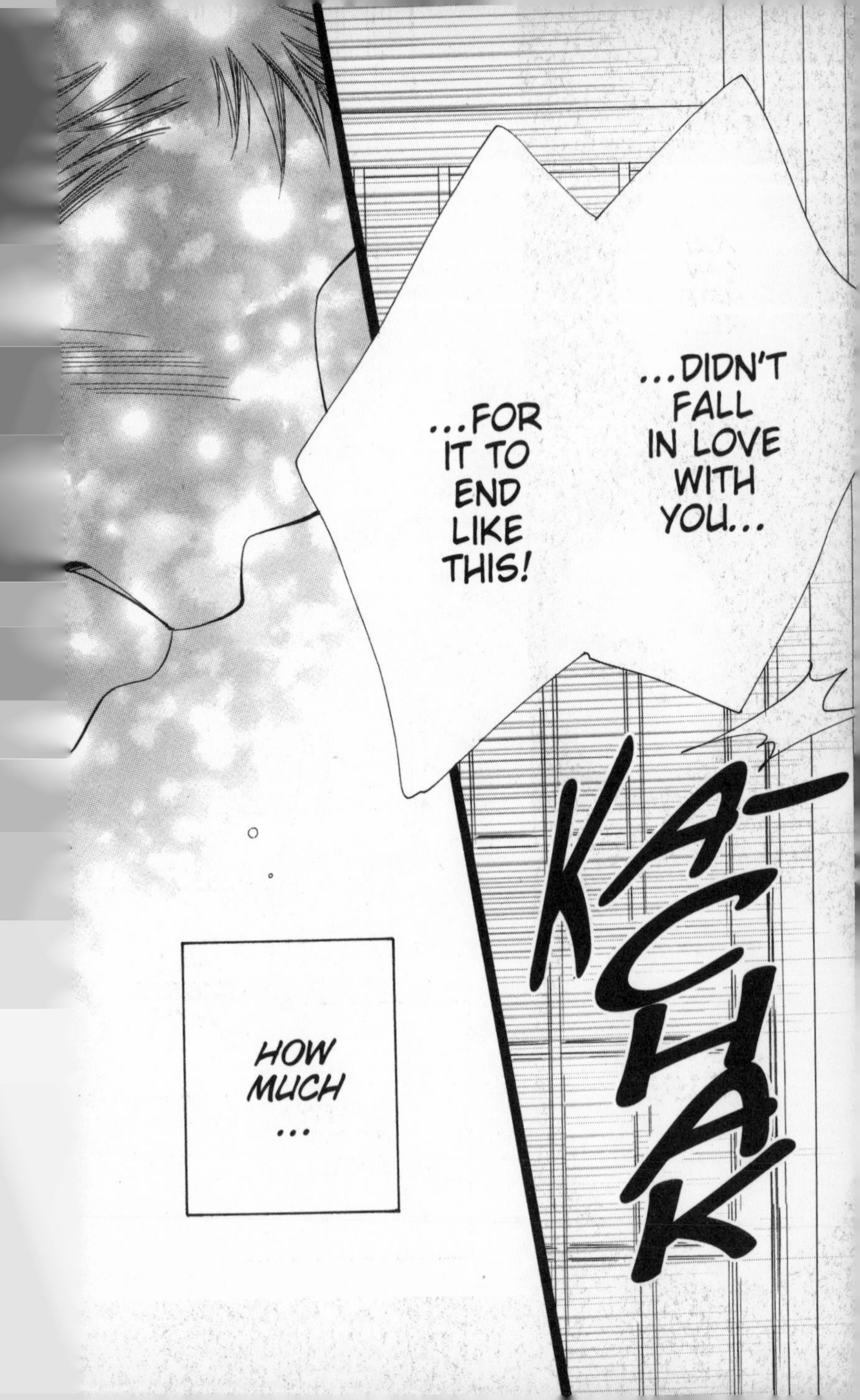
...DIDN'T FALL IN LOVE WITH YOU...
...FOR IT TO END LIKE THIS!
KA-CHAK
HOW MUCH ...

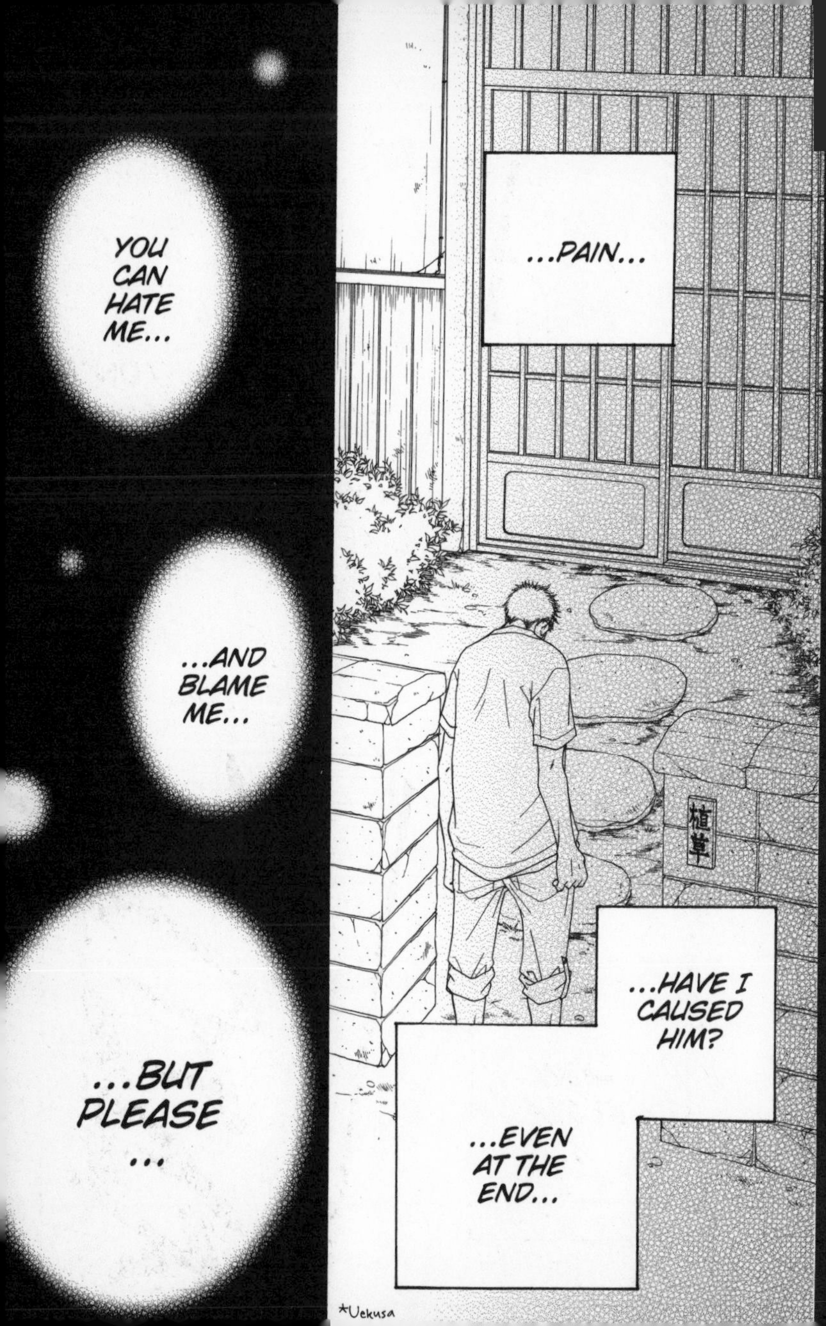
...PAIN...
...HAVE I CAUSED HIM?
...EVEN AT THE END...
植草
*Uekusa
YOU CAN HATE ME...
...AND BLAME ME...
...BUT PLEASE ...

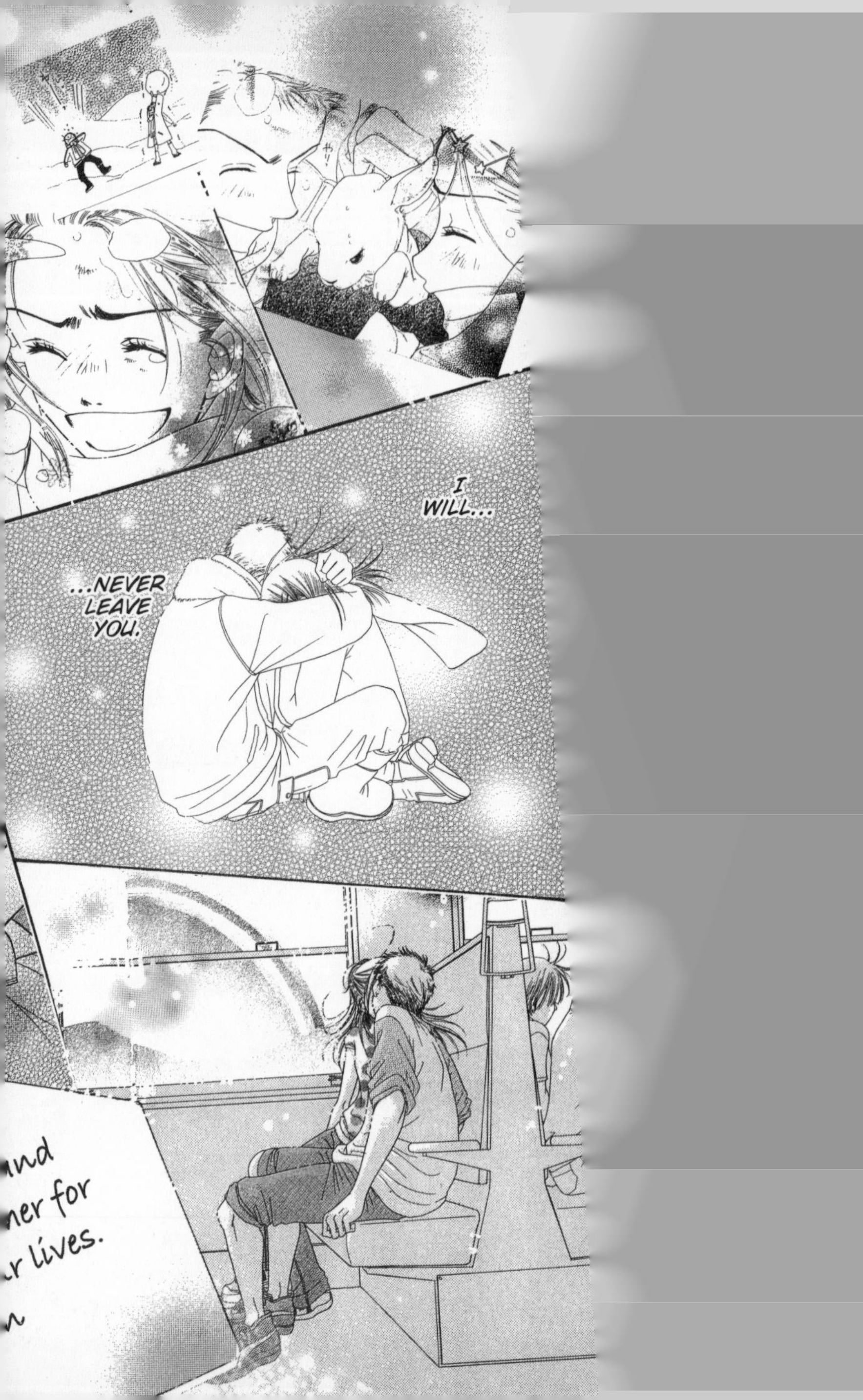
I WILL...
...NEVER LEAVE YOU.
and
ner for
r lives.

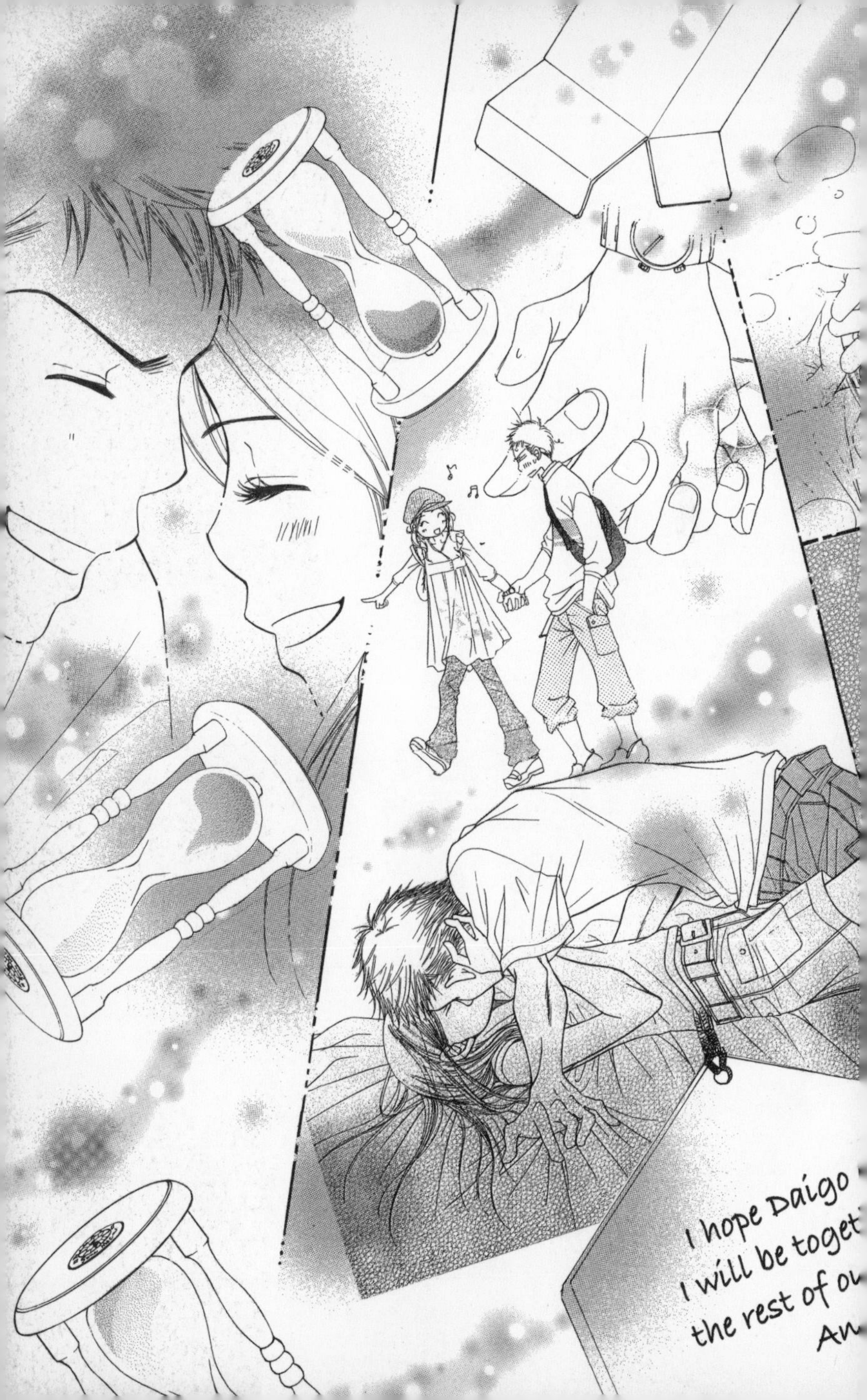
I hope Daigo
I will be toget
the rest of ou
An

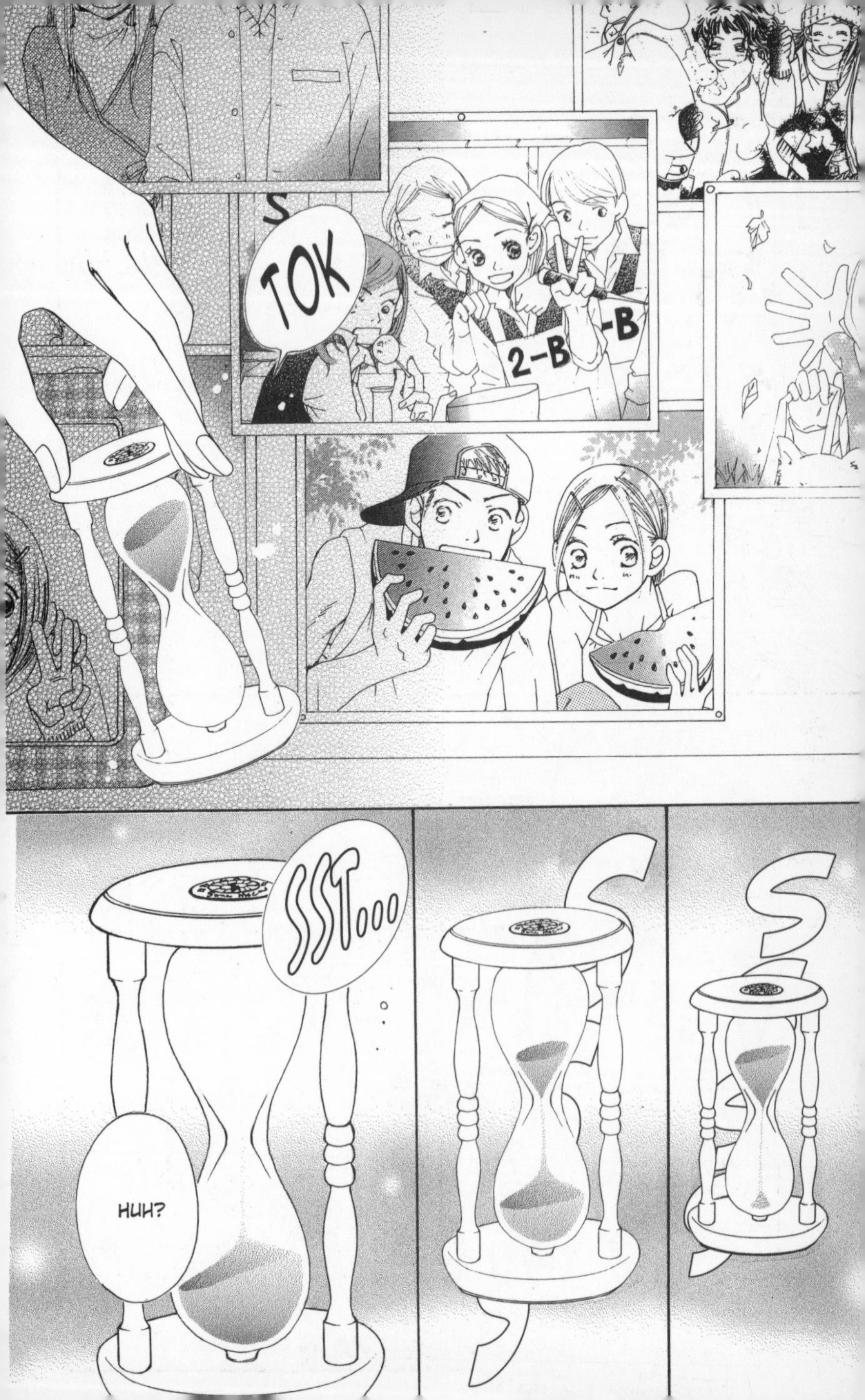
S
TOK
-B
2-B
S
SST...
HUH?

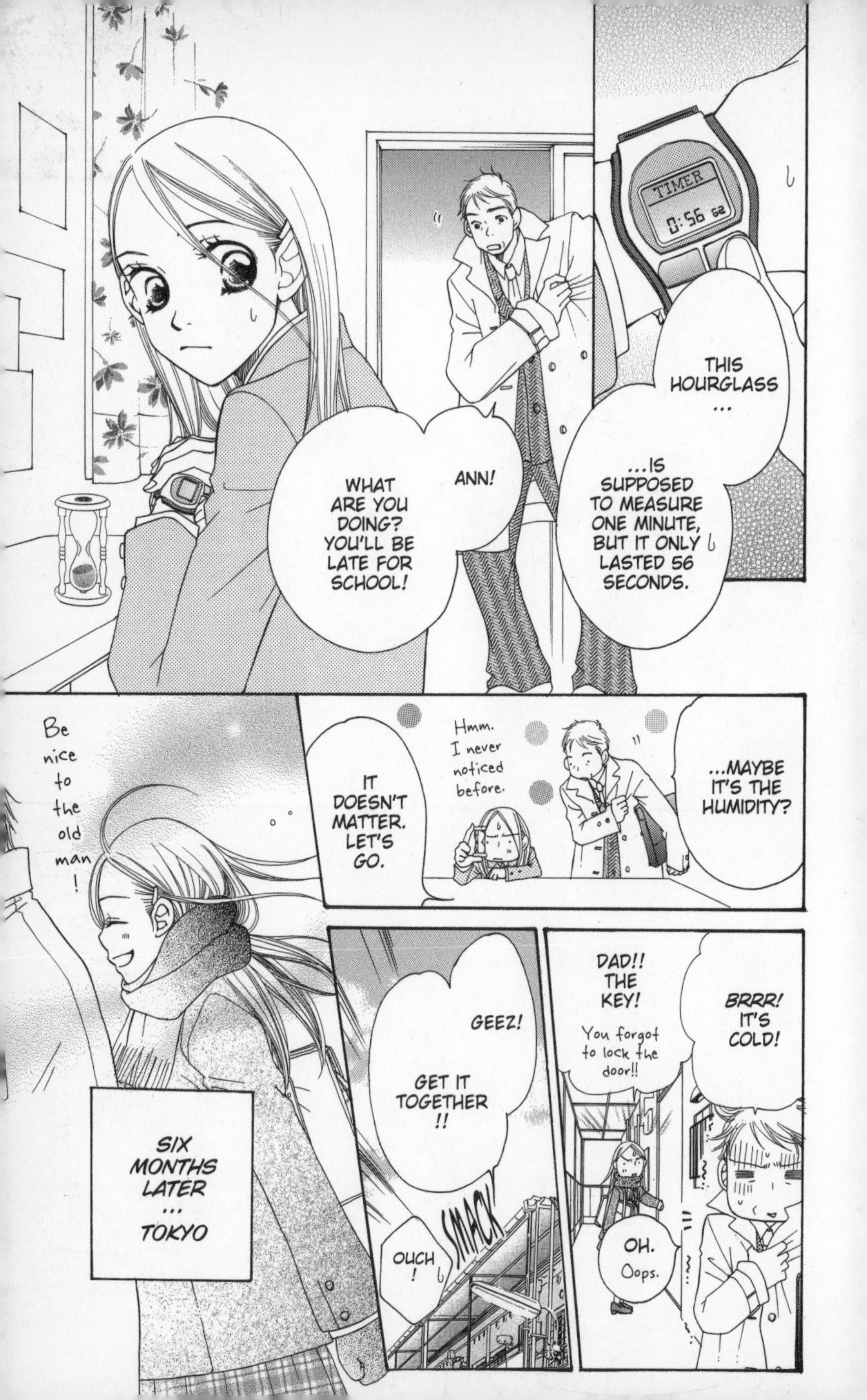
TIMER
0:56 62
THIS HOURGLASS ...
...IS SUPPOSED TO MEASURE ONE MINUTE, BUT IT ONLY LASTED 56 SECONDS.
ANN!
WHAT ARE YOU DOING? YOU'LL BE LATE FOR SCHOOL!
...MAYBE IT'S THE HUMIDITY?
Hmm. I never noticed before.
IT DOESN'T MATTER. LET'S GO.
BRRR! IT'S COLD!
DAD!! THE KEY!
You forgot to lock the door!!
OH. Oops.
GEEZ!
GET IT TOGETHER !!
SMACK
OUCH !
Be nice to the old man !
SIX MONTHS LATER ... TOKYO

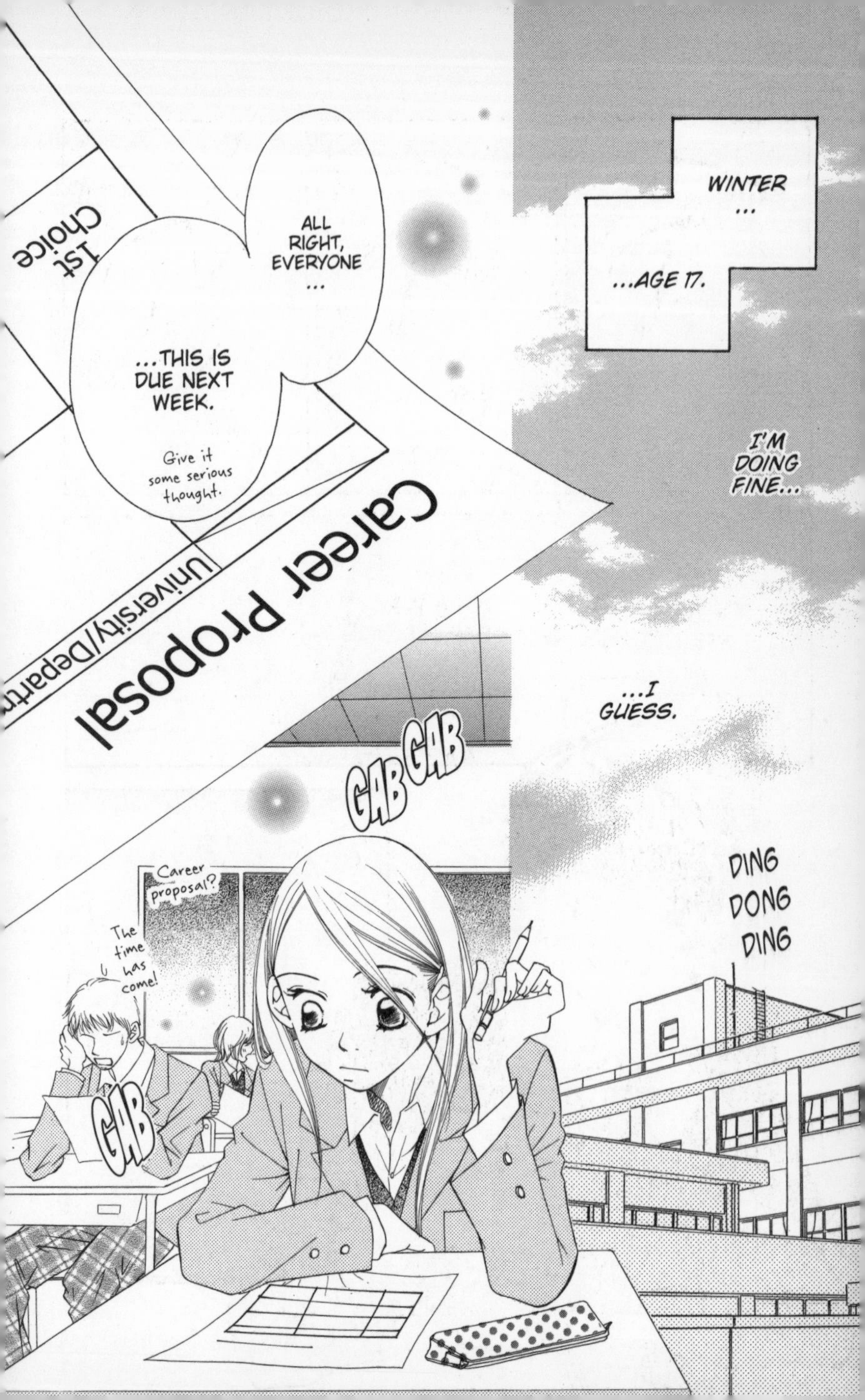

WINTER...
...AGE 17.
I'M DOING FINE...
...I GUESS.
DING DONG DING
1st Choice
ALL RIGHT, EVERYONE...
...THIS IS DUE NEXT WEEK.
Give it some serious thought.
Career Proposal
GAB GAB
Career proposal?
The time has come!
GAB

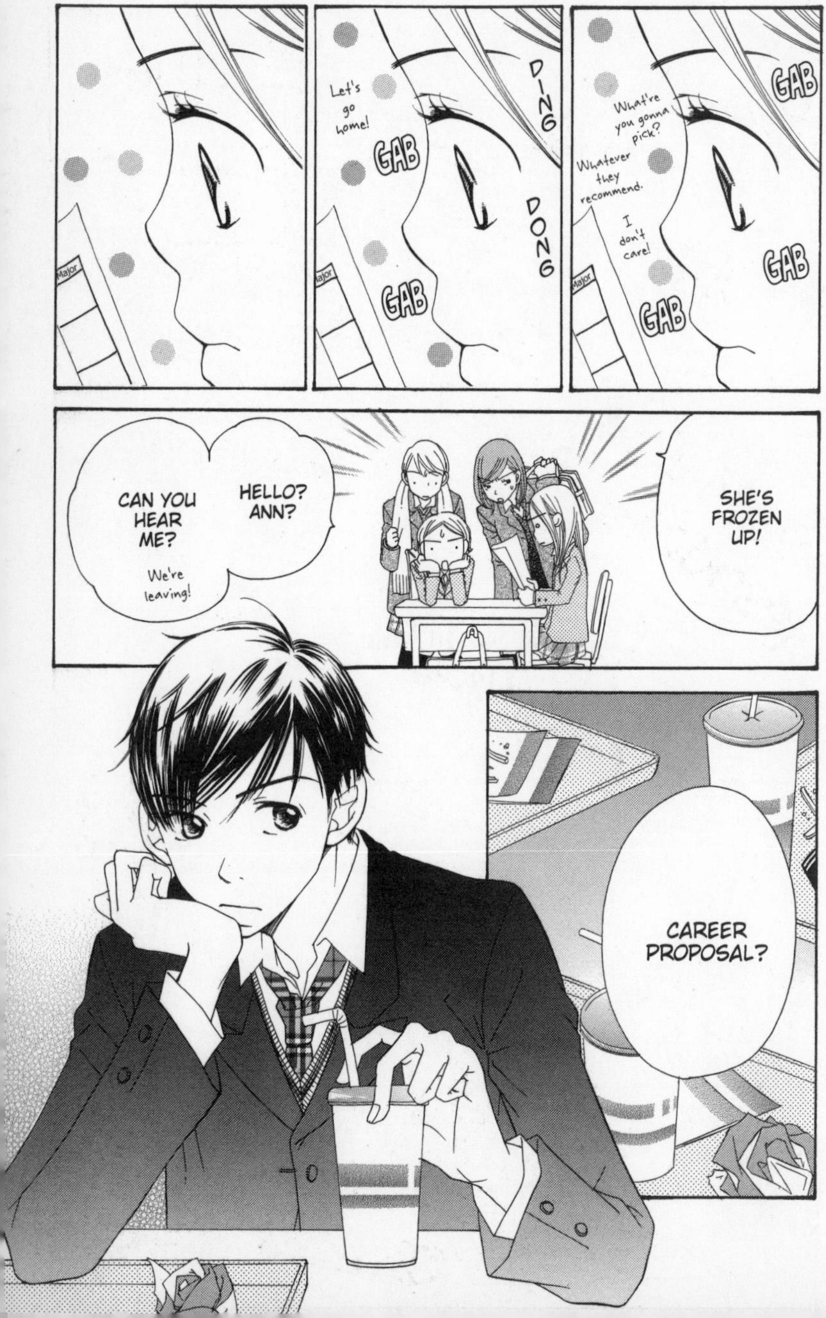
GAB
What're you gonna pick?
Whatever they recommend.
I don't care!
GAB
GAB
Major
DING
DONG
Let's go home!
GAB
GAB
Major
Major
SHE'S FROZEN UP!
HELLO? ANN?
CAN YOU HEAR ME?
We're leaving!
CAREER PROPOSAL?

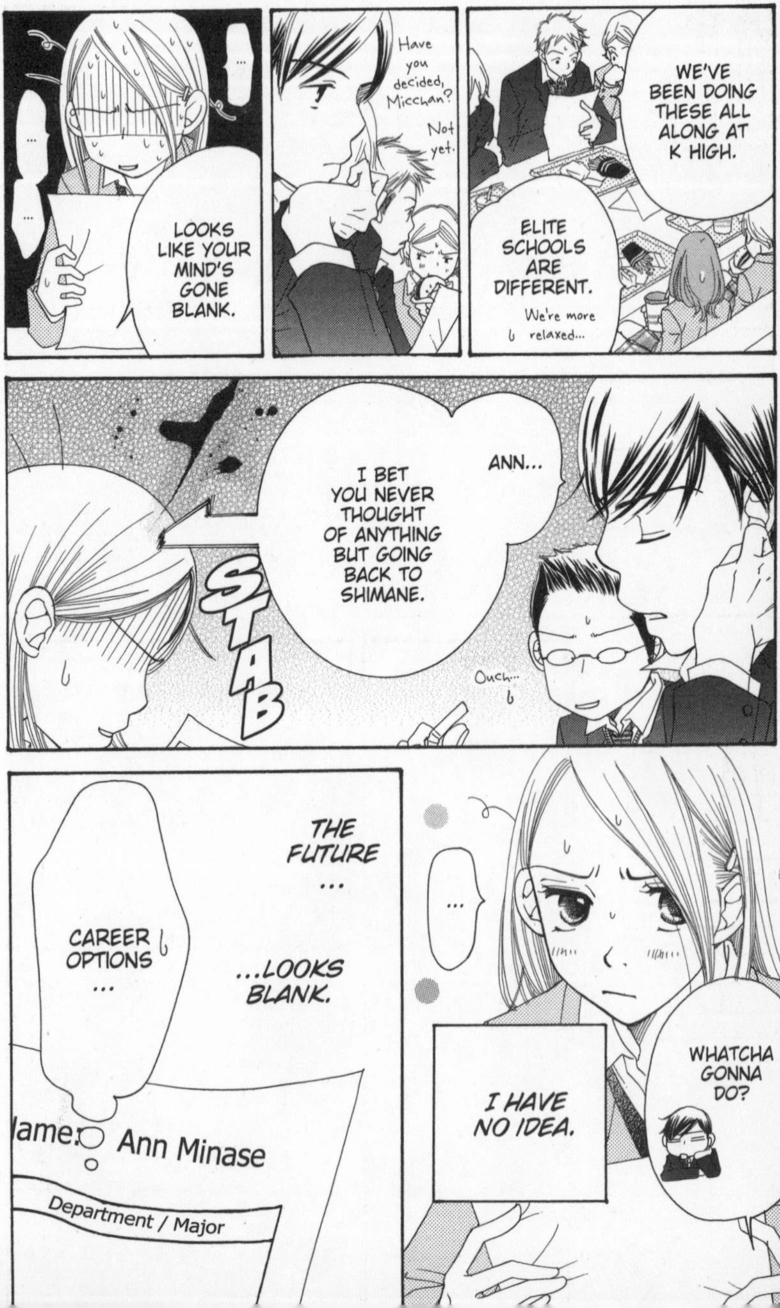
WE'VE BEEN DOING THESE ALL ALONG AT K HIGH.
ELITE SCHOOLS ARE DIFFERENT.
We're more relaxed...
Have you decided, Micchan?
Not yet.
...
...
...
LOOKS LIKE YOUR MIND'S GONE BLANK.
ANN...
I BET YOU NEVER THOUGHT OF ANYTHING BUT GOING BACK TO SHIMANE.
STAB
Ouch...
...
WHATCHA GONNA DO?
I HAVE NO IDEA.
THE FUTURE...
CAREER OPTIONS...
...LOOKS BLANK.
Ann Minase
Department / Major

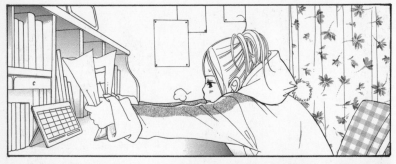

FUJI'S RIGHT.

I WAS GOING TO GO BACK TO SHIMANE AFTER HIGH SCHOOL. THAT WAS THE PLAN WHEN I MOVED AWAY.

I'LL BE BACK IN THREE YEARS!!

I WAS GOING TO RETURN TO SHIMANE...

...FIND A JOB, AND MARRY DAIGO. THAT WAS IT.

Pretty presumptuous of me...

I WAS TOTALLY DEPENDING ON HIM.

I've got to shape up!

December

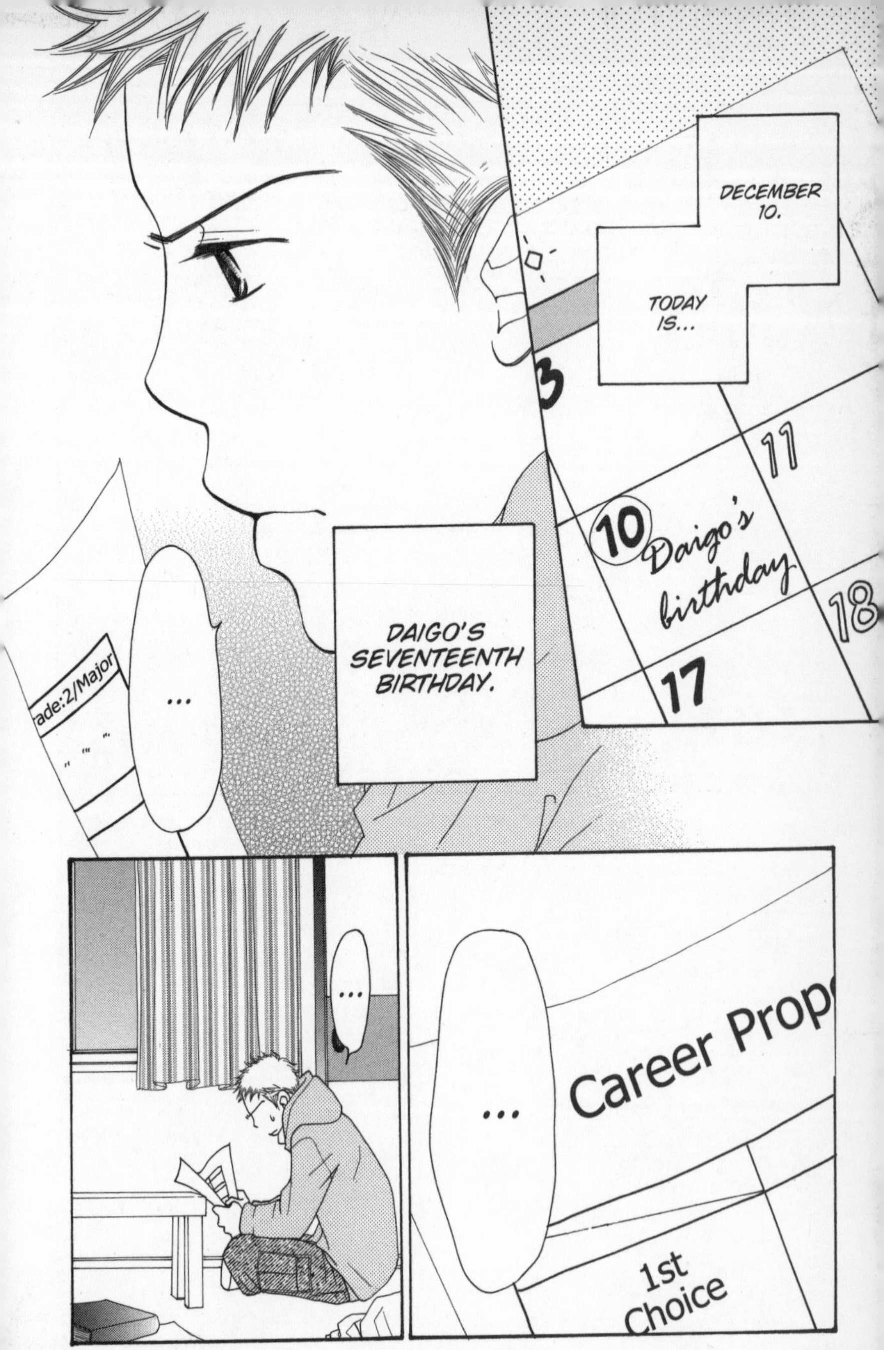
TODAY IS...
DECEMBER 10.
3
11
10
Daigo's birthday
18
17
DAIGO'S SEVENTEENTH BIRTHDAY.
rade:2/Major
...
Career Prop
1st Choice
...
...

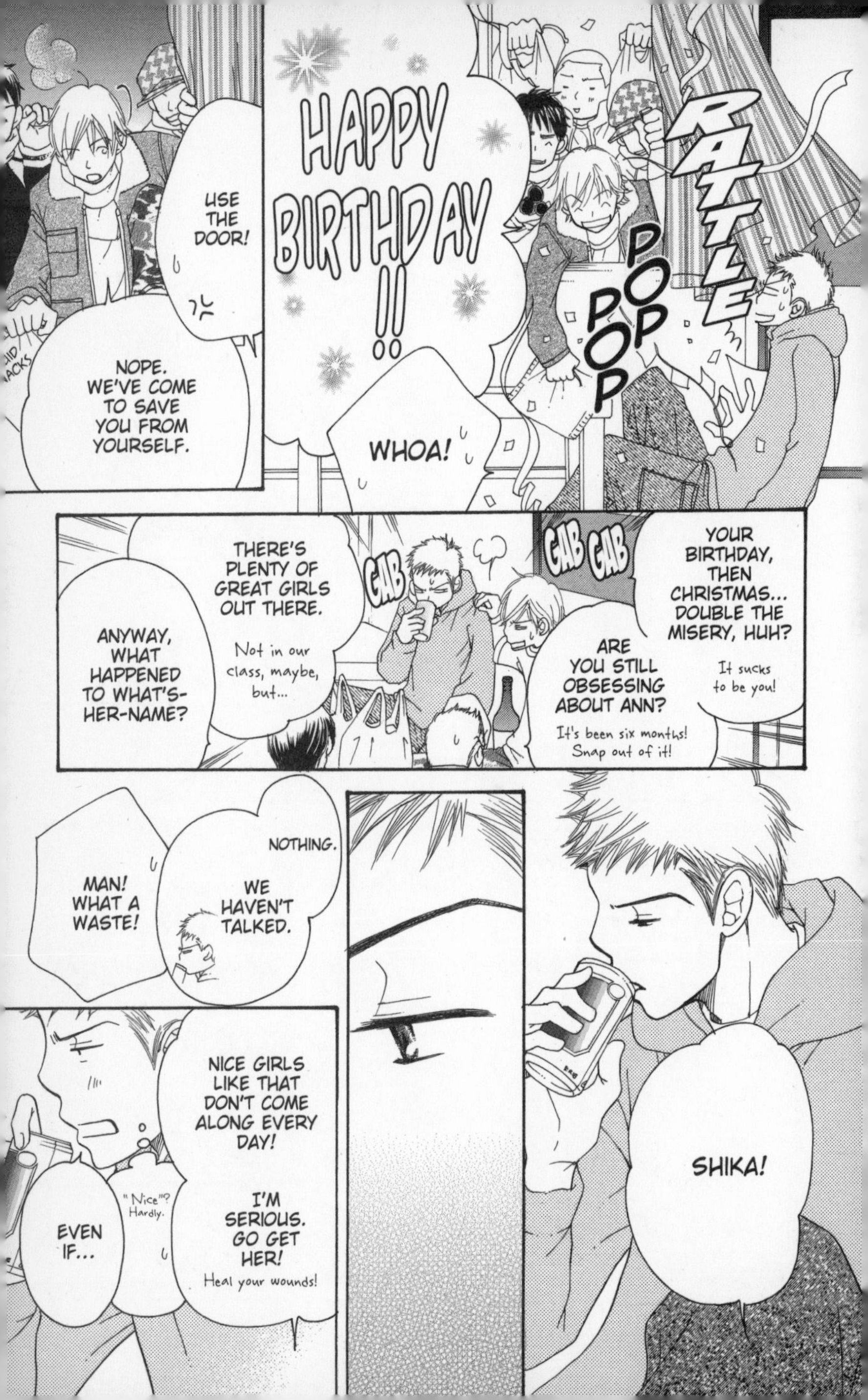
RATTLE
POP POP POP
HAPPY BIRTHDAY!!
WHOA!
USE THE DOOR!
NOPE. WE'VE COME TO SAVE YOU FROM YOURSELF.
YOUR BIRTHDAY, THEN CHRISTMAS... DOUBLE THE MISERY, HUH?
It sucks to be you!
GAB GAB
ARE YOU STILL OBSESSING ABOUT ANN?
It's been six months! Snap out of it!
GAB
THERE'S PLENTY OF GREAT GIRLS OUT THERE.
Not in our class, maybe, but...
ANYWAY, WHAT HAPPENED TO WHAT'S-HER-NAME?
SHIKA!
NOTHING.
WE HAVEN'T TALKED.
MAN! WHAT A WASTE!
NICE GIRLS LIKE THAT DON'T COME ALONG EVERY DAY!
I'M SERIOUS. GO GET HER!
Heal your wounds!
"Nice"? Hardly.
EVEN IF...

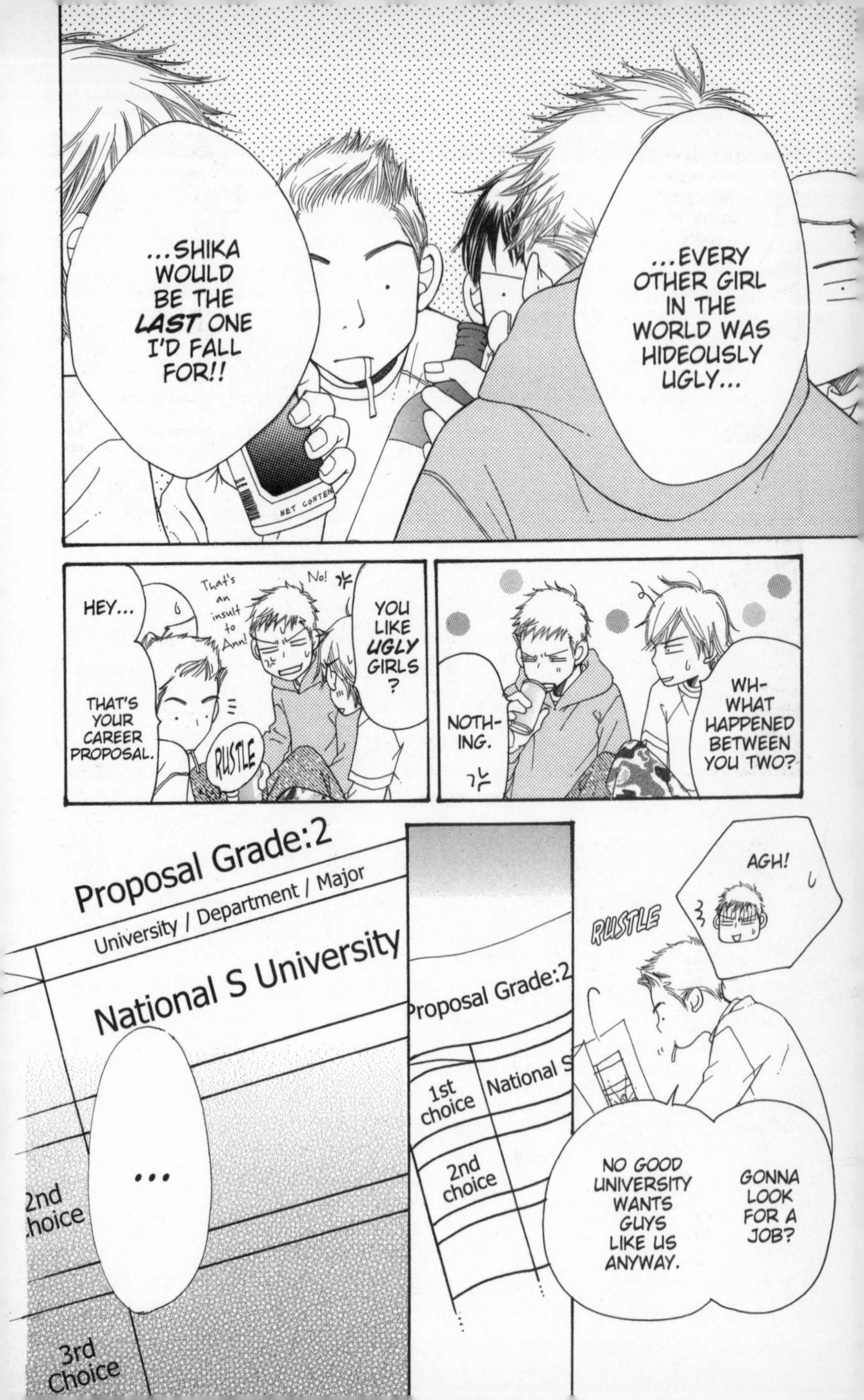
...EVERY OTHER GIRL IN THE WORLD WAS HIDEOUSLY UGLY...
NET CONTEN
...SHIKA WOULD BE THE **LAST** ONE I'D FALL FOR!!
WH-WHAT HAPPENED BETWEEN YOU TWO?
NOTHING.
YOU LIKE **UGLY** GIRLS?
No!
That's an insult to Ann!
HEY...
THAT'S YOUR CAREER PROPOSAL.
RUSTLE
AGH!
RUSTLE
GONNA LOOK FOR A JOB?
NO GOOD UNIVERSITY WANTS GUYS LIKE US ANYWAY.
Proposal Grade:2
1st choice
National S
2nd choice
Proposal Grade:2
University / Department / Major
National S University
2nd Choice
3rd Choice
...

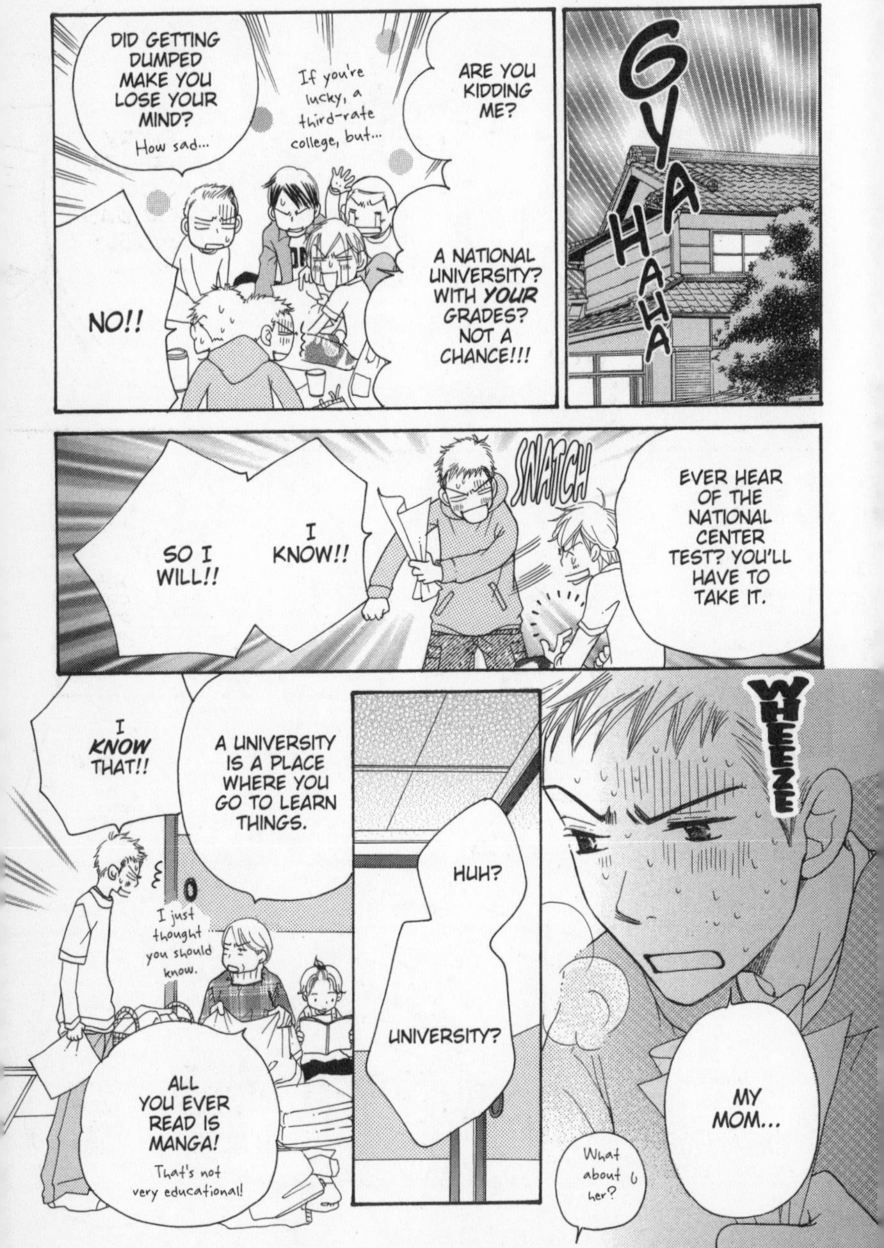
GYAHAHA
ARE YOU KIDDING ME?
If you're lucky, a third-rate college, but...
DID GETTING DUMPED MAKE YOU LOSE YOUR MIND?
How sad...
A NATIONAL UNIVERSITY? WITH YOUR GRADES? NOT A CHANCE!!!
NO!!
EVER HEAR OF THE NATIONAL CENTER TEST? YOU'LL HAVE TO TAKE IT.
SNATCH
I KNOW!!
SO I WILL!!
WHEEZE
MY MOM...
What about her?
HUH?
UNIVERSITY?
A UNIVERSITY IS A PLACE WHERE YOU GO TO LEARN THINGS.
I KNOW THAT!!
I just thought you should know.
ALL YOU EVER READ IS MANGA!
That's not very educational!

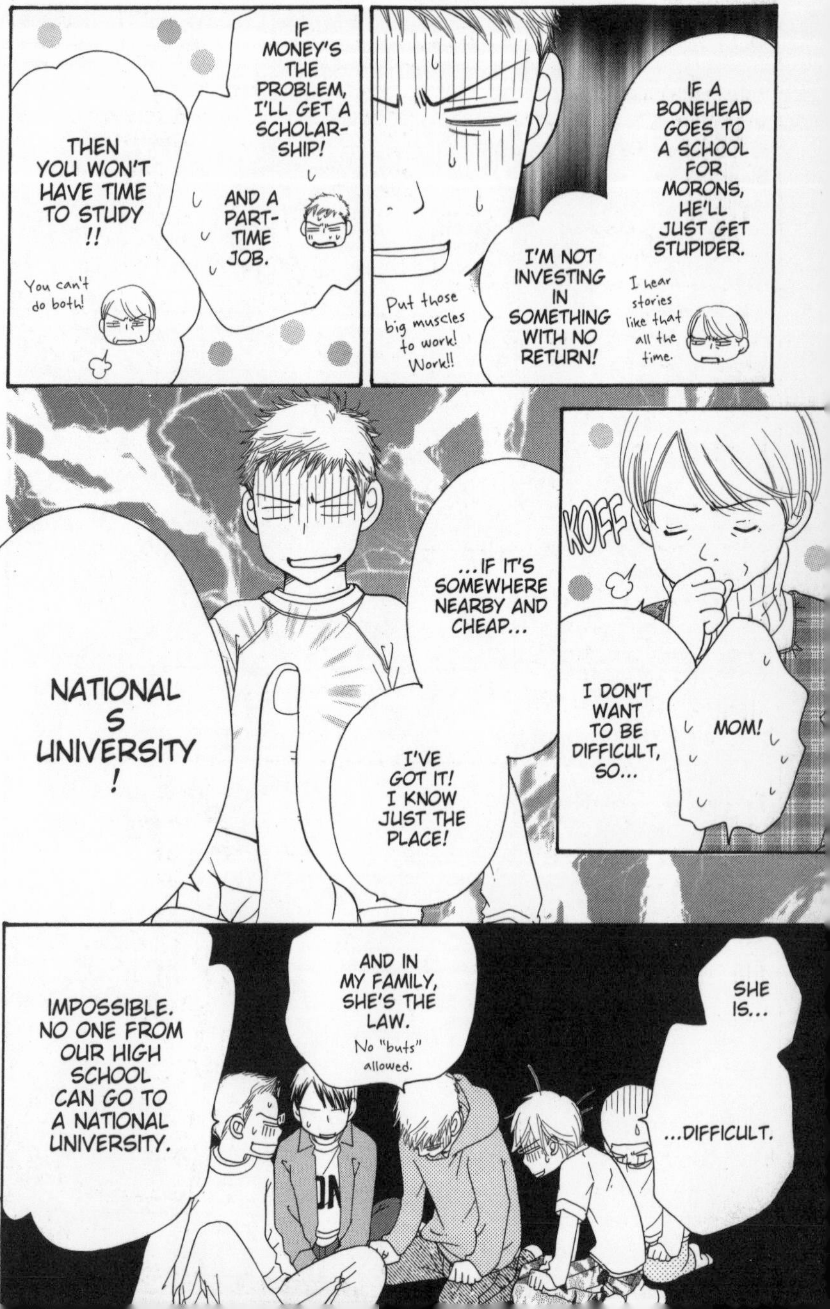
IF A BONEHEAD GOES TO A SCHOOL FOR MORONS, HE'LL JUST GET STUPIDER.
I hear stories like that all the time.
I'M NOT INVESTING IN SOMETHING WITH NO RETURN!
Put those big muscles to work! Work!!
IF MONEY'S THE PROBLEM, I'LL GET A SCHOLARSHIP!
AND A PART-TIME JOB.
THEN YOU WON'T HAVE TIME TO STUDY!!
You can't do both!
KOFF
MOM!
I DON'T WANT TO BE DIFFICULT, SO...
...IF IT'S SOMEWHERE NEARBY AND CHEAP...
I'VE GOT IT! I KNOW JUST THE PLACE!
NATIONAL S UNIVERSITY!
SHE IS...
...DIFFICULT.
AND IN MY FAMILY, SHE'S THE LAW.
No "buts" allowed.
IMPOSSIBLE. NO ONE FROM OUR HIGH SCHOOL CAN GO TO A NATIONAL UNIVERSITY.

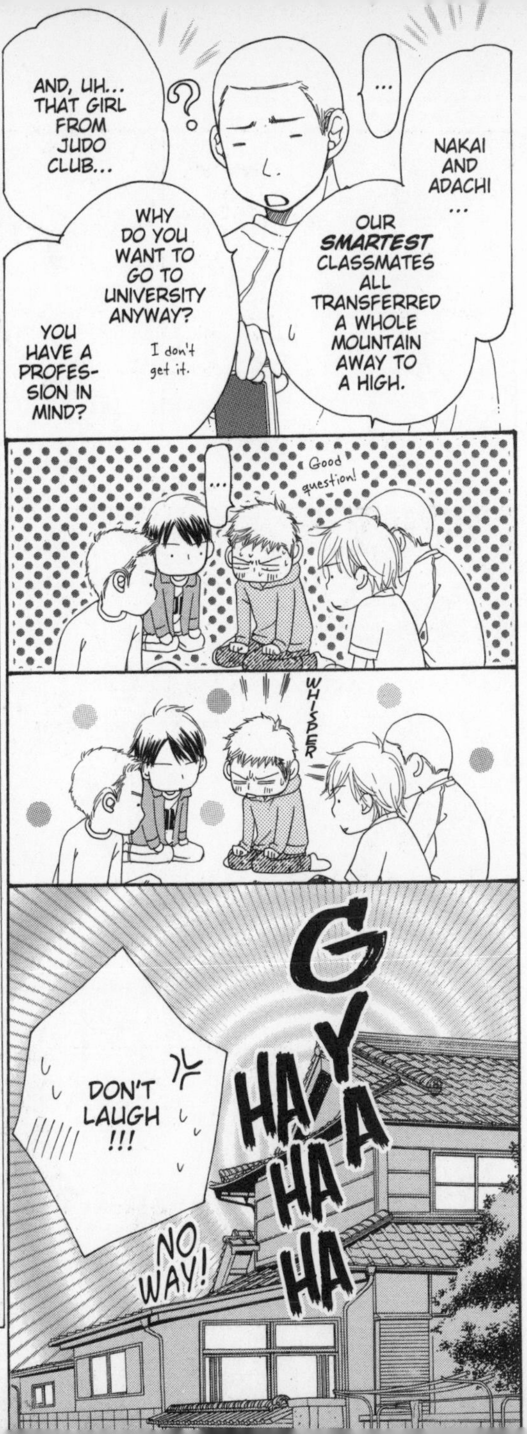
...
NAKAI AND ADACHI ...
OUR SMARTEST CLASSMATES ALL TRANSFERRED A WHOLE MOUNTAIN AWAY TO A HIGH.
AND, UH... THAT GIRL FROM JUDO CLUB...
WHY DO YOU WANT TO GO TO UNIVERSITY ANYWAY?
I don't get it.
YOU HAVE A PROFES-SION IN MIND?
Good question!
...
WHISPER
GYAA
HA HA HA
DON'T LAUGH !!!
NO WAY!

Winter, Age 17: First Love

We've skipped autumn, and now everyone is in the winter of their seventeenth year. Since they'll all have entrance exams soon, I bought a few preparatory books for university entrance exams for reference. I vaguely remember studying this stuff, but now it's all completely incomprehensible. Are these problems really solvable? I have to hand it to university students...they do this stuff all the time!

I first officially (?) fell in love when I was in kindergarten. A good friend told me, "I like A-kun, so you go after B-kun, okay?" So I automatically fell for B-kun. Was I precocious or just suggestible?

I'm planning a tale about everyone at age 18 for volume 6. The pace of this story is starting to pick up. Thank you for reading this far!

October 8, 2004
Hinako Ashihara

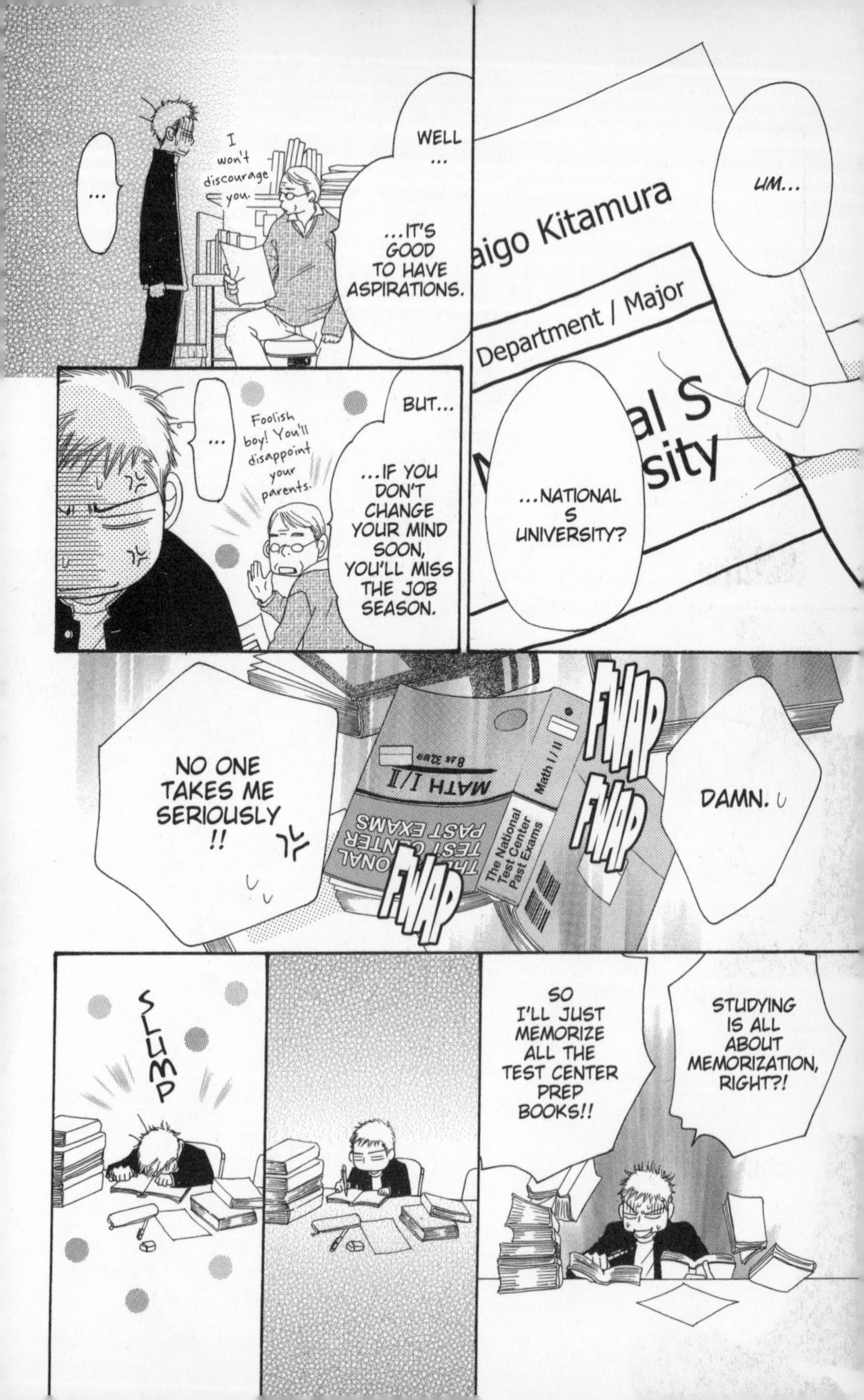
UM...
Department / Major
...NATIONAL S UNIVERSITY?
WELL...
...IT'S GOOD TO HAVE ASPIRATIONS.
I won't discourage you.
...
BUT...
...IF YOU DON'T CHANGE YOUR MIND SOON, YOU'LL MISS THE JOB SEASON.
Foolish boy! You'll disappoint your parents.
...
DAMN.
FWAP FWAP
Math I/II
The National Test Center Past Exams
FWAP
NO ONE TAKES ME SERIOUSLY!!
STUDYING IS ALL ABOUT MEMORIZATION, RIGHT?!
SO I'LL JUST MEMORIZE ALL THE TEST CENTER PREP BOOKS!!
SLUMP

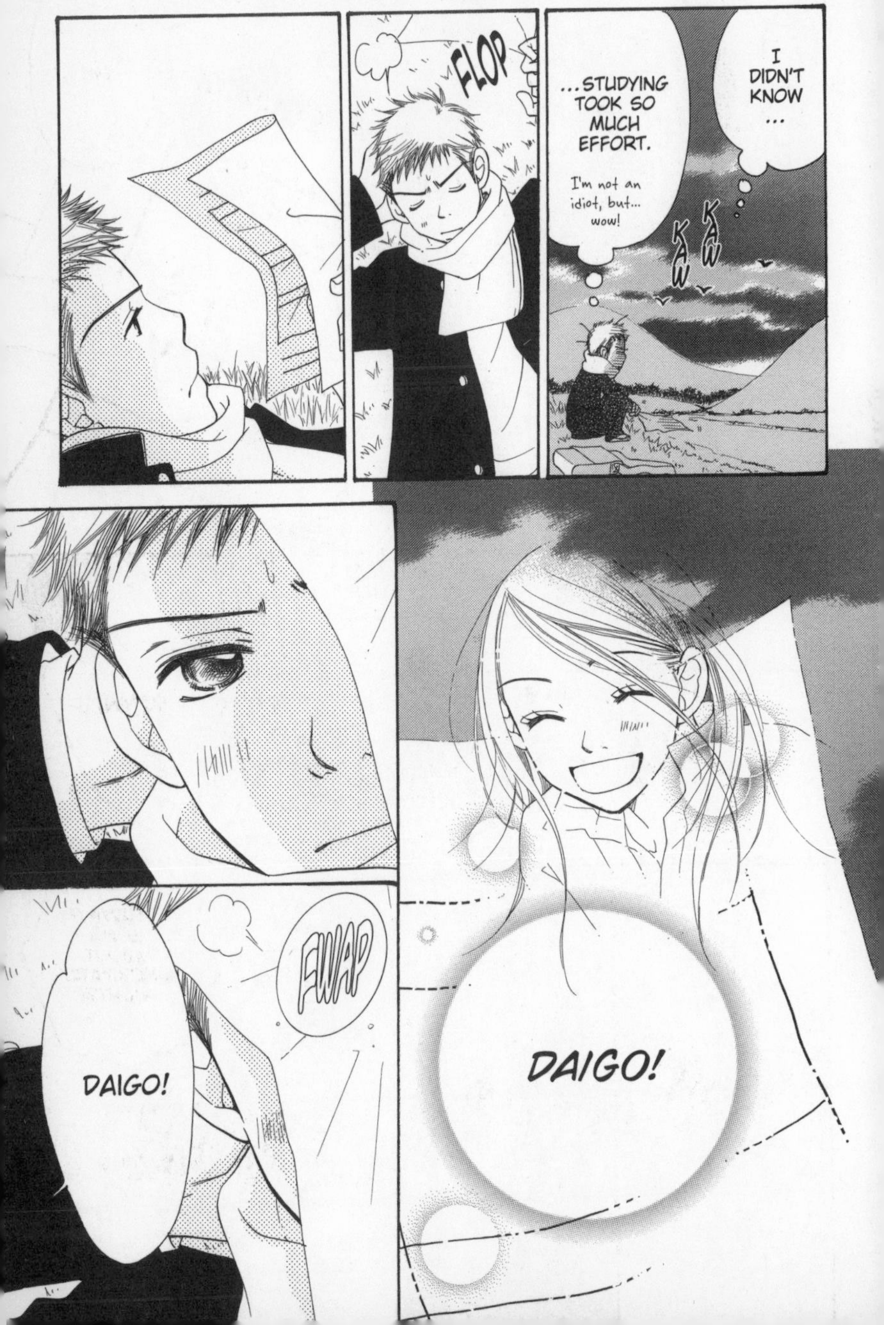
I DIDN'T KNOW ...
...STUDYING TOOK SO MUCH EFFORT.
I'm not an idiot, but... wow!
KAW
KAW
FLOP
DAIGO!
FWAP
DAIGO!

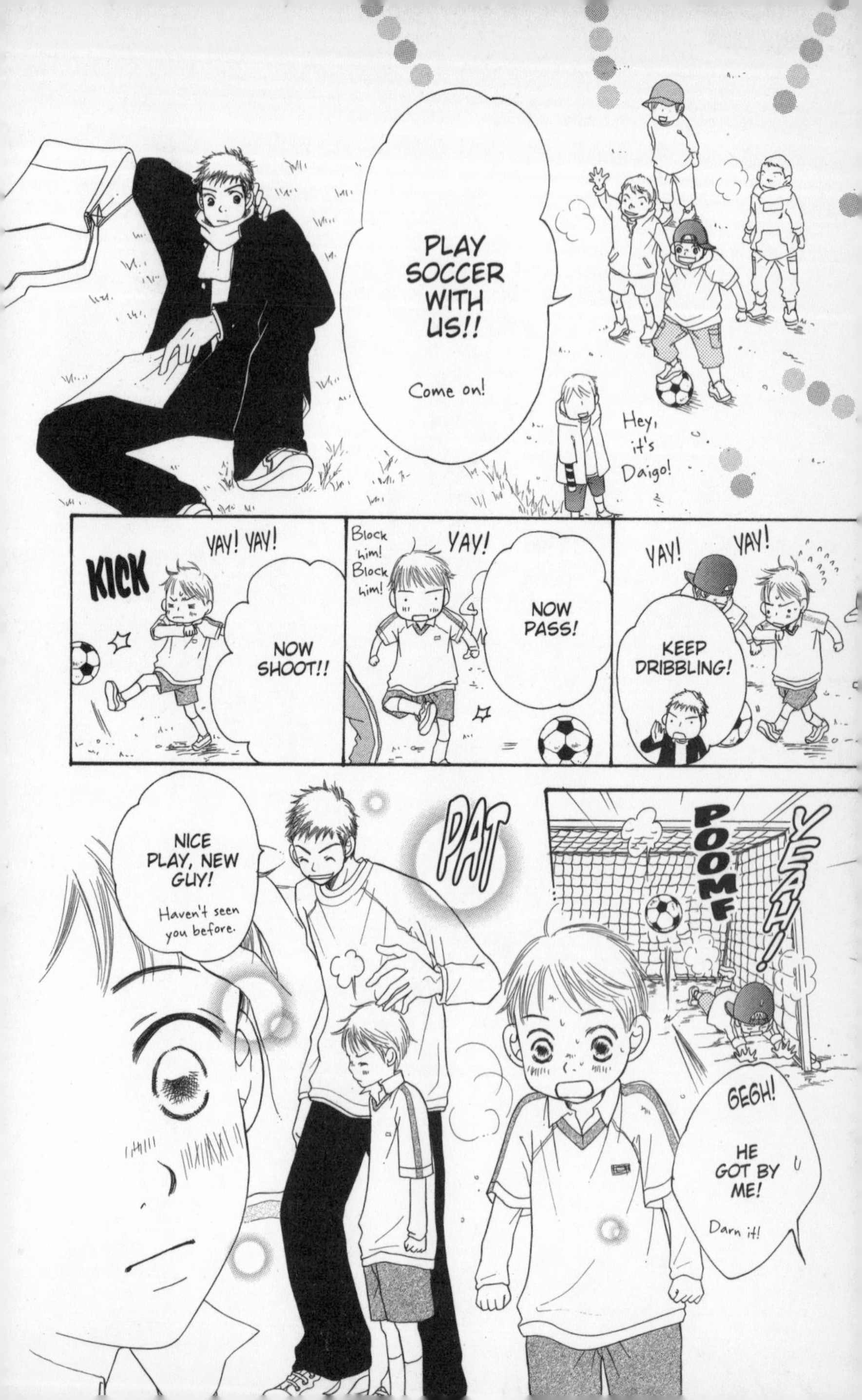
Hey, it's Daigo!
PLAY SOCCER WITH US!!
Come on!
YAY! YAY!
KEEP DRIBBLING!
YAY!
Block him! Block him!
NOW PASS!
KICK
YAY! YAY!
NOW SHOOT!!
YEAH!
POOMF
GEGH!
HE GOT BY ME!
Darn it!
PAT
NICE PLAY, NEW GUY!
Haven't seen you before.

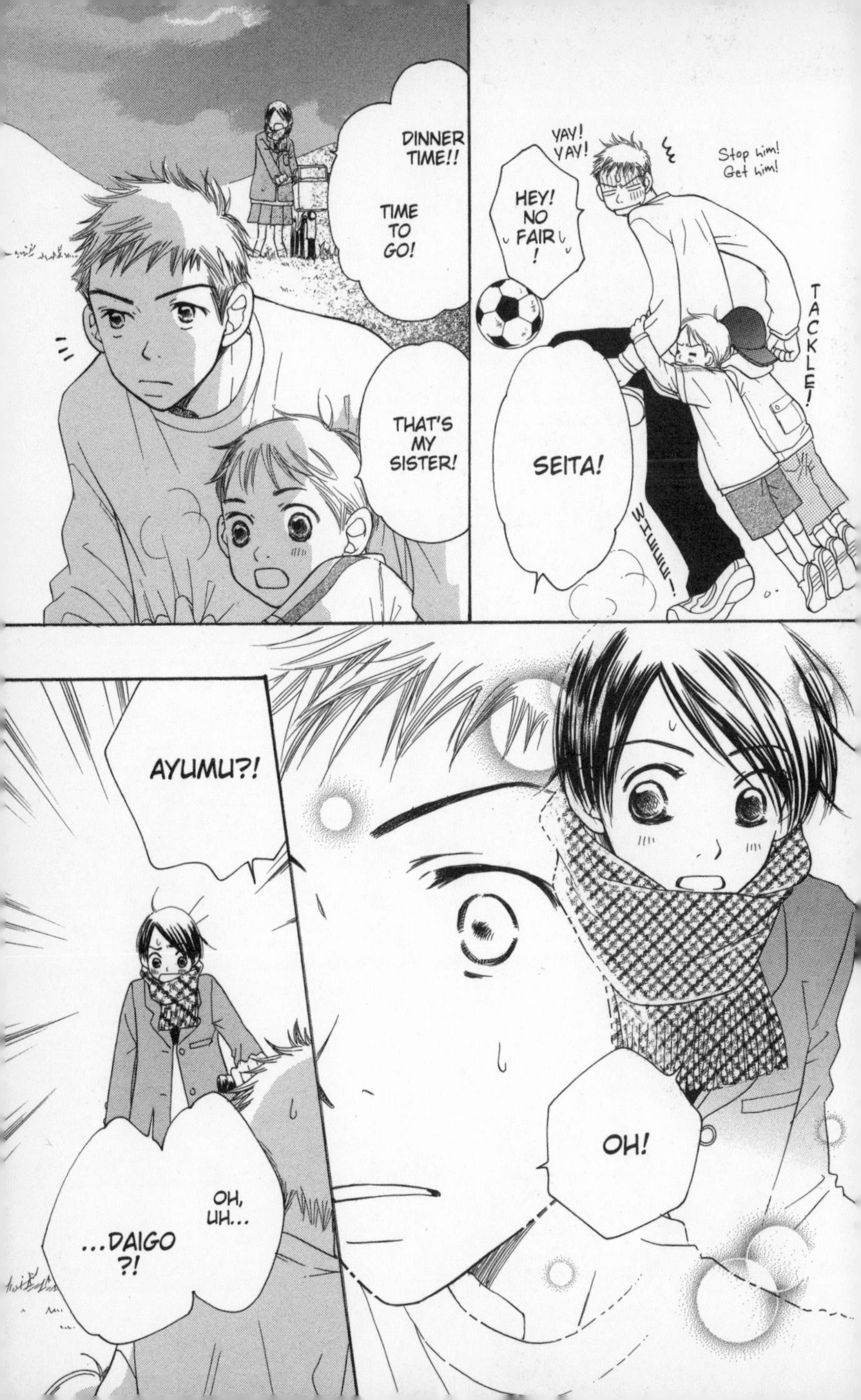
YAY! YAY!
HEY! NO FAIR!
Stop him! Get him!
SEITA!
TACKLE!
DINNER TIME!!
TIME TO GO!
THAT'S MY SISTER!
OH!
AYUMU?!
OH, UH...
...DAIGO?!

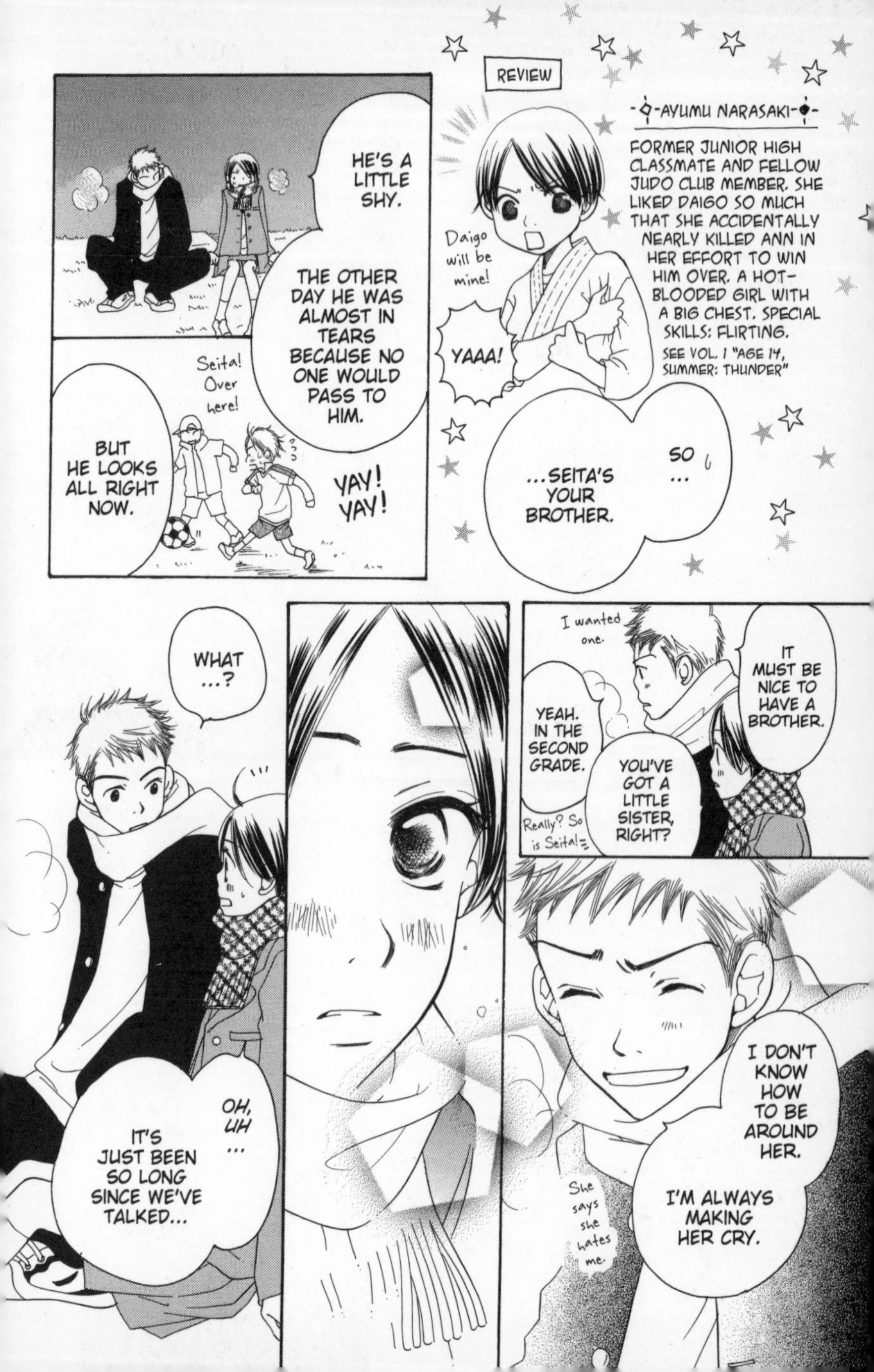
REVIEW
-AYUMU NARASAKI-
FORMER JUNIOR HIGH CLASSMATE AND FELLOW JUDO CLUB MEMBER. SHE LIKED DAIGO SO MUCH THAT SHE ACCIDENTALLY NEARLY KILLED ANN IN HER EFFORT TO WIN HIM OVER. A HOT-BLOODED GIRL WITH A BIG CHEST. SPECIAL SKILLS: FLIRTING.
SEE VOL. 1 "AGE 14, SUMMER: THUNDER"
Daigo will be mine!
YAAA!
SO...
...SEITA'S YOUR BROTHER.
HE'S A LITTLE SHY.
THE OTHER DAY HE WAS ALMOST IN TEARS BECAUSE NO ONE WOULD PASS TO HIM.
Seita! Over here!
YAY! YAY!
BUT HE LOOKS ALL RIGHT NOW.
IT MUST BE NICE TO HAVE A BROTHER.
I wanted one.
YOU'VE GOT A LITTLE SISTER, RIGHT?
YEAH. IN THE SECOND GRADE.
Really? So is Seita!
I DON'T KNOW HOW TO BE AROUND HER.
I'M ALWAYS MAKING HER CRY.
She says she hates me.
WHAT...?
OH, UH...
IT'S JUST BEEN SO LONG SINCE WE'VE TALKED...

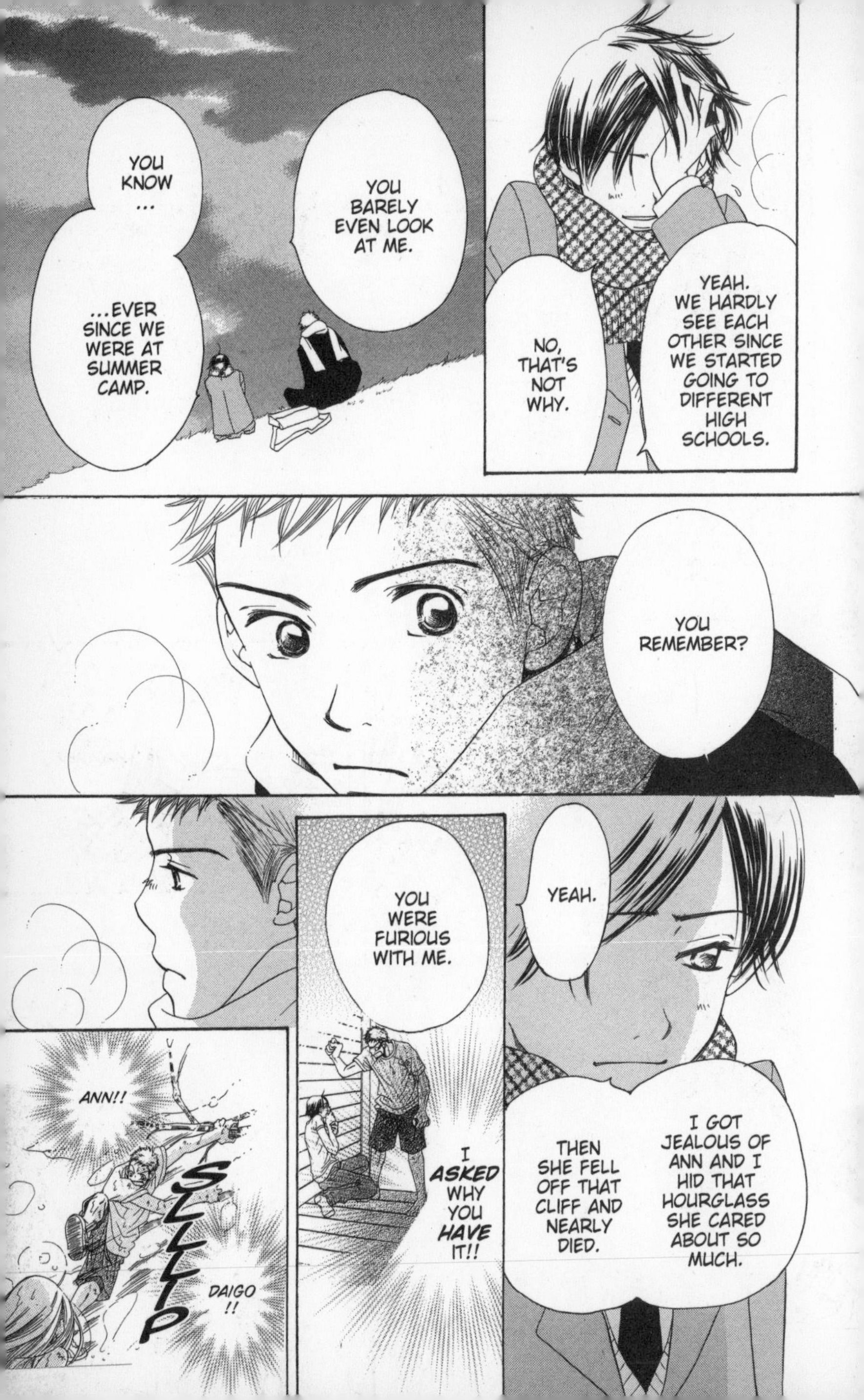
YEAH. WE HARDLY SEE EACH OTHER SINCE WE STARTED GOING TO DIFFERENT HIGH SCHOOLS.
NO, THAT'S NOT WHY.
YOU BARELY EVEN LOOK AT ME.
YOU KNOW ...
...EVER SINCE WE WERE AT SUMMER CAMP.
YOU REMEMBER?
YEAH.
I GOT JEALOUS OF ANN AND I HID THAT HOURGLASS SHE CARED ABOUT SO MUCH.
THEN SHE FELL OFF THAT CLIFF AND NEARLY DIED.
YOU WERE FURIOUS WITH ME.
I *ASKED* WHY YOU *HAVE* IT!!
ANN!!
SLLIP
DAIGO !!

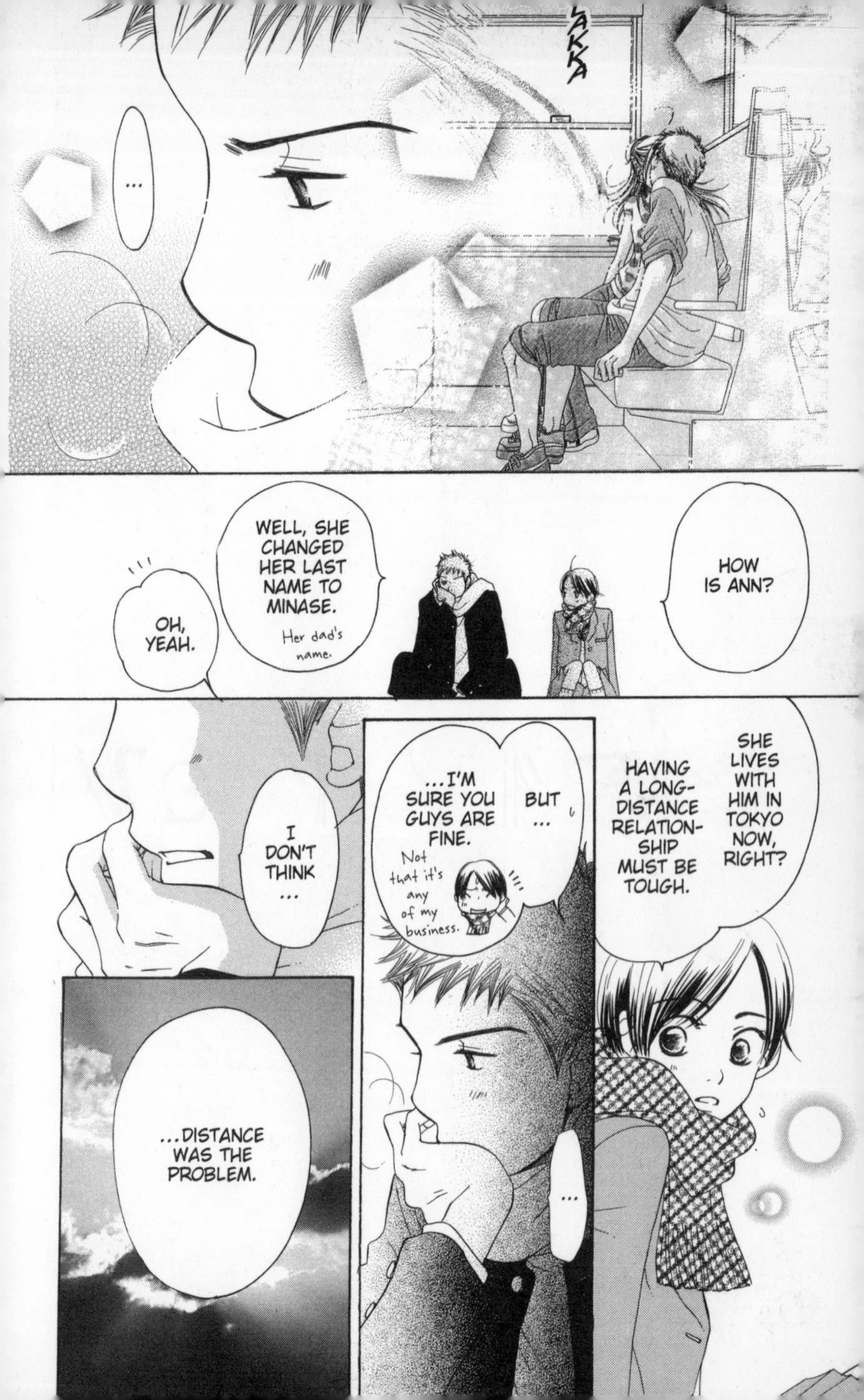
SAKKA
...
HOW IS ANN?
WELL, SHE CHANGED HER LAST NAME TO MINASE.
Her dad's name.
OH, YEAH.
SHE LIVES WITH HIM IN TOKYO NOW, RIGHT?
HAVING A LONG-DISTANCE RELATIONSHIP MUST BE TOUGH.
BUT ...
...I'M SURE YOU GUYS ARE FINE.
Not that it's any of my business.
...
I DON'T THINK ...
...DISTANCE WAS THE PROBLEM.

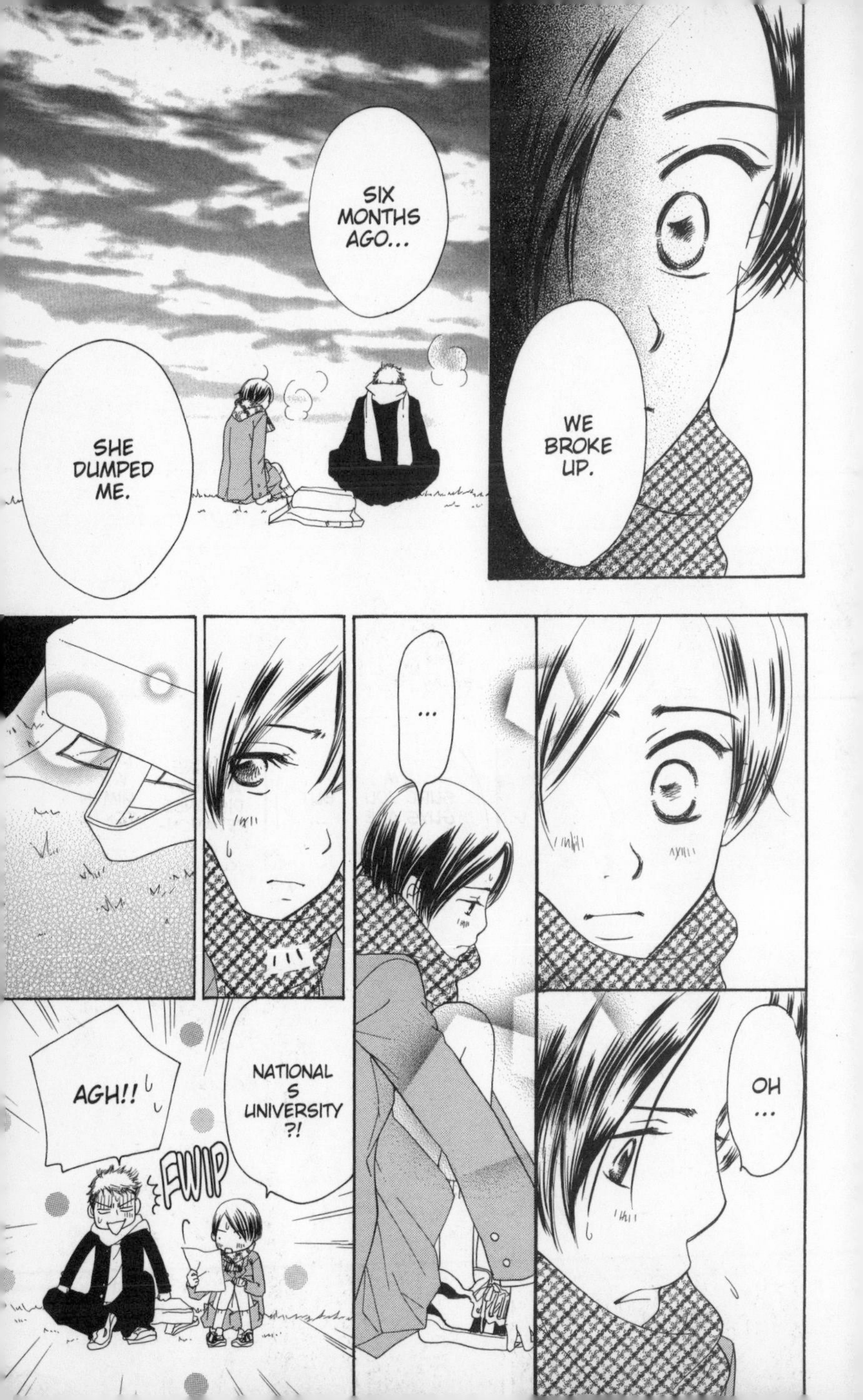
WE BROKE UP.
SIX MONTHS AGO...
SHE DUMPED ME.
OH ...
...
NATIONAL S UNIVERSITY ?!
AGH!!
FWIP

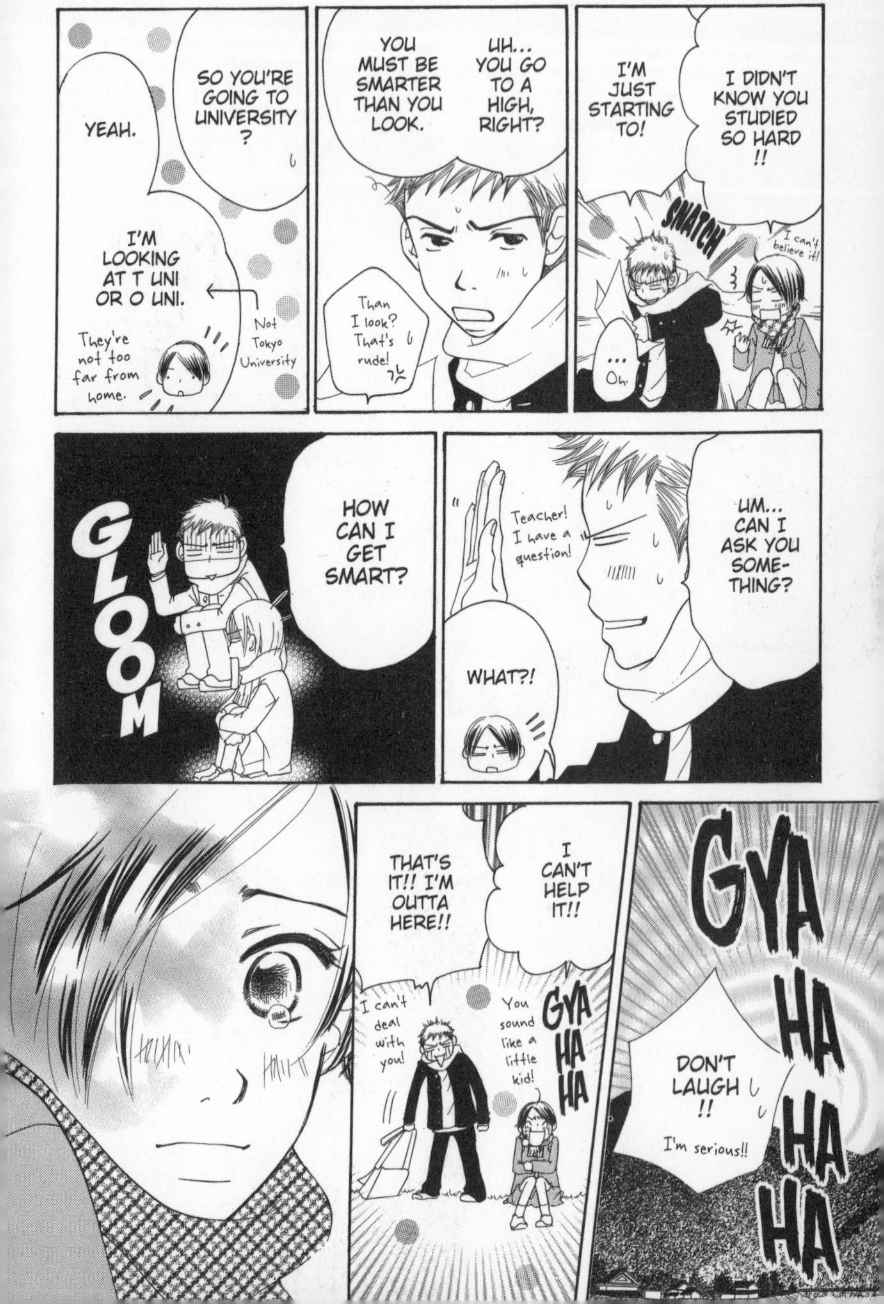
I DIDN'T KNOW YOU STUDIED SO HARD!!
I'M JUST STARTING TO!
SNATCH
I can't believe it!
... Oh.
UH... YOU GO TO A HIGH, RIGHT?
YOU MUST BE SMARTER THAN YOU LOOK.
Than I look? That's rude!
SO YOU'RE GOING TO UNIVERSITY?
YEAH.
I'M LOOKING AT T UNI OR O UNI.
Not Tokyo University
They're not too far from home.
UM... CAN I ASK YOU SOME-THING?
Teacher! I have a question!
WHAT?!
HOW CAN I GET SMART?
GLOOM
GYA HA HA HA HA
DON'T LAUGH!!
I'm serious!!
I CAN'T HELP IT!!
THAT'S IT!! I'M OUTTA HERE!!
You sound like a little kid!
GYA HA HA
I can't deal with you!

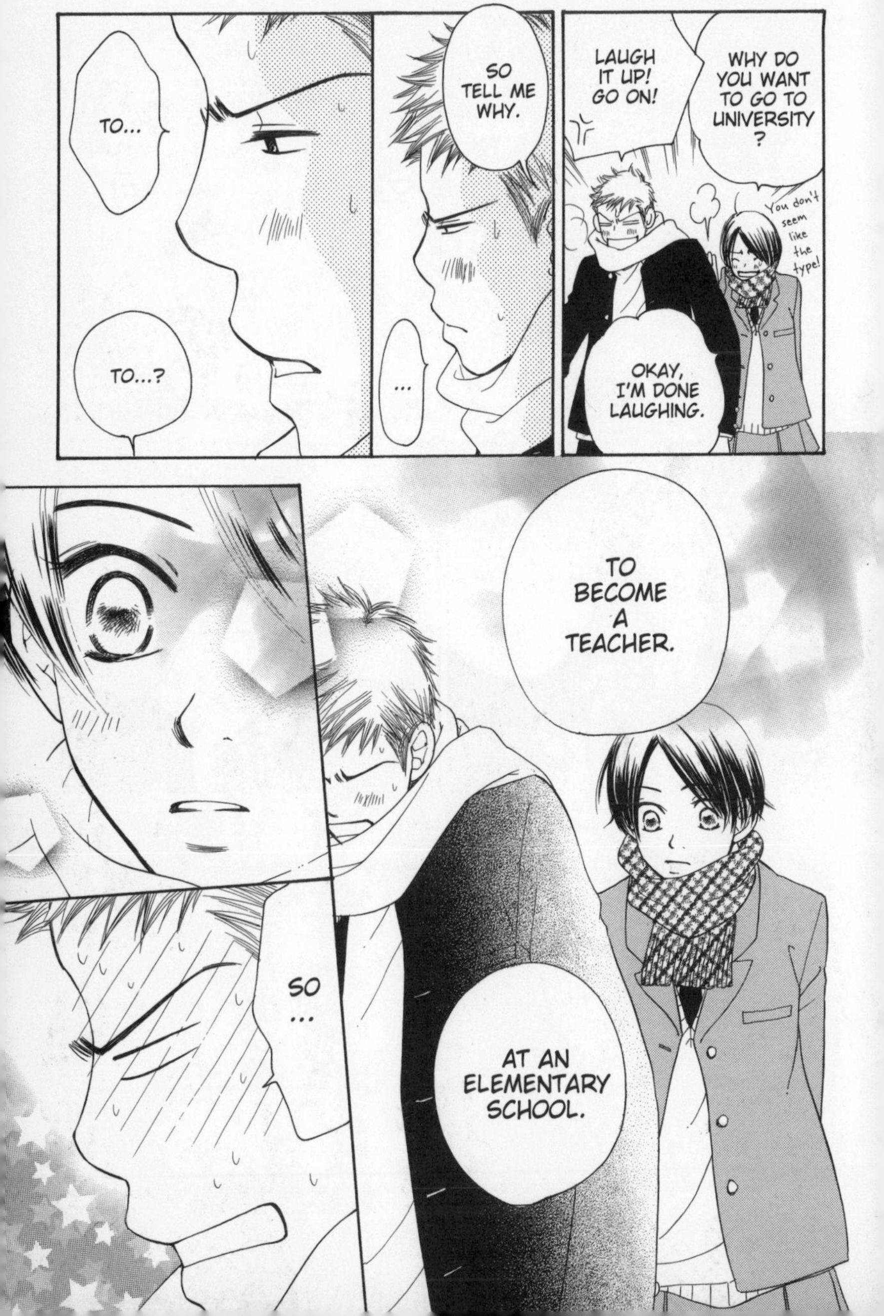
WHY DO YOU WANT TO GO TO UNIVERSITY?
You don't seem like the type!
LAUGH IT UP! GO ON!
OKAY, I'M DONE LAUGHING.
SO TELL ME WHY.
...
TO...
TO...?
TO BECOME A TEACHER.
AT AN ELEMENTARY SCHOOL.
SO ...

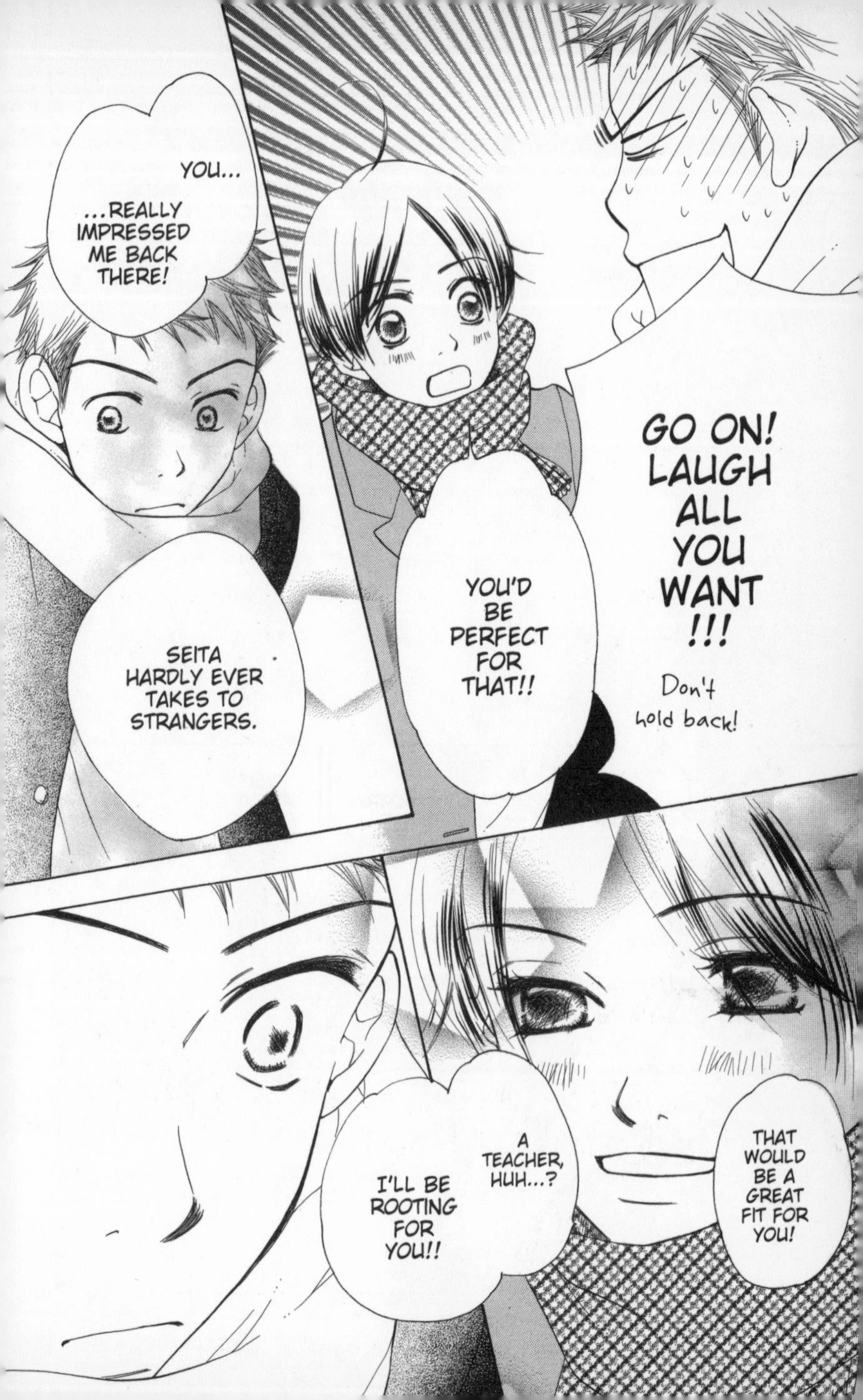
GO ON! LAUGH ALL YOU WANT!!!
Don't hold back!
YOU'D BE PERFECT FOR THAT!!
YOU...
...REALLY IMPRESSED ME BACK THERE!
SEITA HARDLY EVER TAKES TO STRANGERS.
THAT WOULD BE A GREAT FIT FOR YOU!
A TEACHER, HUH...?
I'LL BE ROOTING FOR YOU!!

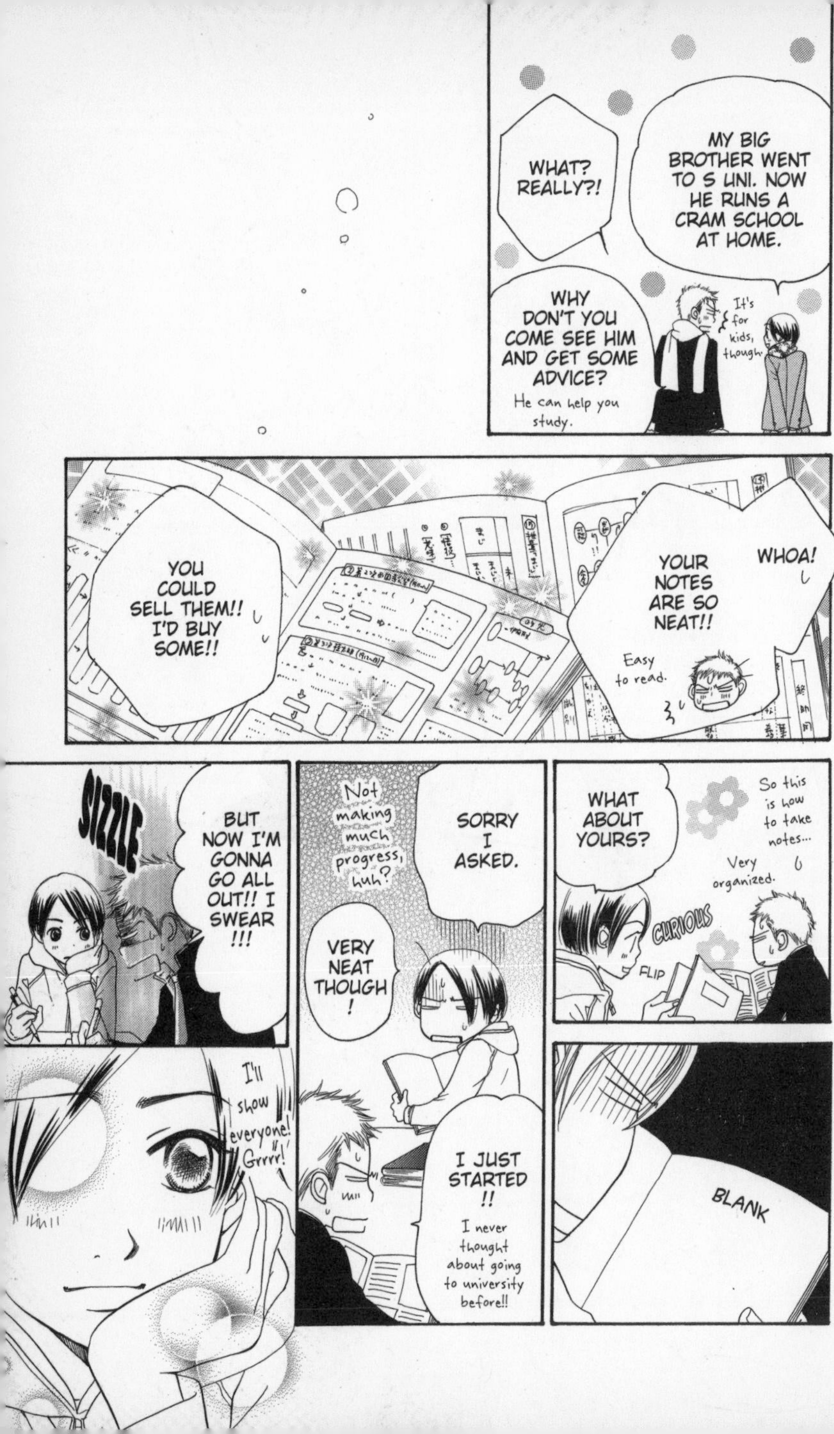
MY BIG BROTHER WENT TO S UNI. NOW HE RUNS A CRAM SCHOOL AT HOME.
WHAT? REALLY?!
It's for kids, though.
WHY DON'T YOU COME SEE HIM AND GET SOME ADVICE?
He can help you study.
WHOA!
YOUR NOTES ARE SO NEAT!!
Easy to read.
YOU COULD SELL THEM!! I'D BUY SOME!!
WHAT ABOUT YOURS?
So this is how to take notes...
Very organized.
CURIOUS
FLIP
BLANK
SORRY I ASKED.
Not making much progress, huh?
VERY NEAT THOUGH!
I JUST STARTED!!
I never thought about going to university before!!
SIZZLE
BUT NOW I'M GONNA GO ALL OUT!! I SWEAR!!!
I'll show everyone! Grrrr!

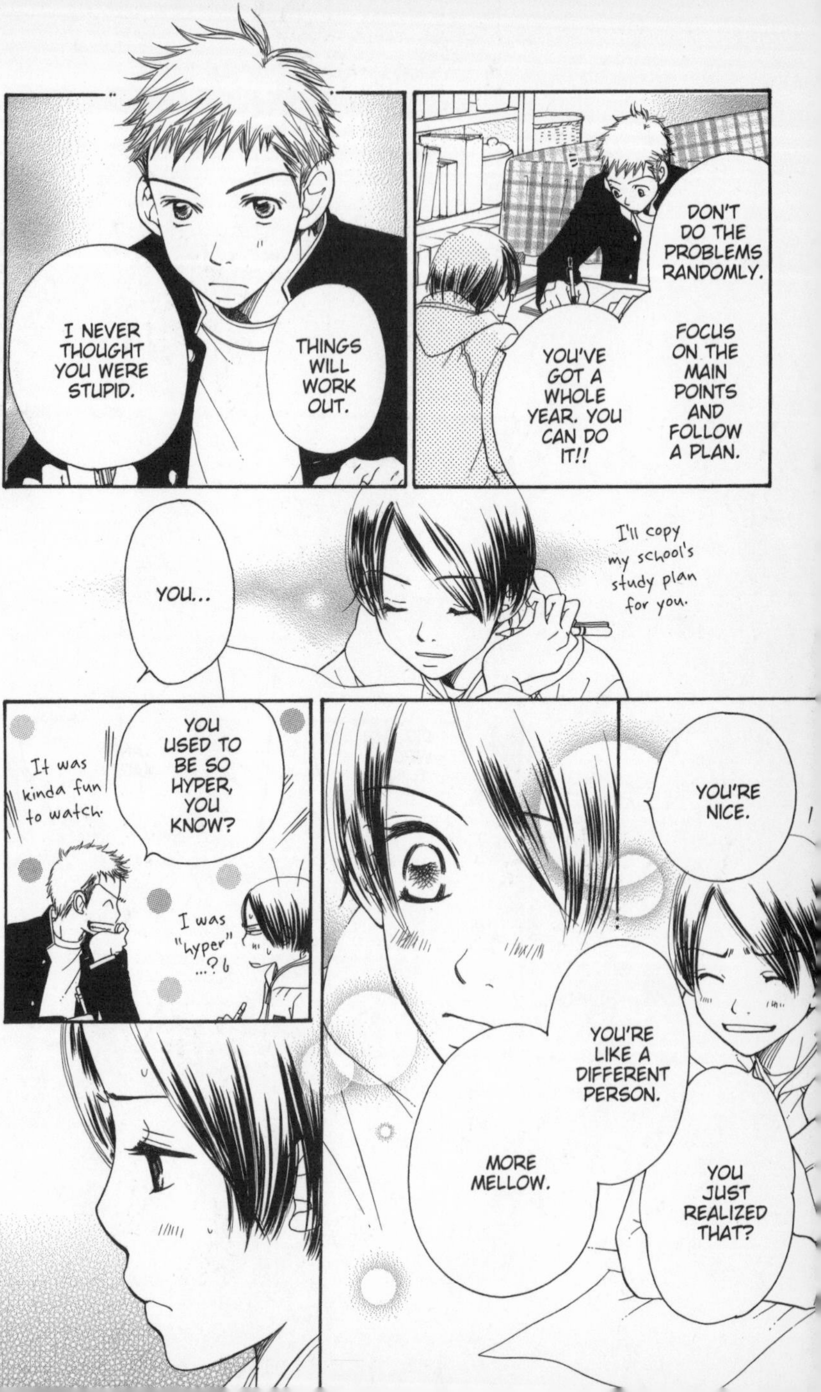
DON'T DO THE PROBLEMS RANDOMLY.
FOCUS ON THE MAIN POINTS AND FOLLOW A PLAN.
YOU'VE GOT A WHOLE YEAR. YOU CAN DO IT!!
THINGS WILL WORK OUT.
I NEVER THOUGHT YOU WERE STUPID.
I'll copy my school's study plan for you.
YOU...
YOU'RE NICE.
YOU JUST REALIZED THAT?
YOU USED TO BE SO HYPER, YOU KNOW?
I was "hyper" ...?
It was kinda fun to watch.
YOU'RE LIKE A DIFFERENT PERSON.
MORE MELLOW.

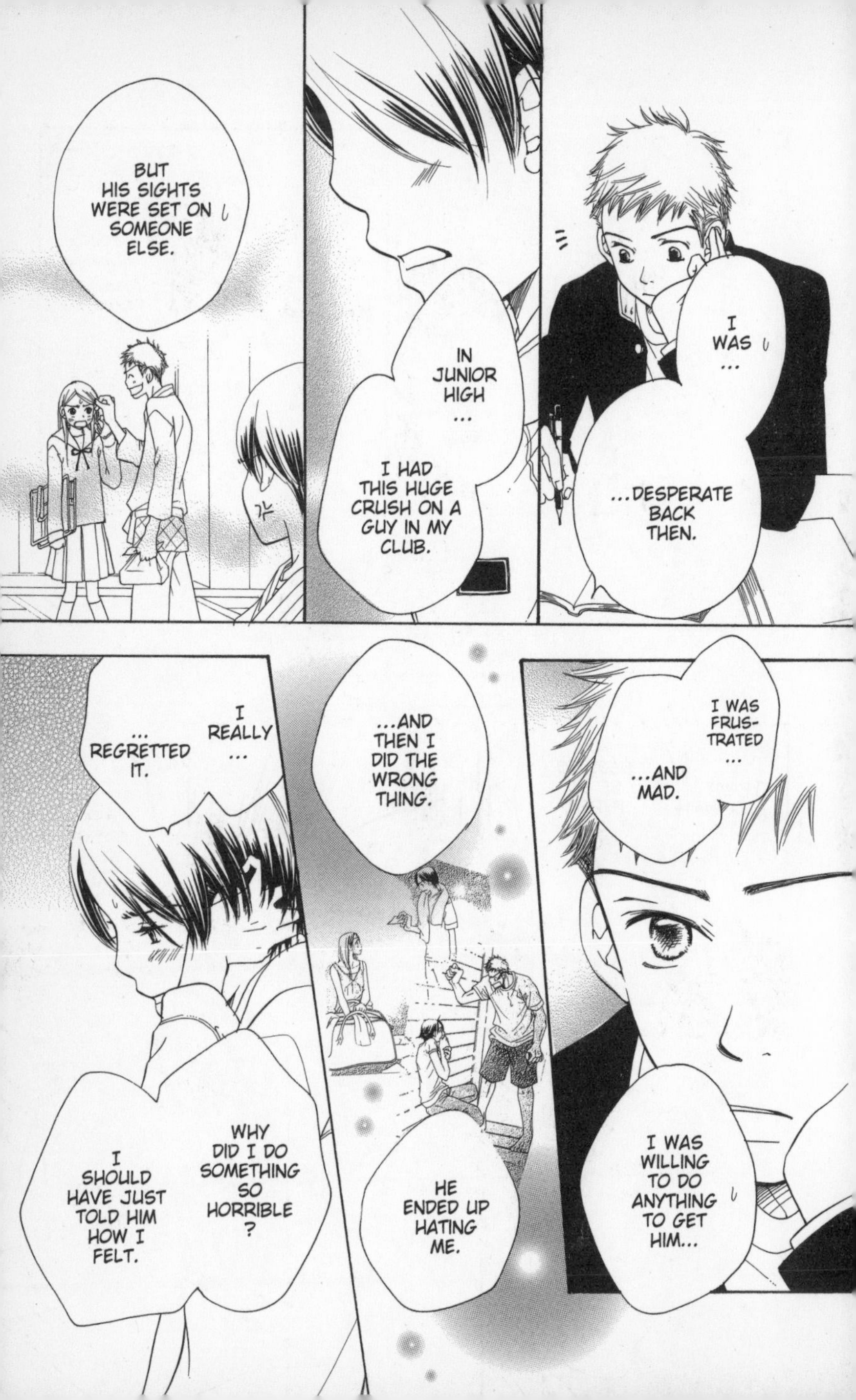
I WAS ...
...DESPERATE BACK THEN.
IN JUNIOR HIGH ...
I HAD THIS HUGE CRUSH ON A GUY IN MY CLUB.
BUT HIS SIGHTS WERE SET ON SOMEONE ELSE.
I WAS FRUS-TRATED ...
...AND MAD.
I WAS WILLING TO DO ANYTHING TO GET HIM...
...AND THEN I DID THE WRONG THING.
HE ENDED UP HATING ME.
I REALLY ...
... REGRETTED IT.
WHY DID I DO SOMETHING SO HORRIBLE?
I SHOULD HAVE JUST TOLD HIM HOW I FELT.

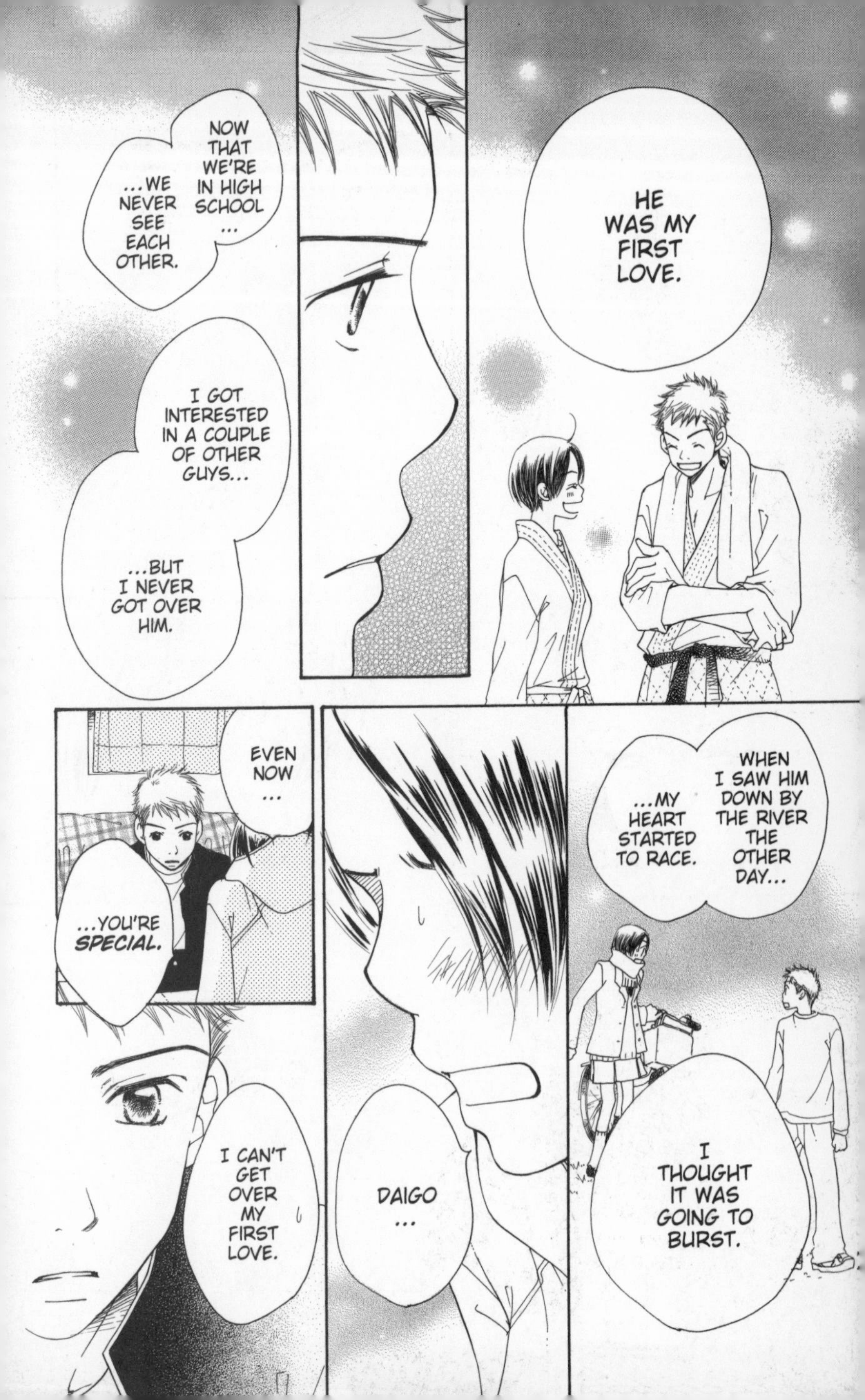
HE WAS MY FIRST LOVE.
NOW THAT WE'RE IN HIGH SCHOOL...
...WE NEVER SEE EACH OTHER.
I GOT INTERESTED IN A COUPLE OF OTHER GUYS...
...BUT I NEVER GOT OVER HIM.
WHEN I SAW HIM DOWN BY THE RIVER THE OTHER DAY...
...MY HEART STARTED TO RACE.
I THOUGHT IT WAS GOING TO BURST.
DAIGO...
EVEN NOW...
...YOU'RE SPECIAL.
I CAN'T GET OVER MY FIRST LOVE.

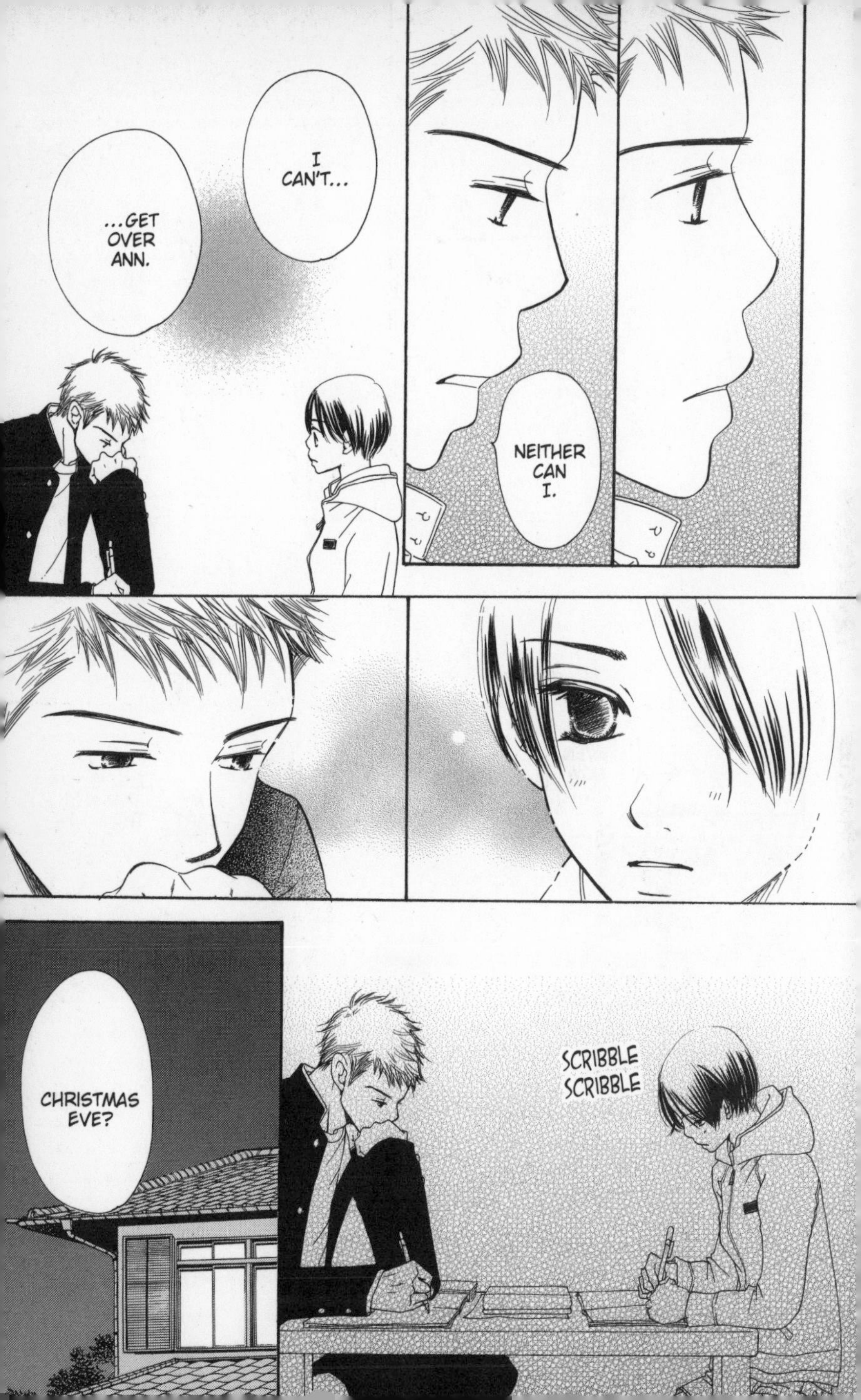
NEITHER CAN I.
I CAN'T...
...GET OVER ANN.
SCRIBBLE SCRIBBLE
CHRISTMAS EVE?

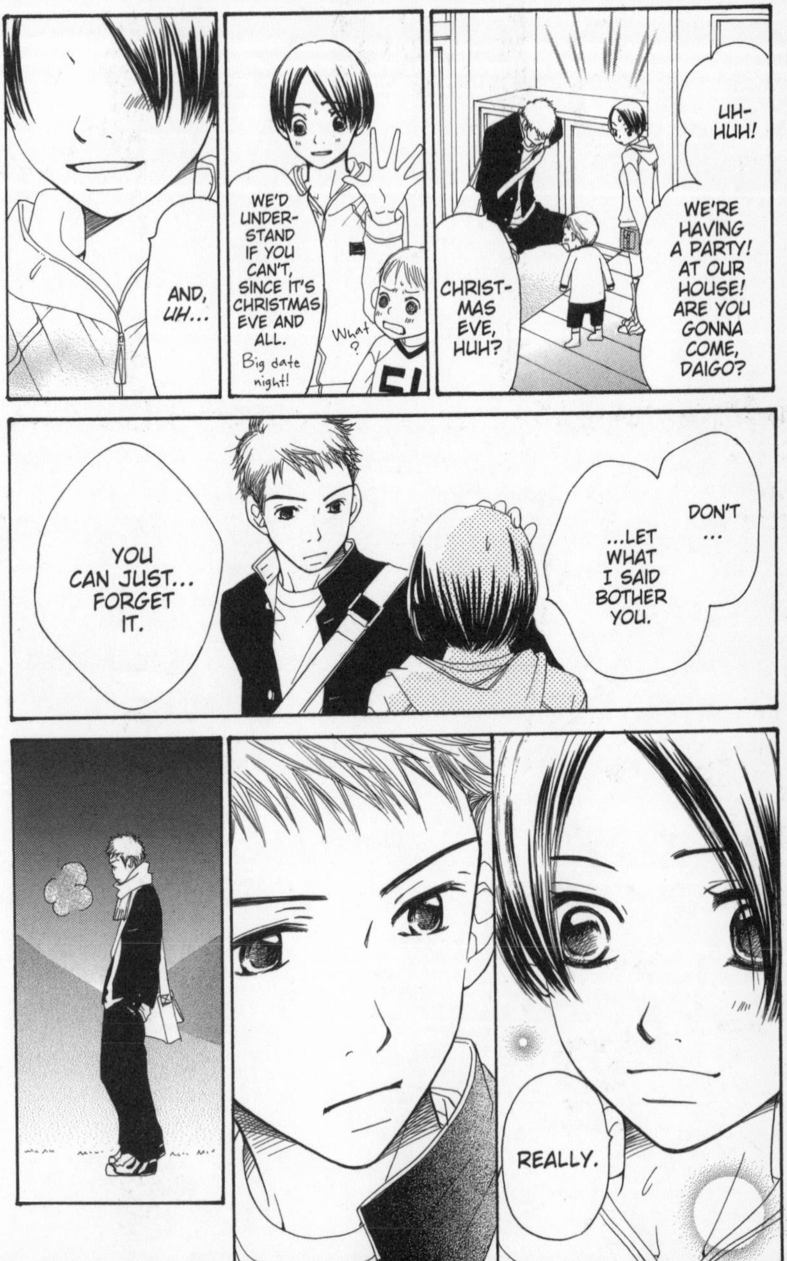
UH-HUH!
WE'RE HAVING A PARTY! AT OUR HOUSE! ARE YOU GONNA COME, DAIGO?
CHRISTMAS EVE, HUH?
WE'D UNDERSTAND IF YOU CAN'T, SINCE IT'S CHRISTMAS EVE AND ALL.
What?
Big date night!
AND, UH...
DON'T...
...LET WHAT I SAID BOTHER YOU.
YOU CAN JUST... FORGET IT.
REALLY.

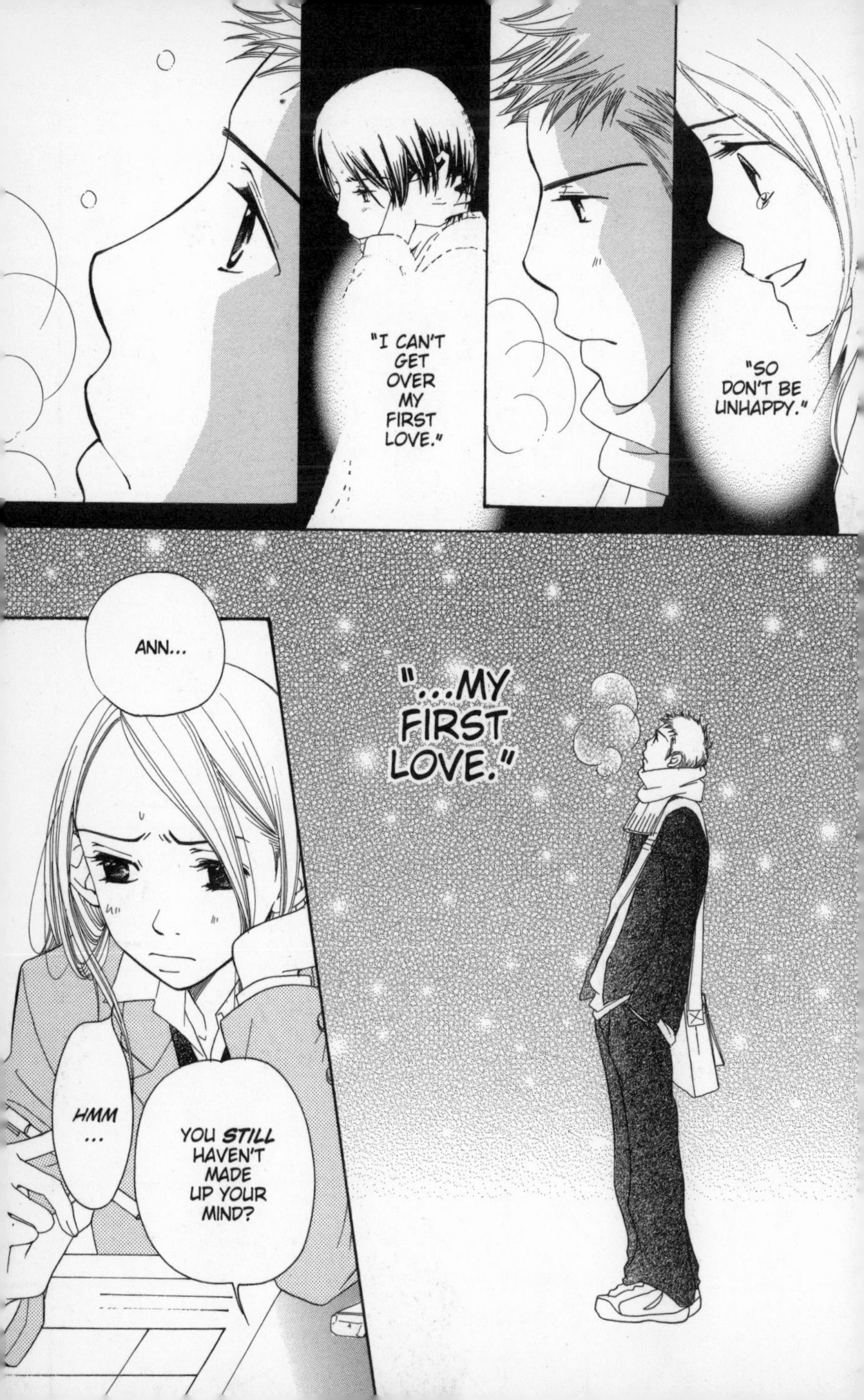
"SO DON'T BE UNHAPPY."
"I CAN'T GET OVER MY FIRST LOVE."
"...MY FIRST LOVE."
ANN...
HMM...
YOU STILL HAVEN'T MADE UP YOUR MIND?

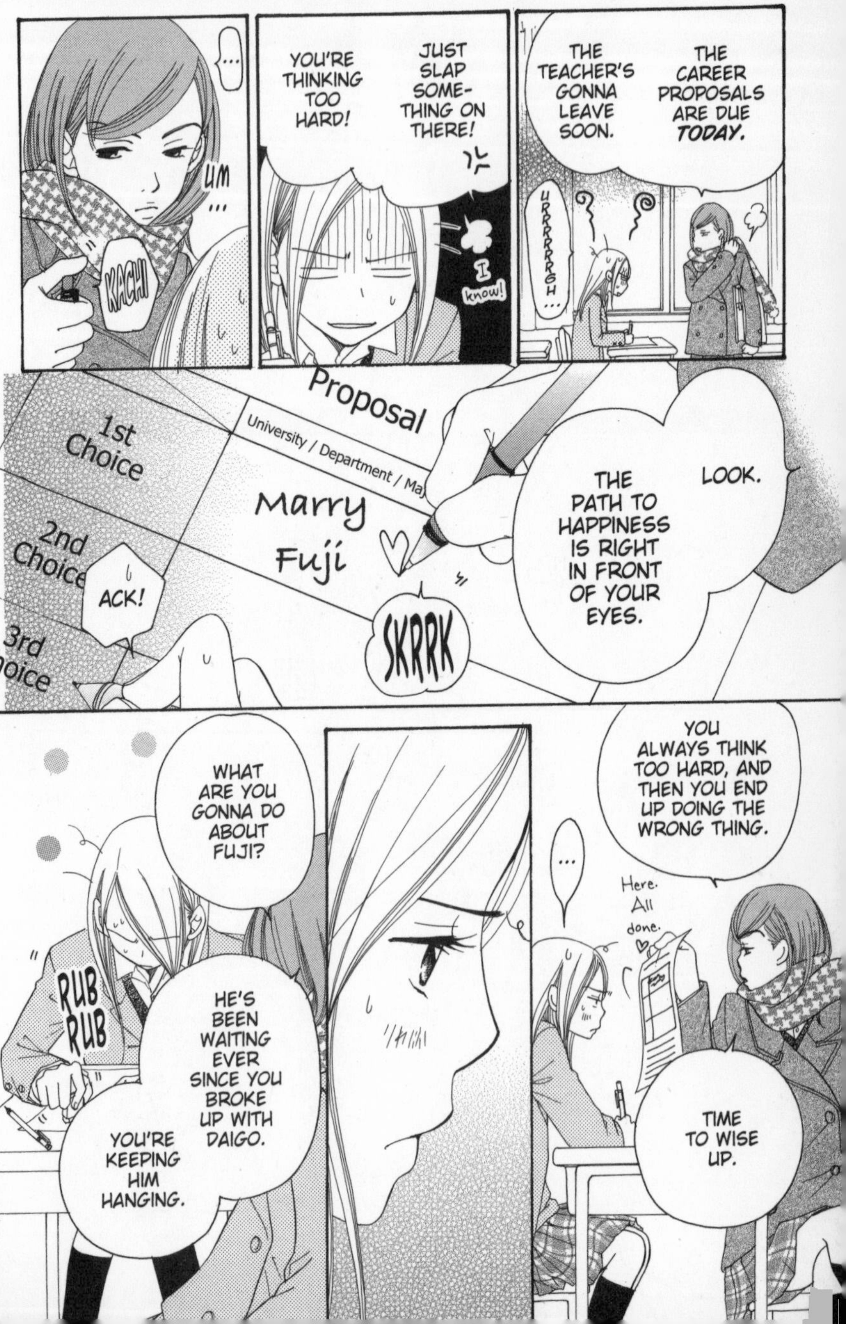
THE CAREER PROPOSALS ARE DUE TODAY.
THE TEACHER'S GONNA LEAVE SOON.
URRRRRRGH...
JUST SLAP SOMETHING ON THERE!
YOU'RE THINKING TOO HARD!
I know!
...
UM...
KACHI
LOOK.
THE PATH TO HAPPINESS IS RIGHT IN FRONT OF YOUR EYES.
Proposal
University / Department / Ma
1st Choice
Marry Fuji
2nd Choice
3rd Choice
SKRRK
ACK!
YOU ALWAYS THINK TOO HARD, AND THEN YOU END UP DOING THE WRONG THING.
...
Here. All done.
TIME TO WISE UP.
WHAT ARE YOU GONNA DO ABOUT FUJI?
HE'S BEEN WAITING EVER SINCE YOU BROKE UP WITH DAIGO.
YOU'RE KEEPING HIM HANGING.
RUB RUB

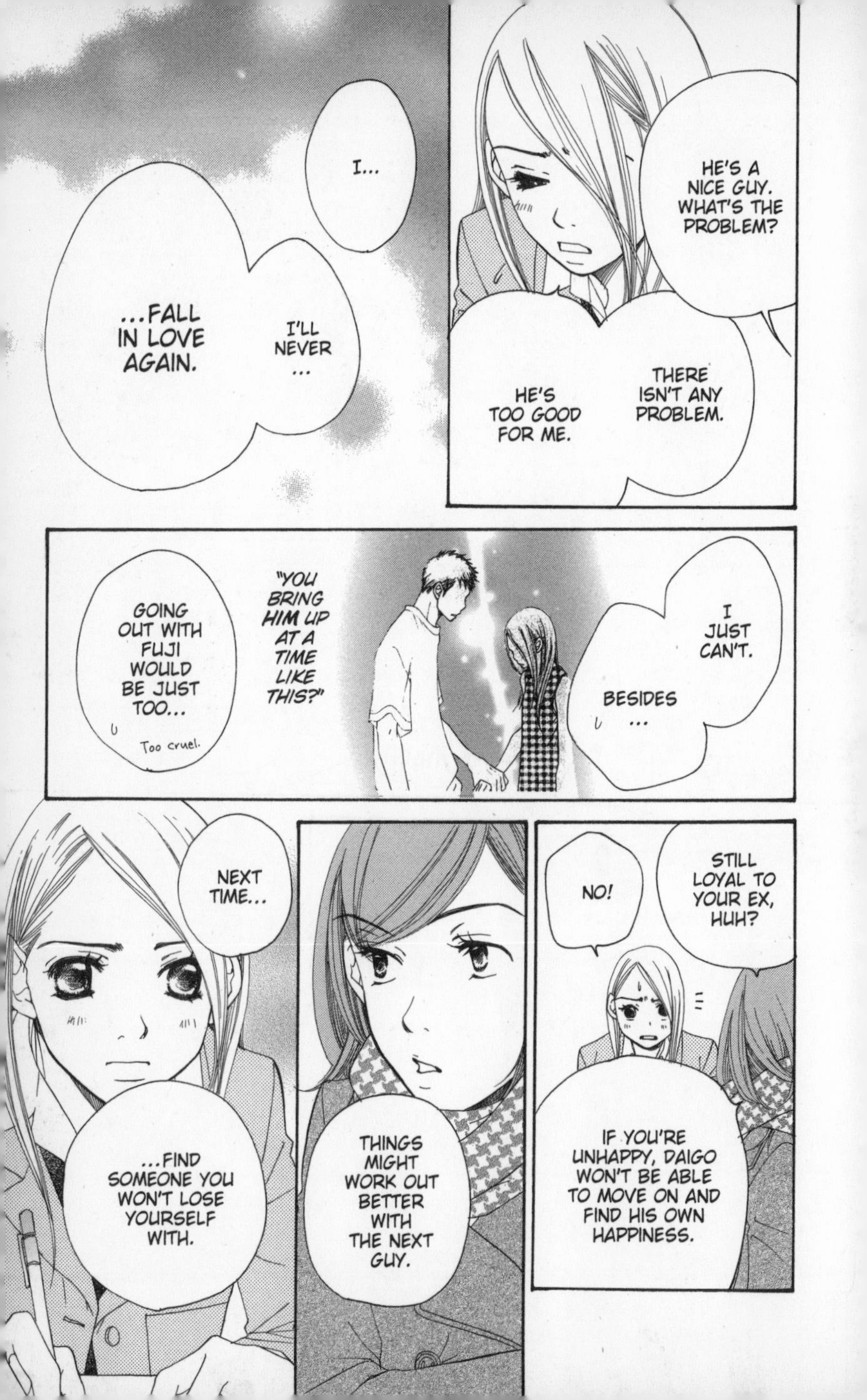
HE'S A NICE GUY. WHAT'S THE PROBLEM?
THERE ISN'T ANY PROBLEM.
HE'S TOO GOOD FOR ME.
I...
I'LL NEVER...
...FALL IN LOVE AGAIN.
I JUST CAN'T.
BESIDES...
"YOU BRING HIM UP AT A TIME LIKE THIS?"
GOING OUT WITH FUJI WOULD BE JUST TOO...
Too cruel.
STILL LOYAL TO YOUR EX, HUH?
NO!
IF YOU'RE UNHAPPY, DAIGO WON'T BE ABLE TO MOVE ON AND FIND HIS OWN HAPPINESS.
THINGS MIGHT WORK OUT BETTER WITH THE NEXT GUY.
NEXT TIME...
...FIND SOMEONE YOU WON'T LOSE YOURSELF WITH.

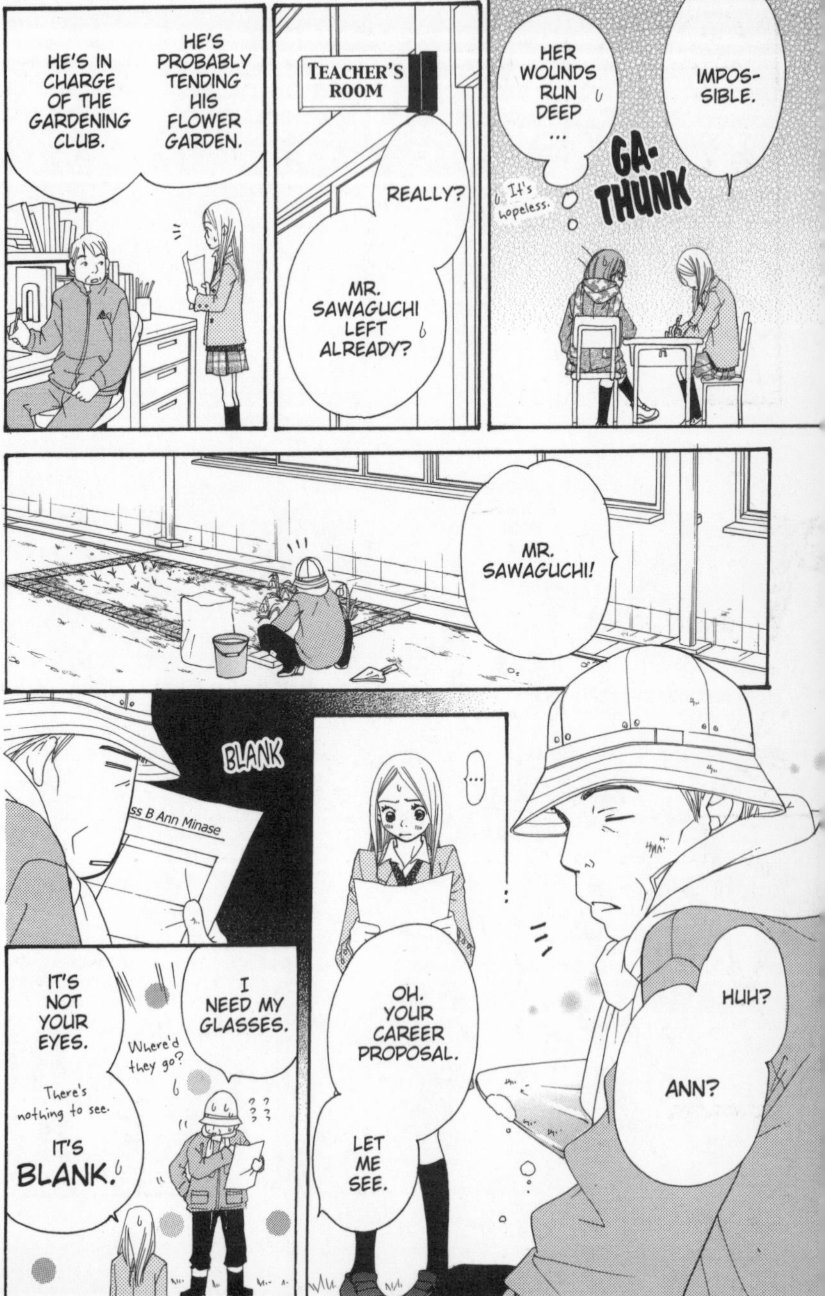
IMPOSSIBLE.
HER WOUNDS RUN DEEP...
GA-THUNK
It's hopeless.
TEACHER'S ROOM
REALLY?
MR. SAWAGUCHI LEFT ALREADY?
HE'S PROBABLY TENDING HIS FLOWER GARDEN.
HE'S IN CHARGE OF THE GARDENING CLUB.
MR. SAWAGUCHI!
HUH?
ANN?
...
OH. YOUR CAREER PROPOSAL.
LET ME SEE.
BLANK
ss B Ann Minase
I NEED MY GLASSES.
Where'd they go?
IT'S NOT YOUR EYES.
There's nothing to see.
IT'S BLANK.

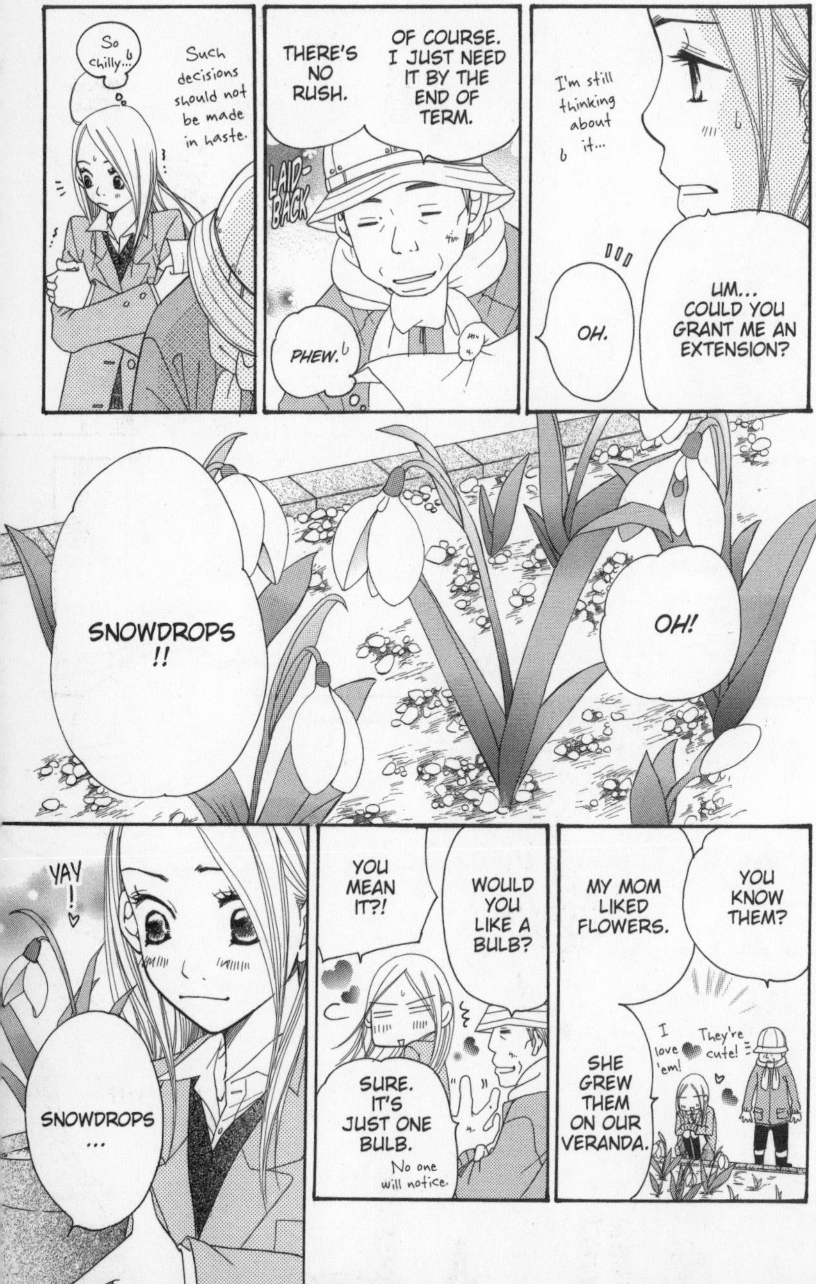
I'm still thinking about it...
UM... COULD YOU GRANT ME AN EXTENSION?
OH.
OF COURSE. I JUST NEED IT BY THE END OF TERM.
THERE'S NO RUSH.
LAID-BACK
PHEW.
Such decisions should not be made in haste.
So chilly...
OH!
SNOWDROPS!!
YOU KNOW THEM?
MY MOM LIKED FLOWERS.
SHE GREW THEM ON OUR VERANDA.
They're cute!
I love 'em!
WOULD YOU LIKE A BULB?
YOU MEAN IT?!
SURE. IT'S JUST ONE BULB.
No one will notice.
YAY!
SNOWDROPS...

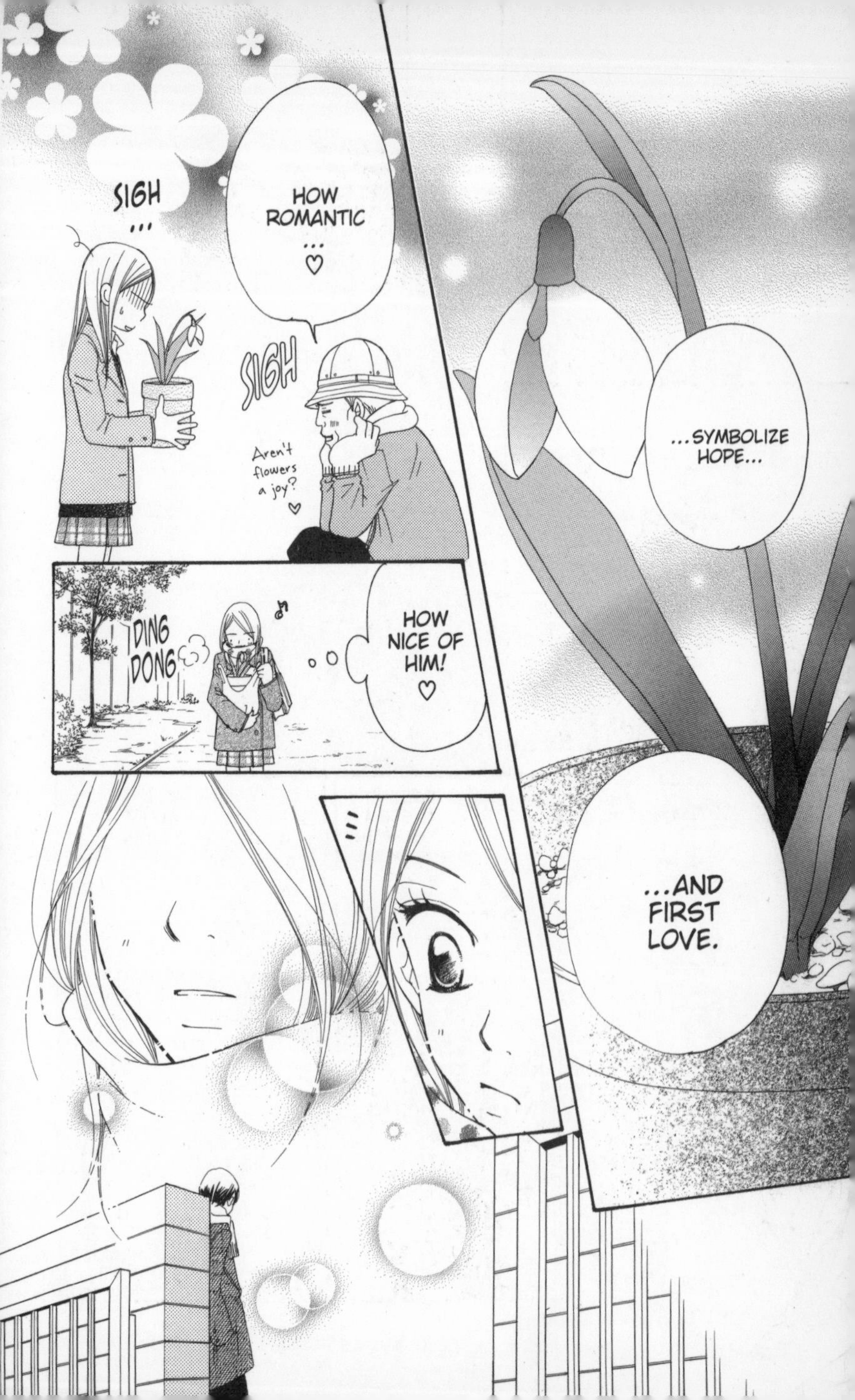
...SYMBOLIZE HOPE...
...AND FIRST LOVE.
HOW ROMANTIC ... ♡
SIGH ...
SIGH
Aren't flowers a joy? ♡
HOW NICE OF HIM! ♡
DING DONG

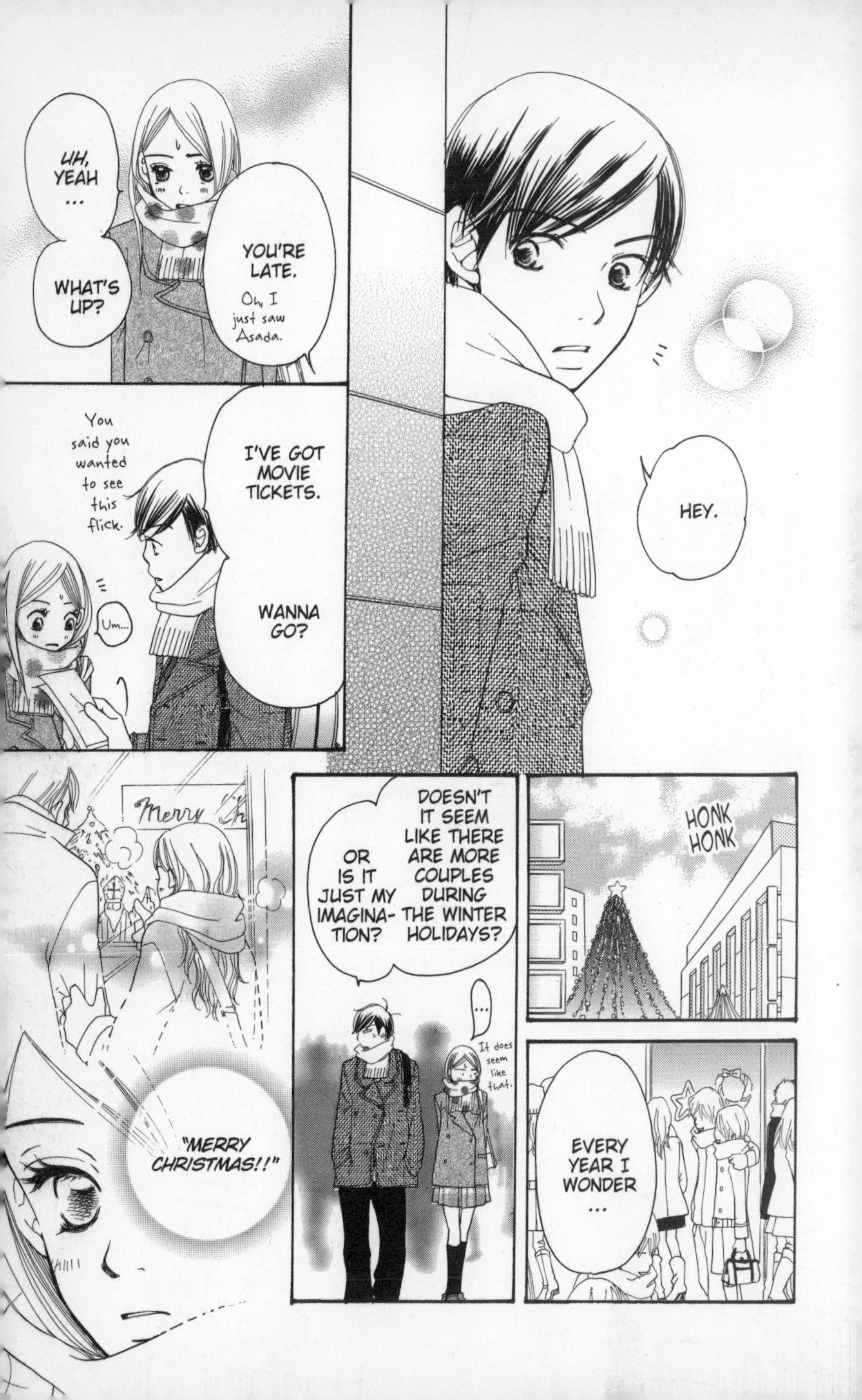
HEY.
UH, YEAH ...
WHAT'S UP?
YOU'RE LATE.
Oh, I just saw Asada.
I'VE GOT MOVIE TICKETS.
You said you wanted to see this flick.
WANNA GO?
Um...
HONK HONK
EVERY YEAR I WONDER ...
DOESN'T IT SEEM LIKE THERE ARE MORE COUPLES DURING THE WINTER HOLIDAYS?
OR IS IT JUST MY IMAGINA-TION?
...
It does seem like that.
Merry Ch
"MERRY CHRISTMAS!!"

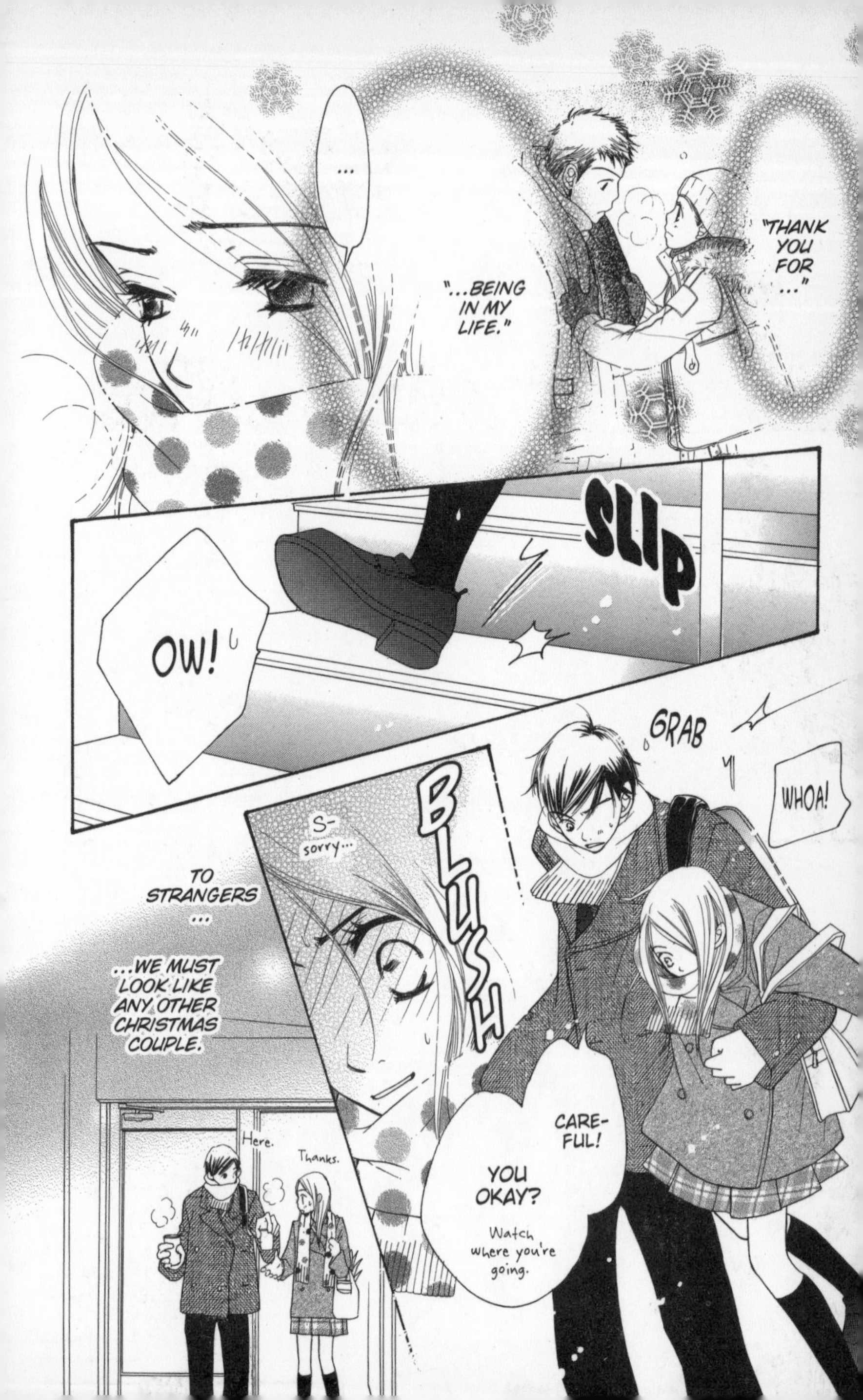
"THANK YOU FOR ..."
"...BEING IN MY LIFE."
...
SLIP
OW!
GRAB
WHOA!
CARE-FUL!
YOU OKAY?
Watch where you're going.
BLUSH
S-sorry...
TO STRANGERS ...
...WE MUST LOOK LIKE ANY OTHER CHRISTMAS COUPLE.
Here.
Thanks.

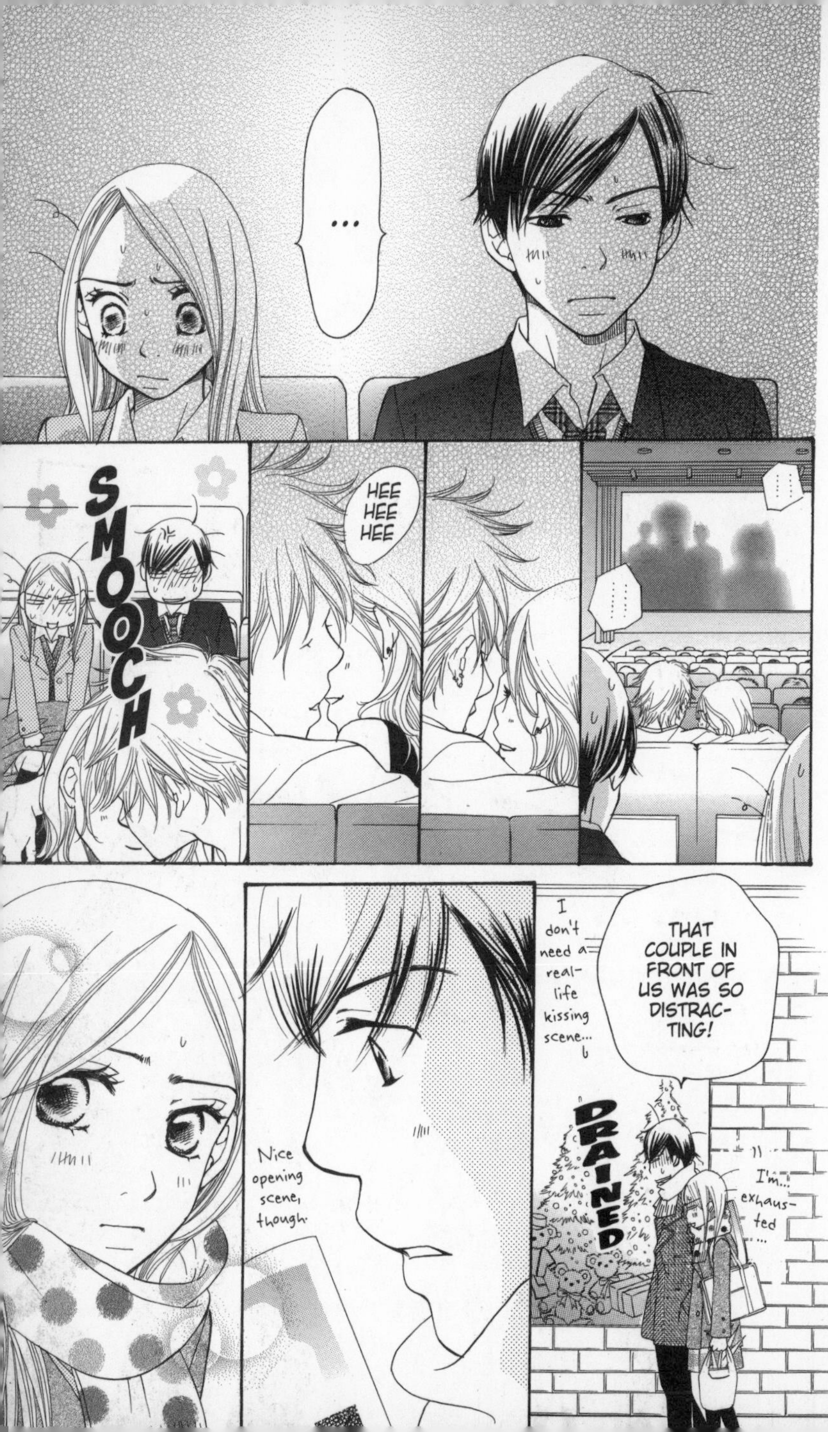
...
......
......
HEE HEE HEE
SMOOCH
THAT COUPLE IN FRONT OF US WAS SO DISTRAC-TING!
I don't need a real-life kissing scene...
DRAINED
I'm...! exhaus-ted...
Nice opening scene, though.

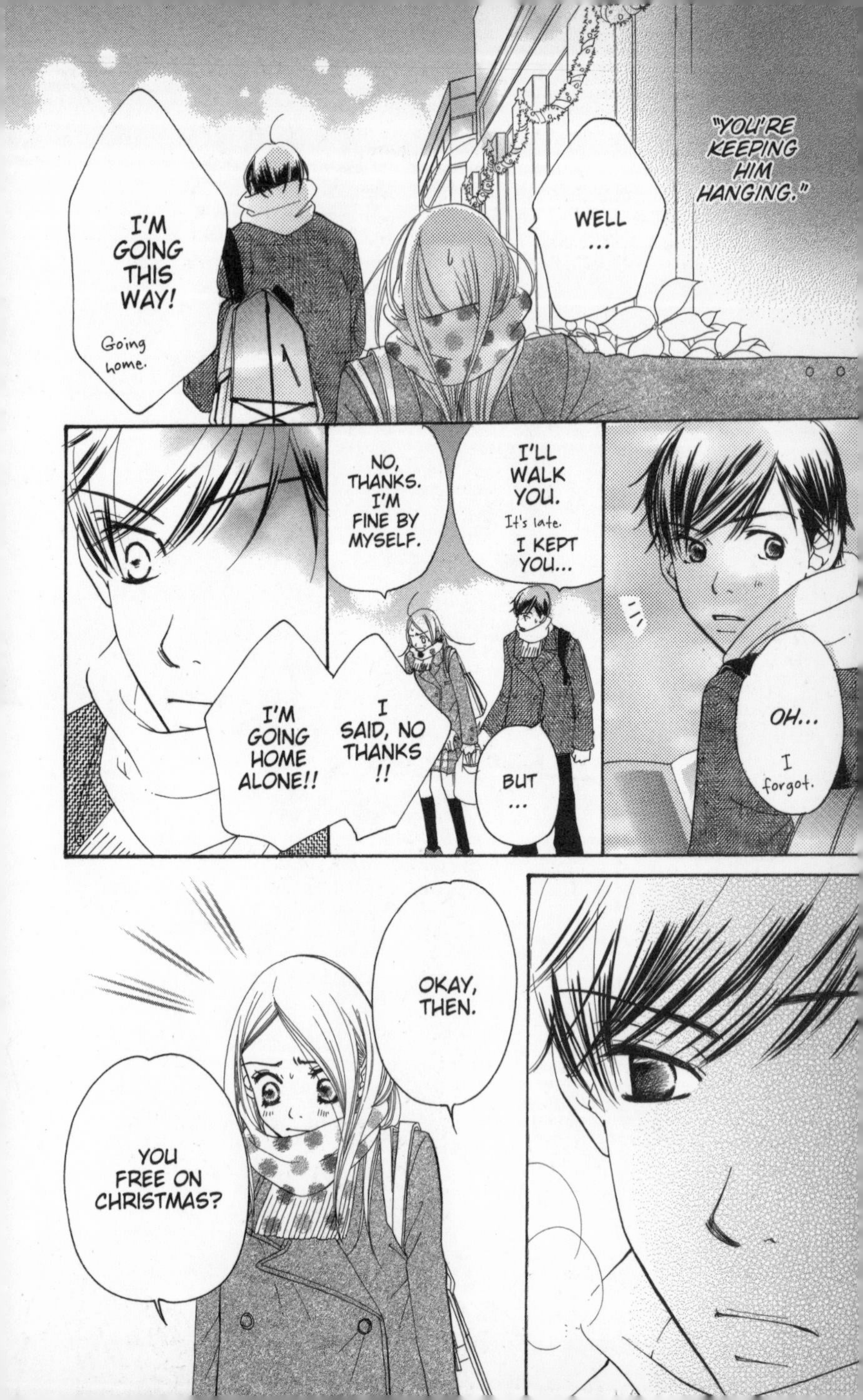
"YOU'RE KEEPING HIM HANGING."
WELL...
I'M GOING THIS WAY!
Going home.
OH...
I forgot.
I'LL WALK YOU.
It's late.
I KEPT YOU...
NO, THANKS. I'M FINE BY MYSELF.
BUT...
I SAID, NO THANKS!!
I'M GOING HOME ALONE!!
OKAY, THEN.
YOU FREE ON CHRISTMAS?

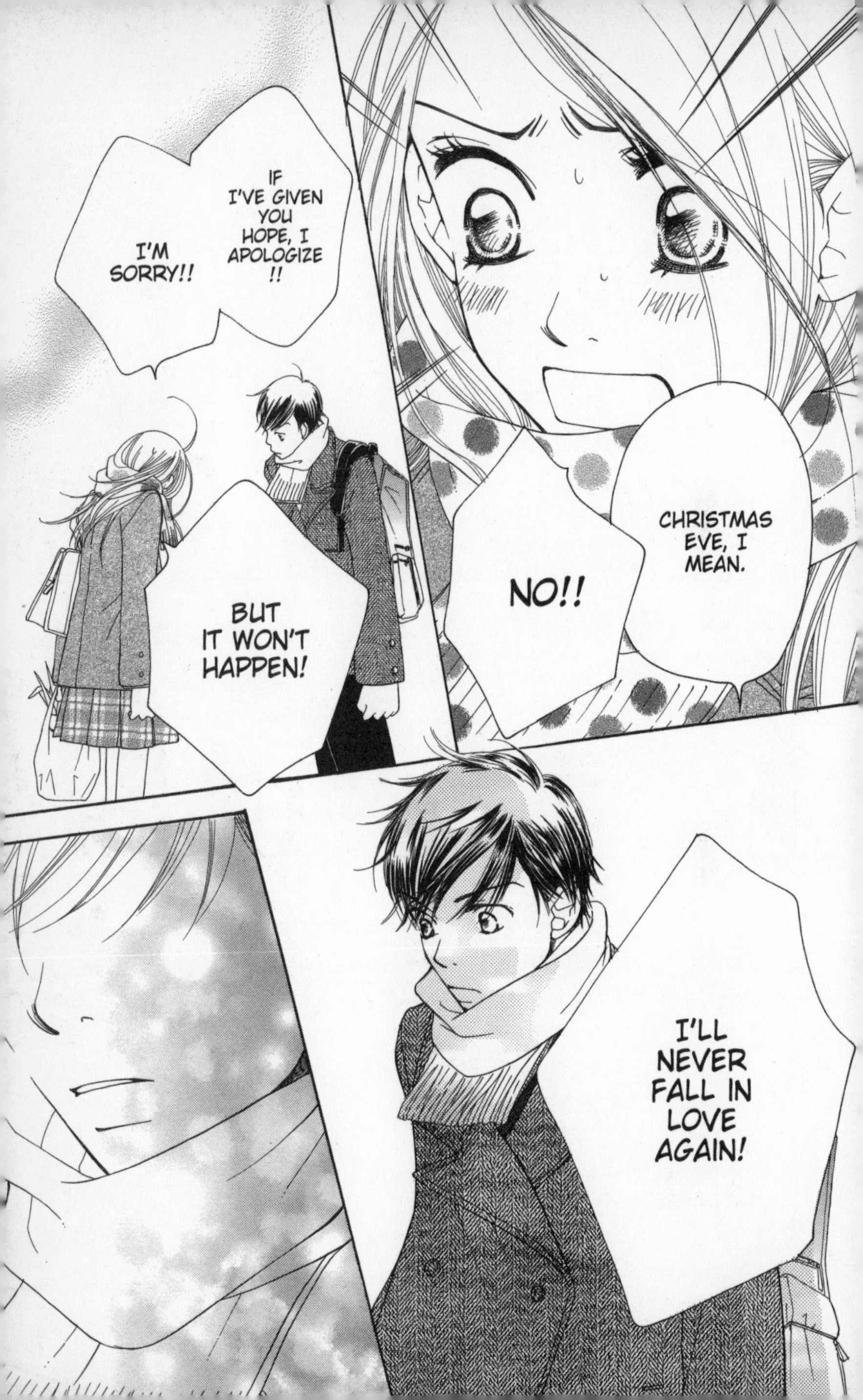
CHRISTMAS EVE, I MEAN.
NO!!
IF I'VE GIVEN YOU HOPE, I APOLOGIZE!!
I'M SORRY!!
BUT IT WON'T HAPPEN!
I'LL NEVER FALL IN LOVE AGAIN!

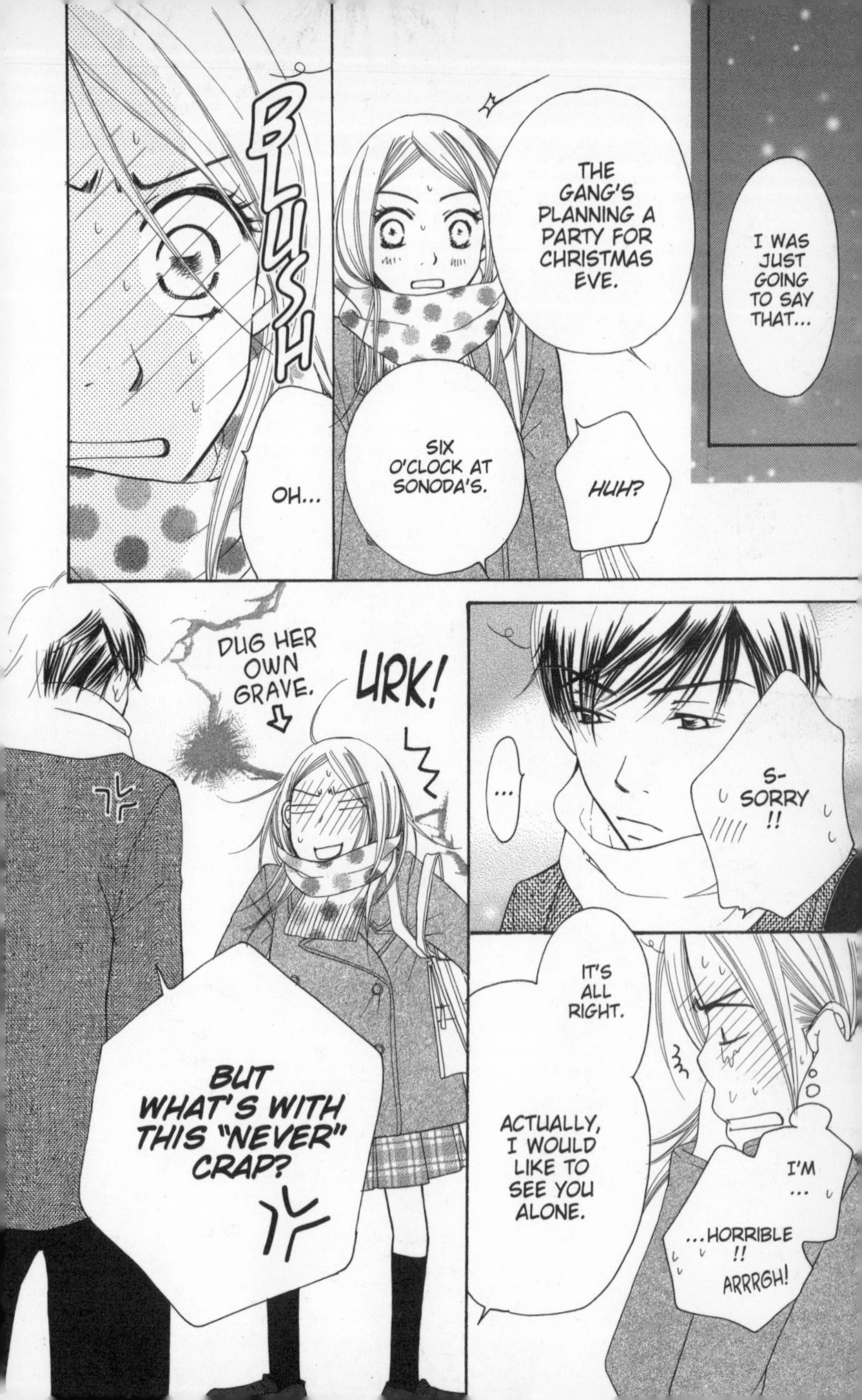
I WAS JUST GOING TO SAY THAT...
THE GANG'S PLANNING A PARTY FOR CHRISTMAS EVE.
HUH?
SIX O'CLOCK AT SONODA'S.
BLUSH
OH...
S-SORRY!!
...
I'M...
...HORRIBLE!! ARRRGH!
IT'S ALL RIGHT.
ACTUALLY, I WOULD LIKE TO SEE YOU ALONE.
URK!
DUG HER OWN GRAVE.
BUT WHAT'S WITH THIS "NEVER" CRAP?

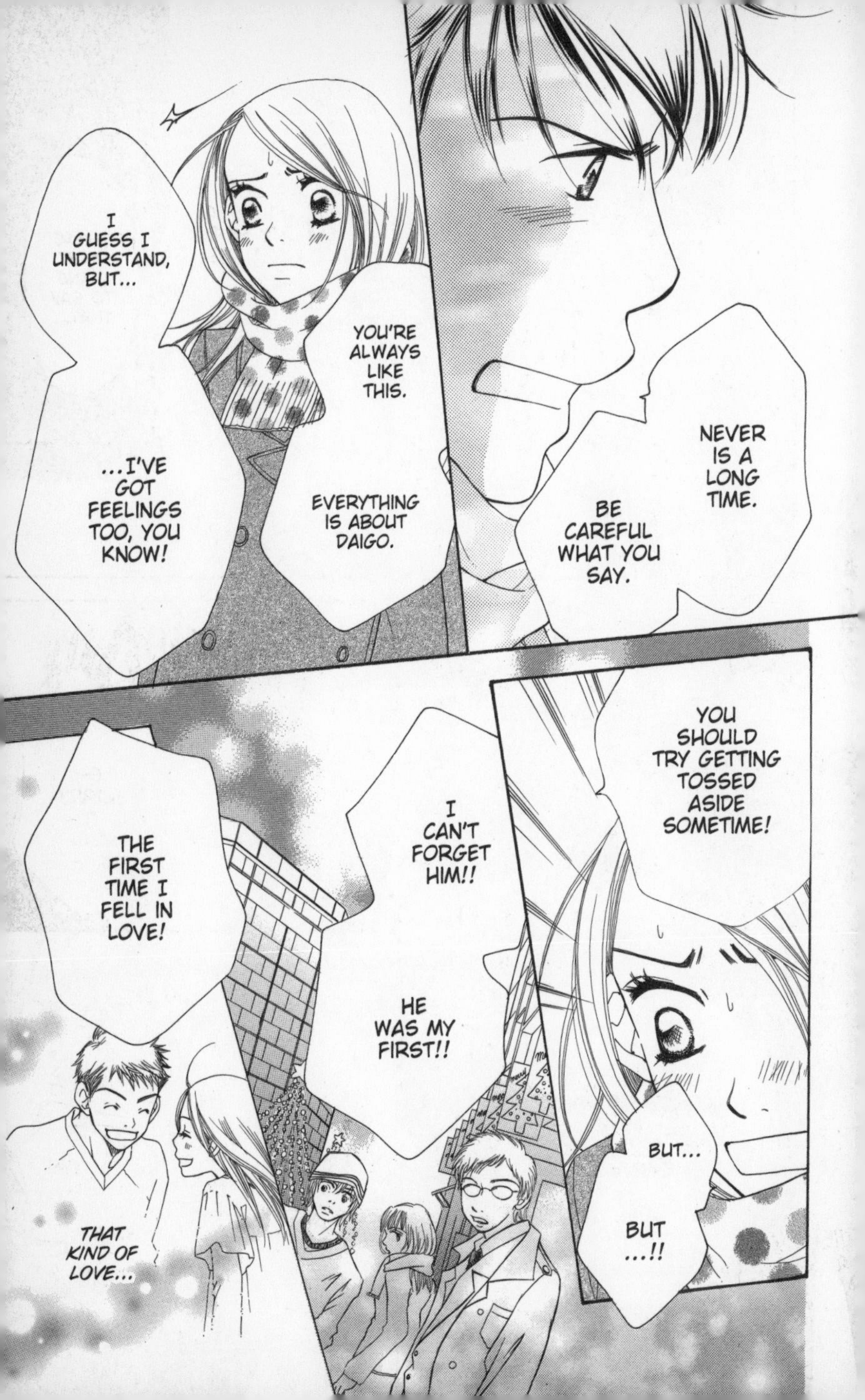
NEVER IS A LONG TIME.
BE CAREFUL WHAT YOU SAY.
YOU'RE ALWAYS LIKE THIS.
EVERYTHING IS ABOUT DAIGO.
I GUESS I UNDERSTAND, BUT...
...I'VE GOT FEELINGS TOO, YOU KNOW!
YOU SHOULD TRY GETTING TOSSED ASIDE SOMETIME!
BUT...
BUT ...!!
I CAN'T FORGET HIM!!
HE WAS MY FIRST!!
THE FIRST TIME I FELL IN LOVE!
THAT KIND OF LOVE...

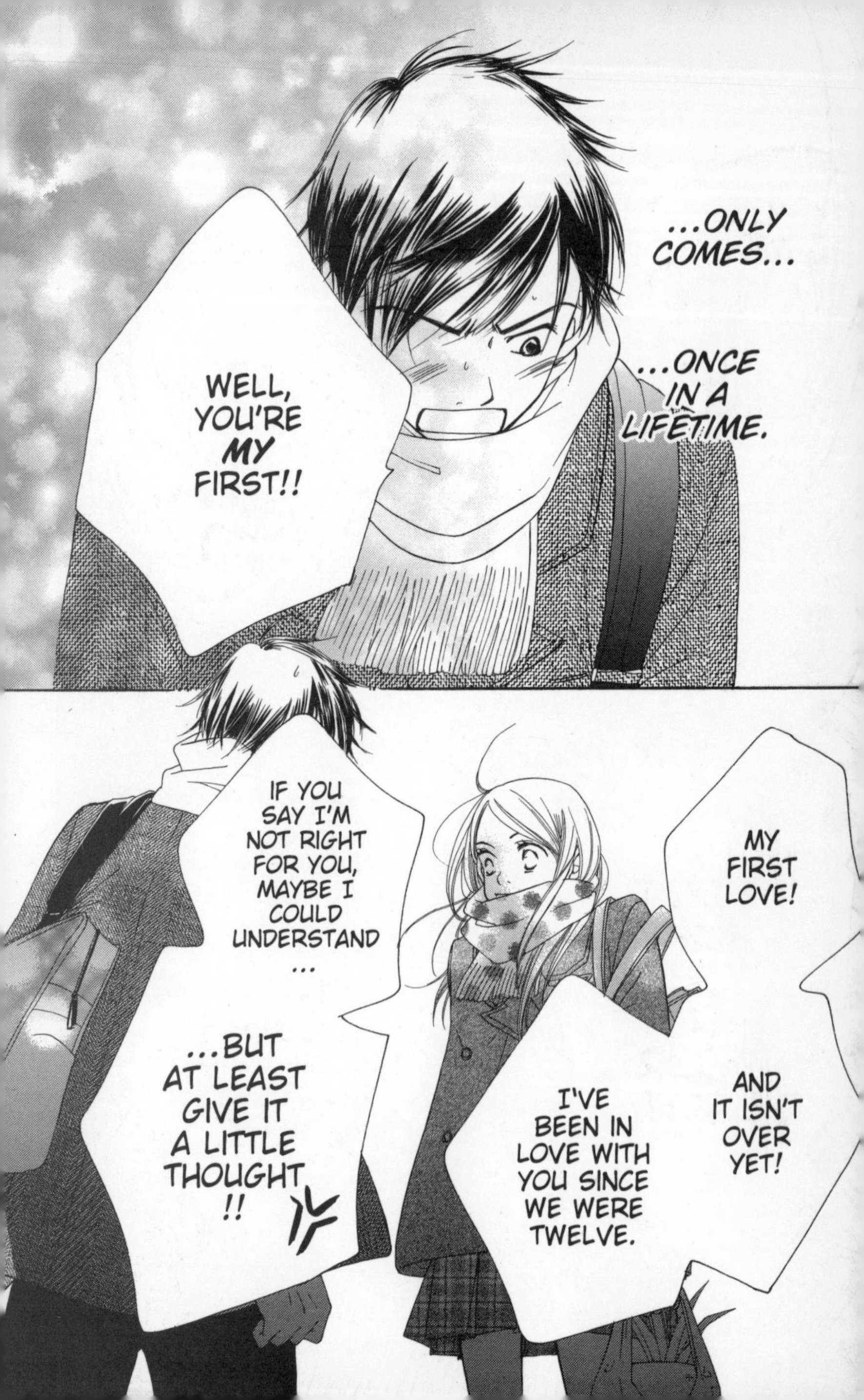
...ONLY COMES...
...ONCE IN A LIFETIME.
WELL, YOU'RE MY FIRST!!
MY FIRST LOVE!
AND IT ISN'T OVER YET!
I'VE BEEN IN LOVE WITH YOU SINCE WE WERE TWELVE.
IF YOU SAY I'M NOT RIGHT FOR YOU, MAYBE I COULD UNDERSTAND...
...BUT AT LEAST GIVE IT A LITTLE THOUGHT!!

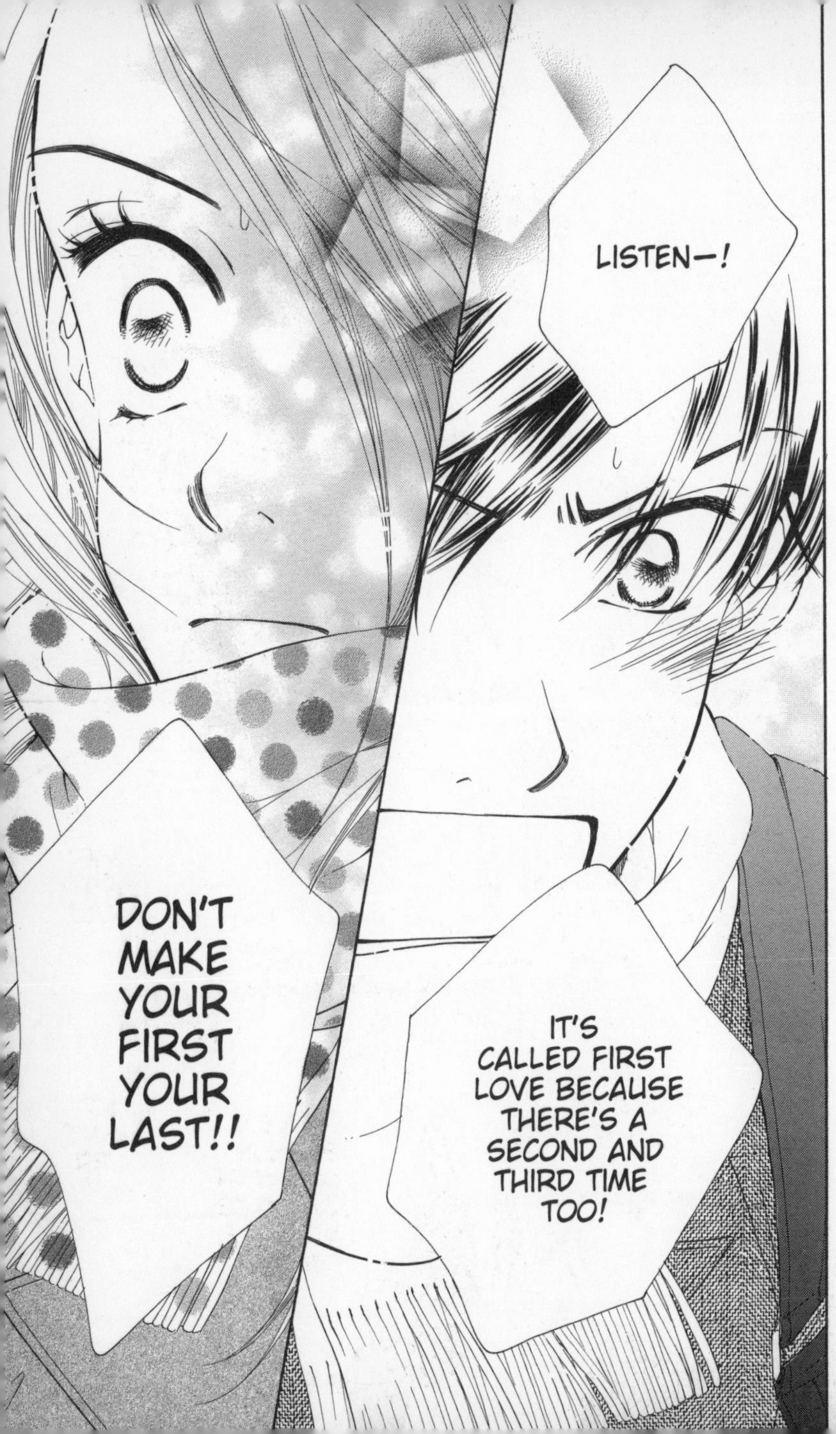
LISTEN—!
IT'S CALLED FIRST LOVE BECAUSE THERE'S A SECOND AND THIRD TIME TOO!
DON'T MAKE YOUR FIRST YOUR LAST!!

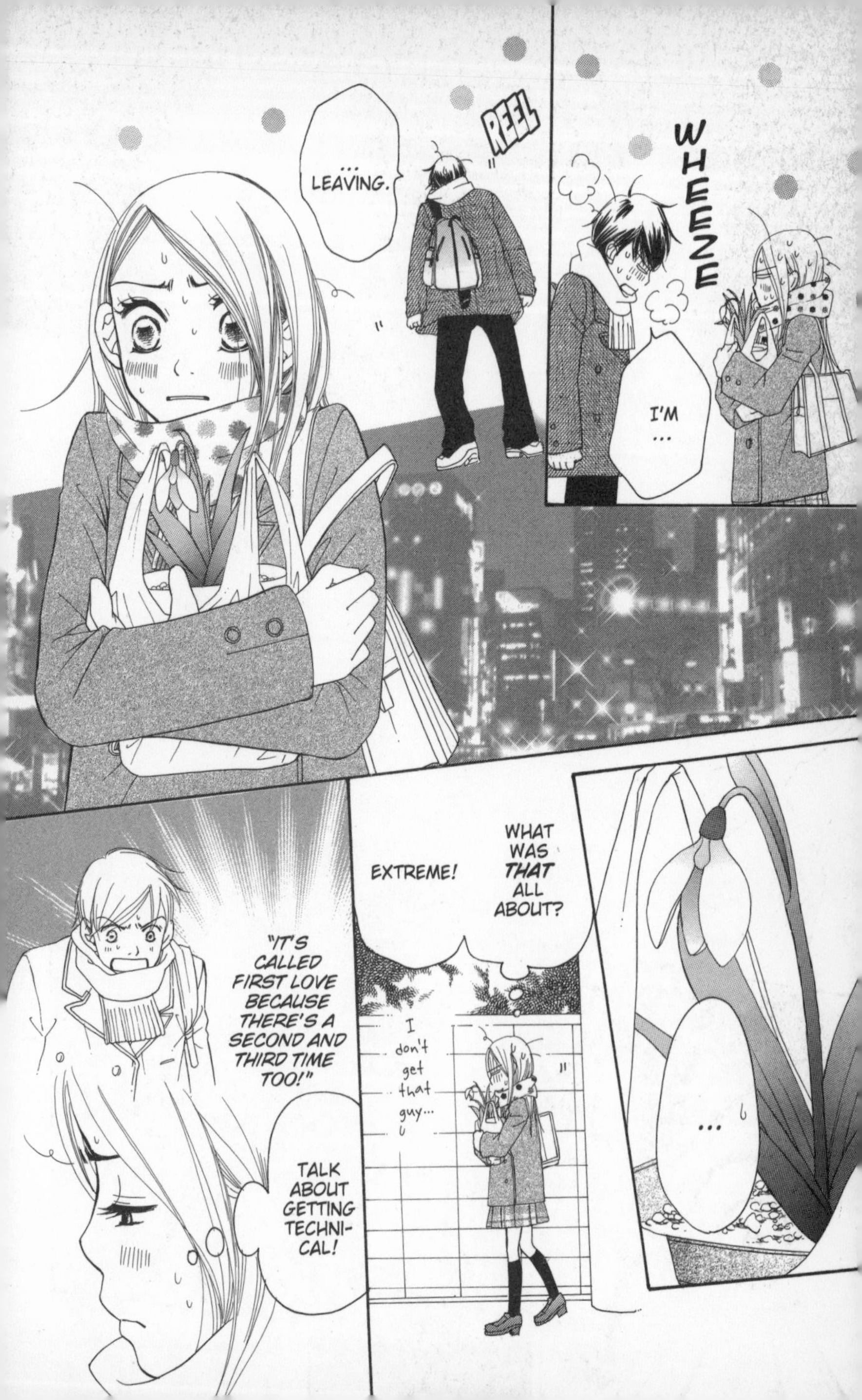
WHEEZE
I'M ...
REEL
... LEAVING.
...
WHAT WAS THAT ALL ABOUT?
EXTREME!
I don't get that guy...
"IT'S CALLED FIRST LOVE BECAUSE THERE'S A SECOND AND THIRD TIME TOO!"
TALK ABOUT GETTING TECHNI-CAL!

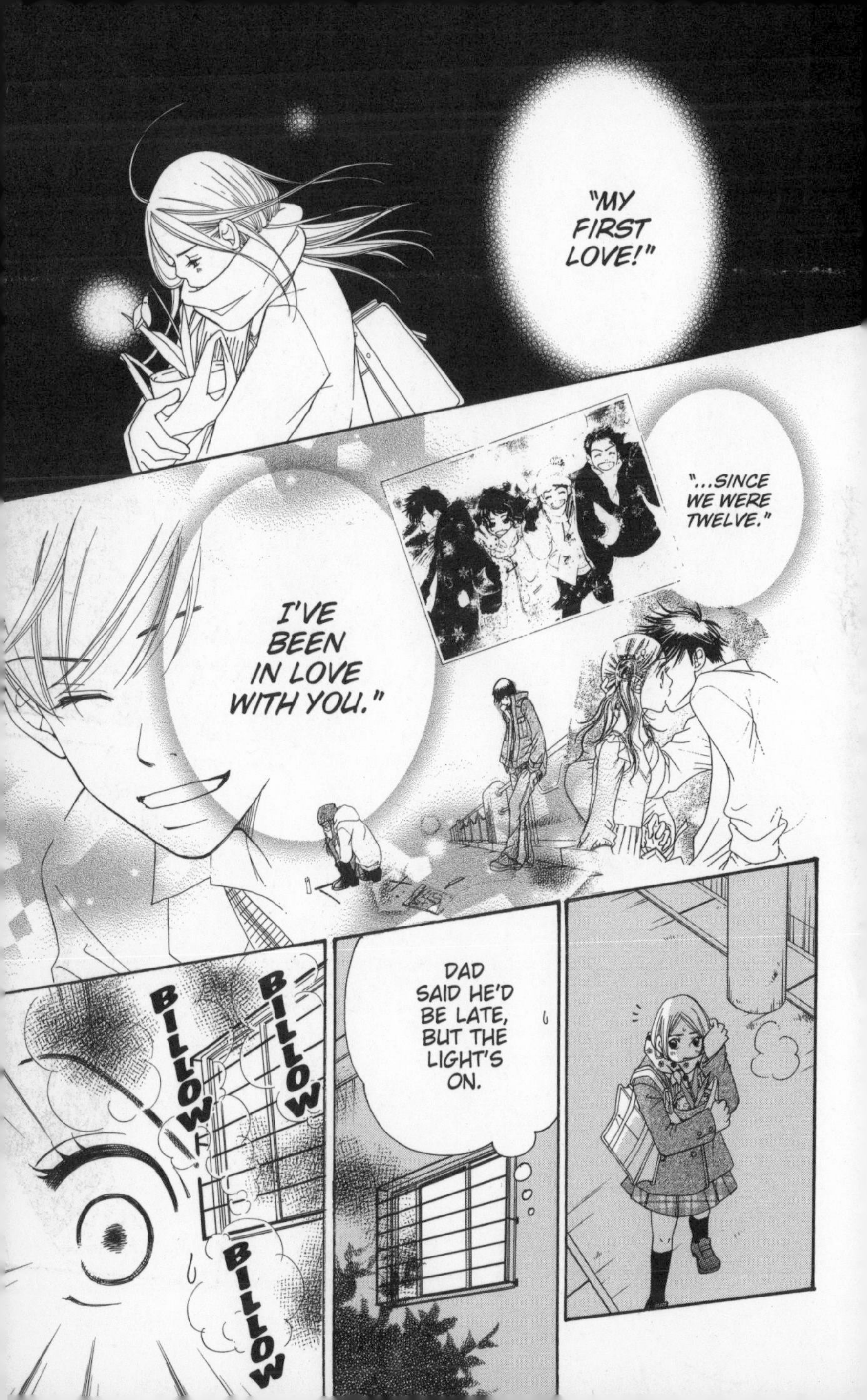
"MY FIRST LOVE!"
"...SINCE WE WERE TWELVE."
I'VE BEEN IN LOVE WITH YOU."
DAD SAID HE'D BE LATE, BUT THE LIGHT'S ON.
BILLOW
BILLOW
BILLOW

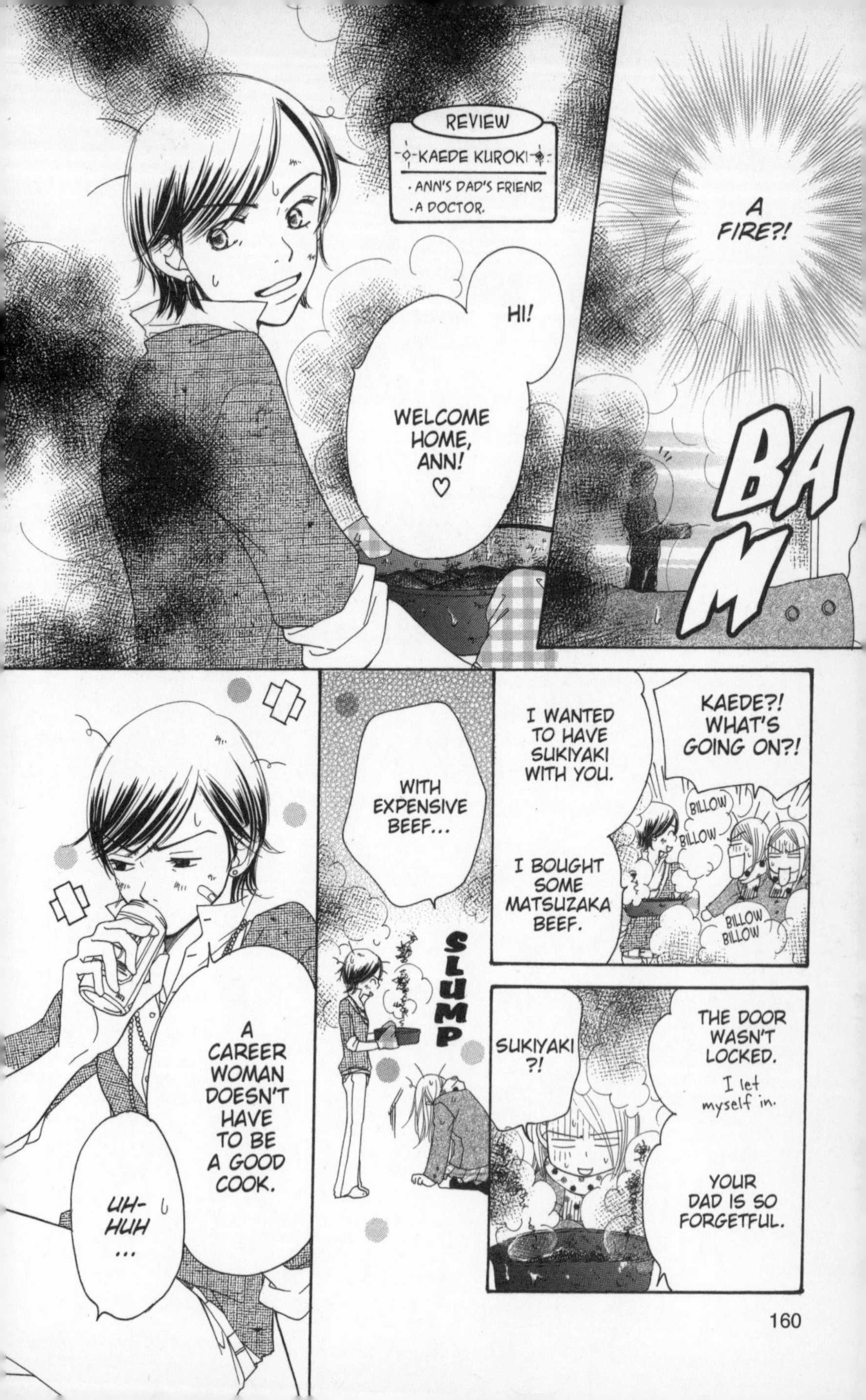
A FIRE?!
BAM
REVIEW
KAEDE KUROKI
· ANN'S DAD'S FRIEND.
· A DOCTOR.
HI!
WELCOME HOME, ANN! ♡
KAEDE?! WHAT'S GOING ON?!
BILLOW
BILLOW
BILLOW BILLOW
I WANTED TO HAVE SUKIYAKI WITH YOU.
I BOUGHT SOME MATSUZAKA BEEF.
THE DOOR WASN'T LOCKED.
I let myself in.
YOUR DAD IS SO FORGETFUL.
SUKIYAKI?!
WITH EXPENSIVE BEEF...
SLUMP
A CAREER WOMAN DOESN'T HAVE TO BE A GOOD COOK.
UH-HUH...

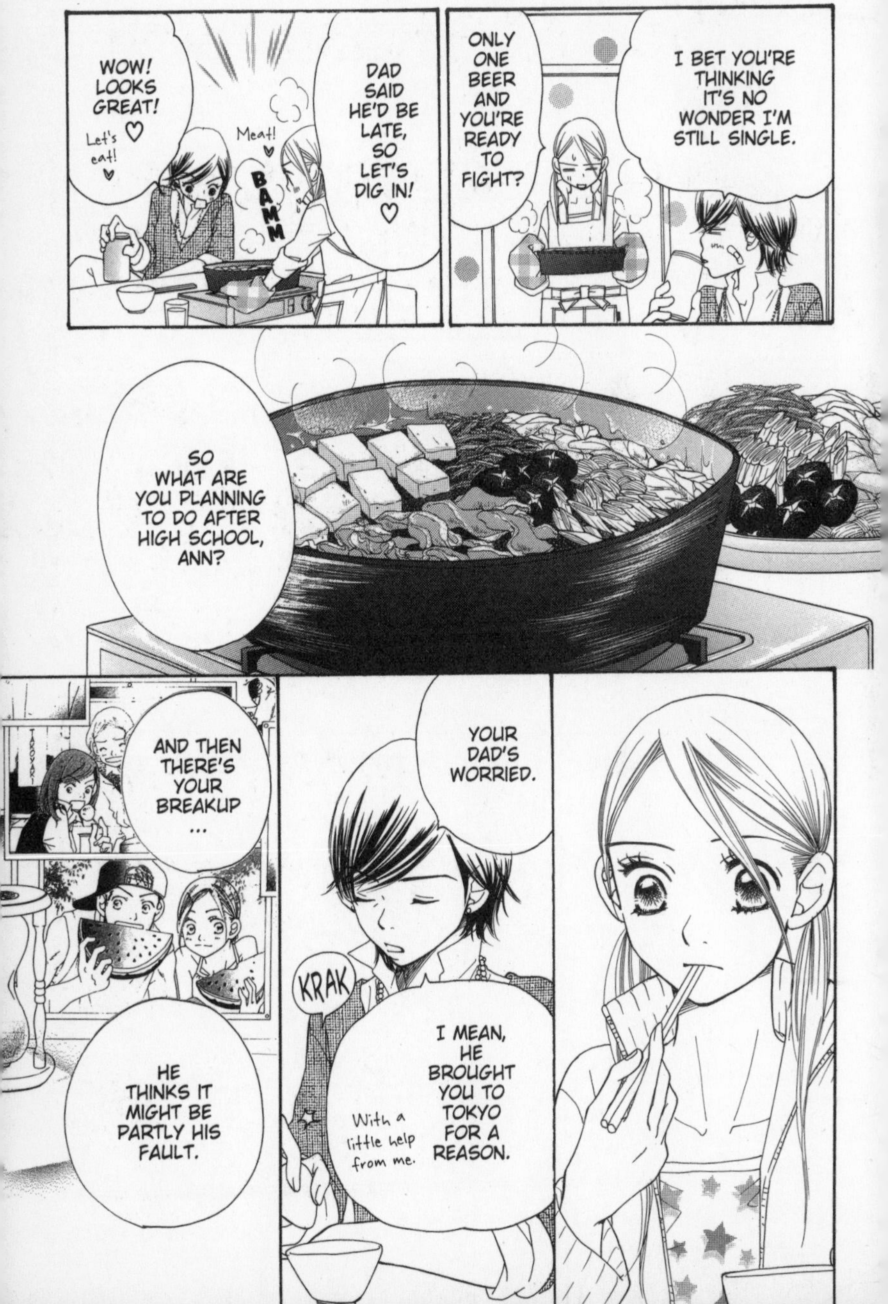
I BET YOU'RE THINKING IT'S NO WONDER I'M STILL SINGLE.
ONLY ONE BEER AND YOU'RE READY TO FIGHT?
DAD SAID HE'D BE LATE, SO LET'S DIG IN! ♡
Meat! ♡
BAMM
WOW! LOOKS GREAT! ♡
Let's eat! ♡
SO WHAT ARE YOU PLANNING TO DO AFTER HIGH SCHOOL, ANN?
YOUR DAD'S WORRIED.
KRAK
I MEAN, HE BROUGHT YOU TO TOKYO FOR A REASON.
With a little help from me.
AND THEN THERE'S YOUR BREAKUP ...
TAKOYAKI
HE THINKS IT MIGHT BE PARTLY HIS FAULT.

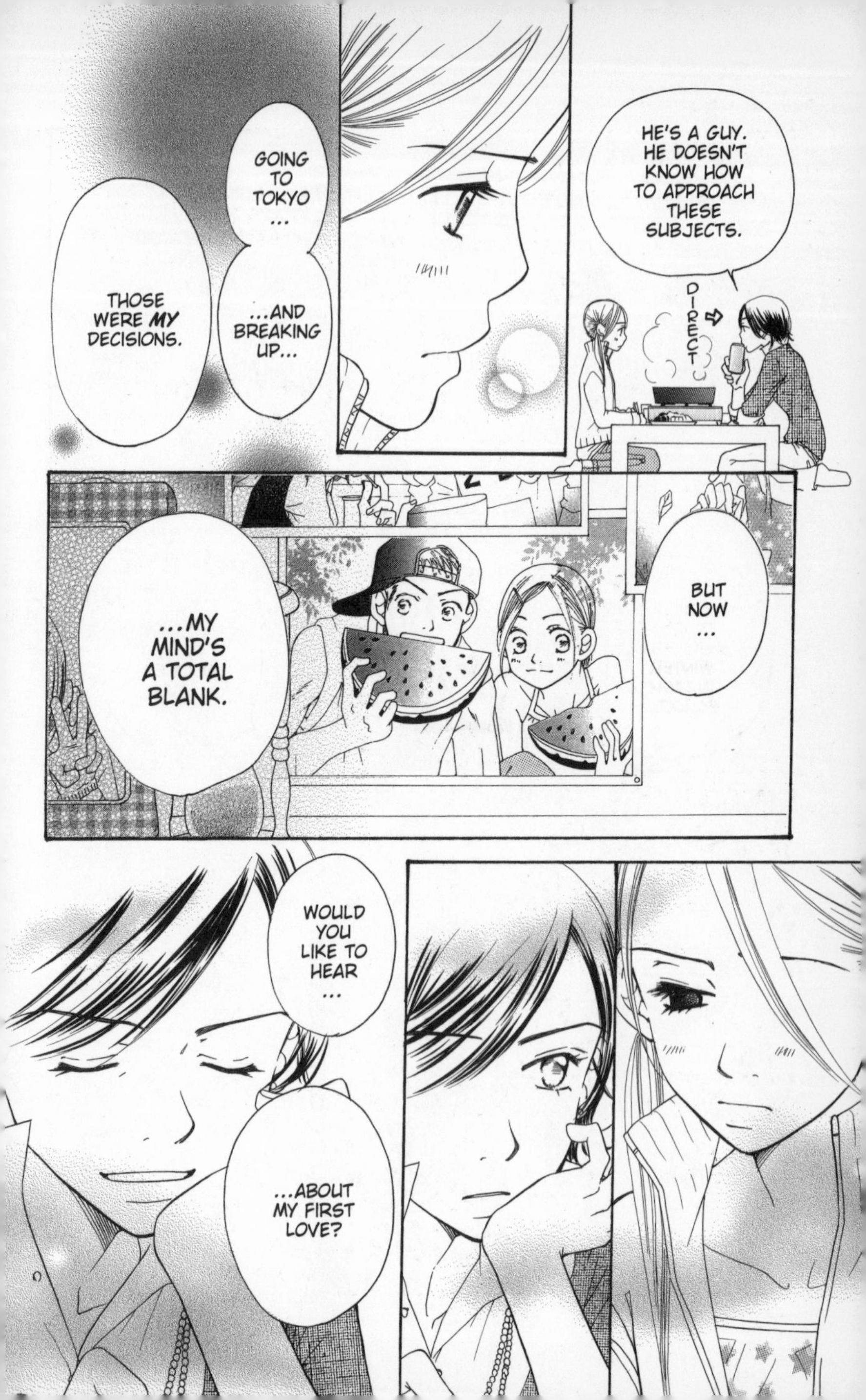
HE'S A GUY. HE DOESN'T KNOW HOW TO APPROACH THESE SUBJECTS.
DIRECT
GOING TO TOKYO...
...AND BREAKING UP...
THOSE WERE *MY* DECISIONS.
BUT NOW...
...MY MIND'S A TOTAL BLANK.
WOULD YOU LIKE TO HEAR...
...ABOUT MY FIRST LOVE?

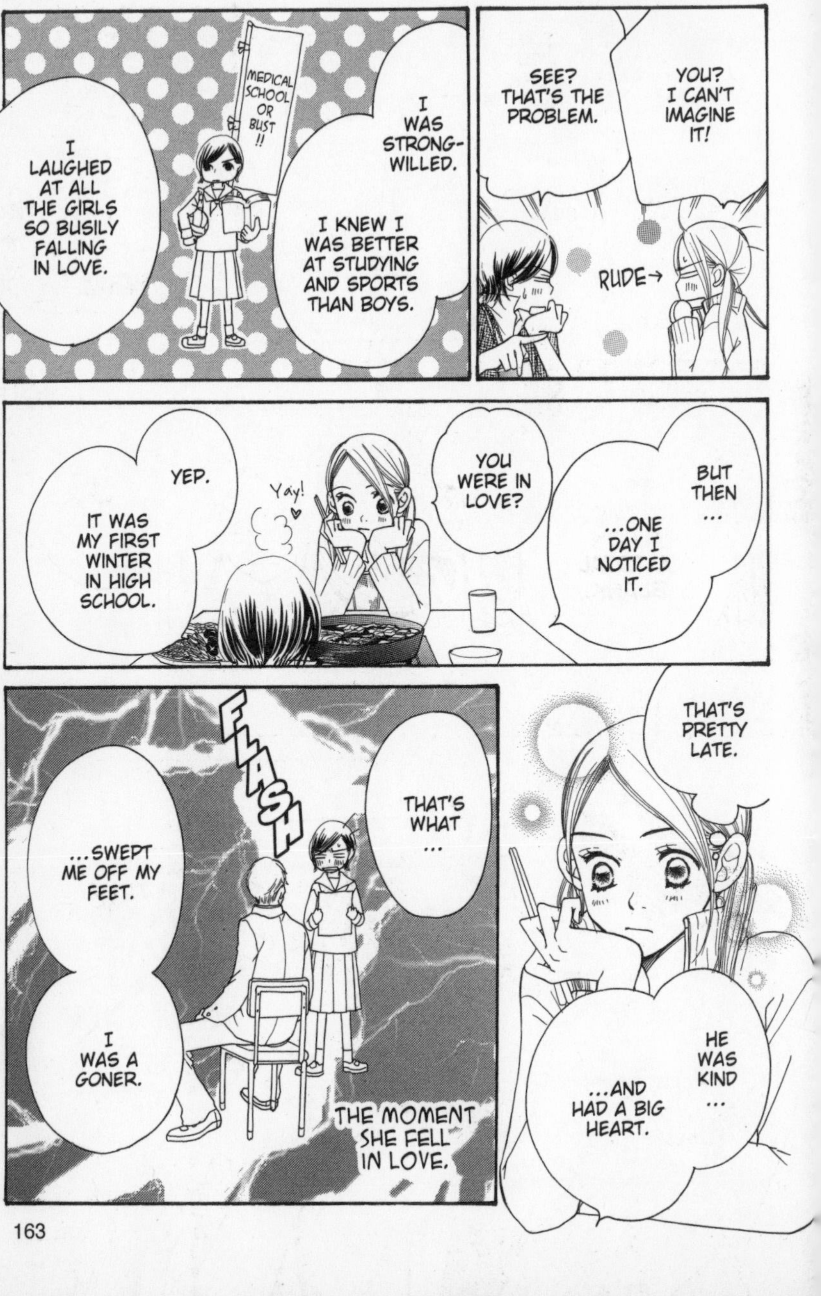
YOU? I CAN'T IMAGINE IT!
SEE? THAT'S THE PROBLEM.
RUDE→
I WAS STRONG-WILLED.
I KNEW I WAS BETTER AT STUDYING AND SPORTS THAN BOYS.
MEDICAL SCHOOL OR BUST!!
I LAUGHED AT ALL THE GIRLS SO BUSILY FALLING IN LOVE.
BUT THEN...
...ONE DAY I NOTICED IT.
YOU WERE IN LOVE?
Yay!
YEP.
IT WAS MY FIRST WINTER IN HIGH SCHOOL.
THAT'S PRETTY LATE.
HE WAS KIND...
...AND HAD A BIG HEART.
FLASH
THAT'S WHAT...
...SWEPT ME OFF MY FEET.
I WAS A GONER.
THE MOMENT SHE FELL IN LOVE.

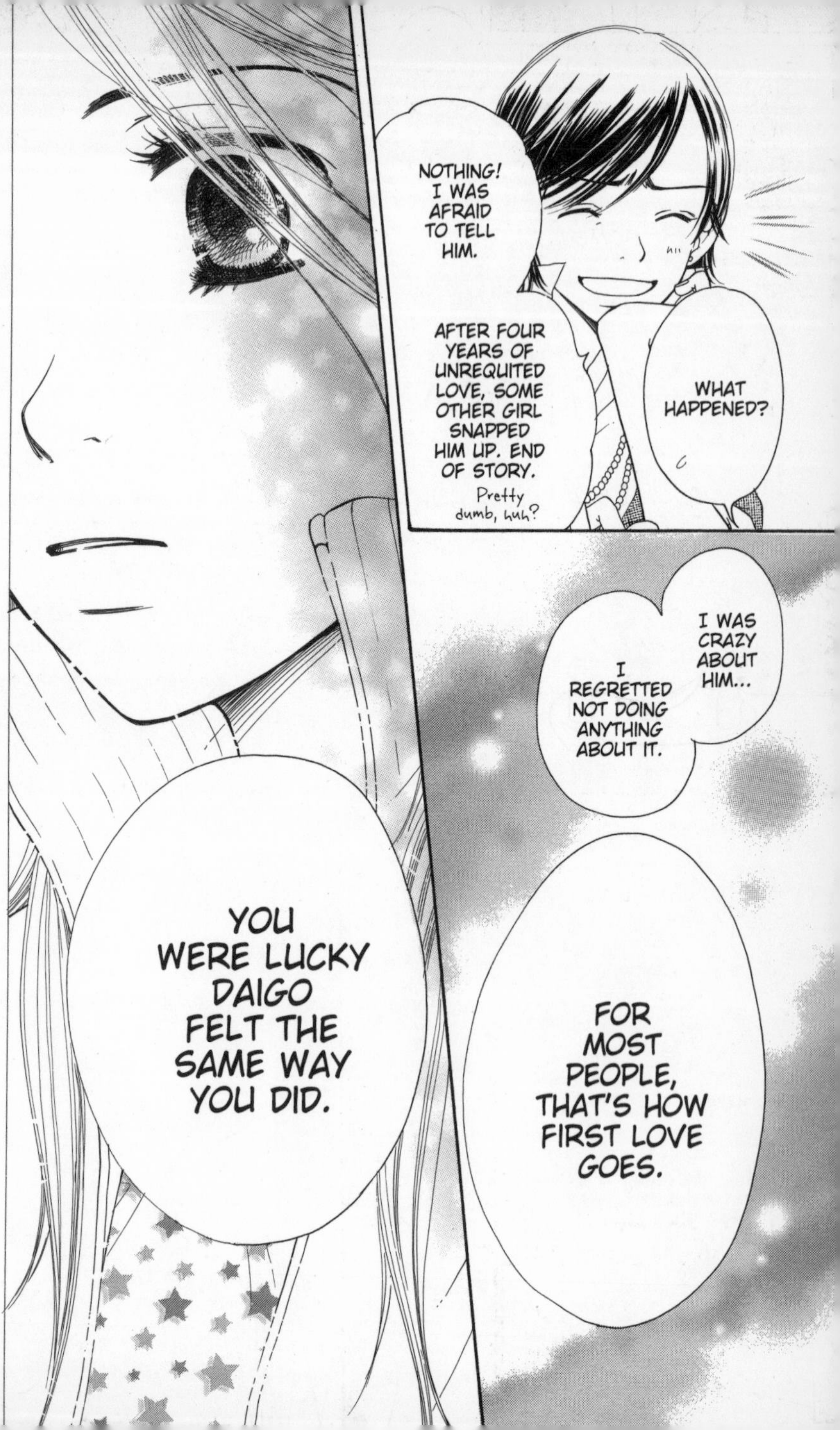
WHAT HAPPENED?
NOTHING! I WAS AFRAID TO TELL HIM.
AFTER FOUR YEARS OF UNREQUITED LOVE, SOME OTHER GIRL SNAPPED HIM UP. END OF STORY.
Pretty dumb, huh?
I WAS CRAZY ABOUT HIM...
I REGRETTED NOT DOING ANYTHING ABOUT IT.
FOR MOST PEOPLE, THAT'S HOW FIRST LOVE GOES.
YOU WERE LUCKY DAIGO FELT THE SAME WAY YOU DID.

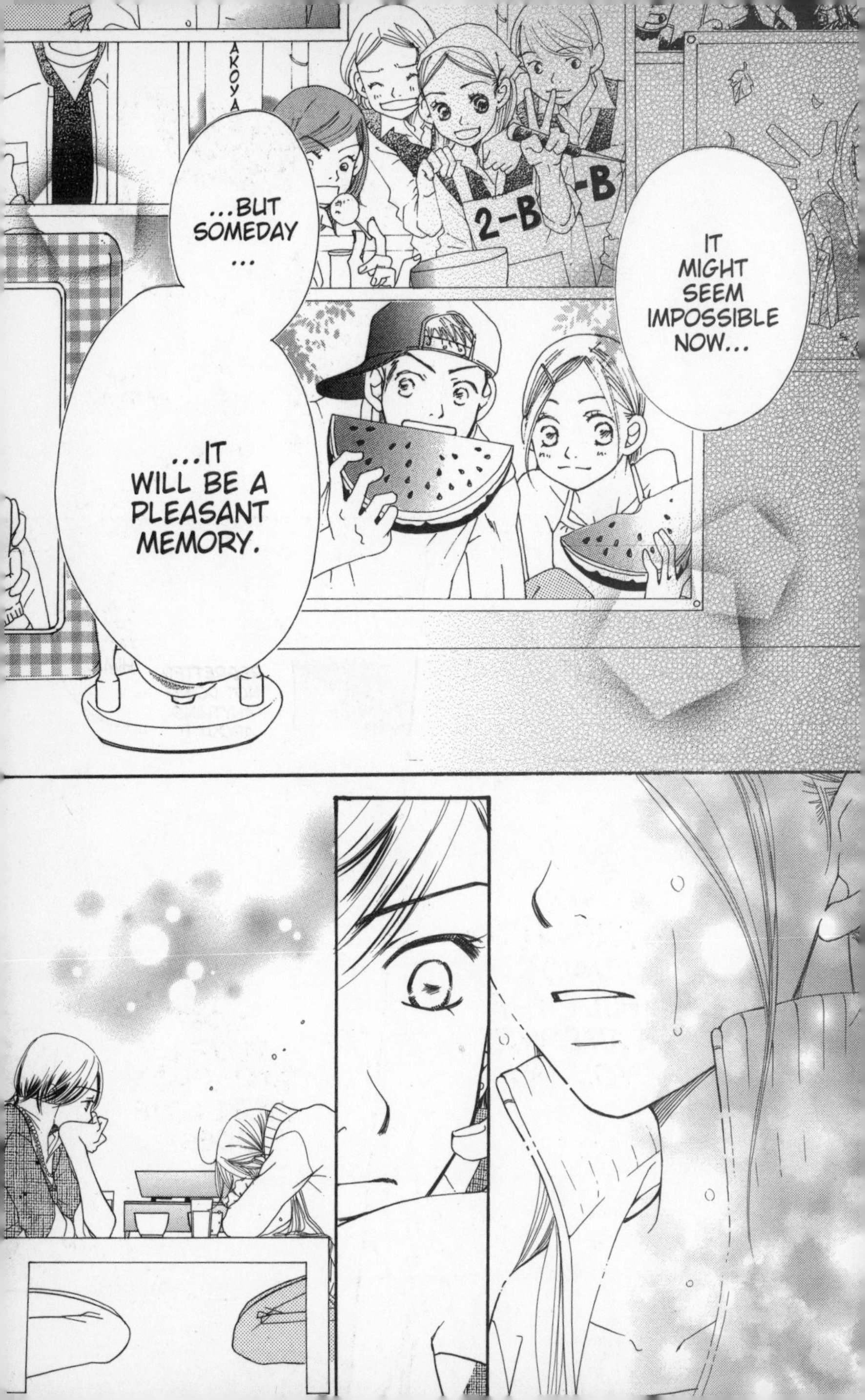
AKOYA
2-B
-B
IT MIGHT SEEM IMPOSSIBLE NOW...
...BUT SOMEDAY...
...IT WILL BE A PLEASANT MEMORY.

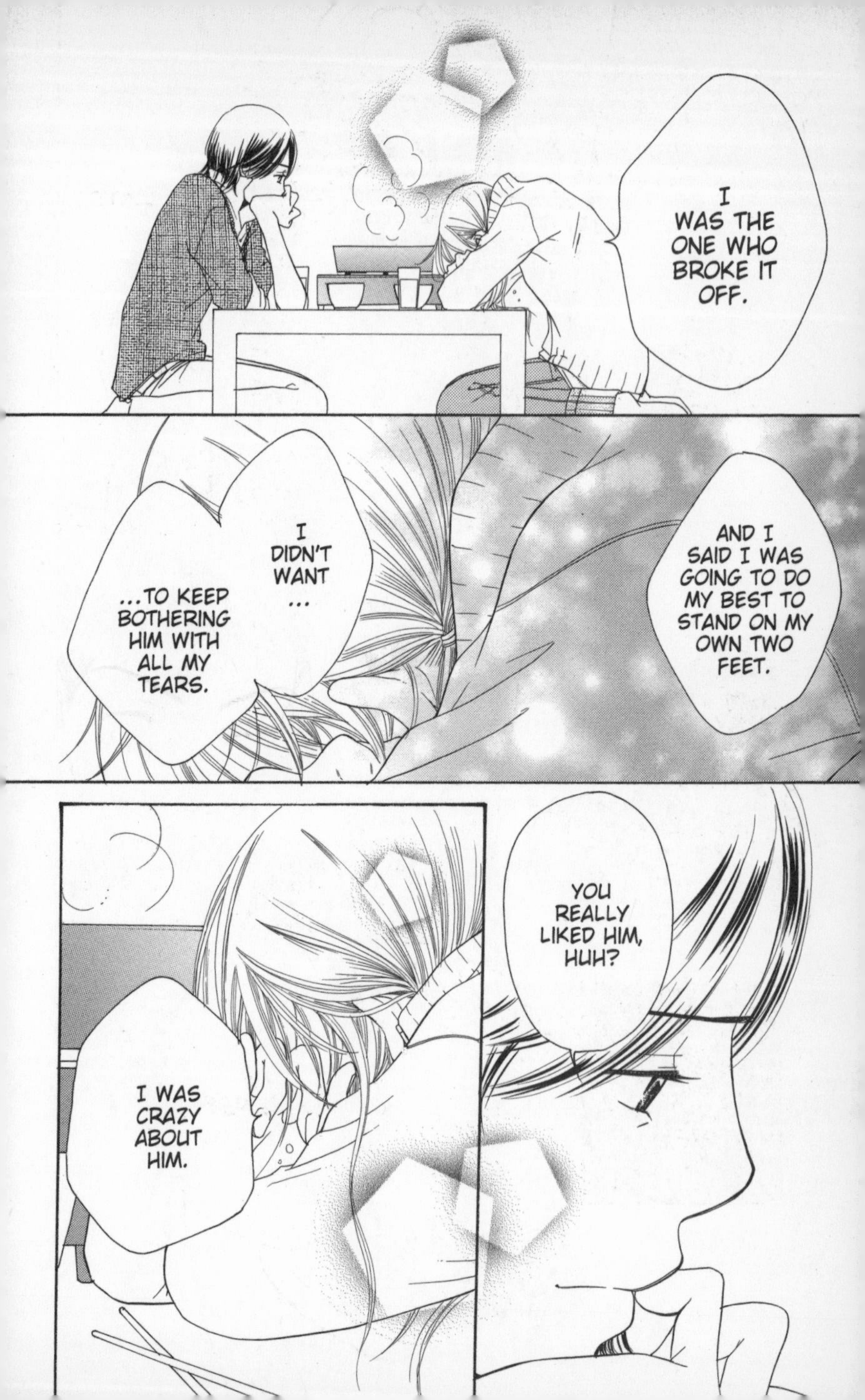
I WAS THE ONE WHO BROKE IT OFF.
AND I SAID I WAS GOING TO DO MY BEST TO STAND ON MY OWN TWO FEET.
I DIDN'T WANT ...
...TO KEEP BOTHERING HIM WITH ALL MY TEARS.
YOU REALLY LIKED HIM, HUH?
I WAS CRAZY ABOUT HIM.

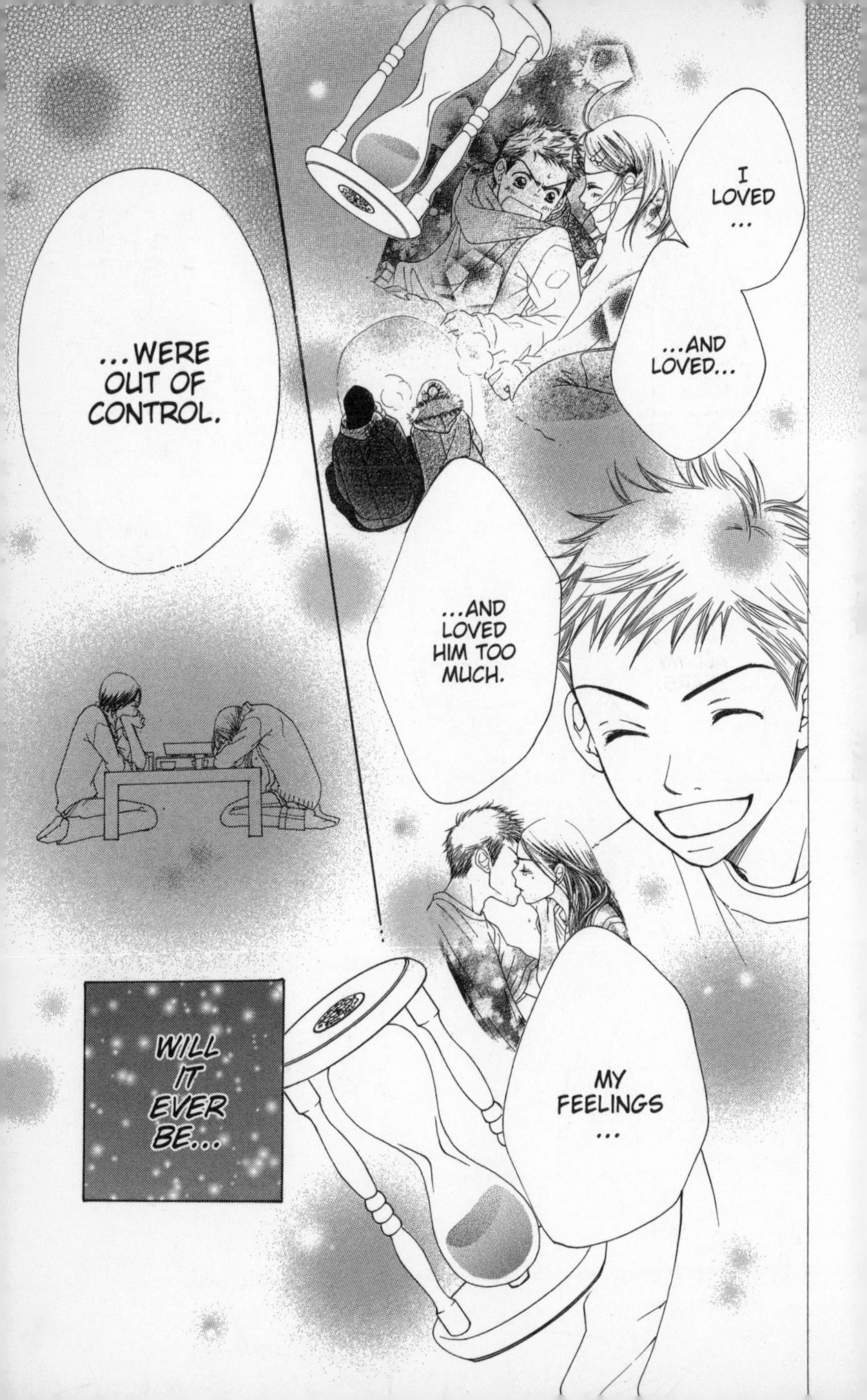
I LOVED ...
...AND LOVED...
...AND LOVED HIM TOO MUCH.
MY FEELINGS ...
...WERE OUT OF CONTROL.
WILL IT EVER BE...

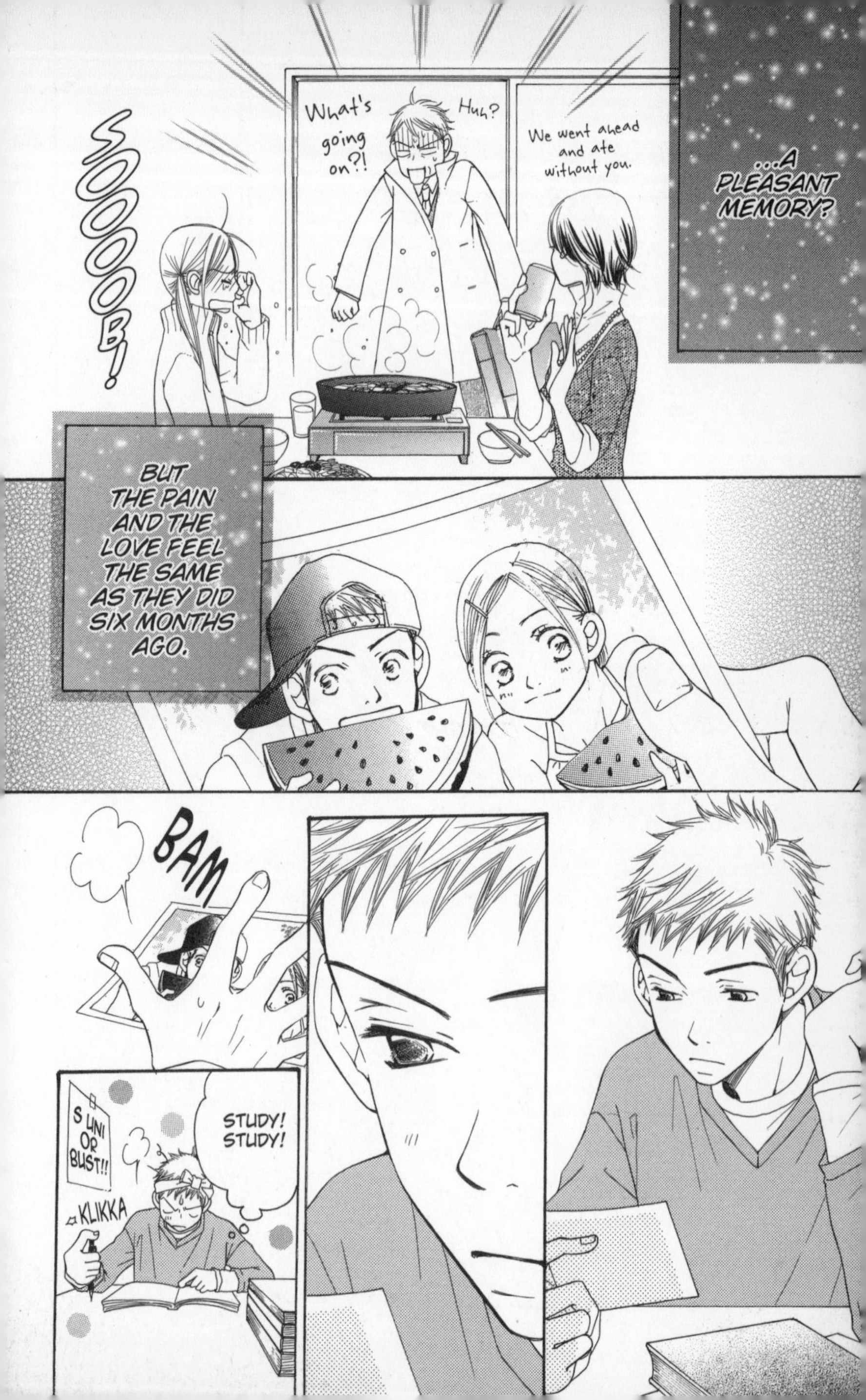
...A PLEASANT MEMORY?
We went ahead and ate without you.
Huh?
What's going on?!
SOOOOOB!
BUT THE PAIN AND THE LOVE FEEL THE SAME AS THEY DID SIX MONTHS AGO.
BAM
STUDY! STUDY!
S UNI OR BUST!!
KLIKKA

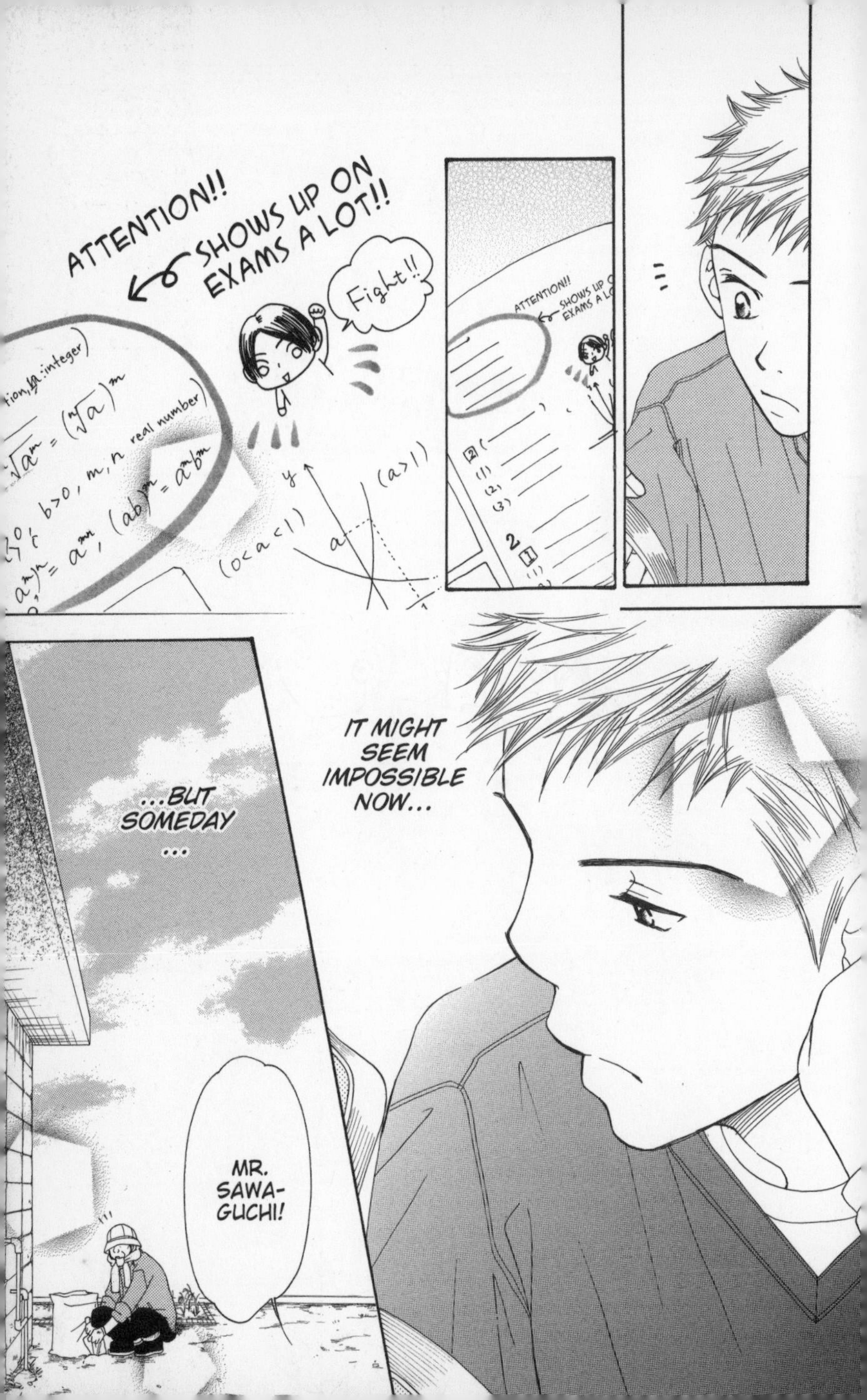
ATTENTION!!
SHOWS UP ON EXAMS A LOT!!
ATTENTION!!
SHOWS UP ON EXAMS A LOT!!
Fight!!
IT MIGHT SEEM IMPOSSIBLE NOW...
...BUT SOMEDAY...
MR. SAWA-GUCHI!

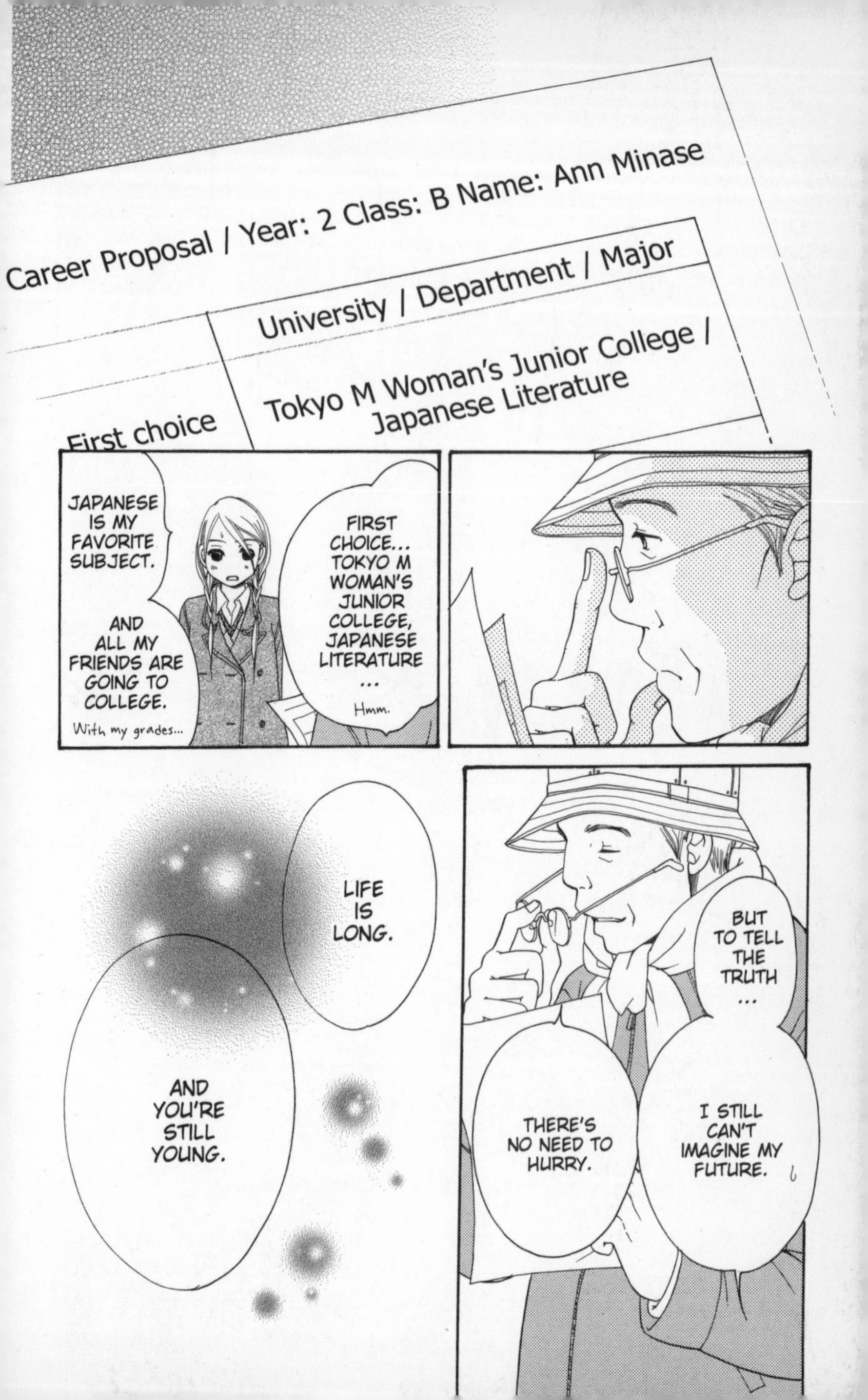
Career Proposal / Year: 2 Class: B Name: Ann Minase
University / Department / Major
First choice
Tokyo M Woman's Junior College / Japanese Literature
FIRST CHOICE... TOKYO M WOMAN'S JUNIOR COLLEGE, JAPANESE LITERATURE ...
Hmm.
JAPANESE IS MY FAVORITE SUBJECT.
AND ALL MY FRIENDS ARE GOING TO COLLEGE.
With my grades...
BUT TO TELL THE TRUTH ...
I STILL CAN'T IMAGINE MY FUTURE.
THERE'S NO NEED TO HURRY.
LIFE IS LONG.
AND YOU'RE STILL YOUNG.

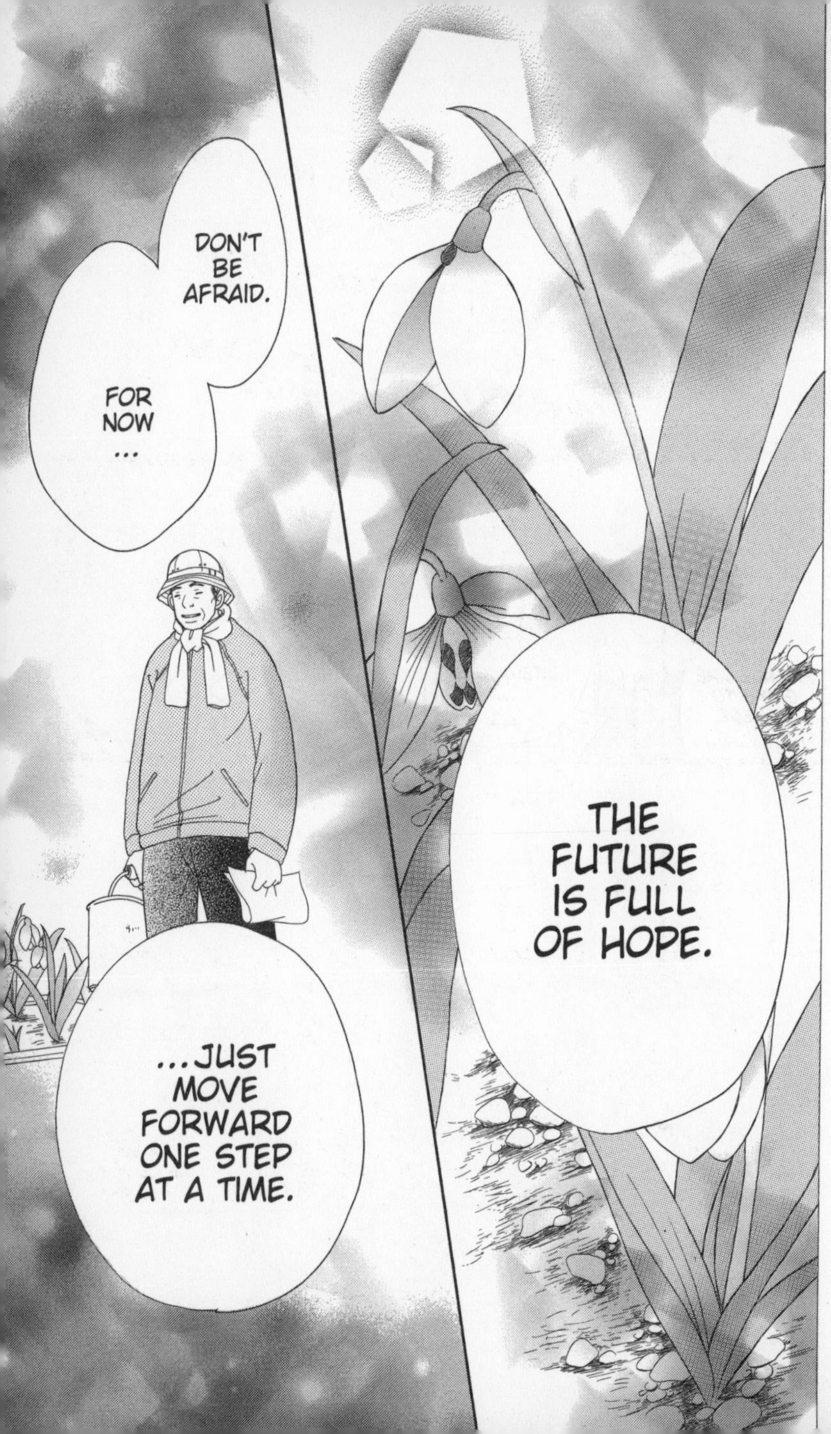
THE FUTURE IS FULL OF HOPE.
DON'T BE AFRAID.
FOR NOW ...
...JUST MOVE FORWARD ONE STEP AT A TIME.

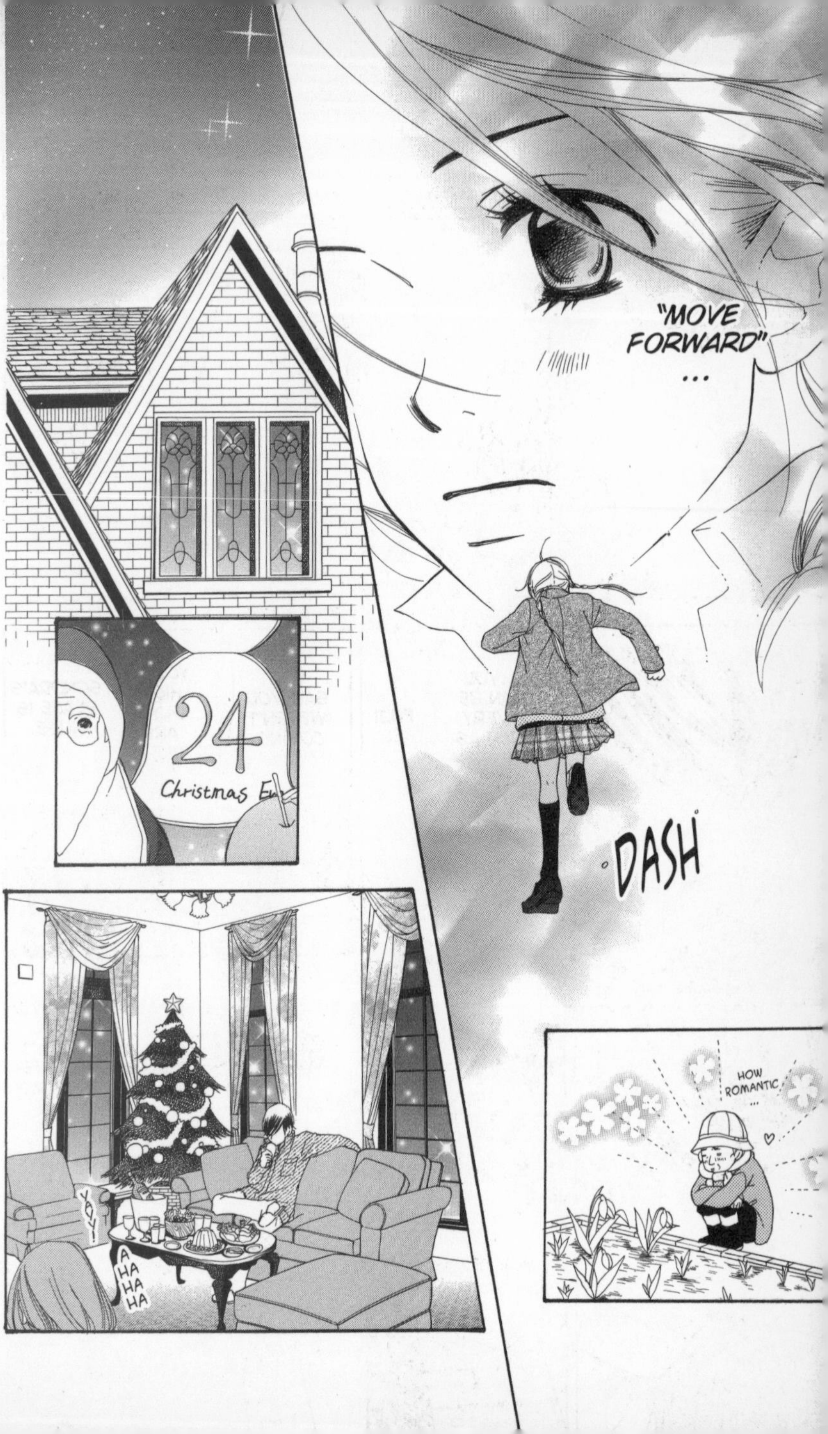
"MOVE FORWARD"
...
DASH
HOW ROMANTIC ...
24
Christmas Ev
YAY!
A HA HA HA HA

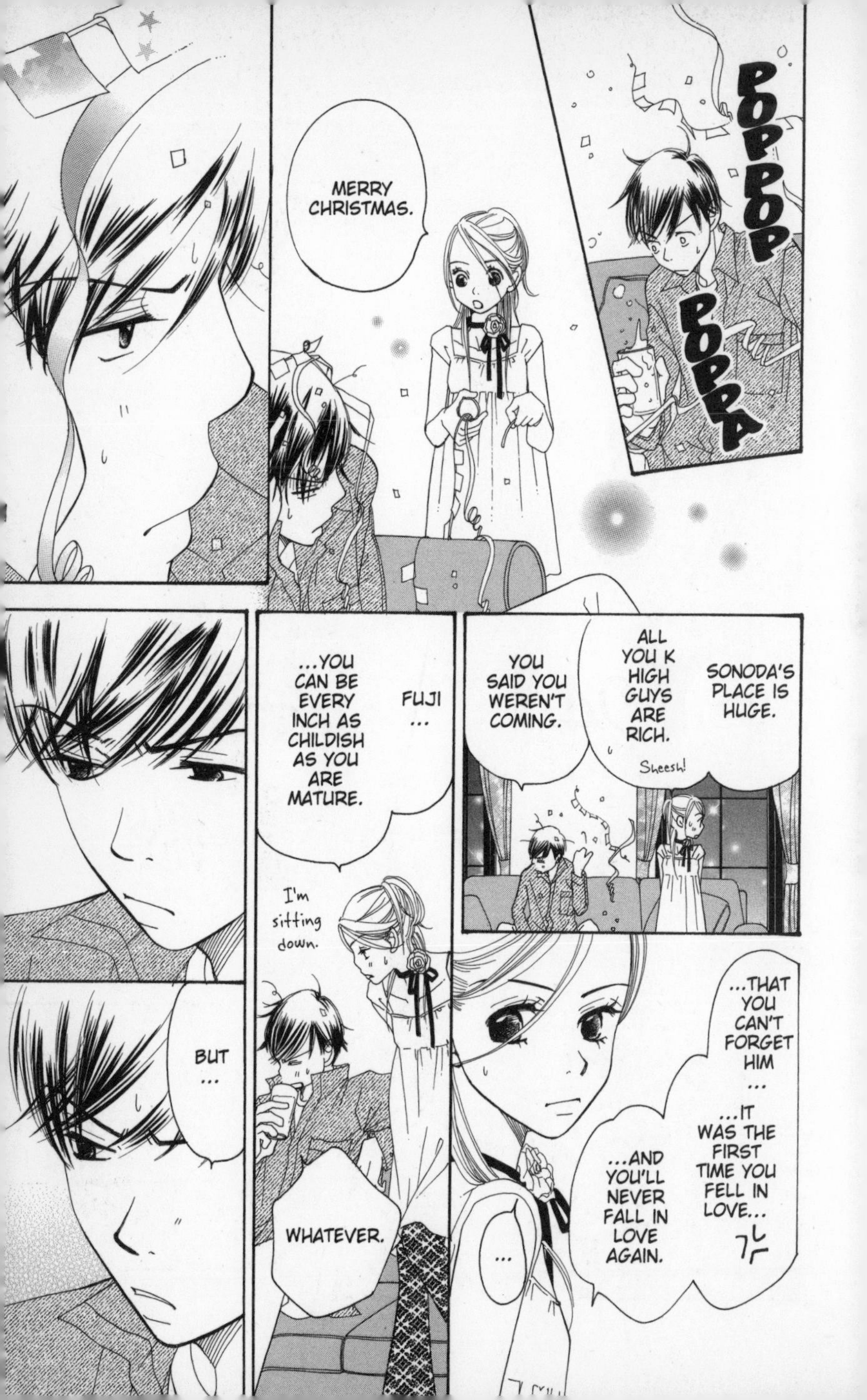
POP POP
POPPA
MERRY CHRISTMAS.
SONODA'S PLACE IS HUGE.
ALL YOU K HIGH GUYS ARE RICH.
Sheesh!
YOU SAID YOU WEREN'T COMING.
FUJI...
...YOU CAN BE EVERY INCH AS CHILDISH AS YOU ARE MATURE.
...THAT YOU CAN'T FORGET HIM...
...IT WAS THE FIRST TIME YOU FELL IN LOVE...
...AND YOU'LL NEVER FALL IN LOVE AGAIN.
...
I'm sitting down.
WHATEVER.
BUT...

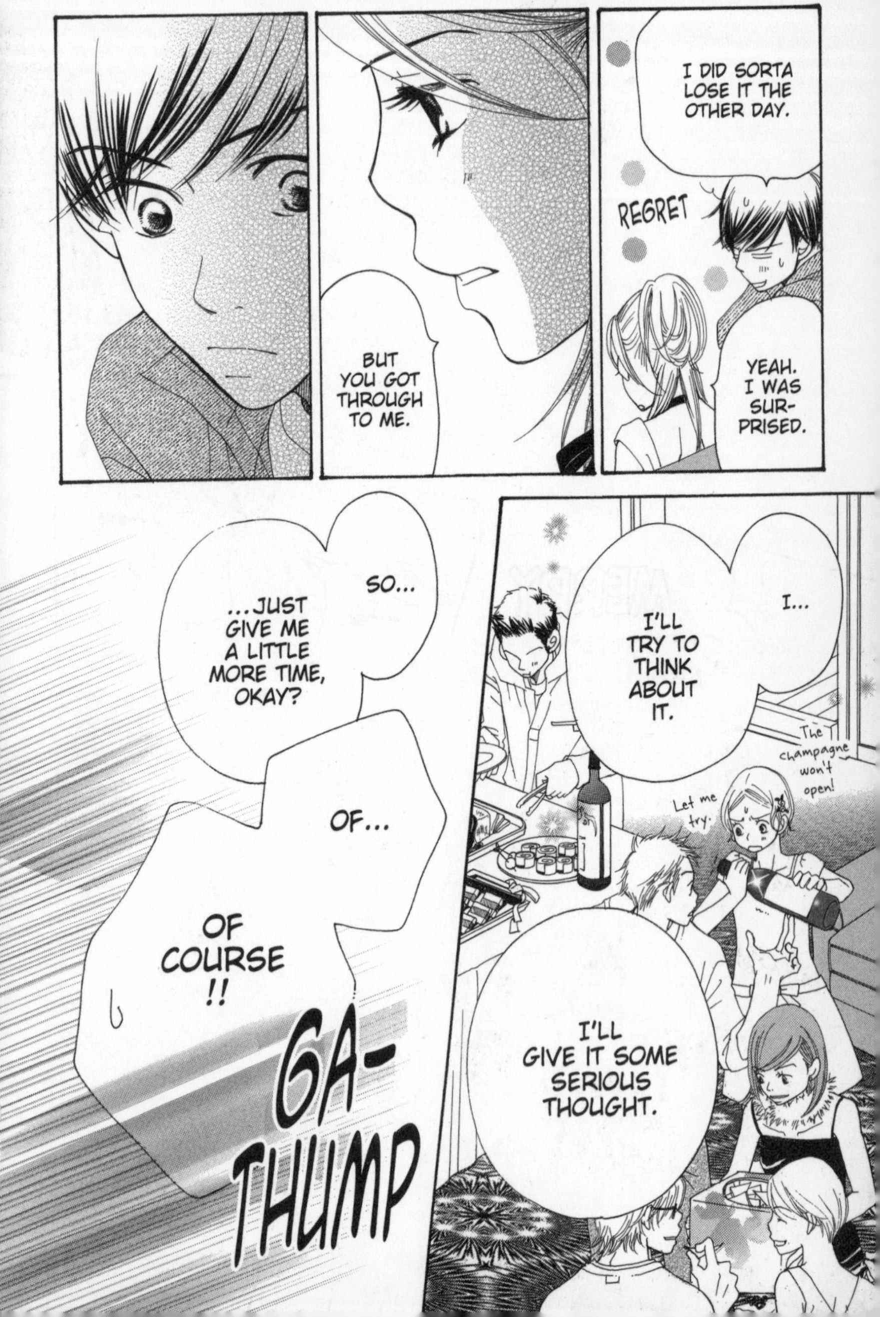
I DID SORTA LOSE IT THE OTHER DAY.
REGRET
YEAH. I WAS SUR-PRISED.
BUT YOU GOT THROUGH TO ME.
I...
I'LL TRY TO THINK ABOUT IT.
The champagne won't open!
Let me try.
I'LL GIVE IT SOME SERIOUS THOUGHT.
SO...
...JUST GIVE ME A LITTLE MORE TIME, OKAY?
OF...
OF COURSE !!
GA-THUMP

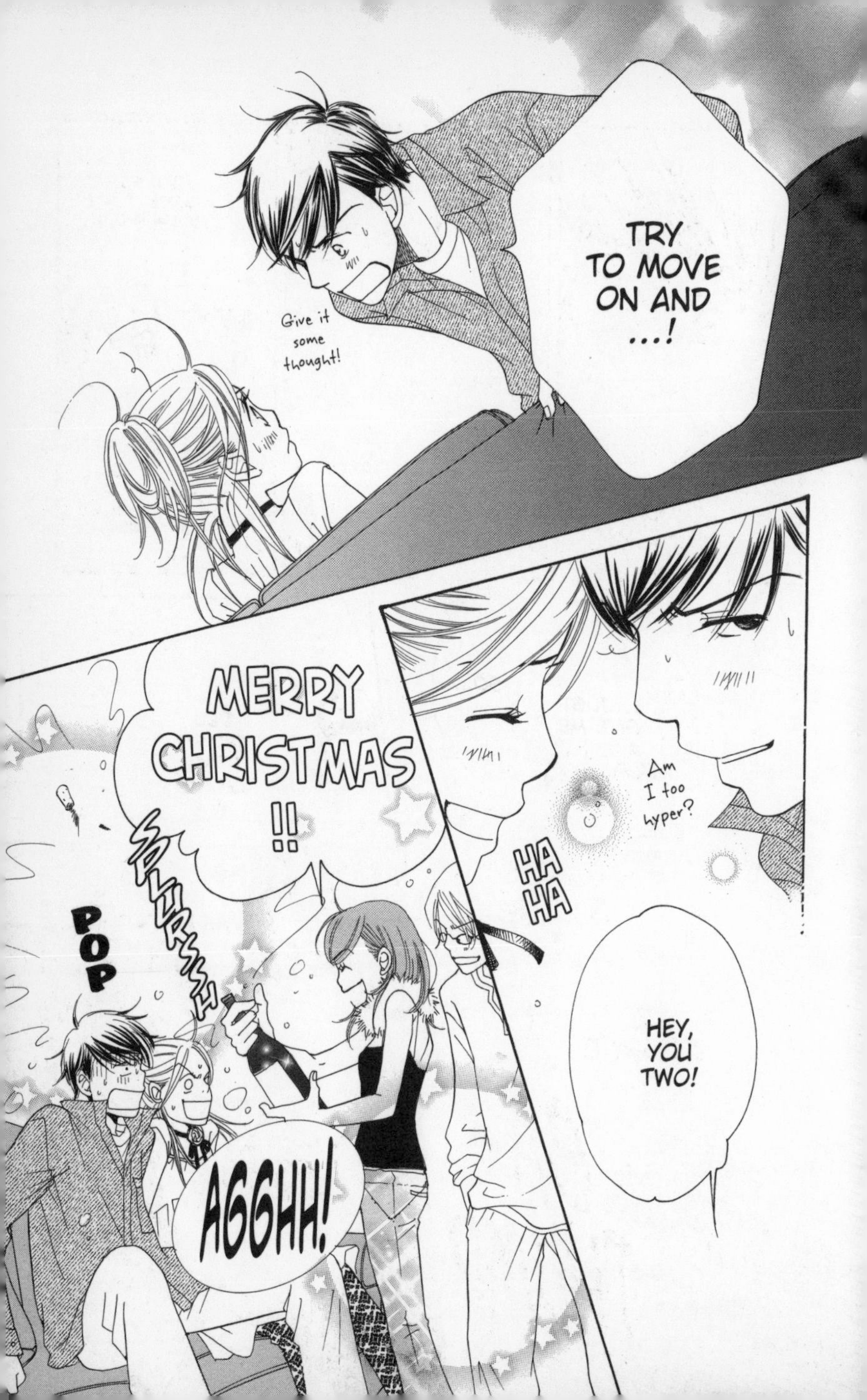
TRY TO MOVE ON AND ...!
Give it some thought!
Am I too hyper?
HA HA
HEY, YOU TWO!
MERRY CHRISTMAS !!
POP
AGGHH!

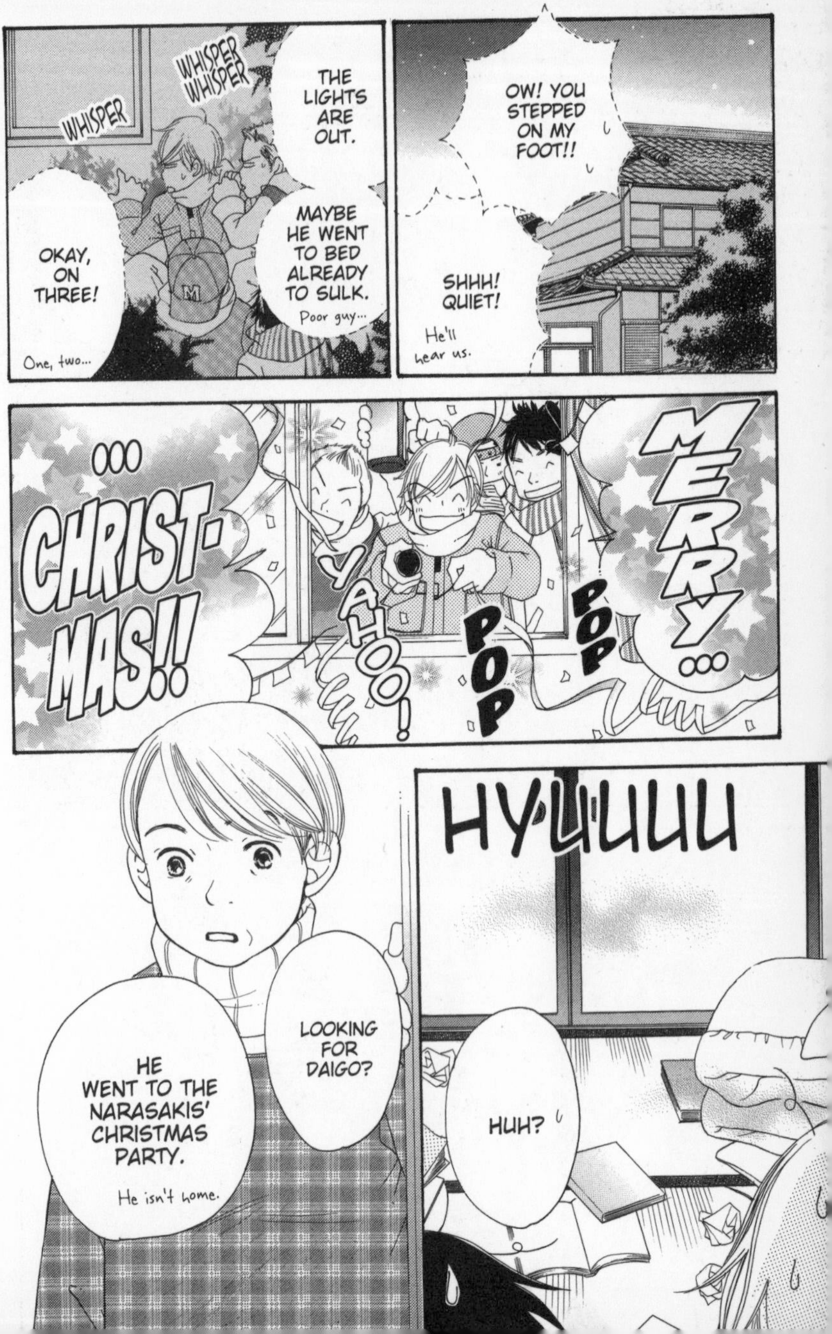
OW! YOU STEPPED ON MY FOOT!!
SHHH! QUIET!
He'll hear us.
THE LIGHTS ARE OUT.
WHISPER WHISPER
WHISPER
MAYBE HE WENT TO BED ALREADY TO SULK.
Poor guy...
OKAY, ON THREE!
One, two...
MERRY...
POP POP
POP
YAHOO!
...CHRIST-MAS!!
HYUUUU
HUH?
LOOKING FOR DAIGO?
HE WENT TO THE NARASAKIS' CHRISTMAS PARTY.
He isn't home.

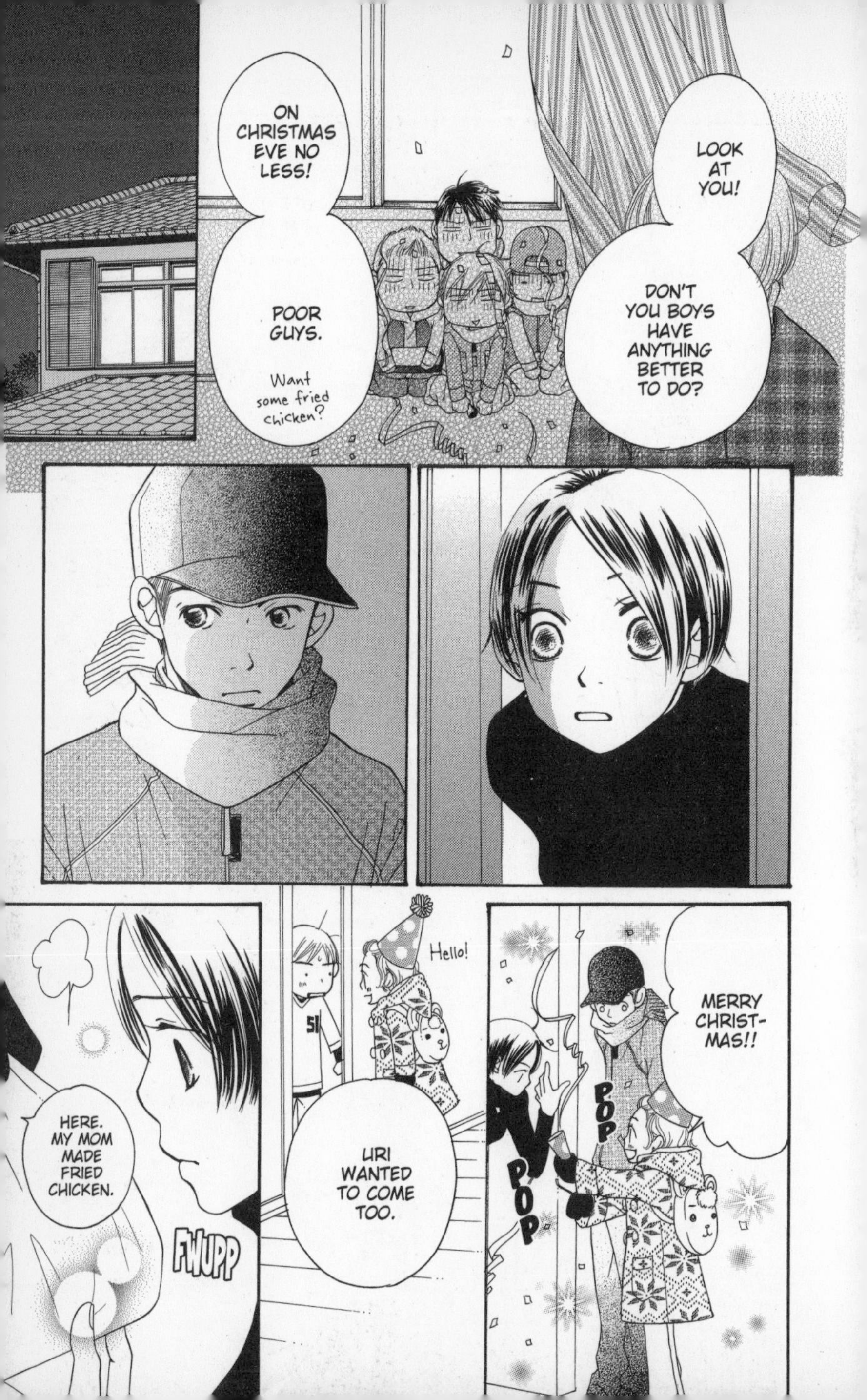
LOOK AT YOU!
DON'T YOU BOYS HAVE ANYTHING BETTER TO DO?
ON CHRISTMAS EVE NO LESS!
POOR GUYS.
Want some fried chicken?
MERRY CHRIST-MAS!!
POP
POP
POP
Hello!
URI WANTED TO COME TOO.
HERE. MY MOM MADE FRIED CHICKEN.
FWUPP

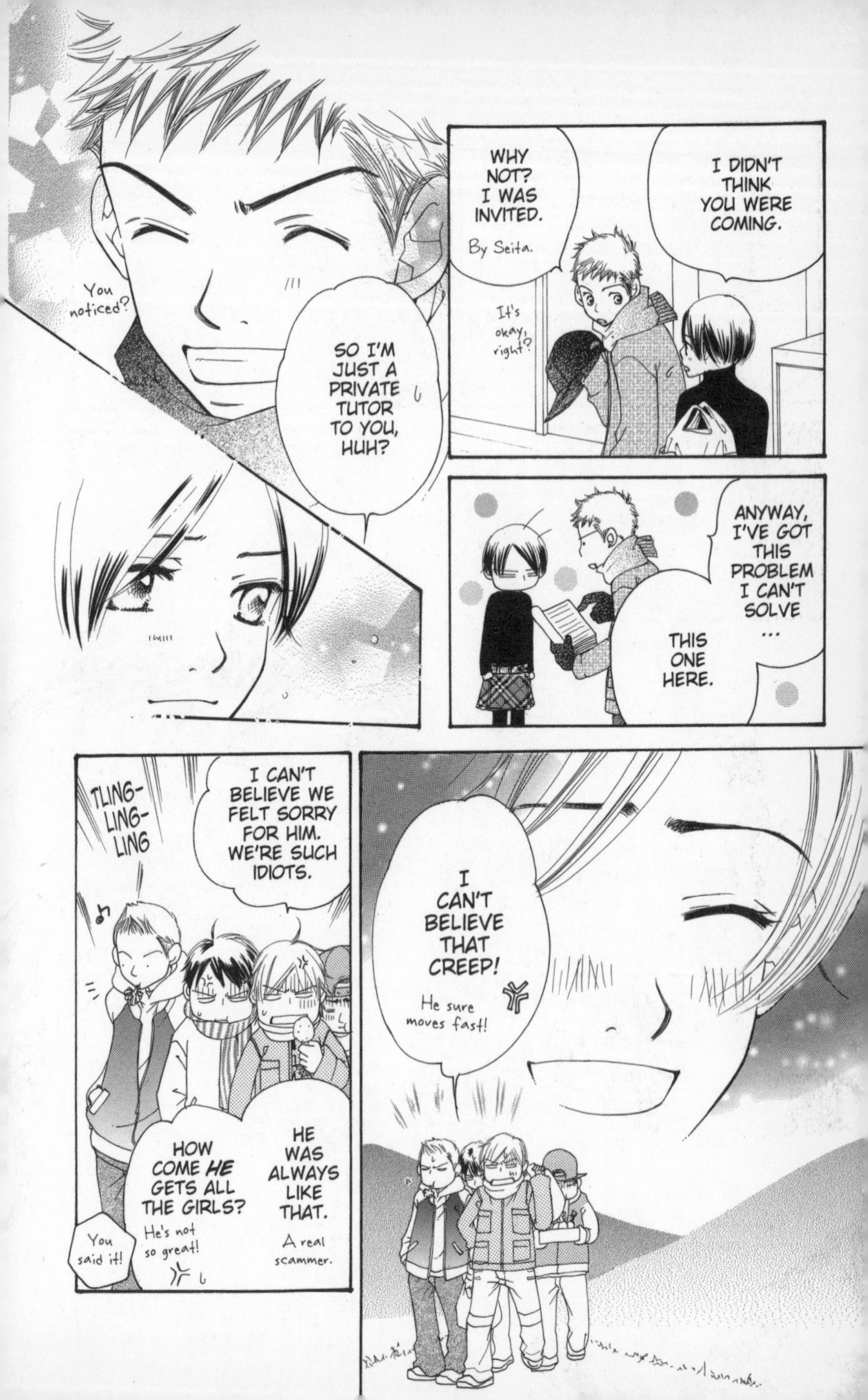
I DIDN'T THINK YOU WERE COMING.
WHY NOT? I WAS INVITED.
By Seita.
It's okay, right?
ANYWAY, I'VE GOT THIS PROBLEM I CAN'T SOLVE ...
THIS ONE HERE.
SO I'M JUST A PRIVATE TUTOR TO YOU, HUH?
You noticed?
I CAN'T BELIEVE THAT CREEP!
He sure moves fast!
I CAN'T BELIEVE WE FELT SORRY FOR HIM. WE'RE SUCH IDIOTS.
TLING-LING-LING
HE WAS ALWAYS LIKE THAT.
A real scammer.
HOW COME *HE* GETS ALL THE GIRLS?
He's not so great!
You said it!

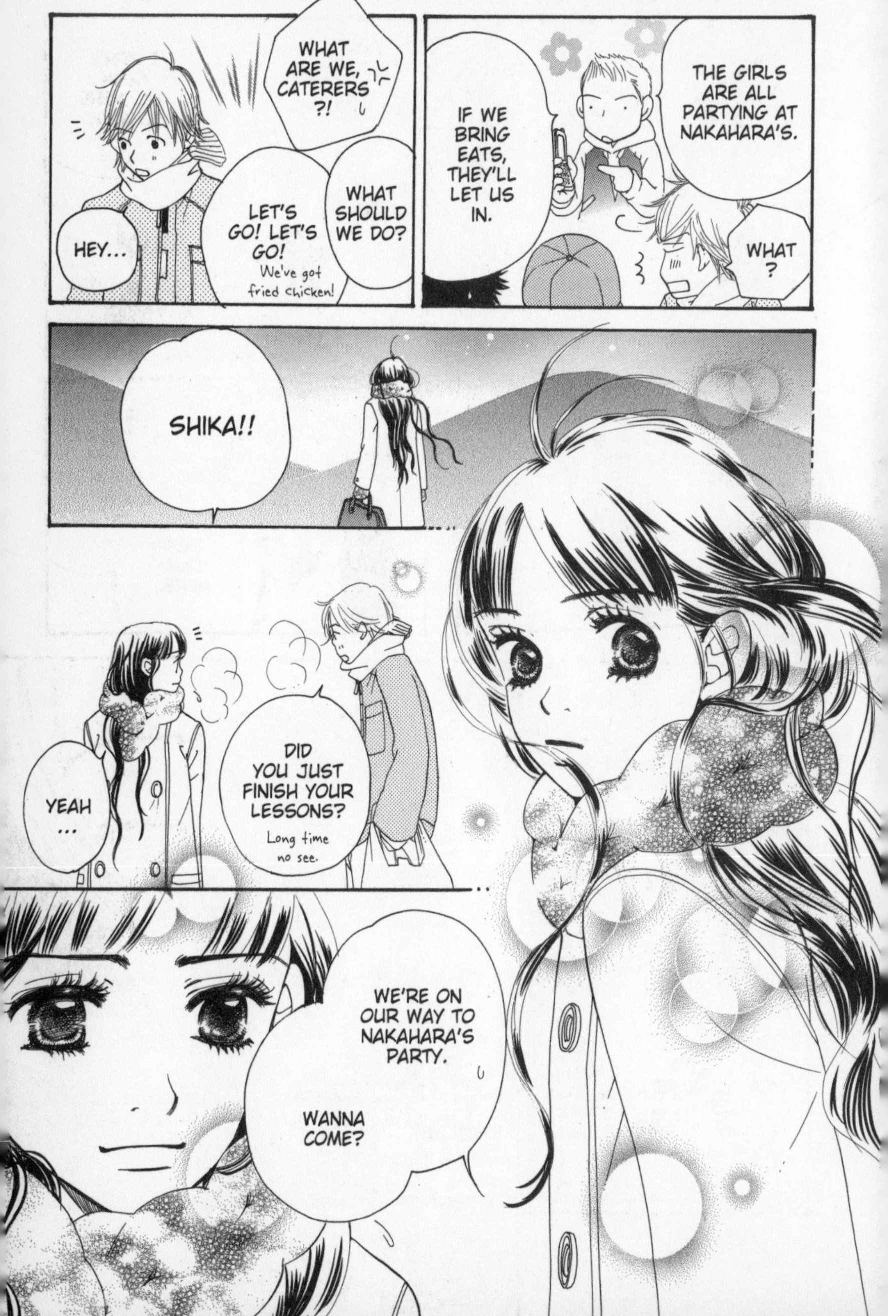
THE GIRLS ARE ALL PARTYING AT NAKAHARA'S.
IF WE BRING EATS, THEY'LL LET US IN.
WHAT?
WHAT ARE WE, CATERERS?!
WHAT SHOULD WE DO?
LET'S GO! LET'S GO!
We've got fried chicken!
HEY...
SHIKA!!
DID YOU JUST FINISH YOUR LESSONS?
Long time no see.
YEAH...
WE'RE ON OUR WAY TO NAKAHARA'S PARTY.
WANNA COME?

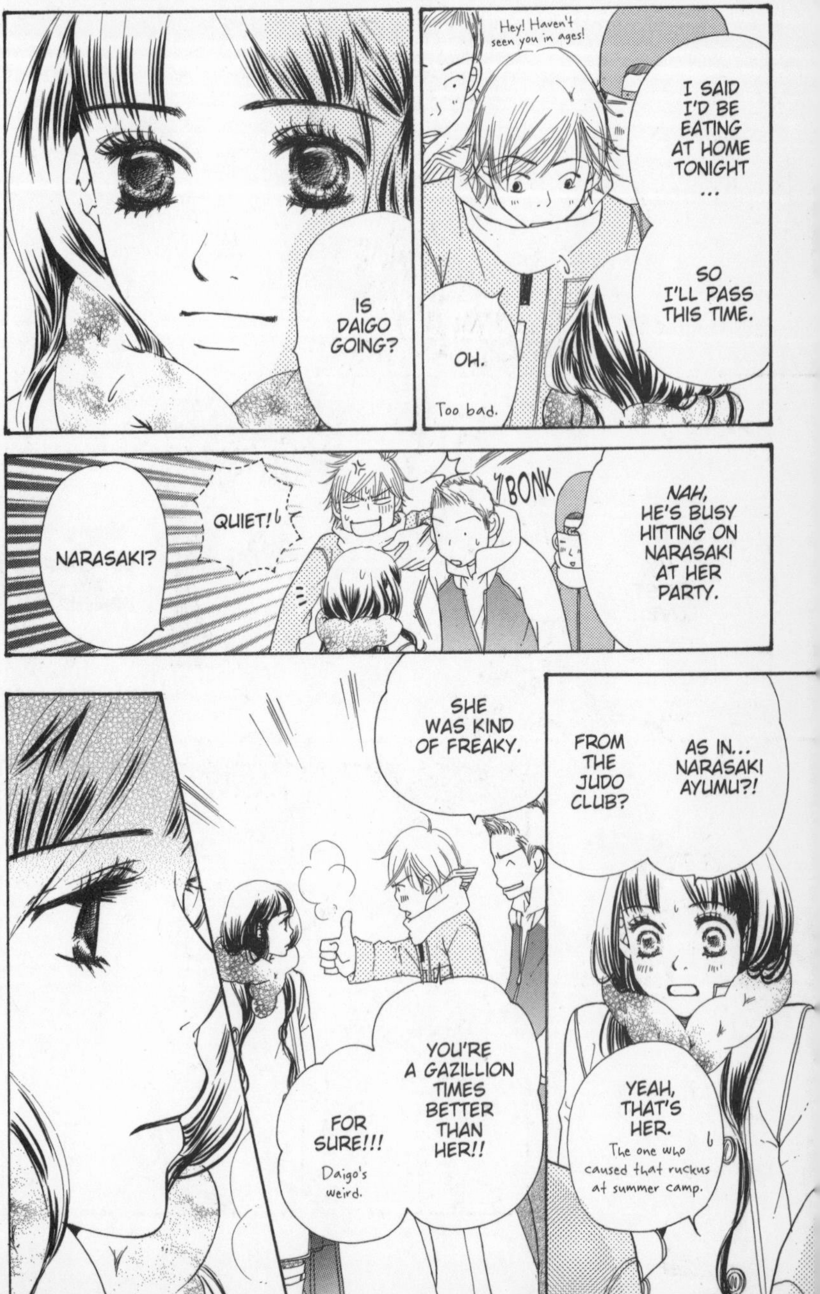
Hey! Haven't seen you in ages!
I SAID I'D BE EATING AT HOME TONIGHT...
SO I'LL PASS THIS TIME.
OH.
Too bad.
IS DAIGO GOING?
NAH, HE'S BUSY HITTING ON NARASAKI AT HER PARTY.
BONK
QUIET!
NARASAKI?
AS IN... NARASAKI AYUMU?!
FROM THE JUDO CLUB?
YEAH, THAT'S HER.
The one who caused that ruckus at summer camp.
SHE WAS KIND OF FREAKY.
YOU'RE A GAZILLION TIMES BETTER THAN HER!!
FOR SURE!!!
Daigo's weird.

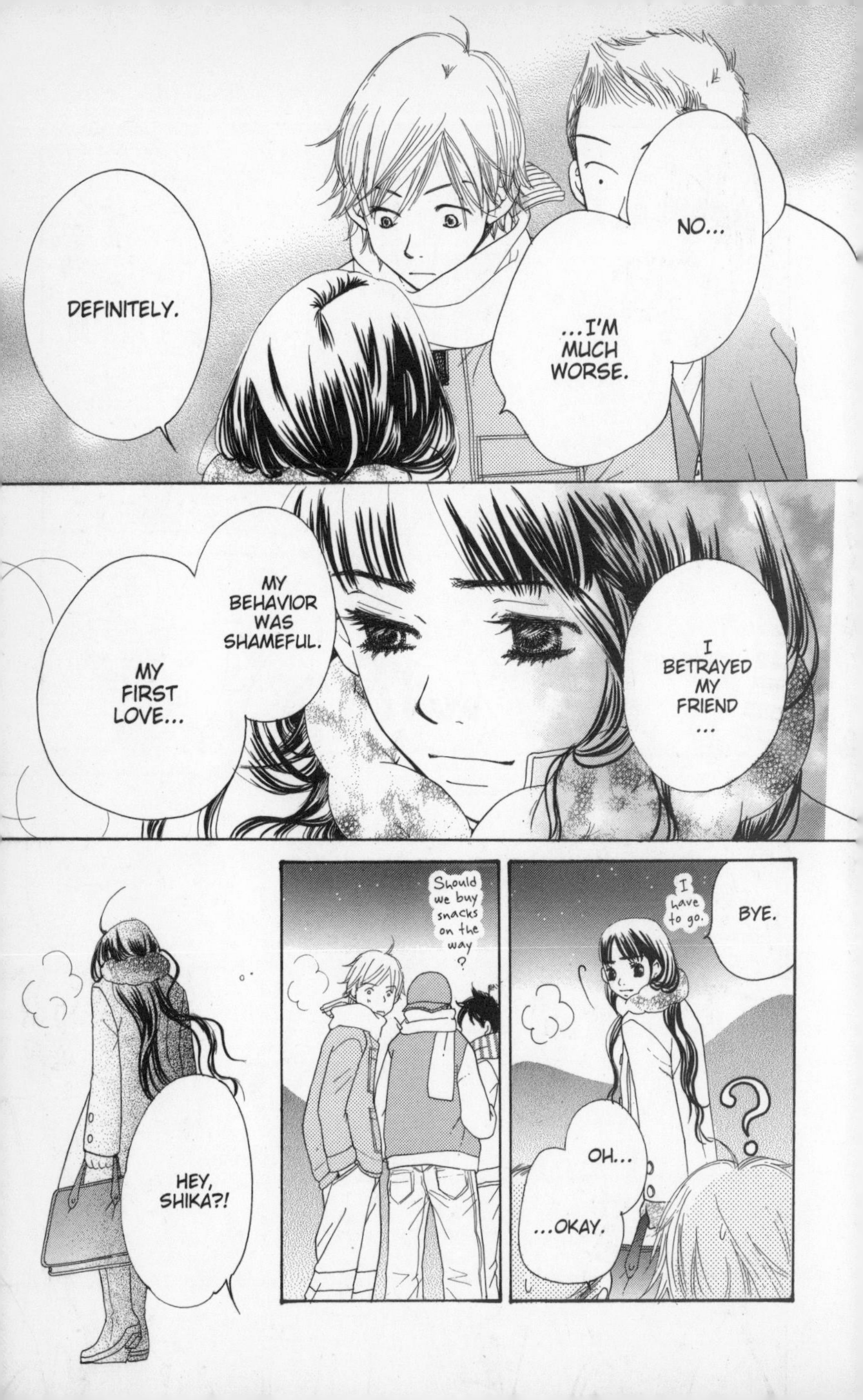
NO... ...I'M MUCH WORSE.
DEFINITELY.
I BETRAYED MY FRIEND...
MY FIRST LOVE... MY BEHAVIOR WAS SHAMEFUL.
BYE.
I have to go.
OH... ...OKAY.
Should we buy snacks on the way?
HEY, SHIKA?!

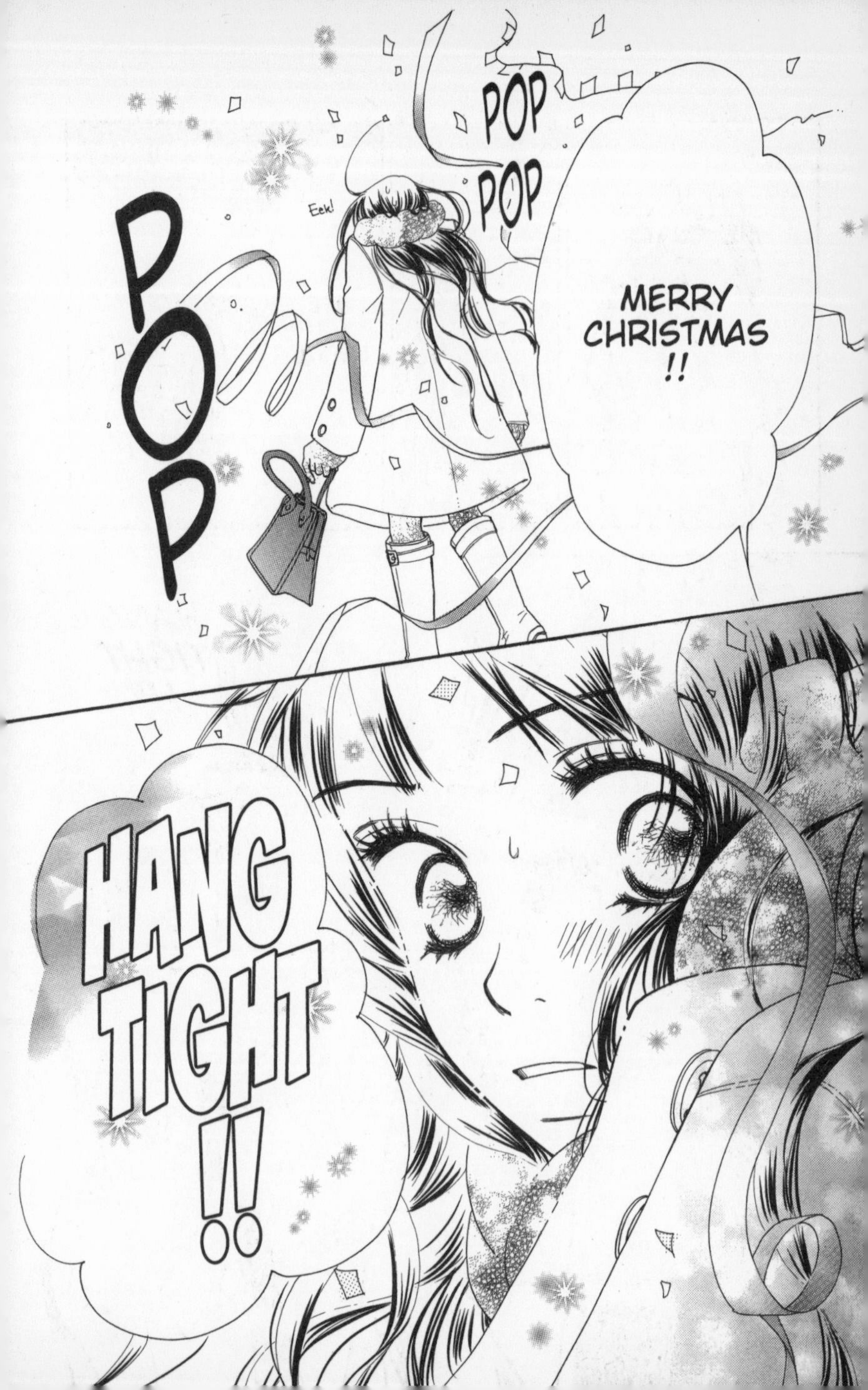
MERRY CHRISTMAS!!
POP
POP
Eek!
POP
HANG TIGHT!!

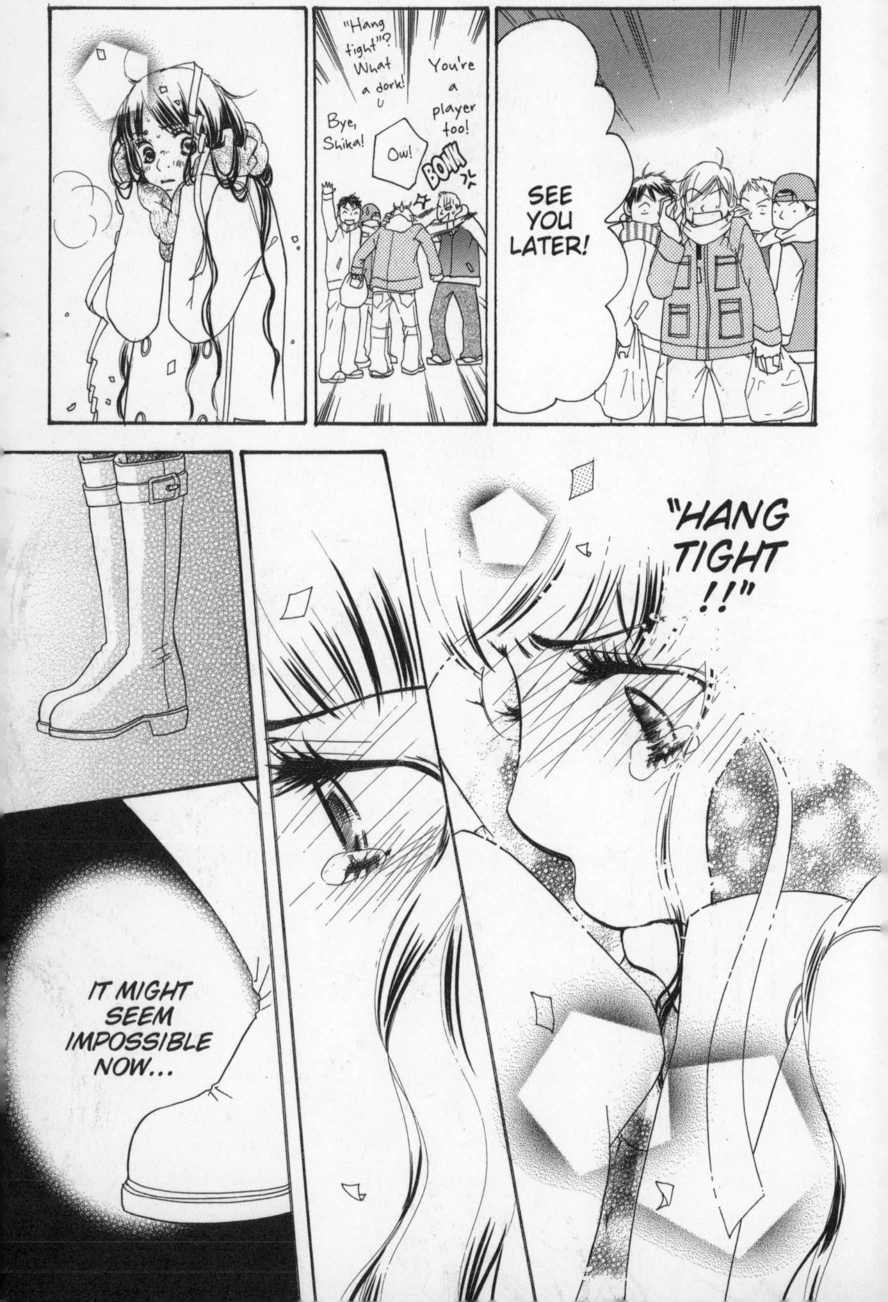
SEE YOU LATER!
You're a player too!
"Hang tight"? What a dork!
BONK
Ow!
Bye, Shika!
"HANG TIGHT!!"
IT MIGHT SEEM IMPOSSIBLE NOW...

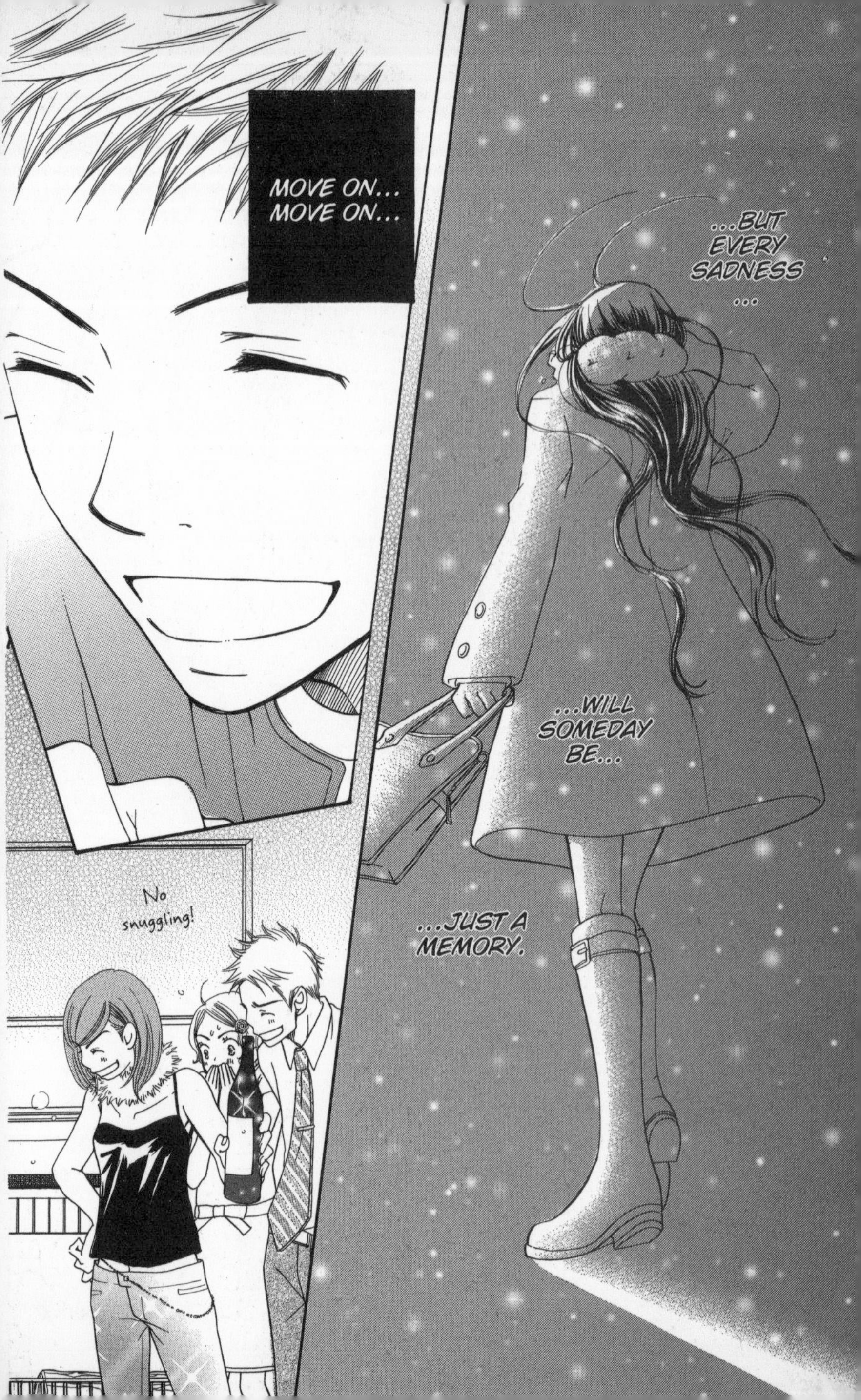
...BUT EVERY SADNESS ...
...WILL SOMEDAY BE...
...JUST A MEMORY.
MOVE ON... MOVE ON...
No snuggling!

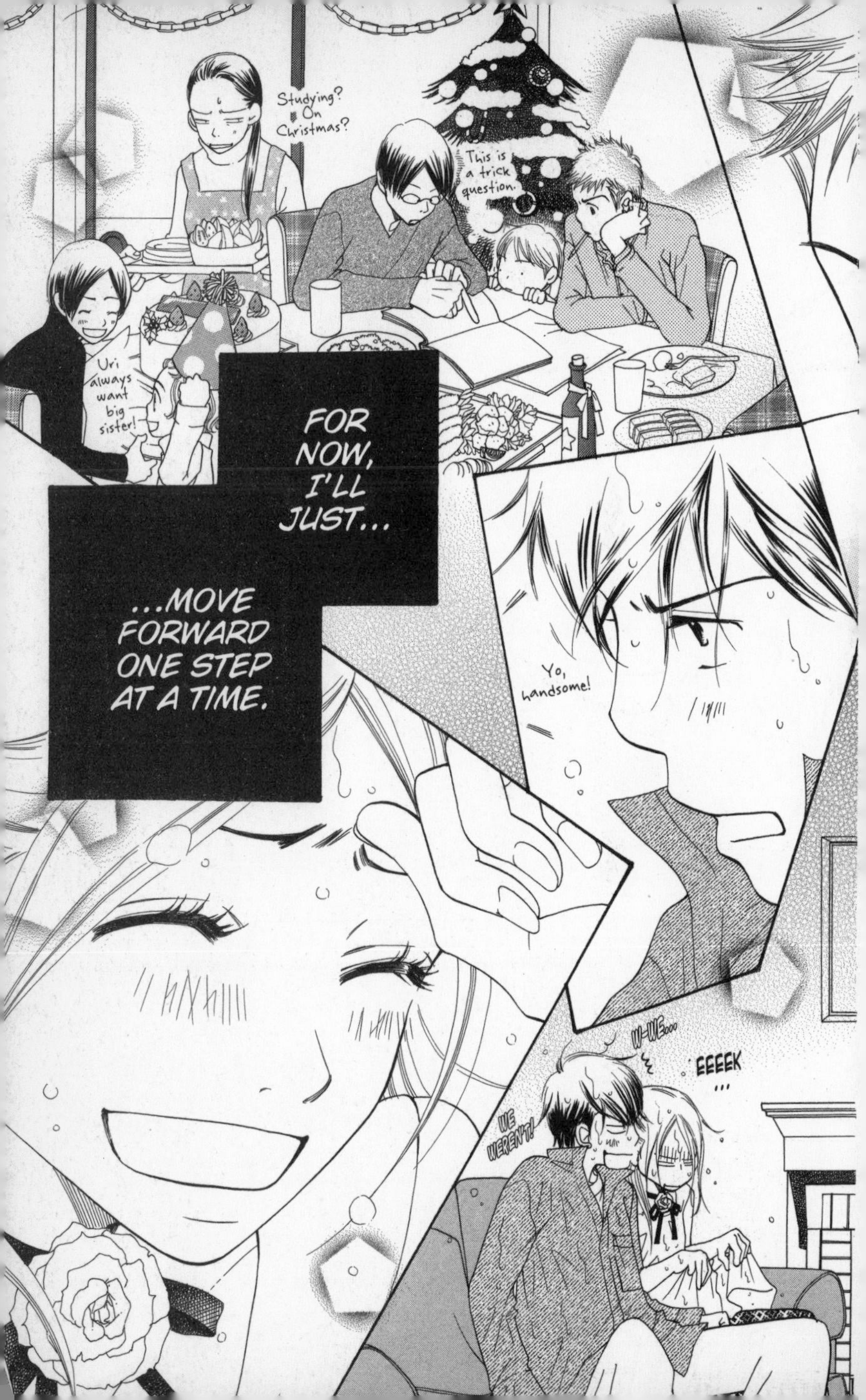
This is a trick question.
Studying? On Christmas?
Uri always want big sister!
FOR NOW, I'LL JUST...
...MOVE FORWARD ONE STEP AT A TIME.
Yo, handsome!
EEEEK...
W-WE...
WE WEREN'T!

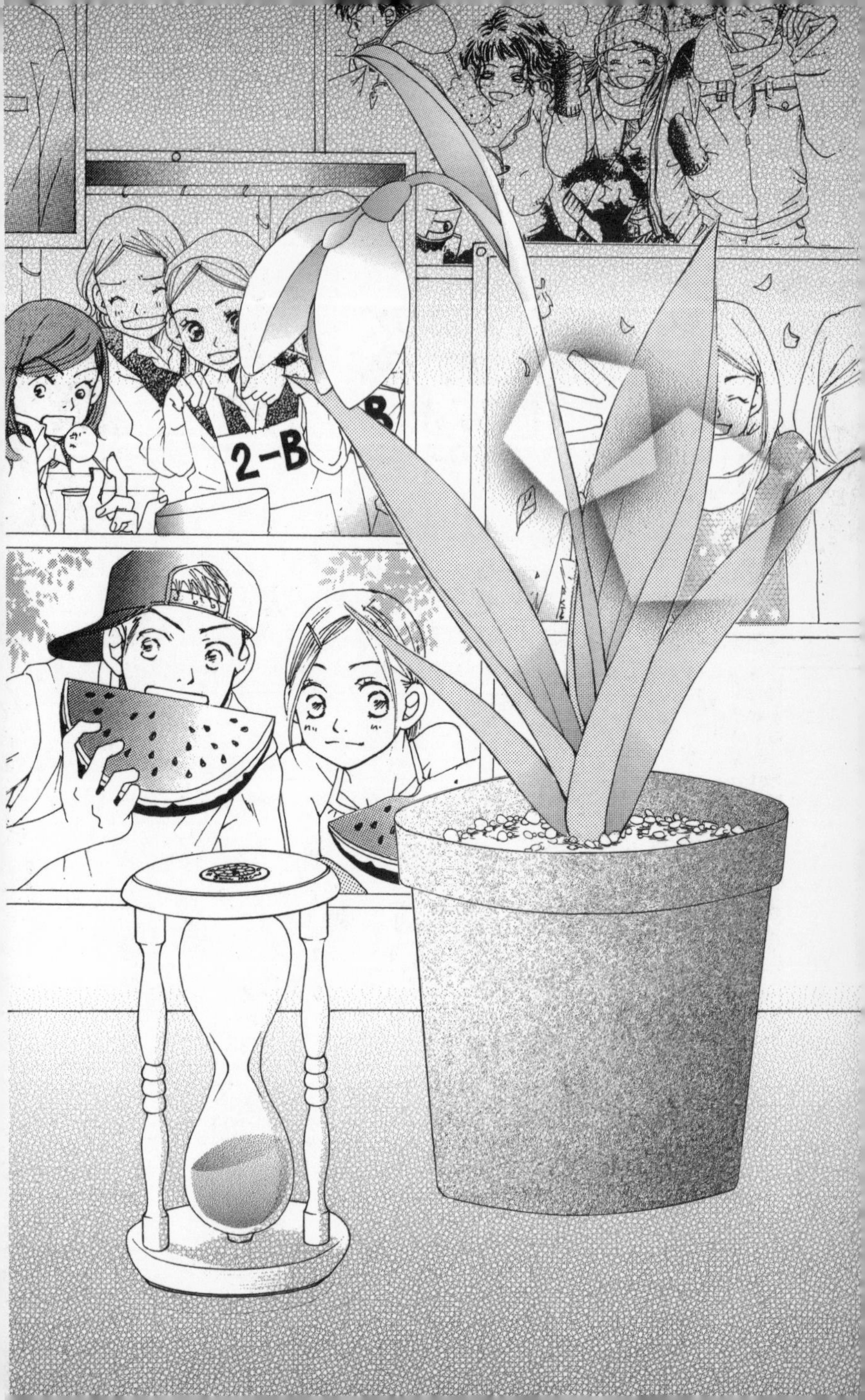
2-B

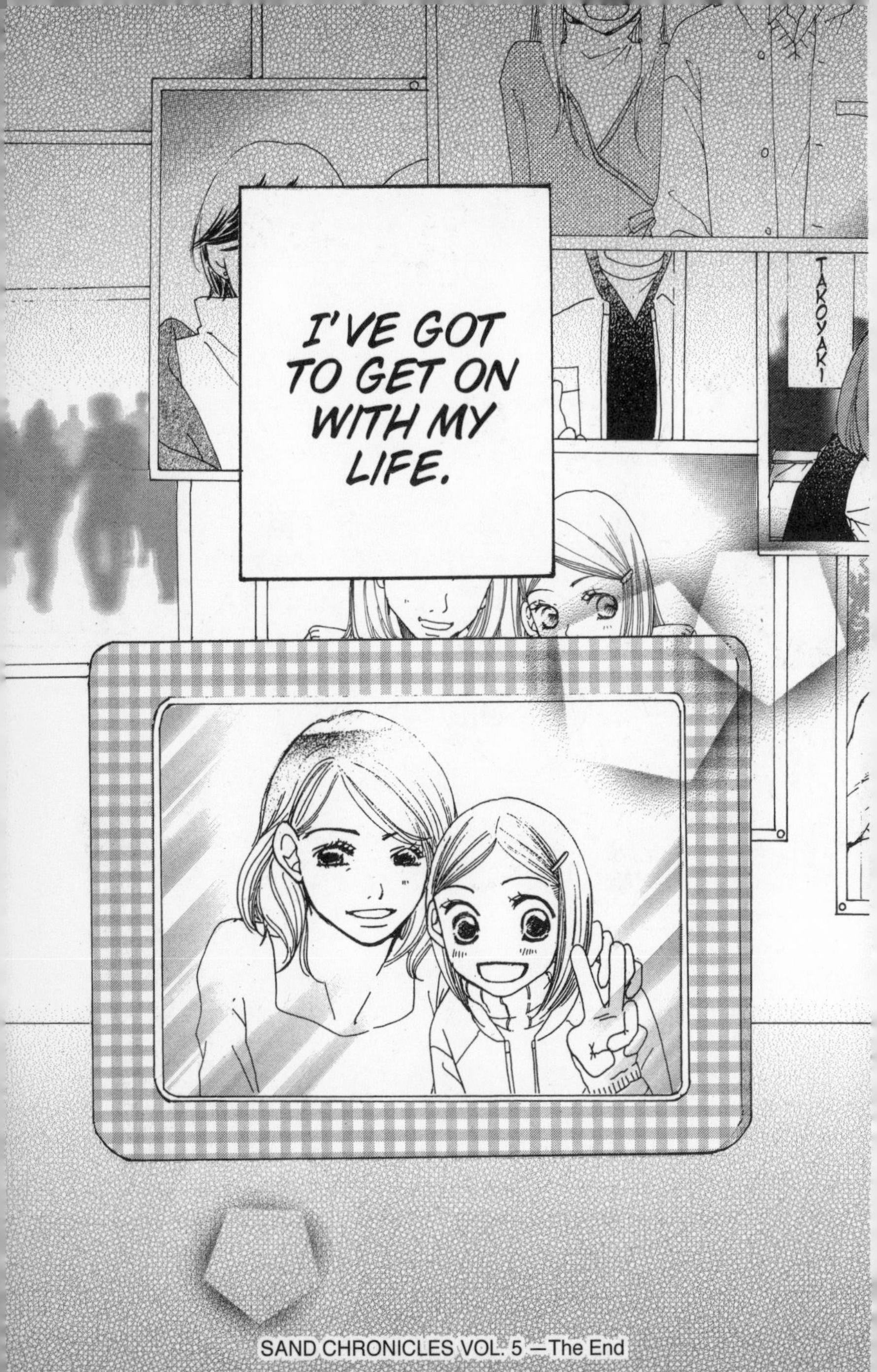
I'VE GOT TO GET ON WITH MY LIFE.
TAKOYAKI

SAND CHRONICLES VOL. 5 —The End

Glossary

If only adolescence came with an instruction manual.
We can't give you that, but this glossary of terms
might prove useful for this volume.

Page 8, panel 2: mizu-manju
Mizu-manju, one of various types of
manju, a traditional Japanese sweet. It
is made of red-bean paste wrapped in a
dough-like jelly of kudzu flour.

Page 12, panel 2: Sonoda-kyun
Translated as Sonoda-babe. His girlfriend
changes the honorific kun from Sonoda-
kun (used for peers and colleagues) to
Sonoda-kyun, which is a cutesy honorific
for a boy. Kyun is also a manga sound
effect used to indicate a surge of love.

Page 21, panel 1: inari-zushi
A fried tofu pouch stuffed with vinegared
rice.

Page 25, panel 1: fu-manju
Fu-manju is a type of manju made of
red-bean paste wrapped in wheat gluten.

Page 59, panel 3: BGM
Background music.

**Page 59, panel 4: The Seven Wild Herbs
of Spring**
These herbs are not just available in spring,
but they have come to be associated with it.

Page 93, panel 1: dragon
A dragon is a firework that you place on
the ground. When lit, it spurts sparks and
flames into the air. They are sometimes
called "fountains" in English. Ann can be
seen holding one of these in panel 4.

Page 116, panel 2: career proposal
This is a form that Japanese students fill
out by listing, in order of preference, what
they want to do after graduating from
high school. The list could include types
of higher education or jobs or both. Their
teacher can then advise them based on
their interests.

Page 160, panel 3: Matsuzaka beef
In Japan, there are three major wagyu
breeds of cattle used for beef. The breeds
get their names from the region they
originated in: Kobe, Matsuzaka, or Oumi.

Page 177, panel 1: fried chicken
In Japan, many families eat KFC fried
chicken on Christmas Eve, perhaps
because Japan's KFCs dress up their
Colonel Sanders mannequins in Santa suits
for the holiday. But Daigo's mother offers
the boys karaage, a Japanese style of fried
chicken often served at parties.

Page 182, panel 2: "Hang tight!"
In Japanese, the original expression was
donmai, which is an abbreviation of
donto maindo, itself a transliteration into
Japanese of the English "Don't mind."

Profile of Hinako Ashihara

A while ago, I was surprised to receive a
fan letter from an old junior high school
classmate of mine. It was my third time
getting a letter or email from an old
acquaintance. It really brought back a lot of
pleasant memories. To think that someone
who knew the old me is reading my manga...
That really keeps me on my toes!
—Hinako Ashihara

Hinako Ashihara won the 50th Shogakukan
Manga Award for *Sunadokei*. She debuted
with *Sono Hanashi Okotowari Shimasu* in
Bessatsu Shojo Comics in 1994. Her other
works include *SOS*, *Forbidden Dance*, and
Tennen Bitter Chocolate.

SAND CHRONICLES
Vol. 5
The Shojo Beat Manga Edition

This manga volume contains material that was originally published in English in *Shojo Beat* magazine, December 2008~February 2009 issues. Artwork in the magazine may have been slightly altered from that presented here.

STORY AND ART BY HINAKO ASHIHARA

English Adaptation/John Werry
Translation/Kinami Watabe
Touch-up Art & Lettering/Rina Mapa
Additional Touch-up/Rachel Lightfoot
Cover Design/Izumi Evers
Interior Design/Deirdre Shiozawa
Editor/Annette Roman

Editor in Chief, Books/Alvin Lu
Editor in Chief, Magazines/Marc Weidenbaum
VP, Publishing Licensing/Rika Inouye
VP, Sales & Product Marketing/Gonzalo Ferreyra
VP, Creative/Linda Espinosa
Publisher/Hyoe Narita

Printed in Canada

store.viz.com

Published by VIZ Media, LLC
P.O. Box 77010
San Francisco, CA 94107

Shojo Beat Manga Edition
10 9 8 7 6 5 4 3 2 1
First printing, May 2009